TERRI'S STORY

TERRI'S STORY

The Court-Ordered Death of an American Woman

DIANA LYNNE

WND BOOKS
AN IMPRINT OF CUMBERLAND HOUSE PUBLISHING, INC.
NASHVILLE, TENNESSEE

TERRI'S STORY
A WND BOOK
PUBLISHED BY CUMBERLAND HOUSE PUBLISHING, INC.
431 Harding Industrial Drive
Nashville, Tennessee 37211

Cover design by Stacie Bauerle, Stones River Design, Murfreesboro, Tennessee

Library of Congress Cataloging-in-Publication Data

Lynne, Diana, 1974–
Terri's story : the court-ordered death of an American woman / Diana Lynne.
p. cm.
Includes bibliographical references and index.
ISBN-13: 978-1-58182-488-9 (hardcover : alk. paper)
ISBN-10: 1-58182-488-2 (hardcover : alk. paper)
1. Schiavo, Terri, 1963–2005. 2. Right to die—Moral and ethical aspects—United States—Case studies. 3. Terminal care—Moral and ethical aspects—United States—Case studies. 4. Coma—Patients—Biography. 5. Medical ethics—United States—Case studies. I. Title.
R726.L96 2005
179.7—dc22 2005020018

ISBN 978-1-68442-183-1 (pbk.)

To

THERESA MARIE SCHINDLER SCHIAVO

December 3, 1963–March 31, 2005

CONTENTS

PREFACE

It's September 12, 2001, all over again for many Americans. As they did on the day after the infamous 9–11, when hate-filled terrorists blasted a hole in the nation's soul, shocked citizens across the country now similarly grapple with a seismic shift in their understanding of what life in America means. The disbelief and denial that lingers months after the slow death by dehydration and starvation of forty-one-year-old Terri Schiavo over the course of thirteen days harkens back to the post-9–11 pall that hung over the country. It's prompted by the same realization that the self-serving agenda of a group of ideologues could threaten the welfare of every citizen in the country, and the awareness that the law, law enforcement officers, judges, and politicians—including the president of the United States—proved powerless to block them.

On March 31, 2005, a brain-injured woman, who was not terminally ill, died as a result of a caregiver's removal of her life-sustaining feeding tube and the accompanying refusal to provide her with oral hydration and sustenance. Her husband believed she would have wanted to die, she would have wanted to be helped along toward what he perceived to be a merciful, dignified end. Although lawmakers, who passed new legislation to facilitate deaths like Terri's, and death-with-dignity lobbyists, who helped craft the legislation, deny that the removal of feeding tubes to cause the deaths of people who are not terminally ill amounts to assisted suicide, those who are intellectually honest see such denial as an act in moral and ethical "hairsplitting," in the words of one prominent death-with-dignity advocate. Another expert characterizes a patient's refusal of nutrition and hydration as "voluntary passive euthanasia."[1]

Terri Schiavo was not the first person to be dehydrated to death as the result of the removal of a gastric feeding tube. Anecdotal evidence relayed by right-to-die proponents suggests thousands across America die in this manner daily and "tens of thousands of other Floridians" forged the trail before her. What creates discomfort for many, and horror for others, is the fact that the medical personnel who withdrew the device from the incapacitated woman's stomach and then neglected to provide her with so much as an ice chip over the near two weeks it took for her to succumb to dehydration were carrying out a court's orders, not an advance directive from Terri Schiavo. The woman had no written instructions regarding the medical care and treatment she would want, or not want, in the event of incapacitation. She never appointed a health-care proxy to make such decisions for her. The determination of whether the woman should live or die fell into the hands of a probate judge who ruled from the bench without the benefit of a jury. He favored death. Consequently a nonterminal disabled woman, who had a life expectancy of at least another decade, according to the medical examiner who performed the autopsy of her body, but whose brain injury rendered her unable to speak for herself, was deemed by our judicial system as being better off dead than alive.

What if the husband was mistaken? Or worse, as some fear, what if he lied? What if Terri Schiavo didn't want to die? Pinellas-Pasco County chief medical examiner Jon Thogmartin called it a "miracle" that Terri survived over an hour without a measurable blood pressure after her heart mysteriously stopped beating on February 25, 1990, and before paramedics succeeded in resuscitating her. The lack of oxygen and poor, or no, blood flow to her brain during those frantic minutes caused massive, "irreversible" brain damage. Thogmartin also found it remarkable she lived fifteen years after this event, and even more remarkable she endured "marked dehydration" over thirteen days before her heart beat its last beat. He called it a "testament" to her strong heart. Others call it a testament to her will to live. If Terri, in fact, wanted to live, then her death becomes a killing. Without the benefit of her explicit written directive on the matter, many have argued it is impossible to know, beyond a shadow of a doubt, which characterization fits her death—assisted suicide or killing.

After Terri Schiavo became incapacitated at the age of twenty-six, the probate court appointed her husband as her plenary guardian, giving him full control over her fate. Years after winning $2.25 million from medical malpractice lawsuits filed on behalf of Terri—money he testified in court he needed to be able to take care of her for the rest of his life—Michael Schiavo recalled his wife had casually commented a couple of times that she didn't want to be kept alive by artificial means and didn't want to be a "burden on anyone."

At the time of her alleged casual statements, feeding tubes were not considered life support in Florida. They are not machines. It's likely Terri Schiavo didn't even know what a gastric feeding tube was until one was surgically inserted into her abdomen, and then it is disputed whether she had the cognition to be aware of the silicone tube attached to her body. What's more, it wasn't until after her husband filed his May 1998 petition to remove the feeding tube that Florida law was changed to include "artificial nutrition and hydration" in the definition of life-prolonging procedures that could be refused or withdrawn by a patient or proxy. In a timely manner the Florida statute was also amended to allow for the withdrawal of life-prolonging medical treatment, even if the patient were not terminal and in the absence of evidence of their wishes, if it was deemed in their "best interest." Such a seemingly subjective evaluation is said to be based on the "consensus of public opinion" that most would likely not want to live in a severely brain-damaged condition. Thus the notion of right to die—which in the minds of most strictly pertains to suffering, terminally ill patients for whom death is imminent and who choose hastened death—was expanded to include the right of nonterminal disabled people to die.

Terri Schiavo was raised in a close-knit family—so close her parents and brother moved to St. Petersburg, Florida, after she and her husband relocated from Pennsylvania, where they both grew up. The Schindlers called the alleged statements about end-of-life care recalled by Michael Schiavo as completely "out of character" for Terri and don't believe she made them. They maintain that, as a lifelong practicing Catholic, Terri believed in the sanctity of life.

One thing the Schiavos and Schindlers are in agreement on is that the media failed to adequately cover Terri's story. Despite the wall-to-wall, 24–7 coverage by the cable news machine during her final days, both sides of the court battle over her life complained that journalists failed to fully and accurately report the facts and adequately delve into the depths of this multifaceted, unprecedented case. Many observers would go so far as to say the media did a disservice to the nation. This book seeks to correct the misinformation and distortion on the part of some news outlets, to fill the gaps in public knowledge about the case left by most, and to place the story in its proper context so as to illuminate its relevance. To accomplish this task, the author conducted more than thirty-five hours of interviews and combed approximately five thousand pages of court records gathered over the past two and a half years. These serve as the primary source material for the pages that follow. Specific case numbers are provided at the end of the preface. Various testimony given in depositions and court proceedings have been quoted liberally. In some instances some individuals were not referenced by their full names. Where possible, these have been supplied, but they were not available in every instance. Additional information gleaned from a survey of supporting medical and legal literature, as well as press accounts of the case, will be cited where used. Efforts were made to solicit comment from all the players in the Terri Schiavo drama referenced in this book. Their remarks are included when they were provided.

With the family members in dispute over Terri's wishes, Pinellas-Pasco County Circuit Court Judge George Greer was called in as referee. He sided with guardian-husband Michael Schiavo and ordered the removal of the feeding tube. He later further ordered she not be given any food or water orally. While it was debated among family members, lawyers, lobbyists, lawmakers, bioethicists, and news commentators as to whether Terri Schiavo would have wanted to live for the past fifteen years in her brain-injured state, it is indisputable she never asked to not be fed. She never declared a desire to be dehydrated to death. If she had, many Americans would expect that her wishes would be respected. Others would question whether such a request, when made while an individual is healthy, would be relevant and still reflect the individual's wishes after he or she had become incapacitated.

But Terri Schiavo never contemplated death by dehydration, as far as any family members, friends, or spiritual advisers were aware. While advocates of an individual's right to die characterize death by dehydration as "pleasant," "peaceful," and "painless," other physicians describe it as "agonizing," "inhumane," and "cruel." Still others would split the difference and describe the final hours of the death process after the person slips into a coma as "peaceful," but the days leading up to them as "torture," during which the patient definitely suffers. Even proponents of physician-assisted suicide and euthanasia admit that slow death by dehydration over the course of thirteen days—not accompanied by healthy, or perhaps terminal, sedation—does not represent "going out flying" or "popping off" in a way to which many would aspire. In fact, the latest techniques pursued by euthanasia advocates involve inhaling inert gas inside a plastic bag, resulting in death within ten minutes, as well as lethal injection—a comparative luxury afforded convicted criminals on death row.

Ironically, the change in Florida law that facilitated Terri's death was birthed out of concern that too many people on their death beds are left to suffer, untreated with proper end-of-life palliative care, which includes pain management. Although she was the first publicized beneficiary of the revised law, likely because of the intense media scrutiny, Terri Schiavo did not benefit from their original stated intent. The medical examiner's autopsy found no trace of morphine or any other opiate in Terri's system at the time of death. This was an incredible discovery considering that pneumonia ravaged Terri's lungs and her organs slowly dried up and shut down during her last days.

Many who perceived Terri's death as tragic complained that they suffered symptoms of post-traumatic stress disorder, which include tension, anxiety, recurring nightmares, and depression as well as feeling powerless, numb, disconnected, and vulnerable. Psychologist Karin Huffer identified such suffering as a result of "protracted litigation perceived to be abusive" as legal abuse syndrome. Judicial-reform activists also warned that the now-discretionary nature of the civil court system more and more often leaves those who come in contact with it "shell-shocked."

In contrast, many other Americans don't recognize the ramifications or the national significance of the Terri Schiavo story. They're comforted to know the law will be on their side if and when they decide they're better off dead and choose to take steps to end their lives. Just as some erroneously conclude there can never be another 9–11 on American soil, or that terrorists will never target their backyard in the future, many dispassionately dismiss Terri Schiavo's fatal dehydration as "her wishes" or as a "private family matter." For those who hold this opinion, the failed intervention by the Florida legislature, Governor Jeb Bush, Congress, and President George W. Bush sparked outrage and resentment.

Although it may have started out as a "private family matter" fifteen years ago when the young woman mysteriously collapsed at home without any prior warning of serious illness, the case of Terri Schiavo shortly became emblematic of a guardianship system overdo for reform. For decades, guardianship advocates have clamored for changes to a paradigm in which guardians acquire dictatorial control over their wards and overburdened courts are loath to upset the apple cart and curb their power. In a familial tug-of-war over the life of an incapacitated loved one, the court-appointed guardian has the upper hand and, in the court's eyes, can do no wrong. It's a system ripe for abuse and neglect and one in which countless incidents of both have been documented.

By 1996 the Terri Schiavo case morphed into a *Roe v. Wade* of sorts concerning "assisted dying" when an attorney promoted as "America's foremost expert on the right-to-die," with ties to the death-with-dignity advocacy organization Choice in Dying,[2] took the stage to assist Michael Schiavo in persuading a court to order the removal of his wife's feeding tube to put an end to her "forced feeding." Attorney George Felos, who admits to having a "fascination with death and dying,"[3] and who considers death to be a "profound mystical process"[4]—but who does not advocate illegal activity, particularly euthanasia—took a page from the playbook of abortion proponents in the 1973 watershed court case and argued that ending Terri's life was necessary to protect her constitutional right to privacy. Felos successfully made the same argument in a prior right-to-die case, resulting in the Florida Supreme Court ruling in 1990 that Estelle Browning, an elderly stroke victim, had a constitutional right to refuse food and water, according to her wishes as outlined in her written advance directive.

"The Florida Constitution has a specific right of privacy," Felos explained. "The Florida Supreme Court said that right of privacy includes the liberty interests we all have in controlling our own bodies. And the Florida Supreme Court has said that you as an individual have the right to refuse any medical treatment . . . because it's part of your liberty interest in controlling your own body."

But unlike Estelle Browning, Terri had left no written advance directive and she was not dying. In this case, Felos had help in making legal history. In 1999 fellow board members at the politically connected Hospice of the Florida Suncoast and colleagues elsewhere within the hospice industry teamed up with prominent death-with-dignity advocates aligned with the pro-euthanasia Hemlock Society and ushered in the changes to Florida law as described earlier. Like its former chairman of the board, Felos, this hospice also had ties to Choice in Dying, which reorganized as Partnership for Caring and later merged with Last Acts to become Last Acts Partnership. The revisions to the law, which became effective October 1, 1999, enabled Felos less than four months later to state in his opening arguments in the first trial, *In re Guardianship of Schiavo,* the "removal of artificial provision of sustenance as medical treatment . . . is the law in Florida." Judge Greer applied the changed law to Terri's case and subsequently issued what's known as his first death order in 2000.

At that point the right-to-die case flashed across the radar screens of pro-life organizations such as Life Legal Defense Foundation, the Alliance Defense Fund, the National Right to Life Committee, the Christian Defense Coalition, and the American Catholic Lawyers Association, which all entered the fray in various ways to bolster the efforts of Terri's parents and siblings to keep her from becoming a "sacrificial lamb on the stage of the right-to-die movement." Judicial reform and victims' advocacy groups like the Justice Coalition also began to speak out against the perceived miscarriage of justice at the trial- and appellate-court levels. Meanwhile, the nation's largest right-to-die organization and euthanasia proponent, the Hemlock Society—

recently renamed End-of-Life Choices—countered the pro-life push with a national advertising campaign centered on Terri's case.

In 2003 *Schiavo v. Schindler* caught the attention of state legislators and Governor Jeb Bush, who were barraged with an estimated 165,000 e-mails on the matter. Their unprecedented actions awoke a slumbering national, mainstream media, which, with prompting from Felos, spun the case as a "private family matter" invaded by self-serving politicians pandering to "fundamentalist right-wing" constituents. The American Civil Liberties Union signed onto the case with Felos to protect the right to privacy of this young woman who was helpless to defend herself from the invasive "over-treatment" of patients perceived to be alarmingly present in our high-tech health-care centers across the country. The reportedly pervasive "over-treatment" problem was cited as the cause of the country's Medicare crisis.

In reality, the proverbial "vast right-wing conspiracy" said to be driving the building momentum to keep Terri Schiavo alive, and acting as a "lynch mob" to get legislators' attention, actually amounted to a grass-roots effort that cut across political, religious, and ideological lines. It was partly orchestrated by a handful of strangers, which included a trio of nurses, a housewife, the mother of a disabled child, a computer guru, a talk-radio journalist, a public relations wiz, a law school classmate, and a group of Franciscan brothers from Minnesota. But other high-profile voices spoke up for Terri, including Lanny Davis, former White House special counsel to President Bill Clinton; Senator Joseph Lieberman (D-CT), former Democratic vice presidential candidate; Senator Barbara Mikulski (D-MD); the Reverend Jesse Jackson, former Democratic presidential candidate; Ralph Nader, consumer advocate and former Independent Party presidential candidate; civil libertarian Nat Hentoff; Senate Majority Leader Bill Frist (R-TN); House Speaker Tom DeLay (R-TX); Focus on the Family founder Dr. James Dobson; Coral Ridge Ministries leader Dr. D. James Kennedy; actress Patricia Heaton; actor-director Mel Gibson; and the late Pope John Paul II.

Despite evidence to the contrary, once Congress and President Bush stepped into the controversy in March 2005, political pundits and the media cast the Terri Schiavo case as the latest battlefront in the new millennium War Between the States—red states versus blue states. For those who believe Governor Bush rigged the 2000 Florida recount of the presidential vote to enable his brother to "steal the election," Terri's death came to represent a vindication of sorts. In the words of *St. Petersburg Times* columnist Mary Jo Melone, Terri's life was "confiscated by [the] agendas of strangers." Even if

Michael Schiavo might have realized he had been mistaken about Terri's wishes, the pro-death train had already left the station.

While the political debate about Terri took on a life of its own, the relatively healthy, nonterminal woman lay dehydrating to death in the small hospice room she had reportedly not been allowed to leave for five years. Five teeth had rotted in her mouth and were extracted. One of her toes was amputated due to a persistent pressure sore that developed into a bone infection. Her body was riddled with contractures because, according to her medical records, for more than a decade she had not received rehabilitative physical therapy to keep her muscles supple.

Although dozens of physicians and caregivers gave sworn testimony that Terri Schiavo was not in a persistent vegetative state but exhibited cognitive awareness and purposefully interacted with her parents, siblings, and others, the testimony of three doctors—one of whom, Dr. Ronald Cranford, is a right-to-die activist who routinely serves as an expert witness in favor of death in right-to-die cases, and who calls himself "Dr. Humane Death"—carried the day in the trial court. Three neurologists led by Cranford concluded Terri Schiavo was in a persistent vegetative state (PVS) and there were no treatments that could restore her cognitive function enough to significantly improve her quality of life so that she would want to remain alive.

Interestingly, however, if Terri Schiavo was in PVS, she beat the odds estimated to be between 1 in 15,000 and 1 in 75,000 by surviving her condition for more than fifteen years, according to statistics provided by the Multi-Society Task Force on PVS, the leading authority on the matter.[5]

Michael Schiavo himself, however, testified in court in 1992 that Terri felt pain and that doctors had told him as much. But people in PVS, by definition, cannot feel pain. Yet Terri was routinely given Tylenol to manage her visible discomfort and moaning during menses, received two small doses of morphine in the initial days of her dehydration, and then acetaminophen throughout her final days. Thus the question remains for many: Why give pain-killers to a person who reportedly has no awareness, no capacity to feel pain?

Even after the autopsy, the Schindlers maintained Terri was in what has only recently been coined MCS (or minimally conscious state). Neuropathologist Stephen Nelson, who assisted with Terri's autopsy, admitted he could not "rule out" that Terri was in MCS, because he found no published studies on postmortem pathological findings that correlate with MCS in his literature review. There is much evidence in the court file, however, that suggests Terri Schiavo was, in fact, an aware but severely brain-injured woman, simply one of the forty-seven million Americans who unexpectedly become disabled through injury. But most of this evidence went unheard by the trial judge, who was persuaded by the court-appointed guardian that his wife was just "a shell of somebody I used to know." In seven years of adjudicating her case, Greer never met Terri Schiavo and could not benefit from his own observations of this key witness's demeanor. Felos and Cranford both eloquently argued, in reference to Terri's condition, "There are fates worse than death." Many Americans agree with this pronouncement. Greer agreed, and as is customary in the American judicial system, appellate court judges presumed the trial judge properly adjudicated the case and didn't abuse his authority, and they affirmed his ruling.

In the autopsy report, Thogmartin waded into this quality-of-life debate. "Her brain was profoundly atrophied. It weighed 615 grams—roughly half the expected weight of [the brains of] a normal human being," he announced at a press conference on June 15, 2005. "This was irreversible and no amount of treatment would have regenerated the massive loss of neurons."

Some experts criticized this as a misleading statement, pointing out the goal of therapy in brain-injured patients isn't to regenerate dead neurons, but to retrain surviving neurons to function in their place.

Others slammed Thogmartin's comment for its perceived appeasement of the right-to-die movement. "No amount of brain injury ever justifies denying a person proper humane care. That includes food and water," Father Frank Pavone, a Catholic priest who was with Terri in the final hours and minutes of her life, stated in a press release. "To remove [food and water] means euthanasia, it means killing," added Cardinal Javier Lozano Barragán, president of the Vatican's Pontifical Council for Health Care. "Let's stop with the euphemisms—they killed her."

While sidestepping the word *vindicated,* attorney Felos told reporters at a press conference following the release of the autopsy report that Michael Schiavo was "very pleased" with its results: "For years, the treating physicians, the doctors—the responsible physicians—Mr. Schiavo, the courts, have said over and over again that there was no rehabilitation therapy or other therapy that could improve Mrs. Schiavo's condition. That was also found by the medical examiner," said Felos.

The Schindlers were unable to make the leap to the conclusion that followed in many minds: Terri needed to die.

"Because her brain damage was at a certain level, it gives us justification for killing her, starving her to death?" Terri's brother Bobby asked rhetorically.

Indeed, the court's death order chilled many in the disabled community, who consider it "dangerous." Some twenty-six national disability rights organizations, led by Not Dead Yet, pleaded for the country to return to its senses.

"'Incompetence' and chronic disability have become the targets for a new eugenics movement that essentially aims to remove most protections for this population that were previously guaranteed by law, tradition, religion or common decency," wrote disability advocate Thomas Nerney. "It is now considered an act of 'kindness' to relieve someone with a significant disability of his or her very life."

The disability rights community sees a deep societal bias against persons with disabilities as the *real* Terri Schiavo story. To them, her death represents the ultimate expression of widespread discrimination against disabled Americans.

Death of disabled persons by the withholding of food and water is actually an old story, dating back to the prominent 1983 court case of Elizabeth Bouvia. After suffering a miscarriage and the dissolution of her marriage, this twenty-five-year-old woman with cerebral palsy checked into a hospital in the Los Angeles area and demanded to be dehydrated and starved to death while sustained by comfort care and morphine. Some of the cast of characters involved in promoting Terri Schiavo's death similarly fought for Bouvia's assisted suicide, including Cranford, bioethicists who filed an amicus brief in both cases, the ACLU, and the Hemlock Society. The key distinction between Elizabeth Bouvia and Terri Schiavo, not lost on those in the disability community, is that Bouvia gave clear and convincing evidence that she wanted to die by dehydration and starvation. Bouvia herself solicited the assistance of the ACLU and hired a Hemlock Society attorney to litigate in favor of her death. Paradoxically, after Bouvia received a court's blessing to commit suicide, she changed her mind.

Elizabeth Bouvia helped the right-to-die movement plant the seed of "better dead than disabled" in American minds. But after the lower courts rebuffed Bouvia's planned assisted suicide, the movement realized it would take a multipronged public education initiative to harvest that seed. A decade-long $200 million campaign to improve palliative care and promote end-of-life choice, primarily funded by the Robert Wood Johnson Foundation and billionaire George Soros's Project on Death in America, was rolled out in the 1990s and then declared no longer necessary by the end of 2003. Terri Schiavo's death came a short sixteen months later.

In response to the Terri Schiavo case, millions of Americans have followed the heed of experts and filled out advance directives to ensure their deaths are hastened rather than needlessly and artificially prolonged in the event of incapacity. While these individuals may consider the advance directive an insurance policy of sorts to assure a death with dignity, the health-care industry and state Medicaid dispensers across the country hail the opportunity to curb the burgeoning cost of keeping the elderly, infirm, and disabled alive in hospitals, nursing homes, and correctional facilities.

In the face of anecdotal evidence that health-care proxies, authorized by patients prior to incapacitation, who seek to keep the patients alive are being replaced with others who seek the patients' deaths, America appears to be sliding down the proverbial "slippery slope" toward involuntary euthanasia. Many fear the fervor over the right to die will be abused in the name of cost cutting as millions of aging baby boomers begin to swamp the already overburdened health-care system. Others grimly report it's already happening and that America has arrived at the point where health-care decisions for those at the end of their lives or rendered incapacitated are being made based on an individual's net worth as computed on a cost-benefit analysis: those lives deemed too expensive to maintain are ended.

"America has been sold a bill of goods," declares former Schindler family attorney Pat Anderson. "In a society that values youth and beauty and the surface over the inner soul, this is the logical outcome. If you're not pretty anymore, if you're not young anymore, you just need to die. You need to move on over."

Former Florida gubernatorial candidate and Jeb Bush attorney Ken Connor believes the Terri Schiavo case, the outcome of which he calls "judicial homicide," holds staggering implications: "I think every human being has . . . a stake in this," Connor said during a Tampa Bay–area radio interview hosted by talk journalist John Sipos last year. "You don't have to be a man or woman of faith to worry about the morality of taking the life of an innocent person. The right to life is the foundation of all other rights. It's that right without which no other right can exist."[6]

In summary, the Terri Schiavo case is more than the sum of all of its permutations—right-to-die, pro-life, disability rights. It is, at its core, a human rights issue. Who decides who lives and who dies and under what circumstances? *In re Guardianship of Schiavo* sets legal precedent that a probate judge, without the added input of a jury, is now an authorized arbiter of life and death. Indeed, America is not the same since Terri Schiavo's death.

Terri's story provides an opportunity for collective introspection. Are we happy with the laws that govern the care of incapacitated and disabled individuals? Should the disabled have the right to die? Are we happy with the level of enforcement of laws designed to protect incapacitated, elderly, and vulnerable adults? Are we happy with how the medical community responds to incapacitation and disability? Are we happy with strangers evaluating our quality of life for us? Are we happy with the courts determining what's in our "best interests" when we cannot speak for ourselves? Are we happy with how the judicial system arbitrates family disputes over incapacitation or disability? What should the role of the courts be in end-of-life issues? Are we okay with dehydrating a forty-one-year-old brain-injured woman to death without her explicit permission? Are we okay with dehydrating a forty-one-year-old brain-injured woman to death at all?

Terri's Story is intended to provoke critical thinking and dialogue about these questions in hopes of arriving at answers that can achieve healing for a divided nation. Failure to do so is to miss the significance of Terri Schiavo's death. As Nobel Peace Prize winner Dr. Martin Luther King Jr. once stated: "Our lives begin to end the day we become silent about things that matter."

Primary sources included the following court opinions:

Schiavo v. Igel, No. 92–939–15 (Fla. Pinellas Cir. Ct. November 10, 1992)
In re Guardianship of Schiavo, No. 90–2908-GD (Fla. Pinellas Cir. Ct. February 11, 2000)
In re Guardianship of Schiavo, No. 90–2908-GD (Fla. Pinellas Cir. Ct. March 7, 2000)
In re Guardianship of Schiavo, No. 90–2908-GD (Fla. Pinellas Cir. Ct. March 24, 2000)
In re Guardianship of Schiavo, No. 90–2908-GD (Fla. Cir. Ct. August 7, 2001)
In re Guardianship of Schiavo, 780 So.2d 176 (Fla. 2d DCA 2001)
In re Guardianship of Schiavo, 792 So.2d 551 (Fla. 2d DCA 2001)
In re Guardianship of Schiavo, 800 So.2d 640 (Fla. 2d DCA 2001)
Schindler v. Schiavo ex rel. Schiavo, 829 So.2d 220 (Fla. 2d DCA 2002)
In re Guardianship of Schiavo, No. 90–2908-GD-003, 2002 WL 31876088 (Fla. Cir. Ct. November 22, 2002)
In re Guardianship of Schiavo, No. 90–2908-GB-003, 2002 WL 31817960 (Fla. Cir. Ct. November 22, 2002)
In re Guardianship of Schiavo, No. 90–2908-GD (Fla. Pinellas Cir. Ct. August 26, 2003)
Schiavo v. Schiavo, No. 8:03-cv-1860-T-26TGW, 2003 WL 22469905 (M.D. Fla. September 23, 2003)
In re Guardianship of Schiavo, 851 So.2d 182 (Fla. 2d DCA 2003)

Schindler v. Schiavo, 865 So.2d 500 (Fla. 2d DCA 2003)
Advocacy Ctr. For Persons with Disabilities, Inc. v. Schiavo, 17 Fla. L. Weekly Fed. D291 (M.D. Fla. October 21, 2003)
Schiavo v. Bush, No. 03–008212-CI-20, 2003 WL 22762709 (Fla. Cir. Ct. November 4, 2003)
In re Guardianship of Schiavo, No. 90–2908-GD (Fla. Pinellas Cir. Ct. November 5, 2003)
Bush v. Schiavo, 861 So.2d 506 (Fla. 2d DCA 2003)
Schiavo v. Bush, No. 03–008212-CI-20, 2004 WL 628663 (Fla. Cir. Ct. 2004)
Bush v. Schiavo, 866 So.2d 136 (Fla. 2d DCA 2004)
Schindler v. Schiavo, 866 So.2d 140 (Fla. 2d DCA 2004)
Bush v. Schiavo, 871 So.2d 1012 (Fla. 2d DCA 2004)
Schiavo v. Bush, No. 03–008212-CI-20, 2004 WL 980028 (Fla. Cir. Ct. May 5, 2004)
In re Guardianship of Schiavo, No. 90–2908-GD (Fla. Pinellas Cir. Ct. July 6, 2004)
Bush v. Schiavo, 885 So.2d 321 (Fla. 2004)
Schindler v. Schiavo, No. 2D04–3451, 2004 WL 2726107 (Fla. 2d DCA November 24, 2004)
In re Guardianship of Schiavo, No. 90–2908-GD (Fla. Pinellas Cir. Ct. February 11, 2005)
In re Guardianship of Schiavo, No. 90–2908-GD-003, 2005 WL 459634 (Fla. Cir. Ct. February 25, 2005)
In re Guardianship of Schiavo, No. 90–2908-GD (Fla. Pinellas Cir. Ct. March 8, 2005)
In re Guardianship of Schiavo, No. 90–2908-GD (Fla. Pinellas Cir. Ct. March 9, 2005)
In re Guardianship of Schiavo, No. 90–2908-GD (Fla. Pinellas Cir. Ct. March 10, 2005)
In re Guardianship of Schiavo, ___ So.2d ___ WL 600377 (Fla. 2d DCA March 16, 2005)
In re Guardianship of Schiavo, No. 90–2908-GD (Fla. Pinellas Cir. Ct. March 18, 2005)
In re Guardianship of Schiavo, No. 90–2908-GD (Fla. Pinellas Cir. Ct. March 22, 2005)
Schiavo v. Greer, No. 8:05-cv-522-T-30TGW (M.D. Fla. March 18, 2005)
Schiavo ex rel. Schindler v. Schiavo ___ F. Supp. 2d ___, No. 8:05-cv-530-T-27TBM, 2005 WL 641710 (M.D. Fla. March 22, 2005)

Schiavo ex. rel. Schindler v. Schiavo, ___ F.3d ___, No. 05–11556, 2005 WL 648897 (11th Cir. March 23, 2005).

ACKNOWLEDGMENTS

PRAISE BELONGS to God for giving my life purpose and for sustaining and empowering me to fulfill that purpose.

Deep appreciation goes to my husband, whom I cherish above all else in this world, for his ceaseless devotion, boundless enthusiasm, and constant faith.

Profound gratitude extends to my mother and sister, whose unfailing love and guidance shaped me as a person and has carried me through a lifetime of goals.

Heartfelt thanks are offered to the rest of my dear family and friends, for whom I am blessed.

Admiration and appreciation go out to Joseph Farah for affording me this opportunity and to Ronald Pitkin, Ed Curtis, Stacie Bauerle, and the rest of the team at WND Books for their publishing expertise and passion and their commitment to excellence.

TERRI'S STORY

1

Terri Schindler Becomes Terri Schiavo

PHOTOGRAPHS SERVE TO KEEP the precious memory of deceased loved ones alive. When strung together, snapshots taken to record major life events or to spontaneously capture random, idle moments form a motion picture reconstruction of a life ended. Perhaps the photograph most often associated with the name "Terri Schiavo" in the minds of the millions familiar with her story is a closeup of a disabled thirty-eight-year-old lying in her hospice bed, seemingly looking up at her mother who is cradling her head in her hands. An apparent expression of love radiates from Terri's face. The photograph was a still frame gleaned from video of an examination performed on Terri in preparation for an evidentiary hearing in November 2002, which was mandated by an appellate court to determine her medical condition at the time and explore her prospects for recovery.

The contentious photograph was derided as "cheap sensationalism" by neurologist Dr. Ronald Cranford, a renowned right-to-die advocate, who testified at the hearing that Terri's brain had atrophied and shrunken to the extent there was little cerebral cortex left, and that her smiling represented an involuntary reflex of a person in a persistent vegetative state. In contrast, Terri's parents, siblings, and a growing legion of supporters cast the photograph as indisputable evidence Terri had cognizant function, recognized her mother, and was purposefully responsive to her. As such, they argued, she was not in a persistent vegetative state and therefore did not meet the criteria under Florida law for her gastric feeding tube to be removed.

Another photograph that often accompanied local press coverage of Terri's story was taken in 1993, three years after the mysterious collapse that resulted in her brain injury. It shows a sophisticated, attractive brunette sitting in her wheelchair inside what appears to be a gift shop. She's wearing a colorful blouse and matching earrings. Her short hair is stylishly cut. Her beautiful complexion is accented with makeup and bright red lipstick painstakingly applied by her doting husband. Her expression is more serious than vacant. What transpired over the nine years between these two photographs is the crux of Terri's story that will be the focus of subsequent chapters.

A collage of photos assembled by supporters of the Schindlers and found stashed inside one of the dozens of boxes of material that represent the court battle to keep their daughter alive serves to introduce the Terri Schiavo comparatively few had the privilege of knowing before her injury as compared to after. Pensive, big brown eyes dominate the baby picture taken within the first year after Theresa Marie Schindler was born on December 3, 1963. Her devoutly Catholic parents, Bob and Mary Schindler, named their firstborn for St. Teresa of Avila, a sixteenth-century Carmelite nun who founded her own order and was later proclaimed the Patroness of Spain and canonized by Pope Gregory XV. The Schindlers' name choice proved somewhat prophetic, as St. Teresa's life was marked by serious illness that drove her into a coma, during which she was thought to be dead. Days later St. Teresa came out of her coma but remained paralyzed in her legs for three years.

Eleven days after her birth, Theresa Marie Schindler was baptized according to the rite of the Roman Catholic Church at St. Henry's Church in Philadelphia, Pennsylvania. Like her namesake, Theresa Marie had an affectionate manner. Her penchant for hugging dates back to her earliest days, as demonstrated in a photograph of her embracing her baby brother, Bobby, as he attempted to crawl across the living room floor. Another photo in the collage captures a pajama-clad Terri, Bobby, and baby sister Suzanne, who came along four years after Bobby and five years after Terri, posing in front of their Christmas stockings hanging from the fireplace mantel. Christmas and holidays were always festive times in the Schindler household, where the large, extended family gathered.

The Schindler family said grace before dinner and went to Mass every week at the local parish church. When she was eight years old, Theresa Marie received her first Holy Communion. She was given a small white "wallet" that contained a rosary and a small book titled *The New First Mass Book* in honor of the occasion. A few years later she and Bobby proudly posed for a picture in their red-and-white confirmation robes after having made their firm profession of faith according to Catholic tradition. Terri's chosen confirmation name, Kathleen, is embroidered on the silk banner draped over her shoulder.

Another photograph in the collage shows the three smiling grade school–aged siblings perched on the sofa with their arms wrapped around each other's shoulders. By now Terri wears thick glasses with heavy frames. Occasionally she would allow her lazy eye to wander in order to torment her mother, who would cry out, "Terri, don't do that!" Sporting a Mickey Mouse T-shirt, the youngster is chubby in comparison to her siblings, foreshadowing the battle she would have with her weight as a teenager. When her mother took her shopping for clothes, she cried.

The shy but friendly and highly likable girl attended Our Lady of Good Counsel, where her infectious laugh sparked a friendship with classmate Sue Pickwell. The two giggled over Terri's crush on a boy named Vincent Mandez. She took to buying his favorite foods so she could trade with him at lunch.

"Think of all the money we spent on you-know-who," Terri later wrote in Pickwell's yearbook.[1] Terri could never have known this secret would be shared with thousands of complete strangers, or that her fourth-grade report card would be submitted as evidence in a court battle waged to save her life. According to the aged document, Terri never arrived late for school and earned good grades. She scored highest in mathematics, spelling, and music.

Terri's graduation from eighth grade was celebrated with a precommencement Mass that included Scripture readings, a responsorial psalm, communion, and prayers. After grade school, Terri and her girlfriends donned green polyester jumpers, green knee socks, and green saddle shoes—the uniform required by Archbishop Wood High School for Girls in Warminster, Pennsylvania, which is part of the archdiocese of Philadelphia. Terri's ninth-grade report card indicates she earned her highest grade in Scripture. Pickwell told the *St. Petersburg Times* she sneaked cigarettes from her dad's shirt pocket, and she and Terri smoked them in the woods. Meanwhile, Terri's perfect attendance record continued, and she earned high marks for conduct.

Another image in the photo collage has the Schindler family posing in front of their four-bedroom Colonial on Red Wing Lane in the middle-class, northwest Philadelphia suburb of Huntingdon Valley. Buck, the yellow Labrador retriever, doesn't cooperate with the photographer and looks away from the camera with ears perked and tail erect. He's obviously spotted something down the street that holds his intense interest. It is still years before the spry family pet would collapse of old age in the driveway, and Terri would attempt to revive him by giving him mouth-to-nose resuscitation.

Her passion for animals also expressed itself in her collection of more than one hundred stuffed animals; a love for horseback riding; and a devotion to Starsky and Hutch, pet gerbils—named for the then popular television show—that routinely wound up in the air-conditioning unit in the basement. After she had gotten her driver's license, Terri came home crying one night, believing she had hit a rabbit or a squirrel with her Trans Am. To spare her grief, Bobby went back to the scene and threw the animal's carcass into the bushes and reported to his sister that he hadn't found anything and she must be mistaken.[2]

Terri's compassion wasn't limited to animals but extended to people. Another longtime girl friend, Diana Meyer, remembers Terri as someone who was nonjudgmental. "Terri is one of those people that you are lucky that you get to know. She is just good," Meyer testified. "I used to say she was the light side of life. I looked at somebody and would say, 'What an ugly dress.' She looked at them and would say, 'But it looks good on her.' I never heard her say anything bad about anyone."

By her junior year in high school the five-foot-three adolescent weighed more than two hundred pounds. She shied away from the camera, hated sports, didn't date, avoided the high-school prom, and spent hours in her purple and white room. She devoured Danielle Steele romance novels and swooned at the sight of *Starsky and Hutch* costar Paul Michael Glaser. Pickwell estimates the two of them wrote hundreds of letters to the actor and squealed with glee when a spokesperson responded. Meyer recalls they watched *An Officer and a Gentleman* with Richard Gere and Debra Winger four times in one day. Likely because of her weight struggles, no photographs chronicle those dreamy high-school years in the collage.

Upon her high-school graduation in 1981, Terri tried multiple weight-loss programs. She lost approximately one hundred pounds and gained a new lease on life. She enrolled in Bucks County Community College with a plan to get a job working with animals. Once again, her infectious laughter made a classmate sit up and take notice of her during a psychology course in her second semester—twenty-year-old Michael Schiavo from Levittown, Pennsylvania.

"I fell in love with her the instant I saw her," Schiavo told CNN anchorwoman Paula Zahn in a March 28, 2005, interview. "She had this persona, this aura about her that just attracted you. . . . Shy and outgoing at the same time, you know? She was just a very, sweet person."[3] Schiavo recalled other juxtaposing traits during a January 24, 2000, trial. "She was a very outspoken person. She believed in what she believed in," he said, "But on the other hand, she had a heart of gold. . . . You would meet her and just be charmed with her."

Michael Schiavo was the first male, outside of her family members, to ever take notice of Terri. He was eight months older and stood more than a foot taller than Terri. His charm and attention swept her off her feet. He was her first kiss and her "officer and a gentleman," as Meyer put it. While they spoke of marriage on their second date, Schiavo waited five months to propose. Because he was not a Roman Catholic, the couple attended prenuptial counseling with the Schindler family's parish priest. Once that was completed, Michael was given a dispensation to marry into the Roman Catholic faith. The night before their wedding, Bob Schindler sat on the floor of his eldest daughter's bedroom and cried. He thought Terri was too young to get married. She was three weeks shy of turning twenty-one. Terri pretended to be asleep as her father wept but later shared the incident with her bridesmaid, Meyer.[4]

Meyer had her own reservations about the marriage, which she expressed in a March 21, 2005, interview with Fox News Channel host Greta Van Susteren. "I didn't like Michael," she said. "I thought Terri deserved more than Michael offered."[5]

Theresa Marie Schindler became Theresa Marie Schiavo during a nuptial Mass at Our Lady of Good Counsel on November 10, 1984, in front of approximately 250 guests. At the end of the ceremony, Terri made a special gesture indicating she dedicated her marriage to the Virgin Mother. Photographs now tucked in an attorney's evidence carton depict a beaming Terri elegantly adorned in a long-sleeved lace wedding gown and old-fashioned bonnet, clutching a large bouquet of white roses sprinkled with pink flowers and baby's breath. As usual, her large brown eyes sparkled. The images of the joyous family occasion bear no hint of the future turmoil wrought by that defining moment. The wedding represented a triumph for the formerly obese and insecure teenager who had only ever dreamed about being in love. She had kept her weight down to 145 pounds and easily fit into a size 12 wedding gown.

Over the course of her first year of marriage, however, Terri regained some of the weight she so diligently lost. She inched up to 155. Michael Schiavo gave court testimony his wife's weight fluctuated in the first years of their marriage. She would lose 20 to 25 pounds and then regain some of it.

Fed up with the cold weather, the couple moved to St. Petersburg, Florida, in April 1986. After that, Terri's weight dipped down to 120, according to her medical records, and stayed in the range of 120 to 123 throughout 1989, the year prior to her collapse. No one knew how Terri managed to lose the weight. Michael Schiavo says he inquired once, and Terri told him she was merely watching what she ate. No one suspected she had an eating disorder.

"To us, she looked like Terri," Schiavo testified.

Terri was happy with her transformation. Shopping for clothes no longer prompted tears—even shopping for bikinis, which she was now wearing for the first time in her life. She loved lying in the hot Florida sun, soaking up its rays. She reappears in the collage of assorted photographs as a slender woman playfully hugging her brother in front of a Christmas tree. Her brilliant smile in another holiday snapshot captures a Terri Schiavo at peace with herself and her life. With burgeoning self-confidence, Terri boldly became a blonde. Three photographs included in the collage exhibit the happy "new" blonde Terri. One depicts her arm-and-arm with her giggling, adoring father. Another has her dressed up in a flattering white dress on the occasion of Bobby's college graduation. A third catches Terri sitting in the backseat of a car with an alluringly warm and serene expression on her face.

Like many newlyweds, the couple had their challenges. While Terri worked as a clerk at Prudential Insurance Company during the day, Michael worked nights in the restaurant industry. By all accounts, their opposite schedules created tension in the marriage. Terri was lonely and restless in the evenings after work and often went out to nightclubs with Bobby. The newfound attention from men evoked by her slim figure and happy aura embarrassed and pleased Terri. She would refer to her brother as her "boyfriend" when men became too amorous. Brian Schiavo also has fond memories of going to nightclubs with his sister-in-law.

"Every time we were together she was a blast," he said. "She was very friendly. She loved to have a good time."

Another brother-in-law, Scott Schiavo, recalled Terri's sense of humor. "In fact, I still to this day have a card she sent my wife on a postcard from Florida of some gentlemen with their back sides bared and a little letter saying to my wife, 'Geez, Karen, these are my four new boyfriends. Do you want to come over?'" he testified in the 2000 trial.

But financial pressures dogged the couple. According to Michael's court testimony, Terri was unemployed for the first couple of months after they moved to Florida, while she waited for her job transfer with Prudential to come together. The couple was dependent on his paycheck, but Michael's employment became erratic. Over the four years they lived in Florida prior to Terri's collapse he worked at six different restaurants. One job only lasted a month. Another lasted three weeks. When Michael was in between jobs, the couple lived off of Terri's income. Terri's office mate at Prudential, Jackie Rhodes, testified Michael's unstable employment record angered Terri. According to Rhodes, Michael would often call the office and tell Terri he was unhappy at his job and planned to quit. Terri, in turn, would plead with him to get another job lined up first.

In a September 27, 1999, court deposition Michael Schiavo was asked whether he usually had another job to go to before he quit one. He responded: "I believe so. I'm trying to remember and I can't recall. I think there was one time that I had a little lapse in a job, but it wasn't for very long."

During their first year in Florida the couple lived in a vacation condo owned by Terri's parents. The Schindlers let them slide whenever they couldn't afford the rent. Michael Schiavo testified in 1999 he thought they had paid "some rent," but he didn't recall. Rhodes testified Terri confessed to her that if it weren't for her parents, she didn't know how she and Michael would manage, because they couldn't afford to pay rent. Upon Bob Schindler's retirement, three months after Terri and Michael had moved to Florida, the Schindlers themselves moved to a townhouse in St. Petersburg. Michael and Terri continued to live in the Schindlers' condo for approximately a year and then rented an apartment on Fourth Street North in the downtown area. Tolly and Shane, Terri's overweight cats, joined them. Bobby Schindler also moved to Florida at that time and rented an apartment in the same complex as his sister and brother-in-law.

Interviewed on his brother's behalf, Brian Schiavo called Jackie Rhodes's testimony "ridiculous" and downplayed the couple's financial pressures. "They weren't professional people. They weren't highly skilled people, and it's not easy to make it here in Florida. Jobs are not plentiful down here, and good paying jobs are even less," he said. "I don't think that there were any other problems than newlyweds trying to make it in Florida."

But marital strife was reportedly a shared hurt that formed a bond between the two office mates. Jackie Rhodes testified about days when Michael called the office and Terri didn't want to take his phone call because they were in the middle of a fight.

"Michael was very controlling," Rhodes told Greta Van Susteren in the March 21, 2005, interview. "[Terri] was not allowed to go anywhere after work. She had to go straight home after work. He would monitor the mileage on her car. And on the weekends, when we'd go anywhere, he would want to know where we were going." Consequently, Rhodes served as designated driver for their customary Saturday outings. They would go shopping, run errands, catch lunch, and every other Saturday they would visit Terri's grandmother in a nursing home while Michael was at work.

Rhodes testified she and Terri both felt overly controlled by their husbands and were unhappy in their marriages. Rhodes's husband had asked for a divorce. Rhodes said she and Terri discussed both getting divorces and moving in together. They reportedly talked about where they would live and what furniture they had.

Bobby Schindler also knew Terri was unhappy in her marriage. Several weeks prior to her collapse, Bobby witnessed Terri have an emotional "breakdown" when they were out at a restaurant with Michael Schiavo and his brother Brian. Terri asked Bobby to go to the rest room with her.

"In the hallway, Terri turned to me and started to cry," recalls Bobby Schindler. "I asked her what was wrong and she said that she wanted to divorce Michael. . . . I didn't know what to say to Terri other than to try and comfort her." Schindler recalled being struck by how much resentment was in her voice when she spoke about Michael. "She had a tough time settling down and kept repeating to me, 'Bobby, I wish I had the guts to divorce him because I would in a second.'"[6]

Mary Schindler also believed the marriage was suffering during the months prior to Terri's collapse. She didn't need to rely on a mother's intuition. Rather, she testified her daughter admitted to her that she was no longer in love with Michael and was considering ending their marriage.

Michael Schiavo denies there was trouble in the marriage and characterizes his relationship with Terri prior to her collapse as "great." "We had a beautiful marriage. It was very loving, very romantic," Schiavo said in an April 25, 2000, interview on *Dateline NBC*. "I'm not going to say it was the most perfect, but it was near-perfect."[7]

"We had wanted kids and that's what we were trying to have when all this occurred," he said in the interview with CNN host Paula Zahn. "[Terri] loved kids. We wanted to have a houseful, just to have a happy, little normal life. We didn't want anything big. We weren't into the glimmer and shine. We just wanted to have a nice little comfortable life together."[8]

Brian Schiavo emphasized that Terri was very close with his mother and his sister-in-law Joan, who lives in Pennsylvania, and said these women would have known if the couple had been having problems.

Terri's faith was a bone of contention in the marriage, according to her father. In a sworn affidavit filed in court, Bob Schindler stated Michael showed no interest in Terri's faith and, on occasion, made derogatory or condescending comments about her going to Mass. For this reason, he said, Terri would go to Mass during the week with girlfriend and co-worker Jackie Rhodes or on Saturday evenings with her parents or her sister while Michael was at work. Mary Schindler stated in a sworn court affidavit that Terri had not fallen away from her faith as an adult but regularly attended Mass. Rhodes also described Terri as a "devout" Catholic. Michael Schiavo testified he and Terri went to Mass together on Sundays every few months. During these occasions, he pointed out that Terri would not receive communion and did not participate in the sacrament of confession. Schiavo would later erroneously tell reporters the Schindlers had never gone to church.

The last time the Schindlers saw their daughter prior to her brain injury was on the eve of her collapse. The family went to the 4:30 p.m. service at St. John's Catholic Church on St. Pete Beach on Saturday, February 24, 1990, and then gathered at the home of Fran Casler for dinner. Casler, a longtime friend of the Schindlers, was very close to Terri and described herself as like an "aunt" to Terri. The two were three weeks into Italian lessons at an adult education center. Casler's houseguest, an Italian chef, had prepared a feast for them. After an evening of good food and plenty of laughter, the Schindlers and Casler parted company, and Terri returned home to her empty, dark apartment.

2

Mysterious Collapse

"I was, for some reason, getting out of bed, and I heard a thud in the hall. I raced out there, and Terri was lying in the hall. I went down to get her. I thought, well, maybe she just tripped or whatever. I rolled her over, and she was lifeless. And it almost seems like she had this last breath."

A soft-spoken Michael Schiavo recounted the torturous details of his wife's mysterious collapse on February 25, 1990. She was twenty-six years old. The couple had been married for five years. They had been planning to start a family. Terri had confided in her mother she was troubled she wasn't getting her period and was frustrated her doctors could not figure out why. Her mother promised the two would go together to find a new doctor after the weekend. By then, Terri needed doctors for a different reason.

With his blond hair complemented by a pale yellow button-down shirt, Schiavo cut a handsome figure on CNN's *Larry King Live*. He appeared exhausted from his drawn-out campaign to carry out his wife's wishes, which he maintained were to end her life. At the top of the program, he expressed anger at the Florida legislature and Governor Jeb Bush for meddling in his private affairs and obstructing Terri's merciful death. The interview evoked sympathy for a man deemed too young to be grappling with a spouse's end-of-life issues, a predicament more often faced in old age.

Schiavo's calm demeanor and casual retelling belied the tense drama surrounding an incident that abruptly changed his life forever and set in motion the circumstances that resulted in her death. In his characteristic style, the talk-show legend leaned forward on his elbows and appeared to hang on Schiavo's every word. It was October 27, 2003, nearly fourteen years after Terri's collapse. Schiavo had told this painful story countless times before for inquiring reporters. But tonight he was reaching an audience of millions.

Explaining that he managed restaurants and worked late at night, Schiavo said he came home from work at about 2:00 a.m. and climbed into bed next to his wife. Terri stirred just enough to tell him good night, and the couple exchanged a kiss. Approximately two and a half hours later, Schiavo found Terri "lifeless" on the hall floor.

"I held her in my arms, and I'm trying to shake her up," he described. "I ran over, I called 911. Her brother happened to live in the same [apartment] complex as we did. I called him. I went back to Terri and from there—six, seven minutes later—the paramedics [arrived]."

"And the way she is now is the way she was that night?" asked King.

"That night she was totally unconscious," replied Schiavo.

Paramedics arrived on the scene at 5:52 a.m. to find Terri Schiavo lying face down and unconscious, half in the bathroom and half in the hallway. Her upper body was in the hall, with her head facing east. Her legs and feet were pointing west on the bathroom floor. Although she showed no outward signs of violence, the paramedics called the St. Petersburg Police Department due to her young age and because "the situation seemed unusual," according to the police report. Two officers arrived on the scene at 6:30 a.m. to find the paramedics still working on Terri. She remained unconscious and was hooked up to a respirator.

Officer Phillip Brewer stated in his report a physical inspection of Terri's body revealed "no signs of trauma to her head or face." Brewer's report indicates he lingered in the apartment after the paramedics and Michael Schiavo had left for the hospital. He wrote that he found nothing unusual inside the apartment, and there were no signs of a struggle or anything that would indicate a crime had been committed. In the kitchen he found various bottles of prescription medications. Only two had been prescribed for Terri. Brewer said he secured the apartment and brought the keys with him to the hospital, where a crowd of family members was gathered in the emergency room.

As with most aspects of the twelve-year court battle between the Schindlers and the Schiavos, the Schindlers tell a starkly different story about that tragic night. According to them, Michael Schiavo, upon the discovery of Terri lying unconscious on the floor, placed his first call to Terri's father, Bob Schindler, and not to 911. Schindler said he instructed Schiavo to call 911, hung up, and then quickly called his son, Bobby, dispatching him to Terri's nearby apartment. Bobby Schindler says he beat the paramedics to the scene by seconds. What he saw still haunts him.

"It's etched in my mind," he said. "Terri was face down on the ground with her arms underneath her and her hands up by her neck. She was like in the fetal position, only facing straight down. She was gasping, kind of making a snoring or gurgling sound," Bobby Schindler recalled. "Michael was frantic."

Terri's younger sibling questioned Schiavo's repeated public accounts of having cradled her "lifeless" body in his arms. "If Michael rolled her over, then he must have rolled her back before I got there," he said. And he must have done so before the paramedics arrived, who also found her lying face down.

THE SCHINDLERS also question why details of Michael Schiavo's account of the horrific early morning hours of February 25, 1990, have changed over the years. For instance, in July 27, 1992, Michael Schiavo stated during a deposition that Terri was not awake when he came home from work between 12:30 and 1:00 a.m. Months later, on November 5, 1992, Schiavo testified he didn't recall whether she was up or not when he arrived between 11:30 p.m. and midnight. He said he "might have" had a conversation with her, but he "didn't remember the conversation." Years later, in the *Dateline NBC* broadcast, Michael Schiavo said, "Terri woke up, gave me a kiss good night, and told me she loved me. And we went to sleep."[1] Then Schiavo told Larry King in the October 27, 2003, interview, "She woke up, said good night, [and] gave me a kiss" when he came home around 2:00 a.m.

Not only does the changing description of Terri's reaction to his arrival home from work and the fluctuating time of that arrival bother the Schindlers, but they are also suspicious about the time stamp Michael Schiavo affixes to her collapse. He told both Larry King in his October 2003 interview and Pinellas–Pasco County medical examiner Jon Thogmartin that he heard a thud and discovered Terri on the floor at approximately 4:30 a.m.

"There is a very troubling gap in time," Schindler attorney David Gibbs III told a crowd of reporters gathered at the medical examiner's office for a press conference. "The 911 emergency call was placed at 5:40. . . . I would like to know what happened from 4:30 when Terri collapsed till 5:40 when he called emergency services. . . . Those 70 minutes are very, very troubling."

In court testimony in 1992, Schiavo pinpointed the time of Terri's collapse at 5:00 a.m. The time gap also aroused the suspicions of Florida Governor Jeb Bush, who announced days after the release of the autopsy report that a prosecutor had agreed to investigate the matter.

"Between 40 and 70 minutes elapsed before the call was made, and I am aware of no explanation for the delay," Bush said in a letter requesting the investigation and faxed to Pinellas–Pasco County State Attorney Bernie McCabe. "In light of this new information, I urge you to take a fresh look at this case without any preconceptions as to the outcome."[2] Bush's renewed action in the case prompted scathing editorials in the local press and the *New York Times,* suggesting such a probe fifteen years after the fact, and months after Terri's death, amounted to shameless political pandering.

"Why is it improper?" Bobby Schindler asked. "Why should we take Michael's word for it that he didn't [cause her collapse]? When you look at his own testimony, he's caught in a series of different stories. It's as though he's not being truthful because he's always changing his story."

Schiavo attorney George Felos deflected the time-gap accusation by explaining his client often confuses dates and times. "There is no hour gap or other gap to the point Michael heard Terri fall and called 911," he said at a press conference.

Offering no explanation himself, Schiavo jumped on the offense: "I have consistently said over the years that I didn't wait but ran to call 911 after Terri collapsed. It is sickening that the Schindlers and Governor Bush, for their own selfish reasons, want to keep this case going."[3]

Another aspect of Michael Schiavo's narrative that varied over the years was the position of Terri's body on the floor. In a July 27, 1992, court deposition, two years after her collapse, Michael Schiavo indicated he found Terri "on her back," according to the transcript:

> ATTORNEY KEN DEACON: When you saw her, how was she lying . . . on her back or—
>
> SCHIAVO: On her back. . . . I was to her within two seconds. I seen she stopped breathing. I ran to the phone, called 911 within five seconds and panicked.
>
> DEACON: What did you do then, after that?
>
> SCHIAVO: I went over to her. I—I thought maybe—I just started talking to her and holding her. I didn't know what to do.
>
> DEACON: Did you try any CPR?
>
> SCHIAVO: No.
>
> DEACON: . . . How did you determine that . . . she had stopped breathing?

SCHIAVO: Because I felt her chest and I heard her gasp once, you know, and—

DEACON: Okay. Then what happened?

SCHIAVO: I immediately went over and called 911.

DEACON: Okay. After . . . 911 and after you were holding her, what . . . was the next thing that happened?

SCHIAVO: I laid Terri down. . . . I remember my brother-in-law lived in the same complex; I called him.

By January 2000, Schiavo's recollection had Terri positioned facedown on the floor. "I was getting out of bed for some reason and I heard this thud. So I ran out into the hall and I found Terri on the floor," he testified on January 24, 2000, according to the transcript. I knelt down next to her and I turned her over because she sort of fell on her face. On her stomach and face. I turned her over going, 'Terri, Terri. You okay?' She kind of had this gurgling noise. I laid her down and ran over and called 911. I was hysterical. I called 911. I called her brother, who lived in the same complex as we did. I ran back to Terri. She was not moving. I held her in my arms until her brother got there. I rocked her. I didn't know what to do. I was hysterical. It was a horrible moment."

When the paramedics arrived, Michael said he moved away so they could work on Terri. "They put the leads on. I heard them say she is flat line. Start CPR. I am standing there going what is happening here? Why is this happening? Why isn't her heart beating? I was just a mess," Schiavo testified.

As he watched the paramedics apply the defibrillator paddles in an effort to restart his sister's heart, Bobby Schindler wondered why Schiavo hadn't attempted to revive his wife. He presumed Schiavo knew how to administer cardiopulmonary resuscitation, or CPR, because Florida law requires restaurant managers to be trained in the life-saving procedure. In fact, Schiavo admits he knew how to administer CPR but failed to do so for his wife because he "panicked."

Terri was rushed to Humana Hospital–Northside in St. Petersburg. En route the paramedics finally succeeded in getting her heart beating again after several attempts at resuscitation. Although paramedics were able to get a pulse at 6:32 a.m., a measurable systolic blood pressure wasn't achieved until 6:46 a.m. By then, extensive damage was done. Her heart had been stopped for more than an hour, starving her brain of oxygen and blood. According to the American Medical Association, the brain cannot survive oxygen deprivation for more than six minutes. How much damage was done to her brain remains in dispute fifteen years later. (That debate will be discussed in chapter 7.)

It would be weeks before Terri would come out of a coma and open her eyes. In the meantime, she suffered convulsions, seizures, and pneumonia and had to be given blood transfusions. She was dependent on a ventilator for a time and then gradually weaned off of it to become free of machines. Doctors inserted a percutaneous endoscopic gastronomy tube, or PEG tube, through the abdominal wall into her stomach to provide hydration and nourishment. It's a simple silicone device that requires surgery and sedation to insert it through endoscopy, but the tube comes out easily with traction. It is considered the best mode of long-term feeding care because it affords fewer complications than tube feeding through the nose.

Terri's long battle with her weight was now completely beyond her control. Instead, she now faced a greater challenge: fighting for her life. The feeding tube connected to her stomach became the crux of the war between her husband and her family. Michael Schiavo sought to have it removed, believing she wouldn't want to live in her condition. The Schindlers fought to keep the tube in place until she could receive therapy, enabling her to eat on her own. (Whether this was reality or wishful thinking also remains in dispute after her death and will be addressed in chapter 7.)

At the hospital, a crowd was gathering. Suzanne Vitadamo, Terri's sister, had come in from out of town, as had members of Michael's family. Coworker Jackie Rhodes was alerted by another co-worker and hustled to the emergency room. The atmosphere was tense. Most seemed dazed. Doctors braced family members, telling them Terri would likely not survive the night. In hindsight, medical examiner Jon Thogmartin called it a "miracle" Terri's heart had restarted.

Michael Schiavo relayed the details of Terri's collapse to Officer Brewer, who entered them in his police report: "Michael Schiavo was awakened by a thud; He thought his wife had fallen down and got out of bed to check on her; He found her unconscious on the floor and called paramedics; He said he didn't know what could be wrong with Terri." Brewer inquired whether there had been any problems at home that would have prompted Terri to attempt suicide. Michael Schiavo reportedly responded there hadn't been any problems, and that he and Terri hadn't had any major arguments lately. Brewer also spoke with Bob Schindler, asking him whether he suspected his son-in-law of any foul play. Schindler reportedly told him, "No."

Michael Schiavo told Brewer his wife had allergic reactions to certain products, like Benadryl, but that she knows to stay away from them. Terri had no history of heart disease. A drug screen revealed no amount of illegal narcotics in her system, and her blood-alcohol level measured at the bottom of the scale. According to Brewer's report, the officer remained at the hospital for the outcome of a CAT scan. It revealed no "mid-line shift" of the brain, which would have indicated an obvious abnormality. Brewer noted additional testing would be necessary to detect a possible aneurysm or pulmonary embolism. Brewer gave Michael Schiavo a business card with the "offense number" written on it and told him he'd call for an update of Terri's condition. Brewer filed his report at 8:55 a.m. The report indicates it was routed to the homicide department. No criminal investigation was ever conducted, likely because Terri did not die that day.

That night, Michael Schiavo spent the first of sixteen consecutive nights camped out at the hospital, sleeping in the waiting room or slumped in a chair beside Terri's bed. According to her hospital records, Terri remained significantly unstable the first few days and did not respond to any stimulation. It took some time before doctors considered her stable enough to be moved from the intensive care unit to the progressive care unit.

3

Bulimia, Bruises, and Bone Scan

WHAT CAUSES A HEALTHY twenty-six-year-old to collapse in the middle of the night? What made her heart stop? These questions remain unanswered. The attending physician at Humana Hospital–Northside and eight consulting physicians, whose fields of expertise ranged from neurology to infectious diseases, who examined Terri during the ten weeks she remained at the hospital were clearly stumped. Her admitting diagnosis was cardiopulmonary arrest. A possible diagnosis of heart attack was briefly entertained but dismissed after blood chemistries and serial EKGs failed to show supporting evidence. Her autopsy later proved her heart was in "excellent" condition, anatomically normal without any areas of myocardial infarction, or death to the heart muscle. A CT scan similarly proved negative for any "acute event." Normal blood gases and chest x-rays dispelled any notion of a pulmonary embolism or other lung cause. Doctors also flirted with the possibility of toxic shock syndrome but later dismissed it.

The laboratory tests taken upon her admission showed Terri had a low potassium level of 2.0, a markedly elevated glucose level of 373, a very low albumin, or protein level of 2.0, and a normal toxic screen without evidence of diet pills or amphetamines. The hospital staff immediately worked to correct the abnormal potassium level, increasing it to 2.9 within two hours of her admission. Potassium is an electrolyte important to the contraction of muscles in the body, including the heart. According to the Web site WebMD, potassium is found primarily in the skeletal muscle and bone and works with sodium to maintain the proper flow of body fluids between the cells in the body. The kidneys regulate the level of potassium in the body through the excretion of urine.[1]

Although he would later testify in the medical malpractice trial that he had no indication Terri had any kind of eating disorder, court documents and medical records from the hospital reveal several discussions between Michael Schiavo and the doctors, during which he shared information to the contrary. Schiavo told doctors Terri had lost sixty-five pounds a few years earlier and remained weight conscious, that she did not eat properly, and that he had to "fight with her to eat a good meal" at times. Additionally, doctors learned from Michael Schiavo that Terri typically drank ten to fifteen glasses of iced tea during the day. Doctors testified Schiavo informed them his wife had an eating disorder.

Because the low potassium level represented the only "striking abnormality" found in an overall "unremarkable" profile, to use physician-speak, the attending physician, Dr. Samir Shah, initially focused on it as the possible cause of Terri's collapse. "At this point it seems that severe hypokalemia could be the triggering cause for her problems," Shah wrote in Terri's admission report, which was dated the same day of her collapse. He added that the "hypokalemia [was] of unclear etiology but could be related to use of iced tea, etc., as well as erratic diet pattern." Hypokalemia is a metabolic imbalance characterized by an extremely low level of potassium in the blood. It is a symptom of diseases that affect kidney function and a side effect of diuretics. Hypokalemia often occurs as a result of rapid loss of urine or sweat without replacement of sufficient potassium.[2]

In the final report filed when Terri Schiavo was discharged from Humana Hospital–Northside on May 9, 1990, a synonym for hypokalemia, hypopotassemia, was listed among her final diagnoses:

- Cardiac arrest
- Anoxic brain damage
- Severe hypopotassemia
- Respiratory failure
- Seizure disorder, secondary to hypoxic encephalopathy
- Pneumonia, secondary to a Staphylococcus aureus
- Right knee fusion

No cause-and-effect relationship between hypopotassemia and the cardiac arrest was discussed in the final report. The cause of Terri's cardiac arrest was unknown.

"Everybody was dumbfounded," Michael Schiavo recalled.

A year later, during the trial of a medical-malpractice lawsuit Michael Schiavo brought against Terri's primary-care physician and gynecologist, jurors latched onto the theory that Terri's potassium imbalance was due to an eating disorder and was the culprit. (More on this trial follows in the next chapter.) Based on the jury's conclusion, Schiavo's attorney, George Felos, repeatedly over the subsequent years called it an "undisputed" part of the case law that Terri's heart stopped beating as a result of the potassium imbalance she developed. But court testimony in 1992 underscored the inconclusiveness of the eating-disorder theory.

"I don't think anybody really can, you know, really tell definitely what caused . . . her heart to stop, but the low potassium may have, may have been a contributing factor," consulting physician Dr. Minquan Suksanong testified. He reiterated this statement later under cross-examination:

ATTORNEY KEN DEACON: Nobody really knows what caused her heart to stop. Is that correct?

DR. SUKSANONG: Correct.

Renowned forensic pathologist Dr. Michael Baden did not accept the eating-disorder-as-the-cause theory. "It's extremely rare for a twenty-year-old to have a cardiac arrest from low potassium who has no other diseases," he said in an interview with Fox News Channel's Greta van Susteren, adding that the medical records reflected that Terri had a healthy heart.

Schiavo himself stressed that the theory remained unproven. In 2000 he testified: "There was speculation made to that, but there was nothing ever proven in court as to that diagnosis." But the theory persisted nonetheless.

"What we can fathom right now is her potassium level was very low. More than likely [because of] bulimia," Schiavo told Larry King in the 2003 interview. According to the surgeon general, bulimia nervosa is an eating disorder that usually arises primarily in adolescent girls. An estimated 3 percent of young women suffer from the binge-eating disorder, which is characterized by episodic, uncontrolled consumption followed by vomiting or laxative abuse to avert weight gain. The causes of bulimia are thought to be a combination of genetic, neurochemical, and psychodevelopmental factors, namely depression, anxiety, substance abuse, and personality disorders.

"Was she a bulimic?" King pointedly asked. Schiavo offered no proof his wife was bulimic—he's never stated he witnessed or heard her vomiting in the bathroom after meals. Nor was there evidence she used laxatives.

"When I was with her, when we were together, Terri would eat and eat and eat," he answered, adding, "Bulimia, from what I've learned over the years, is a very secretive disease."

In court testimony Michael Schiavo described a typical Sunday—the only day of the week he and Terri were able to spend together because of their work schedules. "In the morning she'd wake up, she'd make herself a huge omelet," he said. "And usually we would stop and have lunch somewhere, and then she would eat dinner." Schiavo testified that a couple of times when Terri's weight dipped below 120 pounds, he suggested to her "enough is enough." Similarly, Mary Schindler confronted her daughter about her weight. The response she got was: "I eat, Mom. I eat."[3]

Medical examiner Jon Thogmartin devoted more attention in his ten-page autopsy report to debunking the bulimia theory than any other topic. Summarizing his review of Terri's medical records, court records, and notes from numerous interviews, he wrote: "Her post-resuscitation potassium level and history of remote weight loss appear to be the only evidence that indicate she may have had some type of eating disorder." The operative word in this statement is *post-resuscitation*. Paramedics worked furiously to revive Terri in the early morning hours of February 25, 1990, Thogmartin described. She was intubated within the first five minutes and received seven defibrillations and 1250 cc of fluid, including dextrose solution, epinephrine, lidocaine, Narcan, and dopamine. All of these interventions are known to cause fictitious changes in blood electrolytes and other substances, Thogmartin pointed out.

"Thus it is reasonable to conclude that Mrs. Schiavo's potassium level of 2.0 mmmol/L measured after a period of ventricular fibrillation, epinephrine, and fluid administration was an unreliable measure of her pre-arrest potassium level," he concluded. That leaves her history of weight loss as a teenager as the only other "evidence" of an eating disorder. But he cast doubt on this as well, noting that no one observed her taking diet pills, binging, purging, or consuming laxatives; she never confessed to her family or friends about having an eating disorder; and many other signs and symptoms of bulimia nervosa—such as discolored teeth—were not evident. Addressing Terri's reported iced tea consumption, Thogmartin said caffeine wasn't tested for in the hospital toxicology screening. But he pointed out that the big Italian meal Terri had eaten the night before would have helped her body to absorb the caffeine. Additionally, he doubted that Terri would have gotten up at 4:30 a.m. and "guzzled a quart of tea," which is what she would have needed to do in order for the tea to have been the cause of her potassium imbalance.

By all accounts, Terri was weight conscious prior to her collapse. According to her sister and girlfriends, Terri was under a lot of pressure from her husband to be thin. Diane Meyer said that Terri confided in her that she was worried about becoming fat again and that Michael had warned her after seeing her high-school graduation picture that "if she ever got fat like that again he'd divorce her."

"I said, 'He's probably kidding,'" Meyer told the Associated Press. "But it was upsetting to her."[4]

Meyer was concerned about Terri's eating habits. "She was not eating. Literally was not eating. In the week I spent with her, I saw her eat one bagel," she testified in the 2000 trial. Meyer recalled that during that 1986 visit, Terri had broken up the bagel and eaten a portion of it for breakfast and dinner between Monday morning and Friday evening." In her Fox News interview with Van Susteren, she added, "I had mentioned it to her husband and was told, not so politely, to mind my own business."[5]

Michael Schiavo denied having made such threatening comments to his wife about her weight. He testified he didn't have a preference about whether Terri was thin or heavy. "Terri was my wife. I didn't marry her because of her weight," he said. Michael's brothers, Brian and Scott, point the finger at Bobby Schindler, whom they claim was "hurtful" and teased his sister from time to time about her earlier obesity. They said his comments bothered her. Schindler denies the claim.

Co-worker and friend Jackie Rhodes never noticed anything abnormal about Terri's eating habits, but she also suspected Terri was under pressure from her husband about her weight. She testified that her shared confidences with Terri led her to believe she suffered "mental abuse" in the relationship. Rhodes is now suspicious about having witnessed Terri frequently having bruises on her upper arms and upper legs prior to her collapse. She told Greta Van Susteren in the March 28, 2005, interview she didn't think much of the bruises at the time and dismissed them as "maybe running into the desk at work." Yet she added, "But now, hindsight tells me that I did see them quite frequently and that they may have been more than just a bump into the desk."[6]

Brian Schiavo scoffs at the allegations of domestic abuse: "Mike was three times her size," he told the *New York Times*. "If he was abusing her, there would be some sign of something. She would have taken her two cats and gone to her parents."

According to Rhodes, her last conversation with Terri centered on a fight between Terri and Michael. Rhodes testified she last spoke to Terri on

Saturday, February 24, 1990, the day before her collapse. It had been a running joke in the office the prior week whether or not Terri was going to stay blonde or return to her natural dark brown hair color when she went for an appointment with the hairdresser Saturday morning.

"So I called her Saturday afternoon and asked her, 'Well, are we a blonde or a brunette?'" Rhodes recalled. "She said, 'I'm still a blonde.' But she was very, very upset when I was talking to her. It sounded like she had been crying. I asked her if she was okay. She said she had a fight with Michael. That he was extremely upset with her because she had spent . . . $80 on her hair that day to stay blonde."

When asked whether he had a violent argument with Terri prior to her collapse, Schiavo replied, "How could I? I was at work?" When pressed about Rhodes's testimony, rather than denying the accusation, Schiavo scoffed, "Of course they're going to say that."

Rhodes offered to come over to the apartment to see Terri because she sounded so upset, not her normal jovial self. Terri declined the offer and told her she was headed to her brother's apartment.

Bobby Schindler saw his sister a few hours before she collapsed. "She came over to see me at my apartment. My roommate and I were going out that night and asked if she wanted to come along," he recalled. "She said, 'No.' She was going to go home because she had been fighting with Michael and was going to wait for him to get home that night." After her tearful confession about the state of her marriage weeks earlier, Terri had grown more open with her brother about her troubles with Michael. This compounded his earlier concerns about the marriage, which were based on his observations of her demeanor around her husband. She almost seemed to cower when standing next to him or sitting next to him on the sofa.

Standing six foot six and weighing 250 pounds, Michael Schiavo creates a powerful presence next to most anyone. Combined with a reportedly volatile temper, his presence has frightened many. While Bobby Schindler had stood in the front yard and cheered when Michael arrived to pick Terri up for their first date in September 1982, he says he never grew close to his brother-in-law. He feels the man walked around with a "chip on his shoulder" for some reason. One experience, in particular, soured his opinion about Michael Schiavo. Toward the beginning of Terri and Michael's courtship, Bobby recalled getting into a heated argument with Michael in the family room of the Schindlers' Philadelphia house.

"I remember distinctly that Michael got so upset that he suddenly snapped and grabbed me by the throat and threw me down on the couch," he recalled. "[He] had one hand around my neck and the other was in the air ready to punch me in the face. I couldn't move and I don't know what would have resulted if it weren't for Terri and my girlfriend screaming at him to let me go."

In hindsight, Schindler believes the incident was something he should have taken very seriously. But Terri begged him to not tell their parents about it because it would have upset them too much. Terri was always protective of her parents. Shortly after Terri's collapse, however, Bob Schindler witnessed his son-in-law's temper for himself. Terri's sister, Suzanne Vitadamo, stated she and Michael Schiavo got into an argument while she was temporarily living in the house he and her parents were renting in St. Pete Beach. She didn't recall the specifics of the argument, but she remembered being afraid.

"He went from 0 to 60 in a matter of seconds. Michael started to lunge toward me and I thought that he was going to punch me in the face," she stated. "My father had to step between us before he got to me. I remember how terrified I was and began to run away from him. The house was very large so I had room to run. My parents and I were very disturbed, and I was extremely frightened."

The encounter prompted Bob Schindler to call the psychiatrist who was treating Michael Schiavo at the time. Schindler was reportedly told that Michael was taking antidepressants and was potentially dangerous. The doctor reportedly instructed Schindler that he should call the police in the event of any future episodes.[7] In a 1993 deposition, Schiavo testified the doctor prescribed Wellbutrin, Panlor, Elavil, and Prozac to treat his depression. He said the reason for the medications was that he occasionally felt suicidal after Terri's collapse. According to his testimony, Schiavo filled the prescriptions but didn't take them all, because many of the drugs made him nauseous and clouded his thinking.

Brian Schiavo offered his brother's version of the argument with Vitadamo. He said it happened just after Michael returned to Florida in 1991, after having spent a month in San Francisco, where Terri was undergoing an experimental treatment to stimulate her brain. "Suzanne had asked him if she could have this chest of drawers. He says, 'Sure when I'm done with it you can have it.' He comes home from California and finds every stitch of his clothing [and] all of his personal items heaped on the floor and the chest of drawers was gone. Would I be pissed off? Sure, I'd be pissed off," Brian Schiavo said, adding he believed both of Terri's siblings were "little weasels" who were being coached by their attorney to portray Michael in a bad light.

Bob Schindler described another violent argument with Schiavo in Terri's room over his daughter's rehabilitation funds on February 14, 1993, during which he said Schiavo punched a wall and appeared to be coming after him as if to attack him. Schiavo testified he pushed a bedside table aside and went after his father-in-law, who had cursed him, before storming out into the hallway of the nursing home. At that point Mary Schindler stepped between her husband and Michael Schiavo. While both sides agree the dispute was over money, they offer vastly different accounts of the content of this pivotal argument, which sparked the subsequent family rift. (This will be presented in the next chapter. The Schiavos and Schindlers haven't spoken to each other since this incident, now twelve years ago.)

Others outside of the Schindler family have also expressed a fear of Michael Schiavo. The same day of the argument in Terri's room at Sabal Palms Health Care Center in Largo, Florida, administrator Emily Layton filed for a restraining order to keep Michael Schiavo from entering the property or contacting any of its staff or residents. According to the motion, Michael Schiavo had entered the nursing home two days prior "in a belligerent manner and caused fear of bodily injury to the staff members and/or residents." During that incident, director of nursing Alexa Boyle was alerted on the phone to Schiavo's manner, and she had a conversation with him. Schiavo indicated to Boyle, according to her sworn affidavit filed with the motion for the restraining order, he brought two Largo police officers with him to the facility because "he did not know how he would act and didn't want to go off."

Schiavo dismissed the restraining order as a ploy to oust him as Terri's guardian by staff members who had an axe to grind because he hounded them to improve their care of Terri. He testified he had several "loud conversations" with nurses and a few arguments with the former administrator over numerous grievances he filed with the administration. A court-appointed guardian ad litem, John Pecarek, looked into the allegations of Michael Schiavo's disturbances at the nursing home and inhibiting the care and treatment of the ward. During interviews with thirteen nursing home personnel and caregivers, Pecarek was told about incidents of Schiavo's yelling and screaming in hallways, nurses in tears, and intimidation of the staff by Schiavo. He declared Schiavo a "nursing home administrator's nightmare." But Pecarek concluded that rather than hurting Terri, Michael Schiavo's advocacy and complaining on her behalf resulted in her getting more care and attention than other residents. While attorney George Felos painted Pecarek's comments as a compliment to Michael Schiavo, Sabal

Palms staff members felt he could have advocated for Terri in a more polite, civilized manner.

Two women Michael Schiavo dated after Terri became incapacitated found breaking up with him hard to do. Cindy Shook dated Schiavo for approximately ten months, between late 1991 and the malpractice trial verdict in 1992. She broke a decade of silence on April 25, 2001, and called a local radio station to offer insight into the case dominating the local headlines. She called the station after hearing Michael Schiavo on a competing radio show that morning. As she explained to the *St. Petersburg Times,* hearing people calling into the program and describing Michael Schiavo as a saint prompted her to set the record straight.[8] She told talk-radio host Carrie Kirkland that Michael Schiavo had a definite dark side to him.

"When he would get mad at me, he would tell me, 'I'd rather be with her laying in that bed in the nursing home than with you.' I mean he could be the most incredibly mean person," she said. Shook also told Kirkland that, while they were dating, Michael Schiavo was totally into caring for his wife and spent more time at the nursing home than he would admit. But gradually his demeanor changed. "He was like, '[Terri] has ruined years of my life and she has taken all this time and upset my whole life with this. This is all her fault,'" she said. "It was a complete change. I was just like, 'I don't even know who you are, but get away from me.' . . . I want to take a shower every time I see or hear something about him. I'm just sick."

Shook, who by that time had married and become a mother of two, said she considered trying to get a restraining order against Michael Schiavo. She claimed he stalked her after they broke up, even going so far as to take a job as an orderly at the hospital where she worked.

"Mike's very possessive. He's very jealous," Shook said. "I would look up when I was driving . . . in the rearview mirror and there would be Michael Schiavo," she said, according to court documents. "One time he was behind me in traffic. He got next to me in a two-lane going the same way, and he changed lanes basically right on top of where I was at and I had to swerve not to be hit. I had to swerve off the road. Michael ran me off the road. I considered it as stalking, dangerous, and guessed potentially life threatening."

Upon hearing Shook on the radio, the Schindlers dispatched a private investigator to take her statement. Shook told the private investigator that Schiavo called her as many as fifteen times a day until her husband convinced him to stop. According to the investigator's court affidavit, Shook described Michael Schiavo as violent.

"He would stop at nothing to get what he wants," she reportedly said. "I could tell you a lot of other things that would blow your mind about him, but I am just not willing to jeopardize my family."

After expressing concern about retaliation from Michael Schiavo and fear for the safety of her children, Shook refused to provide a sworn affidavit in support of the Schindlers' court battle. So they subpoenaed her to force her court deposition. The *Times* reported attorneys from both sides had difficulty in finding Shook to serve subpoenas. According to the local paper, Shook claimed the Schindlers were "grasping at straws and twisting her words" to try to save Terri.

"People don't understand. They represent Mike as being this totally unreasonable person and there's two sides to every coin," said Brian Schiavo. He summed up Shook's subsequent backpedaling as, "She basically said the Schindlers were nuts." The Schindlers' attorney Pat Anderson chalked up Shook's alleged statement to the paper to her fear of retaliation.

Trudy Capone also dated Michael Schiavo for several months in 1992. While they were close confidants, they were never romantically involved, according to Capone. She suspected it was because the malpractice trial jury was deliberating over their award, and Schiavo was concerned about what the jury might think of his being involved with another woman. In a sworn affidavit, Capone echoed Shook's sentiment about Michael Schiavo.

"Michael went crazy on me when I ended our friendship," she stated. As Capone described it, Schiavo called her often, and he turned nasty when she avoided his calls at the hospital where she worked. His reported response to her when she ended the relationship was, "You are too old, anyway."

In July 2004 renowned psychiatrist Carole Lieberman offered her services to the Schindler family as an expert witness by releasing a preliminary psychological assessment of Michael Schiavo. In a press release, the author of *Bad Boys: Why We Love Them, How to Live with Them and When to Leave Them* stated that, based on the testimony describing Michael Schiavo's alleged controlling behavior, his alleged stalking, and the observed bruises on Terri prior to her collapse: "Michael fits the profile of an abusive husband. He most definitely [should] be investigated as the perpetrator of the 'incident' that caused Terri's collapse." She compared Schiavo to O. J. Simpson, who was found guilty in civil court of the murder of his wife, Nicole. She called Simpson's "homicidal rage" characteristic of impulsive "men who exhibit pathology in their relationships with women." According to her press release, Lieberman believed Michael Schiavo likely knew that Terri had begun making plans to divorce him and feared her abandonment.

AS ONE person after another came forward to describe an alleged dark side to Michael Schiavo, and in the absence of definitive proof supporting the bulimia theory, the mystery surrounding Terri's collapse began to take on sinister proportions. Court testimony and some of the medical records lend support to suspicions of foul play in the minds of many. Terri's medical records reveal she presented at the emergency room on February 25, 1990, with a "somewhat stiff" neck and all the other muscles in her body were also stiff. X-rays done on her neck showed the normal curvature of the cervical vertebrae had been straightened due to muscle spasms. During his examination of Terri in the fall of 2002, court-appointed independent medical expert Dr. Peter Bambakidis noted Terri's neck still appeared stiff a decade later. Dr. William Hammesfahr, a neurologist solicited by Schindler attorney Pat Anderson, testified the physical and sensory examinations he conducted of Terri's "rigid neck" and the rest of her body suggested she had a vertebral injury and likely also had a spinal cord injury based on symptoms including excessive sweating, facial rashes, and cyanosis in the extremities.

"She has much better control over her face, head and neck, than over her arms and legs," Hammesfahr wrote in his report. "This reminds one of a person with a spinal cord injury who has good facial control, but poor use of arms and legs. It is possible that a correctable spinal abnormality such as a herniated disk may be found that could be treated and result in better neurological functioning." Hammesfahr explained that a neck injury "causes irritation to the sympathetic nerves that control blood flow into the brain." He recommended Terri undergo an MRI to determine any spinal cord abnormality and associated blockage to her sympathetic nerves. Michael Schiavo blocked the Schindlers' request for an MRI.

Hammesfahr gave further testimony about what he concluded was a neck injury during direct examination by Anderson on October 11, 2002:

HAMMESFAHR: There is a neck injury. There may be a spinal cord injury also.

ANDERSON: How were you able to determine a neck injury?

HAMMESFAHR: By physical examination. . . . First, she has very severe neck spasms. That's typical of the body's response, splinting the area to prevent injury to that area.

ANDERSON: Splinting the area?

HAMMESFAHR: Yeah. If you injure your arm, you will move it. Your muscles will contract around it to keep that area [from] moving. Her muscles around the neck area are heavily contracted to help prevent movement around that area. Later on in the videotape, we actually show that it's almost impossible for her to bend her neck. You can pick her entire body up off the bed just by putting pressure on the back of the neck area, which is not typical in brain injury patients but in neck injury patients. In addition, her sensory examination is encephalopathy [brain damage].

ANDERSON: Are you experienced in treatment of patients with spinal cord injury?

HAMMESFAHR: Yes, I am.

ANDERSON: You said that you had never felt a neck like that except for one other patient, right?

HAMMESFAHR: Correct.

ANDERSON: What was the cause of injury in the other patient?

HAMMESFAHR: The person had anoxic encephalous [brain injury due to lack of oxygen] due to attempted strangulation.

A forensics expert, whose opinion was solicited by a supporter of the Schindler family, drew a similar conclusion. "Terri Schiavo's condition is consistent with attempted strangulation," Dr. George McClane, the director of the forensic medical unit of the Department of the Family Justice Center in San Diego, California, stated in a March 24, 2005, e-mail posted on the Schindler family's Web site. "Her healthy heart functioning for the last 12 years is *not* consistent with a 'heart attack from having an eating disorder' having ever occurred."[9]

On *Larry King Live,* Schiavo made a point of addressing the insinuation he had strangled his wife. "The Schindlers made accusations that I strangled Terri," he said. "It confuses me because, before any of this came to light, don't you think the doctors . . . when it first happened would notice marks around her neck?"

McClane has an answer for that. In 1998 he and San Diego assistant city attorney Gael B. Strack wrote an article to help law-enforcement officers and prosecutors detect and prosecute strangulation cases. It stemmed from Strack's review of a random selection of three hundred police reports on attempted and actual strangulation cases submitted over a five-year period. Strack found the vast majority of strangulation cases lacked physical evidence of any crime. In 50 percent of the cases, the victims had no visible injury, and in another 35 percent of the cases the injuries were too minor to photograph. Strack found significant visible injuries—such as red marks, bruises, or rope burns—in only 15 percent of the cases.

Strack discovered 40 percent of domestic incident reports filed by women to the STOP Domestic Violence program described "choking" as part of the abusive conduct at one or more points of their relationship with an abusive man. Yet, despite this frequency, Strack didn't find any associated arrests for choking behavior. Historically, choking is rarely prosecuted as a serious offense because victims of attempted strangulation minimize the incidents themselves, and police and medical personnel fail to recognize it. More recently, strangulation is now recognized as one of the most lethal forms of domestic abuse, and an effort is being made to educate those on the front lines in how to detect it.

According to McClane, strangulation is a form of asphyxia, or lack of oxygen, characterized by the closure of blood vessels and/or air passages of the neck as a result of external pressure on the neck. It only takes eleven pounds of pressure applied for ten seconds to render someone unconscious. As a comparison, it takes eight pounds of pressure to pull the trigger of a gun.

"Depending on the amount of pressure applied to the victim's neck and the neck's position, internal neck swelling can occur with resulting airway compromise," McClane explained. "In some cases, victims may have no visible injuries whatsoever, with only transient symptoms—yet because of underlying brain damage caused by lack of oxygen during strangulation, victims have died up to several weeks later."[10]

Medical examiner Thogmartin ruled out strangulation as the cause of Terri's collapse exclusively based on his review of Terri's medical records. Doctors "were thinking of neck trauma," he noted, and within an hour of her initial hospital admission, they ordered x-rays of her cervical spine, which came back negative.

"Specifically, external signs of strangulation including cutaneous or deep neck injury, facial/conjunctival petechiae, and other blunt trauma were not observed or recorded during her initial admission," he wrote in his report.

"Autopsy examination of her neck structures 15 years after her initial collapse did not detect any signs of remote trauma," Thogmartin added, "but with such a delay, the exam was unlikely to show any residual neck findings."

THE DISCOVERY of a report of a total-body nuclear imaging bone scan done fifty-three weeks after Terri's collapse fueled the Schindlers' and others' suspicions that violence precipitated her collapse. The bone scan came about following a full-staff conference convened February 20, 1991, at Mediplex Rehabilitation in Bradenton, Florida, where Terri had been transferred roughly a month earlier. During this meeting, therapists relayed information that Terri's physical therapy sessions appeared to have become too painful for her. According to nurses' notes, Terri was crying out, "No, no!" and "Stop!" Medical records also indicate Terri's knees were continuously swelling, warm, and causing Terri pain. Her attending physician, Dr. James Carnahan, suspected heterotopic ossification, or HO, had developed in her knees and ordered the bone scan.

According to a report on the medical Web site eMedicine.com, HO is "the abnormal formation of true bone within extraskeletal soft tissues." HO is strongly associated with spinal cord injury. Studies show as many as 50 percent of spinal-cord-injury patients are affected by HO. It was also seen in 20 to 30 percent of patients with traumatic brain injury. HO typically occurs at the joints and usually among the elderly. HO can develop in areas following trauma or surgery. According to eMedicine.com, "the most common sites of HO involvement in patients with traumatic brain injury are the shoulders and elbows, with knees rarely affected. In contrast, knees frequently are involved in patients with spinal cord injury."[11]

Approximately three hours before undergoing a nuclear imaging bone scan, a patient is injected with a tiny amount of a radioactive material, which metabolically acts the same as calcium and phosphate and bone. Because the body processes the radioactive material the same as bone material, it winds up illuminating areas of bone turnover, or growth, during the scan. Bones change rapidly when they are damaged as a result of fractures, cancer, or infection. The areas this "tracer" material lights up are known as "hot spots," or abnormalities in the bones.

The scan request fell to radiologist Dr. W. Campbell Walker. The scan note indicated Terri had a "closed head injury" and instructed Walker to "evaluate for trauma." In a court deposition, Walker explained that, based on the reference to "closed head injury" and the direction given to "evaluate for trauma," he would typically set about looking for evidence that does or doesn't support a hypothesis of trauma. In his report of the scan taken of Terri on March 5, 1991, at Manatee Memorial Hospital in Bradenton, Walker noted "an extensive number of focal abnormal areas of nuclide accumulation of intense type." These "hot spots" suggested fractures in the right and left ribs, the lumbar spine at L1 in her lower back, several thoracic vertebrae, both sacroiliac joints in the hip, her right femur in the upper thigh, and both knees and ankles. The severity and high number of irregularities in the bone scan led Walker to conclude, "The patient has a history of trauma." According to Dr. Thomas Boyle, the radiologist who maintains the popular and award-winning medical weblog CodeBlueBlog.com, "Multiple rib fractures, spinal compression fractures and long-bone injuries are a typical pattern of abuse" and further investigation is warranted in the face of such findings.[12]

Indeed, a follow-up x-ray confirmed the lower lumbar "hot spot" correlated with a compression fracture at L1, or a "broken back" in common parlance, that Walker described as "presumably traumatic." Another follow-up x-ray of the right thigh indicated to Walker the presence of periosteal ossification along the femoral bone, which he said reflected a response to a subperiosteal hemorrhage, or bone bruise. The periosteum is a skinlike layer on the surface of the bone that contains blood vessels and nerve fibers. After concluding the broken back and bruised femur were most likely due to trauma, Walker wrote that he presumed the other multiple hot spots also related to previous traumas. Three physicians who reviewed the report at the request of Anderson concluded Terri was the victim of severe physical abuse.

"Somebody worked her over real good," commented one unnamed physician.

"It's something that should have been investigated in 1991," concluded Baden, the former chief medical examiner for the city of New York.

Even though Mary Schindler was traveling with Michael Schiavo to visit Terri almost every day during the time the scan was done, she never knew about it. The family said it was shocked to learn about the bone scan and angry that they were kept in the dark. They say they only found out about the bone scan in November 2002—eleven years after the fact—when an assistant of Anderson's belatedly found the report in one of the boxes containing Terri's medical records handed over by Schiavo's attorneys. Anderson explained that Hammesfahr's testimony during the October evidentiary hearing about Terri's "suspiciously rigid neck" and Felos's closing statement inquiring as to whether the staff at Mediplex noticed a stiff neck prompted her to undertake a new examination of the "mountain" of Terri's medical records not shared with the Schindlers until late 1999.

Incidentally, multiple boxes of medical documents were handed over to the Schindler's original attorney through the discovery process prior to the 2000 trial. When Pat Anderson took over the case, she found them disorganized and completely out of chronological order. Anderson believes the documents were intentionally "shuffled" by Felos or his associates to make it harder for the Schindler attorney to discover important information, such as the bone scan. This shuffling routine was likely what Felos calls playing the "discovery game" where attorneys "do everything possible to give up as little as they can" and actively thwart the opponent's ability to receive important information. Felos admits to playing the game in his book titled *Litigation as Spiritual Practice.* He described one technique he calls the "avalanche."

"Bury the smoking gun in a mountain of information," Felos wrote. "Your opponent requests 'all documents that may show that the product you manufactured is unsafe.' You strategically place your client's incriminating internal memo among thousands upon thousands of pages of useless but similar looking data. A less-than-diligent opposing counsel may not discover the needle in the haystack."[13]

When the Schindlers filed an emergency motion seeking more information about the bone scan and its implications, Michael Schiavo filed a countermotion to block any further investigation. Felos accused the Schindlers of "continuing to dredge up what has been known before, what has been looked at before." Yet the bone scan was not a part of the case law. It didn't even come up in the 1992 medical malpractice trial, according to the attorney defending the lawsuit.

"There is a possibility that this bone scan represents the true cause of Terry's collapse. Why wouldn't Mr. Schiavo want that investigated? Why wouldn't he bring that up in the malpractice trial? Why would he never mention it in this court?" Anderson argued in support of her motion.

"There are only two people who know what happened that night that she collapsed. And one of them is trying to kill the other, who is too disabled to speak," she commented outside the courtroom at the time.

Felos characterized Anderson's motion as "garbage" and "rank innuendo," and dismissed her recommendation for a probe of the bone scan as a "delay tactic." He argued injuries occurring twelve years prior had "no relevance" to the issue before the court, which was whether new treatment and therapy would offer Terri "sufficient promise of increased cognizant function." In addition, Felos interpreted the bone scan differently than Anderson. He presented the explanation that, with the exception of the "minor fracture" in the "thigh," all the other hot spots represented the development of HO, or abnormal bone growth, "due to the . . . immobile patient's degenerative bone loss."

Felos produced two sworn affidavits by Terri's attending physicians at Mediplex, including Carnahan, which honed in on HO as the explanation for the abnormalities. In his affidavit, Carnahan stated he had ordered the bone scan due to the warmth and swelling in Terri's knees, and he interpreted the results of the bone scan as confirming his suspicions of HO, not trauma, in the knees. According to medical records, Carnahan raised the question of HO in Terri's knees on February 4, 1991, a month before the scan. In his notes of February 12, 1991, Carnahan wrote that Terri's lab work was consistent with HO. In his notes three days after receiving the bone scan report, Carnahan wrote: "Bone Scan reveals subperiosteal area of right thigh—most likely reflects HO. Other areas not explained by disease." Carnahan doesn't specify which of the hot spots he feels are not explained by HO. Four days later he posed the question whether the "bone involvement" revealed by the bone scan was related to the toxic levels of an antiseizure drug Terri was found to have in her blood upon admission at the Mediplex facility.

Carnahan's notes in Terri's medical record demonstrate he completely disregarded Walker's conclusion of trauma. While follow-up x-rays of areas of developing HO would customarily be taken to monitor its progression, according to eMedicine.com, none were done. Carnahan's notes indicate he ruled out trauma without ever consulting with Terri's parents about whether she had a history of breaking bones, falling off of horses, or automobile accidents. Law enforcement was not notified.

"This report got deep-sixed," Anderson concluded.

As if to explain away the one definitive compression fracture confirmed by x-ray, Carnahan said it was common for patients suffering from degenerative bone loss, due to immobility and HO, to sustain fractures from being turned or from physical therapy. In answering reporters' questions about the bone scan, Michael Schiavo used this reasoning and attributed the broken bones to "something that happened during rehab."

Walker testified such physical therapy injuries were "rare." He estimated that over the twenty-three years he had been interpreting radiographs, he had seen fractures in bedridden patients fewer than six times. When asked about Carnahan's conclusion of HO, Walker testified the bone scan was "not consistent" with HO.

"For one thing, I would say the activity in the ribs is not typical," he observed. "Typically heterotopic ossification occurs around the joints because [patients] are not being moved." According to Thomas Boyle's CodeBlue-Blog, radiology residents are taught to recognize hot spots in the ribs as being associated with abuse, particularly when the patient is a child. Boyle further noted that several of the ribs suggested to be broken in the bone scan (no follow-up x-ray was done to confirm the findings) were in Terri's back, near her spine. "It is difficult to fracture your ribs in this area, and it generally takes a direct blow to do it," he wrote.[14]

Under cross-examination by Michael Schiavo's attorney, Walker conceded the broken ribs could have been the result of "aggressive resuscitation" efforts. However, according to the prestigious Armed Forces Institute of Pathology, CPR results in the fracture of *anterior* ribs. "The highly specific posterior rib fracture has never been definitively documented to result from CPR. In an experimental study on CPR in rabbits, no posterior rib fractures could be induced," wrote Lt. Col. Gael J. Lonergan and his colleagues. "Thus, posterior rib fracture is highly specific for abuse and does not result from CPR."[15]

Walker also conceded to Schiavo's attorney that the L1 compression fracture could have been caused by Terri's falling to the floor when she collapsed or by being dropped after her incapacitation. Boyle similarly agreed that dropping a bedridden patient on their bottom could result in an L1 compression fracture.

The knees represented the only point of agreement between radiologist Walker and attending physician Carnahan. Under cross-examination, Walker was willing to accept that the abnormality displayed in Terri's knees could be osteopenia, a degenerative bone loss that happens in the joints of bedridden people in a similar way HO affects them. In fact, an x-ray done of Terri's knees prior to the February 5, 1991, bone scan was interpreted to show "severe osteopenia and degenerative change," according to the doctor's notes.

But Walker wasn't to be completely dissuaded from his conclusion of trauma. He adamantly stressed the femoral bruise was evidence of trauma, and such an injury could only arise from a "direct blow of some sort." Curiously, this bone abnormality was the one cited in the subsequent discharge summary for Terri from the rehabilitation facility in July 1991. The report stated her progress in physical therapy was hindered by the "ossification of the right femur." Remember, HO also forms at sites of past trauma.

When would such suspected abuse have taken place? Although Walker described the hot spots as being "intense," he estimated the damage to the bones occurred within twelve to eighteen months of the scan. This time frame would support the theory the bones were damaged at the time of Terri's collapse. Boyle, however, argued if the radioactive display on the scan was "intense," then that suggests a recent injury, which puts more clout behind the theory Terri was dropped or suffered some trauma at one of the rehab facilities, as Michael Schiavo maintained.

Sixth Judicial Circuit Court Judge George Greer, the primary adjudicator in the Terri Schiavo case, denied Anderson's motion to delve into the findings of the bone scan and hold his standing order to remove the feeding tube in abeyance in the meantime. "The court concludes that while it might be interesting to pursue the issue of trauma as it may have occurred almost 12 years ago, that has nothing to do with Theresa Marie Schiavo in 2002 and the mandate of the 2nd District Court of Appeal," Greer wrote in his November 22, 2002, order.

Special agents with the Florida Department of Law Enforcement were similarly stymied by the passage of time since Terri's collapse. Their investigation into the bone scan and allegations of abuse, neglect, and fraud on the part of Michael Schiavo was shelved by superiors in 2003, who noted the statute of limitations had passed for attempted murder. (Details of this investigation will come in chapter 15.)

Bobby Schindler questioned why Michael Schiavo, who maintained he still loved his wife dearly, didn't want to investigate the bone scan. "Those broken bones got there somehow. We were trying to find out how. It seems to me, if I were her husband, I would want to investigate and find out how they happened," he said at the time the bone-scan report was discovered. After Terri's death, Schindler reiterated his suspicion in an interview with Fox News Channel's host Sean Hannity.

"We still don't know what caused those broken bones," he said. "And what's interesting, Mr. Hannity, if you look back on Michael's testimony and some of the interviews that he's done, he has three different versions—maybe more—of what happened the night Terri collapsed, which is extremely suspect."[16]

Connecting the dots of the reported fight over Terri's eighty-dollar hair appointment the afternoon before she collapsed, the reported bruises seen frequently on Terri, their own observations of Michael Schiavo's reportedly explosive temper, and the bone scan discovered in 2002, the Schindlers have come to suspect a violent altercation between Michael and Terri precipitated her collapse.

"There has surfaced evidence, circumstantial evidence, that something may have happened that was very ugly the night that she collapsed, between her and Michael," said Suzanne Vitadamo during an interview on MSNBC's *Scarborough Country* on March 28, 2005. "We have several speech pathologists on record with the court saying that Terri could possibly learn to speak again. And maybe, you know, Michael doesn't want that to happen."

The other Schindler family members have not been shy about expressing their suspicions. Bobby Schindler draws a comparison with the case of Laci Peterson, the pregnant California woman who disappeared on Christmas Eve 2002 and later turned up dead along with her baby. Her husband, Scott Peterson, was convicted of killing them.

"I saw an interview one time with Scott Peterson's mom," Schindler described. "In it she says, when Laci disappeared, the last person in the world she suspected was Scott. As things sort of unfolded and some strange things started to happen, it became more and more clear to her that Scott could very well have been the person responsible. And the same kind of thing happened with our family. It wasn't until the last few years that we really started suspecting that something horrible could have happened to Terri."

Such insinuations infuriate the Schiavo brothers. "I got so pissed off one day," Brian Schiavo recalled, describing his reaction to hearing Bobby Schindler during a live interview on a local radio station, "I stopped my car and called the radio station and said, 'Are you saying that something my brother did resulted in the condition of your sister? Because if you are, you better have an awful good attorney after this thing. . . . You can't go around and call him a murderer.'"

Equally irate, Felos decried the Schindlers' portrayal of his client as a "smear campaign." Meanwhile, Michael Schiavo summed up the Schindlers' negative portrayal of him as "just useless words from useless people."

In the autopsy, Jon Thogmartin also weighed in on the bone scan. Here again he relied on his review of medical records and interviews to piece together the story. By his count, Terri received twenty-three chest x-rays, three brain CT scans, two abdominal x-rays, two echocardiograms, one abdominal ultrasound, one cervical spine x-ray, and one x-ray of her right knee during her ten weeks at Humana Hospital–Northside.

"No fractures or trauma were reported or recorded," Thogmartin wrote in his report. "Although in the acute phase, rib fractures may be difficult to visualize, any initial rib fractures would have been going through the healing process during the months of hospitalization, and, with the serial nature of the chest radiographs, callus formation from any healing fractures would likely have been visible."

Thogmartin thus concludes that any fractures that occurred concurrent with Terri's collapse would almost certainly have been diagnosed during her initial hospitalization because of the volume of examinations and x-rays she underwent, according to reports and records available to him. He admitted, however, he did not have access to Terri's complete medical record because much of it has been "lost" over the years. His conclusion that the bone abnormalities detected by the bone scan did not come about at the same time as Terri's collapse supported the theory that Terri suffered some kind of trauma during rehabilitation therapy. In fact, Thogmartin stated a compression fracture of the spine is a common and often incidental complication of osteoporosis, which Terri was noted to have developed in her knees. As far as his postmortem findings, which included x-rays and tissue sampling, he found evidence that Terri suffered from heterotopic ossification and marked osteoporosis at the time of her death.

"Such a diagnosis is almost expected of someone in her condition," he wrote. In other words, HO and osteoporosis are sure to set in over fifteen years of immobility. The autopsy, however, could not pinpoint when the condition arose, whether it existed at the time of the bone scan, or if it developed during the last five years of her life. Still, attorney Felos seized Thogmartin's finding as a win for his client. "For years, we have been saying over and over again that the bone scan from 1991 was not evidence of trauma," he told reporters after the release of the autopsy. "It was evidence of bone ossification. That's what the medical findings concluded. That's what the autopsy said."

After ruling out heart attack, bulimia, strangulation, and overt trauma as the cause of Terri's collapse, the only remote possibility in Thogmartin's mind was some kind of drug. "I don't think drugs were specifically ruled out. [Terri] had a toxicology screening, but it was a very specific screening. They conducted a routine test of drugs typically used in drug overdoses," he told reporters during the press conference, adding that the most common cause of cardiac arrest is drug overdose. "We have a lot of drug overdoses come through this office." He said the only way to completely rule out drugs is by having the 1990 blood sample. Thogmartin emphasized, however, that there was no indication Terri took drugs, and she didn't appear to be the kind of person who would. He said everyone he interviewed described her as a "clean-living, hard working woman."

But short of discovering some hospital orderly had secretly frozen Terri's blood sample from February 25, 1990, this lone, lingering hypothesis would go untested. Apologizing to the Schindler family, a deeply frustrated Thogmartin announced he could not determine what caused Terri Schiavo's collapse.

"I was looking for everything I could," he told reporters. "And it just wasn't there. I was grasping at straws."

4

"I Believe in My Wedding Vows"

A GROWN MAN BREAKS down and begins crying on the witness stand, his sorrowful testimony choked by tears. Jurors fidget in discomfort, a few sniffling and teary-eyed. It's the stuff that has made courtroom dramas dating back to Perry Mason days riveting for television viewers. This scene played out in a Pinellas County courthouse in Clearwater, Florida, on November 5, 1992. Michael Schiavo, then aged twenty-nine, was answering questions under direct examination by his attorney, Glenn Woodworth, about how he was handling his wife's incapacitation.

WOODWORTH: You're a young man. Your life is ahead of you. Your future is beyond you. Up the road, when you look up the road, what do you see for yourself?

SCHIAVO: I see myself hopefully finishing [nursing] school and taking care of my wife.

WOODWORTH: Where do you want to take care of your wife?

SCHIAVO: I want to bring my wife home.

WOODWORTH: If you had the resources available to you, if you had the equipment and the people, would you do that?

SCHIAVO: Yes, I would, in a heartbeat.

WOODWORTH: How do you feel about being married to Terri now?

SCHIAVO: I feel wonderful. She's my life and I wouldn't trade her for the world. I believe in my—I believe in my wedding vows.

Michael Schiavo struggled to get the words out, tears piling up in his eyes.

WOODWORTH: You want to take a minute?
SCHIAVO: Yeah.

The courtroom was silent. Everyone waited for Michael Schiavo to summon the courage to continue.

WOODWORTH: You okay?
SCHIAVO: Yeah. I'm sorry.
WOODWORTH: Have—you said you believe in your wedding vows. What do you mean by that?
SCHIAVO: I believe in the vows that I took with my wife—through sickness, in health, for richer or poorer. I married my wife because I love her and I want to spend the rest of my life with her. I'm going to do that.

The heartrending testimony was delivered before a jury hearing the medical malpractice claim Michael Schiavo had brought against Terri's family doctor and gynecologist on her behalf. The family doctor had settled the lawsuit for $250,000 months earlier, but gynecologist G. Stephen Igel chose to defend himself in court. The lawsuit alleged Igel "breached his duty of care" by failing to take Terri's detailed history, including a nutritional and menstrual history, and failing to detect and diagnose a nutritional problem. In his defense, Igel's attorney contended that Terri Schiavo should have disclosed her nutritional history. Igel claimed that even if he had inquired about the stretch marks and loose skin that evidenced significant weight loss on Terri's part, she likely would not have confessed to having an eating disorder if she had one, because bulimics are typically secretive about their behavior.

Needless to say, the parties in the case in 1992 did not have the benefit of the medical examiner's June 15, 2005, autopsy report. Igel's attorney reportedly also never saw the bone scan. Consequently, suspicions of trauma never entered the courtroom discussion surrounding the probable causes of Terri's collapse that included speculation about Terri's medications and toxic shock syndrome.

"I think he liked the bulimia theory," Schindler family attorney Pat Anderson remarked about Igel's attorney, adding that the theory made Terri culpable in her own demise and took the heat off of Dr. Igel. As Anderson described the case, consulting Miami attorney Gary Fox invented the bulimia theory after Woodworth initially saw nothing to pin a case on in Terri's medical records. In fact, when medical examiner Jon Thogmartin undertook the collection of Terri's medical records to launch his autopsy, he reported that he tracked her initial Humana Hospital–Northside admissions records to Fox's office. According to Thogmartin, attorneys on both sides of the malpractice case conceded to the bulimia theory because there was nothing else to "hang their hats on."

Over the course of several days, jurors heard from physicians that Michael Schiavo's wife suffered brain damage as a result of a lack of oxygen to her brain during cardiac arrest more than two years earlier. While doctors testified they didn't know what caused the cardiac arrest, the consensus among them was that, based on information given to them by Michael Schiavo that indicated Terri had an eating disorder, they suspected associated low potassium triggered the heart failure.

Dr. David Baras, who supervised Terri's rehabilitative therapy over the first year after her collapse, testified that Terri suffered "extremely severe and diffuse brain damage." He interpreted the MRI performed on her on July 24, 1990, as showing "profound atrophy with very atrophic appearing cortex, mild white matter disease, abnormal signal in the regions bilaterally."

What does that mean in layman's terms?

"Basically the brain had shrunken, had become very small, and a lot of the tissue matter, the white matter was injured," Baras explained. "Not only the tops of the brain, but also the brain stem had been damaged."

"This amount of damage conveys to me that she has suffered permanent brain injury," he concluded but later offered there was always the slight possibility that she could improve.

"There may be some parts of her brain that have not been injured that are now . . . not functioning at this time and start functioning," he ventured. Based on reports from therapists at the nursing home where Terri was residing, which suggested she was following one-step commands, Baras had recommended she be placed in a more intense rehabilitation program he had put together at Bayfront Medical Center in St. Petersburg, where he was the medical director.

"She could follow some—a one-step command, although that was inconsistent. Nevertheless, that information was very important," Baras told the jury, adding that this indicated to him "that there may be some type of brain function that is returning that would allow her to even have maybe further progress."

Baras noted that Terri was subsequently moved to Bayfront, where she underwent months of intensive rehabilitative therapy, but her neurological status showed little change as far as being able to respond consistently to a stimulus. Terri remained in a persistent vegetative state, totally dependent on others for all her care, he said.

The jurors witnessed a day in the life of Terri Schiavo via a video made at Sabal Palms Health Care Center in Largo, Florida, where she then resided. Michael Schiavo narrated the different segments during playback.

"Right here, basically, you can see she's dressed. She's already had her shower and everything," Schiavo began. "We would get her dressed, put her shoes and socks on. I'm drying out her hands there. . . . Since she's contracted, you have to keep them dry, because infection can set in. And I usually do a little bit of range of motion [therapy] with her." During this therapy Michael explained he had to talk to her, comfort her, because it hurt. "She does feel pain."

In the next segment, Michael Schiavo and Terri's mother work together to transfer her to a wheelchair.

"We'll sit her up on the edge of the bed, and my mother-in-law takes the feet and I'll take the top end, and we transfer her into her chair and slide her down, and usually we're pretty careful about the aligning of her body and her hips," Schiavo continued, pointing out that he held Terri's head back because, "She'll fall forward, and if she falls fast she gets excited. . . . I was told by a doctor she was getting the feeling she's falling."

Elsewhere in the video Michael Schiavo cleaned Terri's teeth, suctioning the toothpaste out of her mouth; applied makeup and lipstick to her face and lips; hooked a bottle of food up to her feeding tube; changed the dressing around the stoma, or hole in her throat left from the tracheotomy performed in the first hours after her collapse, when she required mechanical ventilation; and took her out to a pond for walks and fresh air.

In a somewhat gory section of the video, Terri's podiatrist scraped a blackened area from the top of a toe on her right foot. The jurors learned that she had earlier developed an ulceration on the small toe of her left foot, and the toe had to be removed and the bone taken out.

Throughout the video presentation, Michael Schiavo demonstrated his devoted care of his wife and great attention to details. Dr. Baras described him as "one of a kind," adding Schiavo was perhaps "obsessively devoted" at times. "Throughout the entire time that I knew his wife and cared for his wife, he was always available, and I only have high regards for this gentleman," Baras told the jurors.

Frequent expert witness Lawrence Foreman, from Comprehensive Rehabilitation Consultants, was called in to testify as to Terri's future medical needs. He presented a life care plan he developed for Terri and outlined its cost. Foreman echoed Baras's description of Michael Schiavo. "The impression I got, [nursing home personnel] almost see him as another staff member there and see him as her personal spokesperson and advocate and questions everything and pushes people to the hilt," Foreman said. Sometimes beyond the hilt, he added.

Michael Schiavo testified he had enrolled at St. Petersburg Junior College in September 1990 so he could learn more about how to take care of Terri. He told jurors he wanted to bring his wife home, and that if given the resources, he would do so "in a heartbeat." At the time he began his nursing studies, he and the Schindlers rented a house together and brought Terri home to care for her themselves. Although the video shown in court evidenced the fact that Mary Schindler worked in concert with Michael Schiavo much of the time over the prior years, little testimony was offered describing her high level of commitment to attending to her daughter. In a nonspecific comment, Baras stated he was "impressed with the family." By all accounts, Michael Schiavo and the Schindlers formed a tight, unified family unit, holding fund-raisers and coordinating Terri's care in the early years after her brain injury. This was an extension of their closeness prior to Terri's collapse, when Mary Schindler considered Michael a "second son," and Michael Schiavo called her "Mom." Although they weren't a party to the lawsuit, the Schindlers worked behind the scenes to support the effort.

Approximately three months after the family brought Terri home from the nursing home, they all began to feel overwhelmed by the magnitude of the work involved in caring for a brain-injured person in a residential setting. Mary Schindler was in constant fear something would happen to Terri that she wouldn't know how to handle. They felt inadequately skilled to meet her needs on their own and realized they needed the assistance of home healthcare professionals. They couldn't afford any, however, for any significant length of time. The hope was to win damages from the allegedly negligent gynecologist so they could provide the professional care Terri needed at home for the rest of her life, which was estimated to last beyond age fifty.

Although attorney Woodworth repeatedly instructed the family to not count on getting any damage award, his co-counsel, Roland Lamb, estimated the case was worth between $15 million and $20 million, according to Schiavo. With a view toward the latter, the Schindlers and Michael Schiavo discussed buying a house that had a separate apartment to accommodate

Terri, hiring round-the-clock aides to help manage her long-term care, and taking her for advanced rehabilitation at Shands Hospital in Gainesville, Florida. It was suggested to Michael Schiavo and Mary Schindler during a case-management meeting with doctors on April 17, 1991, that Terri might benefit from a brain-mapping procedure that used a unique machine at Shands. Notes of the meeting in Terri's medical records confirm funding wasn't available for this.

ON NOVEMBER 10, 1992, the eighth anniversary of Terri and Michael's wedding, Woodworth delivered his closing arguments.

"Terri has totally and completely lost the capacity to enjoy life," he told the jury. "We don't know how much she suffers. We don't know how much cognition. . . . There is life, life inside this woman. Something is flickering there. How much we don't know. . . . She is trapped in that body. She's been trapped the last two and a half years. She'll be trapped the next 51.27 years—half a century."

Later that day, the jury reached a verdict. They initially awarded Terri just under $4.8 million and Michael Schiavo $2.1 million. But after calculating that Terri was 70 percent responsible for her condition—assuming it was due to her alleged eating disorder, and factoring in a life expectancy of only seventeen years because of it—the damages were reduced to $1,434,081.30 for Terri and $630,000 for Michael Schiavo, a total of $2,064,081.30. Both sides of the case balked at the figure and immediately filed post-trial motions. Ultimately, they settled on an even $2 million, which was approved by the court on January 27, 1993. Combined with the $250,000 from the out-of-court settlement with Terri's family physician, the malpractice monies totaled $2.25 million. Court documents show that amount was then divided per the jury's original percentages of 70 percent going into Terri's guardianship ($1,563,300) and 30 percent ($686,700) going to Michael to compensate him for his loss of consortium.

Although Woodworth, in his opening arguments, outlined his intentions to bring Terri into court for the jurors to see, he said he decided against it for fear that doing so would be construed as trying to evoke sympathy among the jurors. The videotaped presentation, however, accomplished the same end. "We felt sorry for Terri," one juror confessed to syndicated talk-radio host Glenn Beck a decade later. He subsequently e-mailed Bobby Schindler, telling him that, when he watched Schiavo testify, "There was something about him he didn't trust."

In the months leading up to the malpractice trial and beyond, Michael

Schiavo dated nursing assistant Cindy Shook and licensed practical nurse Trudy Capone. After Schiavo brought his 1998 petition to have Terri's feeding tube removed, both former girlfriends came forward to share their insights into Michael Schiavo. Their accounts of his alleged stalking behavior similarly cast a shadow across the sunny characterization of Schiavo painted for the malpractice-trial jury. In a sworn affidavit dated May 9, 2001, Capone described Michael Schiavo as "very sick and unstable."

Shook entered Schiavo's life first and remained romantically involved with him for about ten months, beginning in late 1991. The two discussed marriage, made plans to live together, and did a bit of house hunting with a Century 21 Realtor. At that time, Michael Schiavo had a veterinarian euthanize Terri's pudgy cats, Tolly and Shane. He asserted it was his mother-in-law's idea. But Mary Schindler disputed this and suggested the likely reason was because the cats wouldn't have gotten along with Shook's dog. While Shook stated Michael Schiavo spent a lot of time at the nursing home and was "real into taking care of her," he also exhibited anger toward her [Terri] and complained that "this had destroyed his life and he was being robbed of a normal life" and "this is all her fault."

Did Terri pick up on her husband's reported anger? Sworn affidavits provided by some of Terri's caregivers over subsequent years suggest she might have. Heidi Law, a certified nursing assistant who attended to Terri at the Palm Garden of Largo Convalescent Center in 1997, described Terri as always upset after visits by her husband. She also reported that Terri would withdraw for hours afterward. Law's co-worker, registered nurse Carla Sauer Iyer, who attended to Terri between 1995 and 1996, echoed her testimony.

"When he left, Terri would be trembling, crying hysterically, and would be very pale and have cold sweats," Iyer wrote in her affidavit. She also attributed callous statements to Michael Schiavo, such as, "When is that bitch gonna die?" She provides more damning testimony about Schiavo, which will be explored in the next chapter.

"In the beginning I felt like Michael really did love Terri," Trudy Capone summarized. "But after time passed, he just wanted his own life and the money. . . . That trial money was everything to him and . . . something happened to him once he received the settlement."

Although Michael used to tell Capone he would never give away Terri's car, because it was special to him, according to her affidavit, as soon as he received his settlement, he went out and purchased a gold Acura and drove it to Capone's workplace to show it to her. "All he could talk about was his new car," she stated.

AFTER $640,734 in attorneys' fees and costs were paid, the Department of Health and Rehabilitative Services was reimbursed for $51,669.21 in Medicaid funds, and other health-care provider and miscellaneous costs of $121,841 were taken care of, approximately $750,000 was placed in the guardianship of Terri Schiavo to pay for her future medical care and rehabilitative treatment. Similarly, after attorneys' fees and costs were deducted, Michael Schiavo received approximately $350,000. As a result of prudent investing in U.S. Treasuries, corporate bonds, and blue-chip stocks, like Coca-Cola, Walt Disney, and Proctor & Gamble on the part of the guardian of Terri's property, South Trust Bank, her trust fund account balance grew by as much as $32,274 the following year, according to the bank's projections. One financial planner estimated that if the principle weren't touched, the fund during the mid-to-late 1990s would have generated an annual interest income of at least $70,000, which would easily have covered the annual cost of a nursing home.[1] In fact, Terri's guardianship account balance swelled to $782,000 by 1998, despite constant outlays in spending. Still, the jury award was a far cry from the anticipated $15 million to $20 million.

"The case went bust and belly up," Schiavo stated in a November 19, 1993, deposition. As a result, he explained, the plans he and the Schindlers discussed regarding Terri's future treatment and care "faded away." Despite his testimony during the malpractice trial, Schiavo admitted a year later that he felt it wouldn't work to bring Terri home again, because it was too much work.

But while the plans may have faded in Michael Schiavo's mind, they were still very real in the minds of the Schindlers. Shortly after Michael Schiavo collected the malpractice-award monies for himself and Terri's guardianship, Bob Schindler confronted Michael in Terri's room at the nursing home—the same facility that had filed a motion seeking a restraining order against Schiavo two days earlier. Terri was sitting in her lounge chair, and Michael was sitting in front of her, working on his nursing studies.

"They came in late," Michael Schiavo recalled. "My father-in-law's usual question to me was, 'How much money am I going to get?' . . . And I said nobody was going to get any money right now. He said, 'What do you mean? This is my daughter.' And he just went on. And to shut him up I said, 'Look, I gave all my money to Terri. I don't have any money.'" Schiavo later admitted in court he had lied about giving away the money and again reiterated he had done so just to "shut him up."

"He looked at me, pointed his finger at me, and then pointed his finger at Terri and said, 'How much money is she going to give me?'" Schiavo continued. "I said to him, 'You'll have to call the guardianship. I'm not the guardian over her property.'"

At that point, according to Schiavo, Bob Schindler cursed his son-in-law and stormed out of the room. That's when Michael Schiavo erupted. He pushed the bedside table aside and lunged toward the door to follow Schindler. Mary Schindler ran over to the door and stood between him and her husband to prevent a violent altercation. The Schindlers and the Schiavos have not spoken to each other since this Valentine's Day showdown in 1993. Michael Schiavo has repeated his version of the argument on *Larry King Live* and elsewhere, claiming the Schindlers' crusade to save Terri's life was motivated by greed. "They don't like me because they want the money," Schiavo told King in the October 27, 2003, interview, then later speculated the Schindlers' "motive" in pursuing the case for so many years was "probably just to make my life hell."[2]

Not surprisingly, the Schindlers' version of the pivotal dispute, which set the stage for the decade-long tug-of-war over Terri's life in the courts, is quite different.

"I [had] asked him a couple times about that money, that it should be going towards Terri," Bob Schindler said in an interview on the Christian Broadcasting Network's *The 700 Club*. "When I finally confronted him, it erupted into a pretty violent argument. He said, 'I [am] the husband. I'll make all the decisions. You have nothing to say." And I said, 'Well, you made a commitment. What about your integrity?' and he took a book, I think it was, and threw it against the wall and started coming after me like he was going to attack me. And my wife, God bless her, she defended me. . . . Yeah, it's all about money—but not for us, it's for Terri."[3]

The Schindlers see a certain irony in Schiavo's accusation they were after Terri's money for themselves. The family has long accused Michael Schiavo of seeking to end Terri's life because he stood to inherit the money in her guardianship upon her death.

"I think, under the circumstances, what he is trying to do is have my daughter put to death to get her money," Bob Schindler later testified in court. "That more than burns me up. He is killing my daughter to get her money."

Michael Schiavo has repeatedly denied the claim—"50 million times," by his count—and often points out he offered to donate all the money to charity to prove "it's not about the money." Schiavo is referencing a settlement offer he extended to the Schindlers upon the suggestion of a guardian ad litem appointed to the case in 1998.

"Unfortunately, the fact that the law makes Mr. Schiavo the recipient of his wife's estate has been utilized to cast suspicion on his motives," Schiavo attorney George Felos wrote in a letter to the Schindlers outlining his client's settlement offer on October 21, 1998. "As it appears that the issue of money may be impeding the release of Theresa from this lingering and extended death, my client makes the following offer to resolve the case." The letter stated Schiavo would donate the "net proceeds" of Terri's estate to a charity of his choice so long as the Schindlers "withdraw their objection to the termination of artificial provision of nutrition and hydration."

Bobby Schindler called it a "hollow offer." "The offer came with the stipulation that my parents agree to let my sister starve to death. Why would we let her starve to death?" he asked rhetorically. The Schindler's letter rejecting the settlement offer written by their attorney, Pamela Campbell, expressed it more diplomatically. "Mr. and Mrs. Schindler respectfully decline the proposed offer. It does not appear that Mr. Schiavo understands their position," Campbell wrote. "If your client is anxious to have this matter resolved, he may want to consider resigning as the guardian and allowing a substitute guardian to be appointed, such as Mr. or Mrs. Schindler or one of Theresa's siblings. Any of the four would be pleased to serve in such capacity." This wouldn't be the first of such suggestions on the part of the Schindlers.

The fallout of this bitter, familial clash was immediate. The nursing home staff, under orders from Michael Schiavo, began refusing to share Terri's medical information with any Schindler family member. Bob and Mary Schindler would later win a court order from Judge Thomas Penick compelling Michael Schiavo to keep them apprised of significant changes in Terri's medical condition. But their efforts to get Judge Greer to enforce the 1996 court order were rebuffed. As of February 14, 1993, the Schindlers were completely out of the loop. Gone was the hope of getting Terri any further rehabilitation. Although Michael Schiavo would later admit in court there were sufficient funds in Terri's guardianship to cover the cost of the recommended treatment at Shands Hospital, he chose not to send her. The brain mapping was relegated as a pipe dream.

Nearly three years to the day after Terri's collapse, her formerly close and unified family splintered. For the rest of her life, the two sides, the Schiavos and the Schindlers, exchanged dialogue with each other only through written correspondence, attorneys, and court motions and petitions.

In June 1993 Michael Schiavo fired what would become the first salvo in the legal arena. Although he had just collected $686,700 for himself from the malpractice trial, and despite admitting in court that the Schindlers had allowed Terri and him to slide on rent prior to her collapse, he hired a new attorney to send a threatening letter to the Schindlers demanding reimbursement of $644.44.

"This is owed to Mr. Schiavo by you for use of his credit card. If this debt is not paid or arrangements made with me to repay this money within ten (10) days from the date of this letter, I will have no alternative but to take whatever legal action is indicated to protect my client's interest," wrote attorney Jan Piper.

Next, in July 1993, Bob Schindler cordially reiterated, in a letter to Michael Schiavo, his demand that Terri's guardianship funds be allocated according to plans that were discussed. "Long before and during the malpractice trial, you made a number of commitments to Mary and myself," Schindler wrote. "One of your commitments was that award money was to . . . enhance Terri's medical and neurological care. You also committed that the award proceeds would be used to provide [a home] for Terri so that Mary and I could live with her, and as her parents, we [committed to providing her] the love and care she deserves on a long-term basis. . . . We would like you to consider giving Terri back." Schindler further politely demanded they be informed of Terri's latest medical and neurological evaluations.

"Regardless of your rationale, we believe you have a moral responsibility [to] include us in determining Terri's welfare," Schindler continued. "Lest you forget, we did raise her for 21 years, and also, from the time of Terri's seizure up to when you [decided] to alienate us, Mary was continually at your side, caring for you and Terri."

There was no response to the letter. Instead, the Schindlers soon learned Michael Schiavo had placed a do-not-resuscitate order, commonly known as a DNR, in Terri's medical chart and attempted to end her life. She only survived because the nursing home intervened. As is common for bedridden patients, Terri had developed a bladder infection. Aware that the infection, if left untreated, would be fatal, Schiavo instructed the nursing home staff not to administer antibiotics. He testified in November 1993 his decision stemmed from a conversation he had with Terri's treating physician at the time:

SCHIAVO: After speaking with my doctor, I gave an order not to treat a bladder infection Terri had.
ATTORNEY JAMES SHEEHAN: Who was the doctor you spoke with?
SCHIAVO: [Patrick] Mulroy.
SHEEHAN: And Mulroy is your doctor or Terri's doctor?
SCHIAVO: Terri's doctor.

SHEEHAN: Tell me about the conversation you had with Mulroy.

SCHIAVO: I talked to him about what he felt Terri's future was. And he told me that Terri is basically going to be like this for the rest of her life, and I was trying to make decisions on what Terri would want.

SHEEHAN: What was her bladder condition? . . .

SCHIAVO: Urinary tract infection.

SHEEHAN: Did the doctor tell you what the treatment for that would be?

SCHIAVO: Antibiotic usually.

SHEEHAN: And did he tell you what would occur if you failed to treat that infection?

SCHIAVO: Yes.

SHEEHAN: What did he tell you?

SCHIAVO: That sometimes urinary tract infections will turn to sepsis.

SHEEHAN: And sepsis is what?

SCHIAVO: An infection throughout the body.

SHEEHAN: And what would the result of untreated sepsis be to the patient?

SCHIAVO: The patient would pass on.

SHEEHAN: So when you made the decision not to treat Terri's bladder infection, you, in effect, were making a decision to allow her to pass on?

SCHIAVO: I was making a decision on what Terri would want.

Terri Schiavo had no living will or other advance directive outlining her preferences in the event of incapacitation. She also never appointed anyone to be her health-care surrogate or proxy to make end-of-life decisions for her. In view of this, some deem anyone else's declaration of her wishes—including that of her husband—mere speculation.

SHEEHAN: How do you determine what she would want?

SCHIAVO: She was my wife. I lived with her. We shared things. We shared a bed. We shared our thoughts.

Schiavo went on to describe one particular conversation he had with Terri in which they discussed her disabled uncle who emerged from a coma "a man that she never knew anymore." He could not walk without use of a cane and was dependent on her grandmother's care.

SCHIAVO: . . . We got into [a] discussion about that, and she said to me, "I would never want to live like that. I would want to just die."

SHEEHAN: So what you're saying is, from that conversation, you have determined that you know what she would want in these circumstances?
SCHIAVO: Yes.
SHEEHAN: And you think that she would have wanted to die?
SCHIAVO: Yes.

As the testimony continued, Schiavo revealed that Sabal Palms Health Care Center had refused to follow his orders because it was against the law. When asked how, as Terri's guardian, he would handle another urinary tract infection in the future, Schiavo responded he would still want to withhold antibiotics but would obey the law. Schiavo also admitted he left the Schindlers completely in the dark about the bladder infection and his intention to end their daughter's life.

SHEEHAN: When you made the decision that you were not going to treat Terri's infection and you were going to in effect allow her to die, did you think that you had any obligation to tell her parents?
SCHIAVO: To answer the question, I probably would have let them know sooner or later.
SHEEHAN: You never did let them know, though, did you?
SCHIAVO: No.

"She would have died without [our] ever knowing. What type of person would do that?" asked Bobby Schindler.

Schiavo swiftly transferred Terri to another nursing home in Largo: Palm Garden of Largo. Six months had passed since he had been awarded the malpractice monies meant to cover Terri's care and rehabilitation for at least the next seventeen years. This nursing-home transfer was eight months after Schiavo told the jury he intended to take care of his incapacitated wife for the rest of his life. Within a couple more months, Schiavo melted down Terri's engagement ring and diamond wedding band to make a ring for himself, and some time that same year a file was completed on Terri Schiavo at a Pinellas County funeral home.[4]

5

"Gulag of Guardianship"

THERESA MARIE SCHIAVO BECAME the ward of Michael Schiavo on June 18, 1990—nearly six months after her unexplained collapse. A common misperception about the Terri Schiavo case is that Michael Schiavo became Terri's guardian automatically, by virtue of being the spouse. This is not the case, however. Guardianship is a legal proceeding in the circuit courts of Florida whereby an individual is adjudicated incapacitated—either mentally, physically, or both—and a judge appoints someone to make decisions for the ward in regards to his or her personal and/or financial affairs. "Incapacitated" is a legal term rather than a medical one.

Under the provisions of Florida Statute 744, which governs guardianship, the court may appoint any person who is "fit and proper and qualified" to act as guardian, whether related to the ward or not. The minimal qualifications consist of being a resident over the age of eighteen, free of a criminal record, and not having a business interest or other conflict of interest with the ward. The statute holds that the court "shall give preference to the appointment of a person who . . . is related by blood or marriage to the ward." According to this language, the Schindlers would have been just as likely candidates to perform the duties of Terri's guardian as Michael Schiavo. But he beat them to the punch.

Sometime within the first seventy-two hours after Michael Schiavo discovered his wife collapsed on the floor and unresponsive, his employer-attorney, Dan Grieco, approached the Schindlers at the hospital, seeking their signature on paperwork that would give Schiavo the sole authority to make the necessary medical decisions for Terri. The Schindlers don't recall any specifics about the documents, other than they were presented to them as a way to expedite critical decision making at a time of crisis.

"At the time, I believed it was done with good intentions," commented Bobby Schindler. "But when you look back now, in hindsight, it could have been done for a different reason. . . . It could have been because [Michael Schiavo] was scared, and maybe Dan Grieco was the one person he could trust to keep things confidential." The paperwork had the effect of sealing Terri's medical records, including the admissions report at Humana Hospital–Northside, from the Schindlers. This, in part, explains why they never knew about or saw the nuclear imaging bone scan until November 2002.

In a September 27, 1999, deposition, Schindler attorney Pamela Campbell explored the origins of the guardianship:

CAMPBELL: Tell me how you became Terri's guardian after the accident.

SCHIAVO: Through attorney Dan Grieco.

CAMPBELL: Was it suggested to you that you become the guardian?

FELOS: Hold on a second. I'd object to the extent that the question is asking him what Dan Grieco may have told him.

CAMPBELL: Or anybody.

FELOS: As far as suggestions by other persons, go ahead and answer the question. As it pertains to suggestions by your attorney that would be confidential communication and you shouldn't answer.

CAMPBELL : Did anybody suggest to you that you become a guardian besides Dan Grieco?

SCHIAVO: No.

CAMPBELL : Did you fill out an application to become the guardian for Terri?

SCHIAVO: I believe we did, yes.

CAMPBELL : What was the reason for you to become Terri's guardian?

SCHIAVO: Because I was her husband.

CAMPBELL : Did you have to take the course at the time to become a guardian?

SCHIAVO: No, I did not. [Family guardians are now required to take an eight-hour training course that covers the legal duties and responsibilities of the guardian, the rights of the ward, and more. Professional guardians, individuals who manage two or more wards unrelated to them, must complete forty hours of instruction and pass an exam.]

CAMPBELL: Have you since then taken any course on becoming a guardian?
SCHIAVO: No, I have not.
CAMPBELL: What was your understanding then of your responsibilities as performing the job of a guardian?
SCHIAVO: To make sure her medical needs are met. Social needs are met.

Three weeks after Terri was discharged from Humana Hospital–Northside, Grieco filed petitions on behalf of Michael Schiavo for the court to determine Terri's incapacity and for his appointment as guardian. Such petitions, according to Florida law, trigger a statutorily mandated process whereby an attorney is appointed to represent the alleged incapacitated person, and notice of a hearing and copies of the petitions must be given to that attorney and to all next of kin identified in the petition. While most states recognize the spouse and the nearest blood relatives as next of kin, Florida statute defines next of kin as "persons who would be heirs at law of the ward . . . and includes lineal descendants" of the ward. The Schindlers say they were never notified of the petition or the associated hearing, despite the fact they were in daily contact with Michael Schiavo at the time. No record of this paperwork or any documents indicating that the Schindlers were notified can be found in the case file.

Court documents reflect an attorney was appointed to represent Terri for the hearing. According to Ron Stuart, the public information officer for the Sixth Judicial Circuit Court in Pinellas–Pasco County, every ward is appointed an attorney for hearings to determine incapacity. The attorney remains on the case through the filing of the guardianship inventory and is subsequently paid out of the ward's guardianship. The case docket indicates Terri's attorney was discharged on August 27, 1990, and the case file was closed three days later. Meanwhile, an examining committee of three physicians, including a psychiatrist, was appointed and reported back to the court on Terri's condition on June 4, 1990. Her condition was determined to be anoxic encephalopathy, or brain damage, and she was deemed still comatose.

Within a matter of minutes on June 18, 1990, and without the knowledge of the Schindlers, Circuit Court Judge Robert F. Michael determined Terri was incapacitated. In his order, the judge stated that notice of the petition and hearing was "given to all known next of kin." There was no reference as to whether "interested persons," which would have assuredly encompassed the Schindlers, were notified of the proceeding. Finding Michael Schiavo had no conflicts of interest, the judge appointed him plenary guardian, or full guardian, which is someone who exercises all delegable legal rights and powers of the ward. Delegable legal rights and powers exclude specific rights that remain expressly reserved to wards, regardless of their incapacitation. Florida guardianship law spells out these rights in F.S. 744.3215 (1). They include the following rights:

- to be restored to capacity at the earliest possible time
- to be treated humanely, with dignity and respect, and to be protected against abuse, neglect, and exploitation
- to have a qualified guardian
- to be properly educated
- to receive prudent financial management for his or her property and to be informed how his or her property is being managed, if he or she has lost the right to manage property
- to receive necessary services and rehabilitation
- to be free from discrimination because of his or her capacity
- to have access to the courts
- to have access to counsel
- to receive visitors and communicate with others
- to privacy

The judge ordered Michael Schiavo to submit to a credit history and criminal background check pursuant to F.S. 744.3135. He was also required to post a bond, for which the order indicates he pledged his and Terri's joint assets. These included furniture and dinnerware collections valued at $29,900. Schiavo was further ordered to place all the ward's personal assets in a restricted account at a financial institution. Her personal property was later inventoried to consist of $4,500 in clothing and $6,600 in fine and custom jewelry.

The Determination of Incapacity and Appointment of Guardian order lists seventeen activities, with regard to the ward's property, that the guardian must not undertake without prior court approval. These include removing any contents of the ward's safety-deposit box; abandoning property; prosecuting or defending claims or proceedings in any jurisdiction; selling, mortgaging, or leasing any real or personal property; and making gifts of the ward's property. Many question whether Schiavo's melting down of Terri's engagement ring and diamond wedding band, admittedly to make a ring for himself, constituted a violation of the prohibition against gifting.

But in a court system overwhelmed by an enormous caseload, little oversight is afforded individual guardianships, and most activities are left to the discretion of the guardian. In fact, as Michael Schiavo's petition to remove his ward's feeding tube traveled through the court system, it seemed to many that this guardian could do no wrong. Most every motion he put forth was granted, including his request to cremate Terri upon her death, over the objections of her parents, who sought a proper burial according to the family's Catholic tradition. Coining this phenomenon as "The Rule of Terri," Schindler attorney Anderson observed, "If it will help her to die, then we definitely observe every nicety in the rule or the statute or the case law. If it will impede her death, we will ignore it completely."

As a rule, guardians hold tremendous power. "Think about if you were under the total control of a guardian," Pasco County clerk of circuit court Jed Pittman posed. "You can't write a check, can't go out the door of your own house—can't even live in your own house. [Guardians] have a lot of power. Sadly, good guardians are far and few between. It's hard to be a good guardian." In situations where a family is at odds over the fate of an incapacitated ward, the guardian who has the upper hand. A key flaw with guardianship, long observed by reform advocates and disability rights groups—and epitomized in Terri Schiavo's case—is that guardians are given total control over their wards. Even doctors and nurses defer to the guardian due to his or her perceived imperial status of being appointed by the court, say critics.

"He controls her body," Bob Schindler once complained to reporters.

"Michael was the doctor in this case," said Pat Anderson. "He threatened all the nurses with loss of their jobs if they crossed him. He just bamboozled [Victor] Gambone." Terri's treating physician, hired by her husband in 1998, testified in 2002 she hadn't received rehabilitative therapy because he deferred to Michael Schiavo's judgment that it was of no value to her. Michael Schiavo justified his stance by explaining that doctors before Gambone had told him physical and occupational therapy were of no use. In fact, Terri's medical records reflect Drs. James Carnahan and Eugene Alcazaran, who oversaw her rehabilitation therapy over a three-month period during the first year of her brain injury, expressed such sentiment. Other caregivers and physicians were more optimistic, however, as will be discussed in chapter 7.

"She has the right, the statutory right . . . to rehabilitation," Anderson stressed in closing arguments in 2002. "Under 744.3215, a person who has been determined to be incapacitated retains this right. This is not a right that her husband exercises on her behalf. She has it."

Dictatorial control over wards by guardians comes about because the system largely insulates them from scrutiny, say insiders. Federal and state agencies and local prosecutors are loath to investigate suspicions of guardianship abuse because there are not enough resources available to back them up if they were to start questioning the system. They don't want to open a Pandora's box. It would be akin to removing two cards from the bottom tier of a house of cards. Doing so results in the whole deck caving in on itself. As a result, auditors typically only look for signs in the annual financial accountings filed with the court of flagrant stealing, and they pay little to no attention to whether wards are being properly cared for.

In re Guardianship of Schiavo was first and foremost a guardianship case. In order to fully grasp the inner workings of this landmark case and its outcome, it is important to place it within the broader context of guardianship and the decades-old struggle for meaningful reform.

In 1989 *Money* magazine dubbed the legal system meant to protect the elderly and disabled in America as the "gulag of guardianship." Editors reached that conclusion after a four-month investigation in which they reviewed hundreds of pages of legal documents and interviewed dozens of attorneys, judges, court offices, elderly persons, and social workers. Among their findings:

- Judges all too often perfunctorily strip individuals of their civil rights and turn them over to guardians who are loosely supervised at best by the overburdened courts.
- The judicial hearings at which people are judged to be incompetent are frequently one-sided, superficial, and last only a few minutes.
- The subjects of most competency hearings rarely show up at them. Some people ignore the hearing notices because they do not understand them. Still others are excused by judges from attending because the people petitioning for guardianship get physicians to certify that going to court would greatly upset the proposed wards.
- Supervision of guardians by the courts is often lax even in those states that require periodic accountings.

"Outside of execution, guardianship is the most radical legal remedy we have," Elias Cohen, a Philadelphia attorney/gerontologist, told the magazine.[1]

Two years before this article appeared, the Associated Press shined a spotlight on the "dangerously burdened and troubled system" with a six-part investigative series in 1987. Based on their review of twenty-two hundred guardianship case files across the country, the AP reported judges were routinely committing people to guardianships without first permitting them access to attorneys or even hearings. The AP also found few safeguards existed to prevent guardians from abusing or stealing from their wards. The investigative series spawned legislative reform in all fifty states.

But lest you think the problem went away, say advocates, think again. Take the case of former attorney Wayne Phillips, who recently pleaded guilty in a Pinellas County court to stealing more than $85,000 from two elderly clients—one of whom had been his teacher in high school. A Florida state judge sentenced Phillips to six months in jail and another six months on work release.[2] Or consider the scandal of attorney Lauren Sill. She was a favorite referral for state social workers because she often accepted poor wards. Eventually she came to be entrusted with the welfare of five hundred wards. Then she set up a "voluntary" guardianship for a woman whose signature was both forged and misspelled, reported the *St. Petersburg Times.* Sill pleaded guilty in December 1993 to stealing $421,000 from several estates.[3] The only bright side to this story of a fallen star is the fact that Sill was caught.

"The exploitation and mismanagement of the assets of the elderly and infirm by their court-appointed guardians is a story as old as Florida," declared the editors of the *St. Petersburg Times* in September 2003.[4] And in Florida, which has more residents aged sixty-five and older (18 percent of the state's population) than any other state, the potential for guardianship abuse and fraud is exponential. And as that population swells to an estimated 22 percent of the total by 2050, the implications for a guardianship system already stretched too thin are dire.

Pinellas County, where Terri Schiavo's guardianship was established, is a case study of what lies ahead for the rest of Florida and other retirement meccas across the country. With a land area of 280 square miles skirting the Gulf of Mexico, Pinellas is the second smallest county in Florida and the most densely populated. The proportion of elderly residents has already surpassed the 2050 prediction for the state overall. According to the 2000 U.S. Census, a total of 921,482 people resided in the county. A significant 23 percent of the population is aged sixty-five and over, and persons with a disability make up another 22 percent.[5] Attorneys skilled in probate, estates, and elder law prosper in this county. And professional guardians make better livings here than elsewhere, because they carry an average caseload of thirty to forty wards. There are an estimated four thousand to six thousand guardianships in the county, representing $50 million worth of assets.

"[Professional guardianship] is an area ripe for fraud and where most fraud abuse has in fact occurred," Karleen DeBlaker, the recently retired

Pinellas County circuit court clerk, testified before a legislative task force in April 2004.

There are endless tales of suspected guardianship abuse tucked away in court documents, correspondence, and property records. Families around the country, and wards themselves, have contacted local advocate Laura Arasmo, with Justice for Florida Seniors, offering disturbing stories. One fairly well-off veteran contacted a local professional guardian to request a voluntary guardianship from the court to handle his financial affairs. Because he suffers from a manic-depressive disorder, the veteran had run up some charges for bad checks, according to Arasmo. The guardian he solicited persuaded the court the man was schizophrenic, and he wound up in a full guardianship.

The bad checks didn't get paid. The veteran wound up in jail, and it took several court appearances before he won his freedom. And the guardian charged the man's estate $1,500 for escorting him to court. The veteran was then placed in an assisted-living facility, the transfer for which he was assessed $2,000 by the guardian. The guardian reportedly failed to collect rent on the veteran's rental property for over a year, and the man lost his GI bill after the mortgage went unpaid. Even though his veteran's income amounted to $40,000 a year, his other bills were either ignored or only partially paid.[6]

"In short, this man lost his house, his vehicles, his freedom, and his shirt," Arasmo summarized. "It's a booming business," she added. "I've got to hand it to people in [the guardianship] business in Pinellas County; they've got it very well organized. They have a certain fleecing program, so to speak. And your parents are vulnerable if they're down here on their own."

During her twenty-four-year tenure as clerk of court, DeBlaker had a bird's-eye view of the system and yearned to fix it. "I've always felt personally that the primary problem is that the initial inventory of the ward-to-be's assets are not accurate in the first place," she said. "If you don't have control at that point . . . a lot of things disappear."

Although state statute calls for a "verified" inventory to be done of the ward's belongings, it provides no guidance for what that means. While relatives of the ward might normally be able to provide a check-and-balance to the guardian's inventory, they're prevented from doing so, because the court seals all guardianship documents. Sealing records serves as a double-edged sword. It protects wards from unsavory elements in the general public who are looking to cash in on the community's vulnerable. But it gives guardians the ability to do the pillaging themselves without detection. And they're given sixty days in which to work. Over the years there has been much documentation to show the temptation proved too great for some guardians to resist. Families of wards complain that precious heirlooms and other property, like an expensive coin collection, were neither accounted for nor ever located if they inquired about them. One family wrote the court to report more than $250,000 in their mother's estate had gone missing.

As a stopgap measure, DeBlaker proposes hiring appraisers to provide a second set of eyes—experienced in the valuation of property—to conduct the wards' inventories. But DeBlaker and her counterpart in Pasco County, who has worked with state legislators for years to tighten guardianship laws and reform the system, largely come up empty at the end of each legislative session.

"Money is the key to a lot of this," Jed Pittman concluded. If legislators were serious about reform, agrees DeBlaker, they'd give courts more funding to hire more auditors.

"The judiciary only has one qualified aide, who is an attorney, who looks over the [guardians'] financial reporting coming from the clerk," DeBlaker explained. "The clerk looks it over the best he or she can and makes a recommendation to the general master. Then [the general master] looks it over as the counsel to the court and makes recommendations to the judges. When you have one person with a number of guardianships that are running through, you can't possibly do everything thoroughly."

But the buck stops with the two judges who oversee all guardianship cases in the county. Judge George Greer is charged with oversight of all the cases that fall in the northern part of the county, and Judge Ray Ulmer is in charge of the cases to the south.

"The last few years of my service as clerk, I was very interested in us beefing up our department to try to catch as much as we could and alert the court about things that look funny," recalls Karleen DeBlaker. "I thought if we put an auditor in the department, we would be able to fix things up. But if the auditor points things out, saying this needs to be looked at further, and the courts don't want to look at it, then things don't get done."

In 2003 DeBlaker recruited the county's internal auditor to dig into her court's guardianship cases. As a result, Robert Melton launched a systematic review of scores of cases and raised questions about some court-appointed guardians. His review led him to compose a top-ten list of "Dirty Tricks of Guardianships." He outlined the list in a lecture at Eckerd College in St. Petersburg. Among the list:

- Guardian creation of a trust, where oversight by the court is a provision of the trust agreement; the guardian becomes trustee with sole discretion to do whatever he or she wants.

- Sell real estate at a low price to a land trust, where nobody knows the beneficiary; watch the property resell a few months later for a huge increase.
- Undervalue the beginning inventory; have a used-furniture "friend" value a house full of antiques for $3,000; "forget" to put some of the more expensive items on the inventory; "forget" to include a $40,000 certificate of deposit.
- Make payment of guardian and guardianship attorney fees the highest priority; disregard mortgage payments, and let ward's home go into foreclosure; squirrel money in the attorney's escrow account for possible future expenses.
- Maintain guardianship at all costs; keep family members uninformed; if family members try to become guardian, accuse them of stealing; use the ward's assets for legal fights to retain guardianship.
- Force incompetency on wards; visit assisted-living facilities and establish employee contacts; obtain voluntary limited financial guardianship; if there is money in the estate, do the paperwork to force declaration of incapacity and get control over everything.
- Pay your attorney well; let attorneys bill their full rate, even for work performed by a paralegal or assistant.[7]

In terms of prosecuting guardianship abuse, there's not much to write home about. Following the report of a 2003 audit of the county's "Ford Motor Company" of professional guardianship agencies, in which Melton accused the guardian of a teenager of sidestepping state laws, not complying with court orders, inappropriate investment practices, and making "questionable expenditures," the Pinellas–Pasco state attorney's office launched a preliminary inquiry one local reporter described as a "whitewash." State Attorney Bernie McCabe was even reluctant to use the term "investigation."[8]

Auditors have since come to suspect there may be something fraudulent about guardians' sales of wards' houses, which often sell for significantly less than appraised value, that resell months later for a significantly higher—and sometimes double—price, according to DeBlaker. McCabe reportedly looked into the auditors' concerns but found nothing he could prosecute.

"House values change. You can't really put your finger on it," said DeBlaker. "It just doesn't look quite right, but you can't prove anything."

Melton's criticism of the local guardianship system, amplified by the local press, created a flap. Pat Hall, executive director for the county's oldest and largest guardianship association, complains Melton painted all guardians with a wide brush. "Some of the family members rake the wards over the coals, but the guardians only have to follow Florida statute," she said, being careful to draw the distinction between family and professional guardianships, the latter of which her organization serves. "Most family members out of state rely on professional guardians and are appreciative." And for those people who have no next of kin, the professional guardian provides an indispensable service. A frequent call that comes into the office of Hall's Guardianship Association of Pinellas County is from people who have noticed newspapers piling up outside the front door of their elderly next-door neighbor's home. The association will dispatch someone over to the house and often find the resident in bad shape.

"These people have no one," Hall said. "Read the obituaries and you'll see how many die with no surviving relatives. It's really hard to see these people dying with no one there to hold their hands."

Guardianship attorneys, backed by the Florida Bar, blasted Melton for his auditing, calling it beyond "the appropriate scope" of his function.[9] Curiously, the judiciary was also critical of Melton. The *Gulf Coast Business Review* reported Judge Greer referenced him as DeBlaker's "hit man" during an interview. Insiders say the judges didn't take kindly to having "low-level clerks" pointing out to them what they ought to be looking at.

"We have to be careful in how we're banging on these professional guardians," Greer told the business journal, adding that he sees more potential for financial abuse by immediate family members who create guardianships than by professional guardians.[10]

During an unprecedented meeting ordered for all Pinellas County guardians, held January 3, 2005, Judges Greer and Ulmer approved a fee increase for professional guardians. At the top end of the scale, those with ten or more years of experience make seventy dollars an hour. Family guardians, meanwhile, get paid twenty dollars an hour. On the heels of the announcement, however, the judiciary sent out a not-so-subtle warning, urging compliance with state laws and court orders, according to Hall, who was at the meeting. "The court has the discretion to adjust fees," the judges reportedly said. "We still have power of oversight."

Melton believes that he has seen progress since he assigned one of his auditors to work full time on guardianships. "We are performing our audits on the cases, and we're providing information to the court, and the court has been taking action on our recommendations," he said. "So, yes, I think the situation has improved."

Melton couldn't comment on whether the guardianship of Terri Schiavo tripped any alarms in his office. A review of the two-inch-thick court docket reveals consistent desk reviews and audits performed by court clerks and Melton's auditor. Records reflect, however, Schiavo had trouble filing his required annual guardianship plan on time. Per Florida Statute 744.367 (5), "Each guardian of the person must file with the court an annual guardianship plan which updates information about the condition of the ward." The annual plan must specify the current needs of the ward and how the guardian proposes to meet those needs in the coming year. The plan is specifically supposed to outline the "provision of medical, mental health, and rehabilitative services in the coming year." Court records reflect, however, Schiavo consistently filed his guardianship plans after the fact, with the blessing of the court. For example, Judge Greer granted him four consecutive extensions of the deadline to file his annual guardianship plans, with the end result being his blueprints for 2002 and 2003 were filed on June 1, 2004. This lack of court oversight in Terri's guardianship is typical, say advocates for reform.

"The fact is that in many places, despite tougher laws, monitoring of guardianships remains lax," the American Association of Retired People (AARP) reported last year. "And although guardians . . . are required to file reports with the courts, those reports rarely get much, if any, scrutiny. Many jurisdictions don't even know how many guardianships there are, much less how well they're being carried out." According to AARP, the majority of the estimated six hundred thousand Americans under guardianship are in family guardianships, and sadly, when it comes to outright abuse, relatives are the most common offenders. But "greedy professional guardians can wreak havoc on a far larger scale," the magazine warned.[11]

As Laura Arasmo describes, families and friends of wards who discover the court-appointed guardian not acting responsibly or stealing from the ward bump up against a "wall of indifference" when they try to get the court-appointed guardian replaced—a probate court system that favors the guardian and a criminal court system that requires a level of proof before action that can only be found in documents sealed by the court.

"When families hire an attorney to petition the court to remove a [court-appointed] guardian and replace him/her with someone in which the family has confidence, these attempts most often fail," noted Arasmo. The Schindlers learned this lesson repeatedly over the last twelve years. They filed several petitions seeking the removal of Michael Schiavo as Terri's guardian, which were consistently denied or never heard. This aspect of the case featured prominently in the minds of many in the disabled community who seek reform of guardianship laws.

"Guardianship . . . has to have limits, especially when the stakes are the very lives of the people under [the] guardians' power. It's important to remember that guardians have power over people, not property, and those people still have rights," stressed Stephen Drake, a research analyst with the disability rights group Not Dead Yet, who himself suffered brain damage at birth and understands the need to retain rights despite disability. Joni Eareckson Tada, a prominent quadriplegic and disability rights activist agreed: "Individual liberties are now inextricably tied to the whims of a legal guardian, and that's not good news for Americans with disability."

DAVID GIBBS III, the Schindlers' lead attorney in the last year of the court battle, commented recently that the "system of justice in America that should have protected Terri . . . focused on the 'system' and completely abandoned any 'justice' in the case." In other words, fundamental commonsense facts fell through the cracks as attorneys and judges apparently failed to see the forest for the trees. That phenomenon set in at the very beginning of the case. The Schindlers' first petition seeking to oust Schiavo from the helm of Terri's guardianship came swiftly after the 1993 bladder infection incident. The couple felt they stood on solid ground: the guardian had admittedly attempted to kill his ward. That incontrovertible fact, however, would get overlooked and somehow lost in the shuffle of motions, hearings, and orders.

In addition to underscoring Michael Schiavo's breach of duty as a guardian by failing to properly care for the medical needs of the incompetent, thereby possibly creating a "life-threatening situation" for her, the Schindlers' July 30, 1993, petition for removal also drew attention to the fact Schiavo had "been engaged in a relationship with a person other than his wife," he had ordered the nursing home not to give out any medical information about Terri to her parents, and his "position as guardian puts him in a potential conflict of interest since he is the heir of the incompetent and stands to gain if she becomes deceased." In response to the Schindlers' petition, the court appointed court investigator Dan Novinsky to assess its merits. Novinsky reported back to the court there were substantial grounds for the guardianship-removal action.

Michael Schiavo's attorney Steven Nilsson filed a countermotion seeking to dismiss the Schindler petition, arguing, in part, it failed to spell out that Schiavo's relationship with a person other than his wife was "improper" and because it failed to provide details about his refusing to treat Terri's bladder infection. Nilsson also pointed out Florida statutes precluded guardians with actual conflicts of interests, not a "potential" conflict of interest. After offering to agree to the appointment of a neutral third party to assume the position of guardian, Nilsson suggested to the Schindlers they drop their case in order to "avoid expensive and divisive litigation that may significantly deplete guardianship funds which should be used for Theresa Marie Schiavo's care." Nilsson could have no idea how ironic this suggestion would be in hindsight twelve years later, after the lion's share of Terri's $750,000 medical trust fund was, in fact, paid out to Schiavo's attorneys.

Circuit Court Judge Thomas Penick Jr. appointed guardian ad litem John Pecarek for the purpose of analyzing Terri's physical condition and well-being, evaluating Terri's living conditions at Sabal Palms Health Care Center, and investigating the nursing home staff's allegations of Michael Schiavo's disturbances and interference in Terri's care and treatment. As previously discussed, Pecarek reported to the court that Michael Schiavo was "a nursing home administrator's nightmare," but that his advocacy and complaining on her behalf resulted in her getting more attention from the staff than other residents.

At a hearing on March 1, 1994, Pecarek testified he felt Michael Schiavo was providing for his ward's medical needs, despite Schiavo's admitted testimony the prior September that he attempted to end Terri's life by not treating her infection. Neither side was allowed to cross-examine Pecarek, and the Schindlers' attorney, James Sheehan, was prevented from pointing out the obvious contradiction: refusing to administer antibiotics to a ward with a potentially fatal infection does not represent providing for a ward's medical needs. Having fulfilled his duties in the mind of the court, Pecarek was subsequently discharged on March 29, 1994, and his fifteen-hundred-dollar fee was paid out of Terri's guardianship.

The Schindlers revamped their petition and filed an amended petition for removal of guardian on March 3, 1994, that addressed the earlier deficiencies illuminated by Schiavo's attorney. However, fear of being crushed by the financial weight of reimbursing Schiavo for his attorneys' fees and costs, should their petition fail, prompted the Schindlers to voluntarily dismiss with prejudice their amended petition on September 14, 1995. Some time over the next couple of months Schiavo would be introduced to George Felos, according to Schiavo, and work would get under way to get court authorization to remove Terri's feeding tube. By February 11, 2000, Michael Schiavo had a ruling from a judge that Terri's wishes were to die. The ruling rendered moot any lingering outrage over his attempt to kill his wife in 1993. After failing to register on the court's radar screen for seven years, the incident was dismissed. How Greer arrived at his 2000 ruling will be presented in the next chapter. Additionally, a blow-by-blow of the legal maneuvering this motion set into play will be provided in chapter 13.

BY NOVEMBER 2002 Terri had survived a sixty-hour dehydration and starvation ordeal, during which her feeding tube was removed pursuant to Greer's affirmed 2000 ruling. At that time, Michael Schiavo had been living with another woman, with whom he purchased a home and fathered a child, for seven years. Another child would soon follow. The Schindlers zeroed in on this relationship in their next attempt to wrest the guardianship of their daughter from the control of her estranged husband. Their November 15, 2002, petition sought the appointment of either of Terri's siblings as the successor guardian. The petition cited Schiavo's public admissions on *Larry King Live* and elsewhere as evidence of his failure to "discharge his duties in protecting the interests of the ward" by violating her right to be treated with dignity and respect and her right of privacy. This charge harkens back to the retained rights of wards in guardianship, regardless of incapacitation, outlined in Florida Statute 744.474.

"Fidelity is a key component of the respect and dignity that our society expects one spouse to afford the other," the petition read. "Yet this guardian believes that Terri's disability releases him of his legal and moral responsibility."

The petition sought a divorce for Terri and further argued Schiavo's admitted adultery violated Florida Statute 798, which makes living in adultery a misdemeanor, and proscribes lewd and lascivious cohabitation. Under the guardianship statute, a guardian found guilty, regardless of adjudication, to any offense prohibited under Florida Statute 435.03, which includes lewd and lascivious behavior, should be removed.

Schiavo attorney George Felos reacted sharply to the petition at the time. "I cannot understand how anyone would take that seriously," he said. "Most people would say that it's understandable that a healthy spouse shouldn't be sentenced to life without companionship." Felos compared Schiavo's situation to that of other clients of his who were dealing with spouses afflicted with Alzheimer's to the point of being institutionalized and no longer recognizing their healthy spouse.

Quoting one of the provisions under the guardianship statute for removing a guardian, the Schindlers' petition also accused Michael Schiavo of "wasting, embezzlement, or other mismanagement of the ward's property" by spending the monies in Terri's medical-care trust fund on Schiavo's litigation to pursue her death. "While exhausting Terri's money for the purpose of killing her, not one red cent could be found by Schiavo to enhance the quality of her life after receipt of the malpractice award. . . . And the expenditure of nothing for therapy that would reduce the pain of contractures, enhance Terri's ability to swallow, or facilitate recovery of basic abilities is the grossest form of asset mismanagement," Schindler attorney Anderson stated in the petition.[12]

As WorldNetDaily reported, the lion's share of the money awarded Terri by the 1992 medical malpractice jury, and from a separate settlement from her family physician, was spent on Schiavo's attorneys' fees.[13] According to petitions for fees filed with the court by the attorneys over the years, and in some cases the attorneys themselves, of the $776,254 reported to have been in Terri's medical-care trust fund on April 6, 1993, $456,816, or 59 percent, was spent on the cost of litigation rather than her medical care. The disbursements are as follows:

George Felos	$358,434
Deborah Bushnell	$80,309
Gyneth Stanley	$10,668.05
Steve Nilsson	$7,404.95

Michael Schiavo himself received $10,929.95 from Terri's fund as reimbursement for expenses, of which $6,000 represented legal costs. Unbeknownst to Terri, monies from her malpractice award also went toward settling her share of "marital debts," WorldNetDaily reported. In late 1994 Judge Thomas Penick Jr. approved Michael Schiavo's petition to pay down a bank loan he and Terri had cosigned months before her collapse. The couple had originally borrowed $11,500, but with Terri incapacitated and not working, Schiavo fell behind on the payments, and the debt mushroomed to $18,000.[14] In his November 1993 deposition, Schiavo testified he didn't recall if he worked at all between 1992 and 1996 while he was attending St. Petersburg Junior College. He also testified he collected Terri's social security checks, which began after her ten-thousand-dollar disability benefits with Prudential were exhausted.

Overall, the balance in Terri's medical-care trust fund defied gravity for the first five years, staying relatively constant, despite outlays to health-care providers one would expect occurred unless the state's Medicaid program was being tapped. This is likely due to the estimated annual interest income of $32,274 projected by the guardian of the property, South Trust Bank. The balance dropped slightly from $776,254 in April 1993 to $761,507 in June

1993, slipped to $692,655 in March 1994 and further down to $610,536 in April 1996. Then the balance rose to $645,738 in April 1997 and further climbed to $713,825.85 in April 1998 and $725,347 in April 1999.

Having been paid a retainer up front, Felos waited until after the January 2000 trial to submit petitions for fees. At that point, the balance dropped precipitously. By October 2003 only $55,000 was left in Terri's guardianship fund, according to Felos. By March 2005 just $40,000 to $50,000 remained, Deborah Bushnell told the Associated Press. There was no way to verify this, however, because trust account records are sealed, as are all guardianship records. Felos also successfully petitioned the court to seal attorneys' fees petitions after the 2000 trial. He scoffed at the claim his client had mismanaged his ward's money: "The charge of embezzlement . . . is ludicrous given that the payment was done per order of the court."

The Schindlers long argued in a variety of affidavits, motions, petitions, and a civil lawsuit that Terri's medical-care funds represented a conflict of interest for Michael Schiavo, who stood to inherit her estate upon her death. Guardian ad litem Pearse made the same argument in recommending that Schiavo's 1998 motion to remove Terri's feeding tube be denied. But as the years of litigation dragged on, and the attorneys' fees mounted, the suspicion that Schiavo was driven by his anticipated inheritance gradually dissipated. In fact, Terri was declared indigent in July 2002, and Judge Greer authorized Michael Schiavo's plan to enroll her in the state's Medicaid program. Attorneys' fees were terminated. Because Terri couldn't afford the roughly eighty thousand dollars a year it cost to stay at the hospice where she was transferred in April 2000, she was allowed to live at the nonprofit facility for free.[15]

Little more than four hours after Terri's death on March 31, 2005, Michael Schiavo petitioned the court to be appointed the personal representative of Terri's estate, which he was summarily granted. According to the petition, the assets in the estate were valued at less than twenty-five thousand dollars. This apparent draining of Terri's guardianship funds by attorneys is a common phenomenon in Pinellas County guardianship, according to auditor Robert Melton. Remember his top-ten list of "dirty tricks" of guardians?

- Make payment of guardian and guardianship attorney fees the highest priority; . . . squirrel money in the attorney's escrow account for possible future expenses.
- Maintain guardianship at all costs; . . . if family members try to become guardian, accuse them of stealing; use the ward's assets for legal fights to retain guardianship.

- Pay your attorney well; let attorneys bill their full rate, even for work performed by a paralegal or assistant."

"[Michael Schiavo] will receive no financial benefit upon Terri's death," attorney Felos told reporters at a press conference on October 23, 2003, adding there was "no insurance to collect."[16] At a press conference the day Terri died, Felos repeated his statement about insurance but added "to my knowledge" and "to my understanding" to qualify his statement.[17] Four months after Terri's death the *Empire Journal* reported a New York literary agent was shopping Michael Schiavo's proposal for a book on the case to publishers.[18]

With the unearthing of the 1991 nuclear imaging bone scan from the volumes of Terri's medical records in November 2002, the greatest perceived conflict of interest in the Schindlers' minds was the suspicion that Terri's mysterious collapse was precipitated by a violent altercation with her husband. The petition for removal raised this specter of suspicion, addressed at length in chapter 3.

Lastly, the Schindler petition alleged Terri's statutorial right as an incapacitated ward to receive "necessary services and rehabilitation" had been violated by her guardian. While Michael Schiavo stated on October 20, 2003, that he spent "more than seven years . . . desperately searching for a cure for Terri," her medical records reflect she had not been given aggressive rehabilitative therapy since April 25, 1991. At that time she was transferred to the long-term-care unit of Mediplex Rehabilitation Center, and physical therapy was decreased to one session a month. As a result, physical therapy notes dated June 5, 1991, and June 13, 1991, indicate she suffered a "significant loss in range of motion at both her hips and knees" and at that time exhibited only limited range of motion in all her extremities. In a "discharge evaluation" prior to Terri's transfer to Sabal Palms Health Care Center, the physical therapist recommended Terri be given aggressive range of motion to all four extremities every day. According to her medical records, however, the physical therapist's recommendation wasn't followed. At Sabal Palms, Michael Schiavo ordered Terri not be given any therapy, according to a sworn affidavit later filed by one of her caregivers at the nursing home.

"I learned as part of my training that there was a family dispute and that the husband, as guardian, wanted no rehabilitation for Terri," Carolyn Johnson stated. "This surprised me, as I did not think a guardian could go against a doctor's orders like that. But I was assured that a guardian could, and that this guardian had gone against Terri's doctor's orders." Johnson noted that everyone at the facility "knew we would lose our jobs if we did not do exactly what Michael said to do." In her affidavit Johnson lamented that the experience made her "look hard at nursing homes" and said she quit her job because she had grown "so disillusioned with the way Terri was treated."

Caregivers came forward from the next nursing home where Terri was transferred after the bladder infection controversy, Palm Garden of Largo Convalescent Center, and echoed Johnson's comments. In a sworn affidavit, registered nurse Carla Sauer Iyer stated rehabilitation had been ordered for Terri by her doctor, but she never saw any being done and had reason to believe any rehab was being given to her.

"I became concerned because nothing was being done for Terri at all—no antibiotics, no tests, no range of motion therapy, no stimulation, no nothing," Iyer stated. "Michael said again and again that Terri should not get any rehab, that there should be no range of motion whatsoever, or anything else."

She wrote that from the time of her employment between April 1995 and August 1996, it was clear to her "that all decisions regarding Terri Schiavo were made by Michael Schiavo, with no allowance made for any discussion, debate, or normal professional judgment."

"My initial training there consisted solely of the instruction, 'Do what Michael Schiavo tells you or you will be terminated,'" Iyer recalled, adding that the atmosphere at the facility was dominated by Schiavo's "intimidation." She described him as using "menacing body language" such as "standing too close to you" and "getting right in your face and practically shouting," which she stated made her fearful for her personal safety.

Iyer said she used to sneak behind Schiavo's back and give Terri range-of-motion therapy when she could. But one time, according to Iyer, Michael Schiavo saw she had put a washcloth in Terri's hand to keep her fingers from curling together, and he made her take it out, saying it was therapy.

But Iyer offered more damning testimony about the appropriateness of Michael's serving as Terri's guardian. Specifically, she characterized Schiavo as being "focused on Terri's death" as exhibited in alleged comments like, "When is she going to die?" "Has she died yet?" and "When is that bitch gonna die?" The caregiver asserts these and similar statements were "common knowledge" at Palm Gardens. She stated Schiavo would be "furious" when Terri wouldn't die and "visibly excited, thrilled even" anytime Terri would be suffering from a urinary tract infection, colds, or fluid buildup in her lungs.

The nurse said she was suspicious that whenever Schiavo visited his wife, he always came alone and always had the door to Terri's room closed and locked while he was with her. Iyer stated that on approximately five occasions she went into Terri's room right after a visit from Schiavo and found Terri "trembling, crying hysterically . . . very pale and [with] cold sweats." It looked to her as if Terri was having a hypoglycemic reaction, and a subsequent check of her blood-sugar level confirmed it had dropped so low the glucometer reading didn't even register. To counteract this, according to Iyer's statement, she would put dextrose in Terri's mouth. During one of these incidents, Iyer recalls finding an insulin vial wrapped up in the rubbish bin in Terri's room.

"It is my belief that Michael injected Terri with regular insulin, which is very fast acting," Iyer stated. She reported her suspicions to the Pinellas County Sheriff's Office, but nothing came of her complaint. Iyer was subsequently fired.

Certified nursing assistant Heidi Law cared for Terri at the same nursing home as Iyer for four months in 1997. She concurs with Iyer that the rule at the facility was no therapy for Terri per Michael Schiavo's orders.

"I know that Terri did not receive routine physical therapy or any other kind of therapy. I was personally aware of [doctor's] orders for rehabilitation that were not being carried out," Law wrote in a sworn affidavit. "Even though they were ordered, Michael would stop them. Michael ordered that Terri receive no rehabilitation or range of motion therapy."

Like Iyer, Law described times when she offered Terri therapy in secret. "I and Olga would give Terri range of motion anyway, but we knew we were endangering our jobs by doing so," she wrote. "We usually did this behind closed doors, we were so fearful of being caught. Our hearts would race, and we were always looking out for Michael, because we knew that, not only would Michael take his anger out on us, but he would take it out more on Terri."

For her part, former Schiavo girlfriend Trudy Capone, who worked with Terri at two different facilities, questioned why he preferred to keep Terri's room dark, with the shades drawn. She said he also wouldn't permit the television in her room to be on, because he was afraid she might hear something "upsetting."

Michael Schiavo has repeatedly and strenuously denied allegations of abuse and neglect. Attorney Felos described Iyer's accusations as "a bunch of garbage." Judge Greer dismissed them as "incredible to say the very least." Felos commented, "The opposition has a pattern of dredging up filth in order to attack my client because ultimately they're going to lose on the merits of the case, which is what the current medical condition of Terri is and what her wishes are."

Dr. Victor Gambone also testified in court that Terri hadn't received therapy since she became his patient in 1998 because Michael Schiavo told him it wouldn't be of value to her. According to Terri's medical records, Gambone recommended on April 20, 1998, that Terri be evaluated for physical therapy to treat her muscle contractures, but Schiavo "declined" the evaluation. Medical records show that by 2000, when Terri was transferred to the hospice against hospice policy to accept only terminally ill patients, her muscle contractures had grown so severe, casual therapy was no longer an option. Notes in her chart in August 2000 and December 2001 state that a caregiver would "attempt" to do passive range-of-motion exercises with Terri but would be thwarted by "severe muscle spasms and contractures" and would abandon the attempt due to Terri's "discomfort as evidenced by moaning, grimacing."

Despite the medical records and court testimony, Michael Schiavo and attorney Felos repeatedly and vociferously asserted the "no therapy" claims were false and that Terri had received therapy. Schiavo's consistent response fell along the lines of what he stated to this author in 2002: "There has been therapy. I had a private aide with Terri until 1996 to stimulate her. . . . I took Terri out to California for experimental surgery in 1991." Over a two-year period the aide took Terri on outings to the mall, museums, and parks to expose her to different kinds of stimulation and for beauty makeovers. When pressed whether Terri had received any rehabilitative or physical therapy since late 1991, which her medical records reflect isn't the case, Schiavo stated: "Before hospice, there used to be monthly evaluations of Terri by physical therapists, occupational therapists. And every month they said, 'Terri will not benefit from therapy.'" The chorus of neurologists and other doctors—nearly all of whom were prevented from examining Terri but allowed to view videotaped footage of a neurologist's examination of her—disputing that there was no hope for Terri grew louder over the ensuing years, but they would never be heard inside the courtrooms.

After Michael Schiavo succeeded in dodging the bullet of several scheduled depositions, in part because the circuit court granted him cover, Anderson finally filed a motion to hear the petition, and Greer agreed to a hearing in November 2003. But it would be July 20, 2004, before the judge ruled that both Michael Schiavo and his fiancée, Jodi Centonze, could be deposed. Amid continued cancellations and no-shows, Anderson asked Greer in August 2004 to compel the parties to appear for scheduled depositions. But

Greer refused. Consequently, the 2002 petition for removal of guardian was never heard.

IN AUGUST 2003 Terri Schiavo again contracted a serious infection that almost took her life. On August 14 she developed vomiting and breathing difficulties and was coughing up blood. She was transported to Morton Plant Hospital in Clearwater, Florida, and admitted. Although she was discharged approximately a week later, her condition had apparently not stabilized, and approximately forty-eight hours later she was again transported from the hospice to the hospital with a recurrence of vomiting and a temperature of 102. She was believed to be suffering from pneumonia in her left lung and sepsis.

As he had prophesied in his September 1993 deposition after the bladder infection controversy, Schiavo did not want to treat Terri's new life-threatening illness. Although by then he had the blessing of the trial court and an appellate court to remove her feeding tube, he was not allowed to deny her antibiotics. Felos filed a motion with Greer to remedy that while Terri was still in the hospital, which Greer denied pending a forthcoming hearing where he was to schedule the second removal of Terri's feeding tube. A trial-court ruling favoring sustaining Terri's life was a refreshing change of pace in the mind of Anderson, who attended the hearing on the motion. Felos argued that treating Terri with antibiotics weeks before her feeding tube would be removed amounted to "unnecessary and futile medical care."

"Mr. Felos, I think that this is totally new from anything we've done before," responded Greer. "I think the guardian certainly does have the right to make this request, but I think he needs to make it in the same manner in which he made the initial request to withdraw the life support. So I'm not going to consider that on an emergency basis."

Chris Ferrara, with the American Catholic Lawyers Association, concurred and holds that seeking the denial of antibiotics from hospital patients "is completely outside the ambit of Florida law." In a federal lawsuit filed the following week, Ferrara took a different tack from the Schindlers' prior actions to counter Schiavo's dictatorial control over his ward. Instead of seeking his replacement as guardian by a member of the Schindler family, he sought the parents' appointment as guardians ad litem. In the suit filed in the Middle District of Florida in Tampa, Ferrara alleged Michael Schiavo and George Felos conspired with the Hospice of the Florida Suncoast (the owner of Hospice Woodside, which housed Terri) and Morton Plant Hospital to hasten Terri's death. Ferrara called the "premature discharges" from the hospital and Terri's resultant shuttling between hospice and the hospital part of an "exit protocol."

The lawsuit expanded the earlier claims of medical neglect on the part of guardian Michael Schiavo by determining them to be violations of the Rehabilitation Act of 1973, which prohibited discrimination against an "otherwise qualified" handicapped individual, and the Americans with Disabilities Act (ADA), which provides that necessary and appropriate rehabilitation services and physical/motor skill therapy not be denied a substantially disabled patient. The ADA specifically states, "Nothing in the Act . . . authorizes the representative or guardian of an individual with a disability to decline food, water, medical treatment, or medical services for that individual." This section of the federal regulation, in Ferrara's view, spoke not only to Schiavo's denial of physical therapy for Terri over the years but also to his ongoing attempt to withhold the antibiotics necessary to treat her pneumonia, as well as the imminent withdrawal of her feeding tube. Hospitals and hospices that accept federal Medicare and Medicaid funding are subject to the act.

Ferrara further argued that, regardless of the state appellate court's mandate that Terri's feeding tube be removed, the Fifth and Fourteenth Amendments to the U.S. Constitution give Terri "an independent right to life." In addition, Terri's due-process rights under the Fourteenth Amendment were asserted to have been violated, because she wasn't afforded a guardian ad litem or her own lawyer throughout most of the duration of the decade of legal proceedings.

The federal lawsuit also claimed Michael Schiavo had repeatedly violated Terri's First Amendment right to freedom of religion. The complaint cites Schiavo's interference with the Reverend Monsignor Thaddeus Malanowski's ministering to Terri during her hospitalization, as he had done during hospice visits the prior three years. When queried about his decision to temporarily ban the priest from Terri's bedside by a reporter at a press conference, Schiavo responded, "If I want Terri to have a priest, I'll supply that priest." The lawsuit further argued that Florida's statute on removing artificial nutrition and hydration was unconstitutional, because it ran counter to Terri's Roman Catholic Church doctrine.

On October 7, 2003, Florida Governor Jeb Bush filed a court brief to bolster the Schindlers' efforts. Three days later, U.S. District Judge Richard Lazzara ruled he lacked the jurisdiction to hear the lawsuit and dismissed the case. Eleven days later Malanowski was prevented from giving Terri what was believed would be her final Holy Communion, a tiny cracker that represents the body of Jesus Christ.

Nearly six months later the Schindlers would be dropped from Michael Schiavo's approved-visitors list for Terri, based on the insinuation they were behind five "puncture wounds" found on both of her arms. A press release sent from Felos's office at 8:40 p.m. on March 29, 2004, titled "Schiavo Puncture Wounds Found After Parents' Visit," stated that holes apparently caused by a hypodermic needle were discovered immediately after a forty-five-minute visit from the Schindlers. The press release said medical personnel found Terri in a "disheveled state, with her feeding tube wrapped around her back." The purple cap from a hypodermic needle was found in Terri's gown, according to the release, "confirming the belief the puncture wounds were caused by a hypodermic needle." The release implied Terri's parents had either withdrawn blood or injected her with some substance. Terri was promptly taken to the hospital for toxicology testing and other blood work. The release said a forensics team had examined the "crime scene," and the Clearwater Police Department was investigating. The Schindlers would learn about the incident after the media had received the press release. Anderson decried the incident as "staged."

WorldNetDaily reported the wounds were actually discovered several hours after the Schindlers visited Terri, when she was dressed in street clothes, not a gown. The toxicology exam concluded there were no unauthorized substances in her system. And the Florida Agency for Health Care Administration investigators dispatched to Terri's bedside on April 1 could not confirm the presence of needle marks on her arms. Six weeks later the Clearwater Police Department announced it found no evidence of a crime. But it would be several more weeks before the visitation rights of the Schindlers were restored. Shortly before Mother's Day, Schiavo proposed his in-laws could see their daughter if they hired an off-duty police officer to stay in the room with them during the visit. The idea sparked outrage. "No mother should have to pay an admission fee to see her child on Mother's Day," Anderson retorted.[19]

When the Schindlers were reunited with their daughter, they found her missing five of her back teeth. An oral surgeon had extracted the teeth due to discoloration, which is indicative of deterioration. The discoloration of Terri's teeth was an issue raised in a court hearing in February 2002. Terri's treating physician, Gambone, testified in October 2002 that he didn't know whether Terri's teeth had been cleaned since 1998. Medical records reflect her last cleaning was in 1995.

On April 26, 2004, Anderson filed a petition for writ of quo warranto seeking a "show cause" hearing in which guardian Michael Schiavo would have to prove his worthiness to act on behalf of his ward, and the court would determine whether he had exceeded or abused his guardianship authority by restricting the Schindlers' visitation. Quo warranto means "by what authority." In addition to referencing the extracted teeth, the denial of physical therapy as evidenced by Terri's medical records, and attempts to socially "isolate" Terri by restricting visitation, the petition discussed Schiavo's "dereliction of duty"—condoned by the court—with respect to the mandatory filing of his guardianship plans. It offered as an example Schiavo's receiving approval on May 8, 2002, for a care plan filed February 1, 2002, meant to outline care for the year ending June 30, 2001. In other words, the plan was nineteen months late.

"Since 1990, [Michael Schiavo] has *never* received approval for a care plan on a prospective basis," the petition underscored. "No guardian may exercise the delegated rights of his ward except pursuant to such a plan."

"No provision is made for the elimination of rehabilitative services or medical treatment or elimination of visitation," the petition added.

After determining the Schindlers' petition was "legally sufficient," Greer granted a "show cause" hearing and ordered Michael Schiavo to appear. In a countermotion, Felos referenced the Pandora's Box justification described earlier for local prosecutors' reticence to press charges against criminal guardians. Felos argued the "public detriment" of granting the Schindlers the opportunity to prove Michael Schiavo lacked the legal authority to serve as Terri's guardian exceeded their private benefit.

"If this court were to enter the judgment that the [Schindlers] seek—that [Michael Schiavo] has no power to act because he has not filed his annual guardianship plan—then all similarly situated guardians in this circuit who have applied for and received an extension to file their annual guardianship plans would be powerless to act on behalf of their wards. Potentially hundreds of wards in this circuit would be left with no duly authorized guardian to act on their behalf," wrote Felos in a June 1, 2004, motion to dismiss the petition and dissolve the writ of quo warranto. Remember the two judges providing the oversight for the estimated six thousand Pinellas County guardianships, and therefore granting filing extensions, were Greer and Ulmer. Felos also argued quo warranto was an extraordinary remedy "unavailable to a party who has a sufficient remedy at law."

Greer ultimately agreed with Felos's arguments and on July 6, 2004, issued an order dismissing Anderson's petition and canceling the "show cause" hearing, arguing it was duplicative to the November 2002 petition for removal of guardian—the petition that would never come to be heard.

"Logic and reason would lead us to conclude that an extraordinary remedy should not be afforded where an ordinary one is available," Greer wrote in his ruling, adding that granting the writ would result in "confusion and disorder."

In January 2005 the Schindlers filed one last petition to roust Schiavo from his guardianship perch, followed up with another request for Terri's divorce on February 28, 2005. By then some eighty-nine charges of neglect, abuse, and exploitation of Terri had been lodged with the state social service agency statutorily mandated to protect "vulnerable" citizens, the Department of Children and Families (DCF). Nothing would come of the complaints, which dated back to 2001. Incredibly, all the charges were deemed "unfounded." DCF was but one of several social service and law-enforcement agencies to which the Schindlers appealed to intervene on Terri's behalf. The organizations uniformly refused. (Reasons for this will be explored in chapter 15.) By the time this last effort was made, Terri had been largely sequestered in her small, reportedly dark hospice room for nearly five full years, due to a broken wheelchair. A security guard was posted outside her door much of the time.

The Schindlers' latest attorney, David Gibbs, argued the same four conflicts of interest highlighted in prior actions existed to justify Schiavo's removal from his post as guardian: personal conflict, due to adultery; legal conflict, due to his failing to provide Terri with her own lawyer during the course of five years of litigation; financial conflict, due to Schiavo's exhausting Terri's medical-care funds on litigation expenses; and religious conflict, due to Schiavo's active lack of respect of Terri's faith.

"Any one of these four conflicts of interest should provide the court with a sufficient reason to terminate Mr. Schiavo's guardianship and appoint a replacement guardian," Gibbs commented at the time.[20]

But the court denied the petition without hearing it on March 10, 2005.

"He's trying to kill Terri. That's the bottom line. And for the past ten years he has tried to kill Terri in one form or another," Bob Schindler summarized in 2002.

"My aim is to carry out Terri's wishes," Schiavo retorted. "If Terri would even know that I had somebody taking care of her bodily functions, she'd kill us all in a heartbeat. She'd be so angry," he added.[21] In published reports, Michael Schiavo consistently justified his intransigence over remaining both Terri's husband and guardian by explaining he needed to ensure her wishes to die were carried out. Yet he offered a different reason during a September 27, 1999, deposition:

ATTORNEY PAMELA CAMPBELL: Have you considered turning the guardianship over to [Robert and Mary] Schindler?

SCHIAVO: No, I have not. . . . Basically, I don't want to do it . . . because they put me through pretty much hell the last few years. . . . Just their attitude towards me because of the litigations. There is no other reason. I'm Terri's husband and I will remain guardian.

Michael Schiavo kept his pledge. And he was praised for it. In August 2005 the Florida State Guardianship Association awarded him its Guardian of the Year award. "He was an ordinary guardian who carried out his duties in extraordinary ways," the association's past president Joan Nelson told the *Orlando Sentinel*. "Oh, my God, that's offensive," the paper also quoted Brother Paul O'Donnel, a Franciscan friar who served as a Schindler family spokesman, as saying. "Michael Schiavo . . . basically let her rot."

The honor was bestowed on Schiavo at the organization's eighteenth annual conference. "I'm not much of a speechmaker," Schiavo told the audience after accepting the diamond-cut crystal award. "I don't like to talk much. But on behalf of my wife, Theresa, I thank you."[22]

6

Terri's Wishes

WHAT DID TERRI SCHIAVO want? What would *you* want if you were incapacitated—immobile, unable to speak, totally reliant on others? These two questions perplexed attorneys, judges, politicians, pundits, media commentators, and the public over the past fifteen years. In the minds of many, the questions became entangled. Right-to-die advocates argued the two questions are one and the same and have lobbied legislators across the country to change state laws to reflect a "best interest" standard. They succeeded in Florida in 1999, and this will be examined in depth in chapter 12.

Court documents, medical records, and public statements suggest the two questions were also intertwined in the mind of Michael Schiavo. Former girlfriend Cindy Shook testified that he was thoroughly confused in 1991 as to what to do about Terri. He reportedly told her several times that he and Terri never discussed end-of-life issues.

"How the hell should I know? We never spoke about this," Shook recalled an exasperated Schiavo saying. "My God, I was only twenty-five years old. How the hell should I know? We were young. We never spoke of this."

Shook's court testimony occurred after Michael called a radio talk show on the morning of April 24, 2001, the day Terri's feeding tube was removed for the first time. On the air he declared he was carrying out Terri's wishes as they had discussed them prior to her collapse. When Shook heard callers describing Michael Schiavo as a saint, she reportedly determined to set the record straight and called another local radio station to offer a rebuttal. After hearing Shook on the radio, the Schindler family promptly dispatched a private investigator to obtain her statement. She reportedly told Bob Schindler that Michael Schiavo had told her he planned to divorce Terri and leave her care to her parents, but all that changed when the malpractice trial verdict came in. So did Shook's relationship with Michael; she said it ended that day.

In her sworn affidavit, Trudy Capone similarly stated that while she and Michael were dating in late 1992 and early 1993, he often confided to her that he didn't know what Terri would want him to do. "He would ask me what I thought he should do," she stated. "I swear to you he never knew what Terri wanted."

Terri's friend Fran Casler also filed a sword affidavit with the court stating that Schiavo indicated he didn't know Terri's wishes during the early years of her incapacitation. Casler described a conversation in which Schiavo was reportedly "complaining that he did not know the answers to question he was being asked" by the lawyers gathering information for the medical malpractice trial.

"I specifically remember Michael's saying, 'How should I know whether she wanted to die? How should I know what she wanted?' He was gesturing at the time in a somewhat grandiose way," Casler wrote in the affidavit.

"I would have to say at this time—before the medical malpractice trial—when Michael was living with Bob and Mary Schindler in their home, that Michael was like a broken record, complaining about the effect on his life of Terri's collapse," Casler continued. "His complaining became tiresome for those around him, me included. We all felt sorry for him, but he seemed to be wallowing in his own misery and wasn't making any progress in facing the reality of the situation."

Over the years, according to medical records and his testimony, Michael Schiavo received input from Terri's doctors and caregivers. Those of the opinion that Terri's life was useless apparently stood out in Michael's mind. Dr. David Baras, who treated Terri during the earliest days of her incapacity and who testified about her condition during the malpractice trial, reportedly told Michael Schiavo that even if Terri were to come out of her coma, she would be a total quadriplegic. Based on this comment, Michael testified, he declared to the Schindlers that it was not in Terri's best interest to regain consciousness.

"At the point of the coma that Terri's in now, she's a total quadriplegic. Okay? In my own feelings, if Terri were to wake up and see herself the way she is now, she wouldn't even want to live like that," he said during the November 1993 deposition. In the minds of those within the disability community, this apparent bias against people with disability is the essence of the Terri Schiavo story. Advocates who joined in the cause to keep Terri alive regard this attitude that Terri's brain injury rendered her life meaningless as pervasive throughout society. (More on that follows in chapter 10.)

Medical records show Terri was in a coma for several weeks after her collapse. Once her eyes opened, she was diagnosed as being in a persistent vegetative state. (More on the distinction between these two states of unconsciousness will follow in chapter 7). Although nurses and therapists reported Terri had advanced to the point of saying "yes," "no," and "stop that" during therapy sessions; was following one-step commands on occasion; and exhibited a slight visual tracking ability, according to Terri's medical records, doctors wanted to see more "meaningful progress." As early as April 1991—fourteen months after her collapse—Dr. Eugene Alcazaran, according to Terri's medical file, met with Michael Schiavo and Mary Schindler and "explained [Terri's] lack of progress at length." During this meeting, Schiavo reportedly expressed he felt two and a half months at the Mediplex rehabilitation facility was too short to "give Terri a chance." But Alcazaran stressed that, due to the original severity of the brain injury, he didn't see how formal physical therapy or occupational therapy would facilitate any more "meaningful progress." He recommended she receive only maintenance care.

"No benefit presently seen to therapy plan," Dr. James Carnahan similarly concluded a week later, basing his recommendation on the lack of improvement in Terri over the prior four months. Terri was promptly transferred from the aggressive rehab section of the facility to the long-term care unit, where physical therapy was decreased to one session per month. As a result of the physical therapy protocol being stepped down, nurses' notes indicate Terri began to suffer severe contractures in her legs, which eventually became pervasive throughout her body. (More discussion of Terri's medical condition will follow in chapter 7.)

Fast forward to July 1993 and Dr. Patrick Mulroy's suggestion, according to Schiavo, that he not treat her urinary tract infection, which would, in effect, cause her to die. Then on November 18, 1993, Schiavo met with a referred physician who reportedly advised the removal of the feeding tube. Schiavo testified the next day about their conversation:

> SCHIAVO: Dr. Harrison [said] to me, when the EEG was done, sat me down in the office, and he says that her EEG is so depressed and why do you let her live. And he said to me that this woman died four years

ago, and it's such a tragic thing. And he said to me, I noticed you've taken her to Largo Medical Center for some treatments, and he says that the next time she gets an infection, not to treat it. And then we started talking about—he said, remove the feeding tube. And I told him I couldn't do that to Terri. . . .

ATTORNEY JAMES SHEEHAN: Was it Dr. Harrison's suggestion the feeding tube be removed?

SCHIAVO: It wasn't a suggestion; it was just talk. He just mentioned it.

SHEEHAN: How did he mention it? What did he say?

SCHIAVO: He was talking about removing the feeding tube, and I said I couldn't do that to Terri.

SHEEHAN: Was this the first—this was the first time she had seen Dr. Harrison?

SCHIAVO: Yes, it was.

SHEEHAN: Do you know Dr. Harrison at all?

SCHIAVO: No, I do not.

SHEEHAN: Other than a referral from Dr. Lyles?

SCHIAVO: Just a referral from Dr. Lyles.

According to Schiavo, his reaction to the first suggestion of removing Terri's feeding tube in late 1993 was, "I couldn't do that to Terri." His statement reflects a sense that it was morally wrong to remove her feeding tube. But his opinion on the matter changed sometime during the next couple of years, and pulling the feeding tube morphed from a moral wrong to a moral imperative. And while the near one million dollars in Terri's guardianship was accruing interest, Michael was losing interest in her welfare, according to caregivers Carolyn Johnson, Carla Sauer Iyer, and Heidi Law.

In 1994 Michael Schiavo began to date Jodi Centonze, with whom he would father two children. He began living with her at her home in 1995, and eventually they purchased a house together in 1999. Schiavo was often questioned over the years whether his longstanding relationship with Centonze presented a conflict of interest for him in pursuing the motion to end Terri's life.

"Does it hurt the situation, do you think, as the way the public might look at you?" Larry King asked during the October 27, 2003, interview.

"From their side, I'm sure," Schiavo responded. "But you know something? I'm fortunate to have two women in my life that I love very much." He then went on to assert his girlfriend had done more for Terri than Mary Schindler had. The claim outraged the Schindlers, and they flatly denied it.

By all accounts, the Schindlers encouraged Michael Schiavo to date and move on with his life. Calling Bob Schindler a "conniving and manipulating person," Brian Schiavo believed Terri's father had an ulterior motive when he reportedly suggested Michael should seek the company of another woman as soon as two weeks after Terri's collapse.

"I looked at him in shock," Brian Schiavo said. "He said, 'No, no. I mean it.' I believe that he was starting to think how he could be involved in this and trying to get Michael out of the picture back then."

Indeed, Bob Schindler's July 1993 letter reflects it was his hope that Michael would move on with his life and give "Terri back" to her parents so they could see that she received proper care "long term." Michael Schiavo did move on, but he didn't give Terri back.

"I moved on with a part of my life," Schiavo stated in 2002, "I'm sorry that the Schindlers can't move on with any of theirs."

Centonze was obliquely referred to as Michael's fiancée in his mother's July 1997 obituary, which was published in her hometown newspaper in Pennsylvania. Only her first name was given. While the funeral notice listed the spouses of Michael Schiavo's four brothers, it failed to mention Terri. Nonetheless, Clara M. Schiavo's passing on July 2, 1997, served as a pivotal event in Terri Schiavo's life. Michael Schiavo later stated that it was his mother's death that prompted his battle to carry out Terri's wishes to die.

"I never wanted Terri to die. I still don't," he said in a written statement released on October 20, 2003. "After more than seven years of desperately searching for a cure for Terri, the death of my own mother helped me realize that I was fooling myself. More important, I was hiding behind my hope, and selfishly ignoring Terri's wishes. I wanted my wife to be with me so much that I denied her true condition."

The statement raised the ire of the Schindler family and their supporters. Casler declared Michael Schiavo a "liar." "He suddenly remembered that he knew what Terri's wishes were. But when I was with him after Terri's collapse, he repeatedly said to me and everyone else that was within earshot that he didn't know what Terri's wishes were," she said.[1]

"Which Michael are we to believe?" Bobby Schindler asked. "The one who promised he would take care of his wife for the rest of his life, or the one who says these were Terri's death wishes?"[2]

During the 2003 appearance on CNN's *Larry King Live,* Michael Schiavo was confronted by a caller who challenged him to take a lie detector test to prove the veracity of his recollection of Terri's end-of-life wishes. Schiavo responded, "I'll refrain from answering that right now."[3]

Schiavo's written statement—released five days after Terri's feeding tube was removed for the second time, and one day before Florida Governor Jeb Bush signed an executive order directing its reinsertion—served as an answer to questions arising over the apparent delay in his recollection of Terri's wishes. His original petition to remove Terri's feeding tube was filed in May 1998, eight years after her collapse and subsequent diagnosis of persistent vegetative state. This "troubling aspect" of the case had prompted the Florida House of Representatives to pass "Terri's Law," which, when signed off by the Florida Senate, empowered the governor to intervene.

Prominent pro-life attorney Ken Connor, former president of the conservative Family Research Council, raised the issue in his defense of Governor Bush and the constitutionality of "Terri's Law." "Why didn't Mr. Schiavo testify under oath before the jury where he sought millions of dollars about Terri's desires to die under these circumstances?" Connor posed in a radio interview with Tampa Bay talk journalist John Sipos on April 20, 2004. "The closing line in the direct examination of Michael Schiavo in that case was something to the extent, 'I take my marriage vows very seriously, and I plan to spend the rest of my life with Terri Schiavo.' How on earth can one possibly reconcile that statement with Michael Schiavo's unrelenting efforts to bring about the death of his wife and to reconcile that with his living with another woman by whom he has fathered two children? How on earth that indicates a respect for his marriage vows and a continuing intention to live with his wife and take care of his wife is just a mystery to me."[4]

While Clara Schiavo's death, which resulted after a doctor removed her from the respirator sustaining her life in accordance with her written advance directive, may have helped justify the decision, in her son's mind, to similarly bring about Terri's death, Michael Schiavo's decision to end Terri's life was clearly made at least a year earlier. In a petition seeking the reimbursement of fees to be paid out of Terri's guardianship funds, Schiavo's guardianship attorney, Deborah Bushnell, indicated she contacted right-to-die attorney George Felos on December 13, 1995. Felos gained notoriety for his legal advocacy of another Floridian woman's right to die in the late 1980s, Estelle Browning.

On March 5, 1997, Schiavo signed a contract authorizing Felos to represent him "in connection with the withdrawal and/or refusal of medical treatment." Aside from this paper trail, Michael Schiavo publicly confirmed in the original 2000 trial that he arrived at his decision to withdraw Terri's feeding tube around the time Felos became involved in the case. He revealed this information during direct examination by Felos about the 1993 urinary tract infection incident.

SCHIAVO: The doctor recommended that we don't treat the infection and that Terri should have a "Do Not Resuscitate" order in place.
FELOS: How did you feel about that when you heard that?
SCHIAVO: I was emotional, but I felt it was what Terri would want.
FELOS: Did you bring up the subject of the DNR order, not treating the infection, first?
SCHIAVO: No. The doctor did.
FELOS: Did you make a decision to implement, institute a Do Not Resuscitate order and Do Not Treat Infection?
SCHIAVO: Yes. I did. . . .
FELOS: Did the nursing home react to it at all?
SCHIAVO: Yes. They did. They started getting all upset. Telling me it was against the law to do something like that. . . .
FELOS: Did you back off of the decision at that time?
SCHIAVO: Yes. I did. I had the nursing home, I had the [Schindler's] petition [to remove him as guardian], and my emotions were running. So I backed way off.
FELOS: Why didn't you pursue the removal of the feeding tube?
SCHIAVO: Because at that time my emotions were running. I couldn't—I was ready to do the natural thing. I was not ready to pull the feeding tube at that time.
FELOS: Even though you knew Terri wanted it?
SCHIAVO: Yes. . . .
FELOS: The Schindlers dismissed their petition with prejudice in September 1995, and this petition was filed in—your current petition to remove artificial life support was filed in May of 1988 (*sic*). Why did you wait two and a half years to file the petition?
SCHIAVO: I did not wait. I met you in the beginning of 1996, I believe. I was talking to another attorney.
FELOS: Well, okay. I have to caution you not to testify as to any communication you might have with your attorney because of attorney/client privilege. Let me ask it this way. Did you seek to put into motion your decision to remove the feeding tube before the petition was filed in May of 1988 (*sic*)?
THE COURT: You keep saying '88.
FELOS: '98. Thank you, Your Honor.

FELOS: When did you make the decision and start putting it in motion?

SCHIAVO: In 1995. End of 1995. . . .

FELOS: Mr. Schiavo, you mentioned that your mother passed away. When did that occur?

SCHIAVO: 1997. July.

FELOS: Did that experience at all affect your decision to bring this petition?

SCHIAVO: My mother gave me a gift when she was dying. We stopped her feeding because that is what she wanted, and her medications. She gave me that gift that it was okay to die.

FELOS: Mr. Schiavo, why have you filed this petition? Why are you asking the Court for permission to remove Terri's feeding tube?

SCHIAVO: Because that is what Terri wanted, and it's my responsibility because I love her so much to follow out what she wanted.

FELOS: Thank you. No further questions.

This testimony, with its verbal cues such as "Let me ask it this way," gives the appearance that Felos is trying to lead Michael Schiavo to convey the message he ultimately conveyed in his October 20, 2003, written statement: his mother's death in July 1997 prompted his recollection of Terri's wishes to die under her current circumstances and made him realize he was being selfish if he didn't ensure that her wishes were carried out. When Schiavo apparently deviated from the script and revealed their meeting in late 1995, Felos peremptorily admonished him to divulge no more. After Schiavo finally drew the parallel between his mother's situation and Terri's, the direct examination abruptly ends. After a ten-minute recess, Felos approached the bench and requested Greer remove the members of the media from the courtroom, saying, "My client requests that the proceedings not be recorded by the media, and he believes that it would impair the privacy rights of the ward."

Greer declined to expel the media, stating, "I don't know of any legal authority for them to not be here." In hindsight, it didn't matter. Schiavo's apparent bungling of the script, and Felos's apparent tooth pulling was overlooked by the local press, who dutifully conveyed Felos's intended message: Clara Schiavo's death was the turning point for Michael Schiavo, the moment when he realized he must allow Terri to die with dignity as his mother had.

OVER THE next five years, "Terri's wishes" became a mantra synonymous with "she wants to die" for Michael Schiavo, his family members and attorneys, and Florida judges. During the 2000 trial, Schiavo relayed a conversation he had with Terri in the mid-1980s, while they were traveling by train from Pennsylvania to Florida. Terri's grandmother was in ill health and had taken a turn for the worse, and Terri was feeling conflicted about leaving town at that time.

"Terri was reading a book," Schiavo began. "She put the book down and looked at me. She says, 'I'm kind of concerned about leaving.' I told her, 'Your mom said to go.' She says, 'Well, I'm concerned about my grandmother. What if she dies? Who is going to take care of my uncle?'"

Schiavo later explained that Terri's uncle had lived with the grandmother ever since he had become disabled in a severe car accident. He was paralyzed in his arm, had slurred speech, relied on a cane to get around, and walked with a severe limp. His mental faculties were also impaired.

"She says, 'If I ever have to be a burden to anybody, I don't want to live like that,'" Schiavo recalled. "I told her that she should remember that for me too."

Schiavo also testified that Terri made a couple of casual statements along the same lines when they were watching television documentaries depicting both adults and children being kept alive on ventilators and tube feedings and medications through IVs.

"She made the comment to me that she would never want to be like that. Don't ever keep her alive on anything artificial. She did not want to live like that," Michael Schiavo told the court.

Following the filing of Schiavo's petition to remove Terri's feeding tube in May 1998, the court appointed a second guardian ad litem in the case, attorney Richard Pearse Jr., to give a recommendation as to whether the petition should be granted. In his final report, filed December 29, 1998, Pearse took issue with the scant evidence provided to him in supporting the notion that Terri would have wanted her feeding tube removed.

"The only direct evidence probative of the issue of the ward's intent is the hearsay testimony of her husband, Mr. Schiavo," Pearse wrote. "However, his credibility is necessarily adversely affected by the obvious financial benefit to him of being the ward's sole heir at law in the event of her death. . . . Since there is no corroborative evidence of the ward's intentions, and since the only witness claiming to have such evidence is the one person who will realize a direct and substantial financial benefit from the ward's death, the undersigned guardian ad litem is of the opinion that the evidence of the ward's intentions developed by the guardian ad litem's investigation does not meet the clear and convincing standard."

Pearse further made a revealing comment about Schiavo in his report: "It is apparent he has reached a point where he has no hope of the ward's recovery and wants to get on with his life." Pearse recommended Schiavo's motion to remove the feeding tube be denied. He then filed a petition requesting he either continue to represent Terri or another guardian ad litem be selected. After Felos accused Pearse of bias, due to his personal conviction against pulling feeding tubes, Judge Greer dismissed Pearse's request to stay on as guardian ad litem and discharged him without appointing a replacement. According to court documents, Pearse was paid $4,511.95 in fees out of Terri's guardianship.

By the summer of the following year, Felos found corroborative evidence in Michael Schiavo's brother, Scott, and their sister-in-law, Joan, who both gave depositions offering recollections of statements allegedly made by Terri and similar to those recalled by her husband. When Scott Schiavo took the stand in the 2000 trial, he recalled a conversation from a family luncheon after his mother's funeral in July 1997.

"We were kind of upset about the way that she left the world. It was not her wish, the way she wanted to live," Scott Schiavo told the court, explaining that when his mother suffered a heart attack, because the doctor did not have her DNR in her hand, CPR was performed, and she was kept alive on a ventilator until the DNR was produced.

"She was only being kept alive by a machine. She was pretty much gone. It upset us all because it was not the way she wanted to be kept alive. To see her like that, it was not the memory that we all wanted," he continued. "And Terri made mention at that conversation that, 'If I ever go like that, just let me go. Don't leave me there. I don't want to be kept alive on a machine.'"

Joan Schiavo relayed two conversations she allegedly had with Terri about artificial life support. As she explained, a friend of hers had a baby who was born sickly. She and her husband had to put the baby on a ventilator and machines to keep the baby alive. A few months later they made the decision to take the baby off the machine.

"They took all the tubing and everything off the baby," Joan Schiavo testified, adding that Terri told her that she and Michael would have made the same decision because "she would not want to put the baby through anything like that."

On another occasion, Joan recalled that she and Terri were watching a movie in which a man was in a coma and there was no hope for him. She said they both agreed they wouldn't want to go through anything like that.

"This whole perception that she has a death wish is completely uncharacteristic of who she was," argued Bobby Schindler. "I believe 100 percent in my heart that Terri was an advocate for life. She believed in her religion. As a Catholic she would never agree to such a thing." Mary Schindler and Terri's childhood friend, Diane Meyer, testified to that extent at the trial. Both recalled that Terri stated she didn't agree with the decision made by the parents of Karen Ann Quinlan to remove her from her life-sustaining respirator. Meyer shared her recollection of an incident she had with Terri during the summer of 1982 after their high-school graduation when the two became best friends and spent every day together. While they were riding in her car, Meyer made a cruel joke about the young woman who had been in a persistent vegetative state for six years before her parents won their bitter court battle. The joke reportedly angered Terri.

"Do you remember what the joke was?" Schindler attorney Campbell asked Meyer during direct examination.

"I apologize for the joke," Meyer prefaced. "It was, 'What is the state vegetable of New Jersey?' And the punch line was Karen Ann Quinlan." Meyer testified that she had seen a television movie about Quinlan in the lounge at her school in Scranton, Pennsylvania. She believes that was what had prompted the joke. Meyer told the court she distinctly remembered the incident because Terri had never lost her temper with her before. But this time she did.

"She went down my throat about this joke, that it was inappropriate." Meyer later told the Associated Press, adding that she remembered Terri wondered aloud how Quinlan's parents and doctors could possibly know what Quinlan was feeling or what she would want. "Where there's life, there's hope," she recalled Terri stating.[5]

In court depositions, Bobby Schindler and Suzanne Vitadamo said they felt obligated as Catholics to abide by the will of God, and Terri should have access to all types of medical treatment available to keep her alive, because that represents God's will. Vitadamo stated that taking away life support amounted to murder.

Father Gerard Murphy, an ordained Roman Catholic priest who counseled families at hospitals on how to handle end-of-life issues and medical treatment decisions on behalf of the Diocese of St. Petersburg, disputed Terri's siblings' perception of the Catholic faith. Serving as an expert witness for Michael Schiavo, the priest cited the teachings of Pope Pius IV in 1953 that "Catholics are mortally bound to respect life and to care for life, but not at all costs." Murphy discussed the pontiff's concept of "extraordinary versus ordinary means," and he interpreted that to mean a Catholic is morally bound to take advantage of ordinary means, but not extraordinary means. Murphy said that distinguishing between the two depended on the perception of the patient—whether the patient perceived a medical treatment to be too emotionally draining, too psychologically repugnant, too expensive, or providing little or no hope of recovery.

"My belief in the health care system is that technology is a two-edged sword," Murphy testified. "The wonderful technology meant to heal and save people and get them back on the road can also interfere with nature." Murphy told the court it had become his mission to educate Catholics about the conditions under which they could refuse medical treatment in order to avoid resorting to assisted suicide, which he predicted would become legal in Florida. He emphasized that suicide was wrong, but patients still had the right to die by refusing medical treatment. He cited the example of his own father, who opted to quit going through chemotherapy but agonized over whether he was committing a sin.

The priest, who admitted he had no formal training as a moral theologian or medical ethicist, was asked on direct examination by Felos to assume that Terri had told her husband that, if she were dependent on the care of others, she would not want to live like that, then asked whether the removal of her feeding tube was consistent or inconsistent with the position of the Catholic Church under these circumstances. Murphy responded, "After all that has transpired, I believe, yes, it would be consistent with the teaching of the Catholic Church." Many Catholic bishops—and even the late Pope John Paul II—would later dispute Father Murphy's testimony, but to no avail.

On February 11, 2000, Greer issued a ten-page order authorizing Michael Schiavo to "proceed with the discontinuance of said artificial life support for Theresa Marie Schiavo." Based on the language of the order, it is clear his call was far from close.

"The court . . . heard from witnesses who ran the gambit of credibility, from those clearly biased who slanted their testimony to those such as Father Murphy whom the court finds to have been completely candid," Greer wrote, later making it clear he was referencing testimony in support of the Schindlers as "vague and almost self-serving." In contrast, he found the testimony of Scott and Joan Schiavo to be completely reliable and noted that neither of them "appeared to have shaded his or her testimony or even attempt to exclude unfavorable comments or points." Greer also made a point to defend Michael Schiavo's actions. "It has been suggested that Michael Schiavo has not acted in good faith by waiting eight plus years to file the petition which is under consideration. That assertion hardly seems worthy of comment other than to say that he should not be faulted for having done what those opposed to him want to be continued," Greer wrote.

Then Greer chided the Schindlers for good measure: "It is also interesting to note that Mr. Schiavo continues to be the most regular visitor to his wife even though he is criticized for wanting to remove her life support." The slight did not go unnoticed by the Schindlers.

"Michael and his family want to paint this picture that because we didn't go visit Terri when this initially happened, which is completely false, that this is reason enough to kill her," said Bobby Schindler. "It's as though they're trying to rationalize pursuing her death. In other words, 'Because you abandoned Terri, we're going to take steps to kill her.' The argument is completely false. But let's just say the family did in fact abandon Terri. Does that mean we have the right to kill her? It's not logical."

When Felos presented newspaper clippings to Mary Schindler to establish that Terri was only eleven years old in 1975 when the Quinlan court battle was decided, that persuaded Greer to dismiss both her testimony and that of Diane Meyer. It wasn't until March 2005 that an attorney noticed Greer's math was "fuzzy," based on his assumption that Quinlan had died immediately after she was taken off her respirator. In fact, Quinlan remained in a coma for nearly nine years. She was still alive, therefore, in 1982 when Meyer testified she had seen the docudrama. This fact also explained the troubling aspect, in Greer's view, of Meyer's switching in and out of present and past tense during her testimony, which led him to conclude that her testimony wasn't credible and was "slanted."[6]

After disregarding the testimonies of Mary Schindler, Diane Meyer, and part of Joan Schiavo's testimony—about the baby—Greer found her other statements as well as those of Scott and Michael Schiavo amounted to "Terri Schiavo's oral declarations concerning her intention as to what she would want done under the present circumstances." He further declared the statements "clear and convincing evidence" of Terri's wishes.

Needless to say, the ruling shocked the Schindlers. "The whole thing was ludicrous," Bob Schindler observed. "I actually believed it would be thrown out of court. Even when the trial started, I thought Greer would just throw it out. Everything seemed like a grade B or grade C movie. Everything seemed so weak that they were presenting to the court. I just didn't see how that could ever happen."[7]

It was inexplicable to them that Greer found Terri's alleged oral statements sufficient to order her death. "The legislature put this 'clear and convincing' standard on these cases in Florida—to be able to starve someone to death—which was a high standard," commented Bobby Schindler. "For Judge Greer to take casual conversations based on hearsay evidence seven years after the fact, resulting in close to a $1 million payday for Michael Schiavo, while he was engaged to another woman . . . it really makes you wonder what the heck was going on here and, additionally, has really lowered the bar for anyone to walk into a courtroom and do what Michael Schiavo did."

For sure, the family stressed, Terri would never elect to be dehydrated to death. "Terri's a scaredy cat . . . if you went 'boo' to Terri, she'd jump ten feet off the ground. If a bee flew in the house, she ran into a closet," her father reminisced during a CBN interview in October 2003.[8]

"My sister was very fun-loving and carefree. She was afraid of a bee sting. Terri would never, ever want to be starved to death, never," Vitadamo echoed in a March 28, 2005, interview on MSNBC's *Scarborough Country*.[9]

The family determined to fight the ruling to the bitter end, which came five years later. Over those five years every aspect of Greer's ruling was disputed, from the veracity of Michael Schiavo's testimony, to the true nature of Terri's medical condition and prognosis, to the presumption of her wishes and the position of the Catholic Church on the matter. Dozens of physicians, the Florida legislature, Governor Jeb Bush, the U.S. Congress, and President George W. Bush ultimately weighed in on the Terri Schiavo case before a federal district court judge pounded the final gavel, sounding the death knell for the brain-injured woman. Greer's opinion that Terri wanted to die proved impenetrable. The court's endorsement of Michael Schiavo's efforts to end Terri's life catapulted the debate beyond the sphere of a private family matter and gave the case national significance. And the bigger the case grew, the more determined Michael Schiavo became to carry out what he perceived to be Terri's wishes. He would later challenge President Bush and Governor Bush to visit Terri after they intervened in the case.

"The overriding issue in this case was her choice," Felos summarized on the day Terri died. "Whether you might disagree with the evidence, or the quantum of proof, or the reliability of the witnesses . . . whatever opinion you may have, the court, through a grueling process, found by clear and convincing evidence—through testimony of three witnesses, relaying seven conversations—that Mrs. Schiavo said, 'No tubes for me.' 'I don't want to remain artificially.' I think affording a patient their choice to die in the manner they choose is . . . certainly a death with dignity."[10]

Curiously, toward the end of his ten-year court battle, on March 20, 2005—two days after Terri's feeding tube was pulled for the third and final time—Michael Schiavo contradicted himself during another interview on *Larry King Live*.

"I won't give it up. Terri is my life. I'm going to carry out her wishes to the very end," he said. "This is what she wanted. It's not about the Schindlers. It's not about me, not about Congress. It's about Terri."

Roughly five minutes later, when King asked whether Michael could understand Terri's family's feelings, he said: "Yes, I do. But this is not about them. It's about Terri. And I've also said that in court. We didn't know what Terri wanted, but this is what we want."[11]

Did Schiavo's contradiction amount to an innocent slip of the tongue made during an emotionally trying and sleep-deprived time in his life? Or was it a Freudian slip, as some speculated? It didn't matter.

"From a legal perspective, it doesn't really matter what Mike does," Deborah Bushnell said on CBS's *The Early Show* the next day. "The court has already made its decision. That court order that the judicial branch has put into place is going to be carried out."[12]

The Second District Court of Appeals also recognized Terri's court-ordered death no longer had anything to do with her guardian. In fact, Terri's wishes ceased to matter. Instead, all that mattered was Terri's adjudicated will, as determined by Judge Greer and subsequently rubber-stamped by the three-judge panel of the appellate court. "The trial court's decision does not give Mrs. Schiavo's legal guardian the option of leaving the life-prolonging procedures in place. No matter who her guardian is, the guardian is required to obey the court order because the court, and not the guardian, has determined the decision that Mrs. Schiavo herself would make," the panel, led by Chief Judge Christopher Altenbernd, wrote in a March 16, 2005, opinion.

7

"Plant" or Disabled Person?

THE WOMAN LIES SLUMPED to one side of her hospice bed, leaning toward the direction of the warm sunlight streaming through the nearby window. Traces of gray dust her brown hair, subtly documenting the passage of time. She is now thirty-eight years old and has been in this incapacitated state for twelve years. She looks older than her years, her face and neck somewhat disfigured as a result of brain injury. Her atrophied, contracted arms are curled up just below the healed stoma in her neck, which is a permanent hole cut into her windpipe to facilitate the mechanical ventilation she needed the first days after her brain injury. Her mouth hangs open and reveals gorgeous white teeth. Her big brown eyes stare vacantly in a wide-eyed fashion. While she breathes on her own and maintains blood pressure, there is little sign of life in the face of Theresa Marie Schiavo.

As the video plays, viewers see Mary Schindler approach her daughter's bedside. She places her face within inches of Terri's, almost rubbing noses, and greets her with a cheery, "Hi, baby. How are you?" Like watching the digital colorization of an old black-and-white movie, signs of life instantly seep into the formerly empty expression. Terri's countenance appears to warm and soften. The corners of her mouth curl up, and her lips spread into a smile, revealing more pearly whites. Her eyelids relax, and the vacant stare is replaced with an apparent expression of complete happiness. As Mary Schindler coos and fusses with Terri's pillow, holding her head in her hands and kissing her forehead, Terri gives a short vocalization then a squeal. The sounds appear to be Terri's verbal responses to her mother's questions.

Or perhaps Terri's vocalizations are in response to her mother's loving touch on her cheeks? Does she recognize her mother? Can she see her mother? Can she smell her mother's perfume and body lotions? Can she sense the caring presence and positive energy at her bedside? What is her medical condition? These questions remain in dispute months after Terri Schiavo's death and autopsy.

For those who accept the court's ruling that Terri wouldn't want to live dependent on artificial life support, with no hope of recovery, the diagnosis and prognosis of her medical condition are a crucial element in the decision to end her life. Was Terri an unconscious "plant" or a neglected, aware disabled person? The fault line between these two starkly different bodies of thought ran down the middle of her family. To Suzanne Vitadamo, Terri was still Terri.

"She is severely brain damaged," Vitadamo said, "but she's in there. You go in, and she lights up like a Christmas tree when she sees my mother. So she's there. She does the best that she can to let us know. I truly believe she's very much aware. She shows us all the time that she's in there just by her reactions. I see her just as my sister."

But Michael Schiavo didn't see his wife there anymore. "I see a shell of somebody I used to know. Somebody I loved and adored very much," he said years before her death. "And now she's a shell, just somebody that is really not living; she's existing. That's not life." His brother Scott described Terri as resembling "a beat-up old car." Michael's attorney, Felos, likened Terri to a plant.

"A plant is alive. A plant has photosynthesis reflexes. If you shine a light, it moves. Shut off the light, it moves the other way," Felos posed in his closing arguments during the 2000 trial. "There is a difference between life and consciousness."

The vegetative state is "the strange combination of being awake but unaware with no evidence of a working mind," according to Dr. Bryan Jennett, a professor of neurosurgery at Scotland's University of Glasgow and the man who, along with colleague Dr. Fred Plum, coined the term "persistent vegetative state" in 1972. The term's derivation stems from the notion that the patient "remains with the capacity to maintain the vegetative parts of neurological function but . . . no longer has any cognitive function." The vegetative state is said to be "persistent" one month after an acute brain injury and "permanent" after a year. The terms "persistent" and "permanent" as applied to the vegetative state tend to be used interchangeably, however. The one-year benchmark that distinguishes vegetative state from permanent vegetative state is the point at which the brain damage is declared irreversible.

Some coma patients evolve into this state of wakeful unconsciousness, or vegetative state, which is announced by the opening of their eyes. "Whilst eye opening is a positive and uncontroversial feature of the vegetative state, the crux of the rest of the definition is essentially negative—the lack of any evidence of awareness, by meaningful responses or activity," Jennett wrote in *The Vegetative State.* "However, the wide range of reflex responsiveness in vegetative patients, and the tendency for this to become more marked as time passes in most patients, can give rise to some such activity being interpreted as evidence of returning consciousness."

Jennett goes on to point out that some vegetative patients do recover consciousness and progress to a state of minimal consciousness, or MCS. But because some vegetative patients regain a "wide repertoire" of reflex responsiveness without recovering any evidence of awareness, the boundary between these two states of consciousness is hard to pin down.[1]

In fact, studies show a high rate of misdiagnosis of PVS. A retrospective study published in *BMJ,* which formerly stood for *British Medical Journal,* in 1996 found a 43 percent misdiagnosis rate of PVS. Of forty patients referred to a twenty-bed rehabilitation center between 1992 and 1995 who were considered in a vegetative state—including seven who were believed vegetative for a year and three in PVS for over four years—seventeen patients were found to have been misdiagnosed.[2]

Although Jennett and Plum coined the term PVS in 1972, it wasn't until 1994 that experts hammered out a protocol for clinical diagnosis to give neurologists a road map through this "elusive" field of study. The Multi-Society Task Force on PVS—which included representatives from the American Academy of Neurology (AAN), the Neurological Association, the Association of Neurological Surgeons, the Academy of Pediatrics, and the Child Neurology Society—published a report spelling out the criteria for PVS diagnosis that became the gold standard in the United States. The Multi-Society Task Force defined the vegetative state as "a clinical condition of complete unawareness of the self and the environment accompanied by sleep-wake cycles with either complete or partial preservation of hypothalamic and brain stem autonomic functions." The task force listed the criteria for diagnosis as:

1. No evidence of awareness of self or environment and an inability to interact with others

2. No evidence of sustained, reproducible, purposeful, or voluntary behavioral responses to visual, auditory, tactile, or noxious stimuli
3. No evidence of language comprehension or expression
4. Intermittent wakefulness manifested by the presence of sleep-wake cycles
5. Sufficiently preserved hypothalamic and brain-stem autonomic functions to permit survival with medical and nursing care
6. Bowel and bladder incontinence
7. Variably preserved cranial-nerve reflexes, and spinal reflexes[3]

But even with this published criteria, considerable debate remains within the medical community over what behaviors reflect cortical activity and how much cortical activity amounts to awareness. While some experts, according to Jennett, consider lack of response to a visual threat to be one criterion of the vegetative state, others accept that some vegetative patients respond at a subcortical or reflexive level. Response to visual threat, therefore, is not considered per se evidence of awareness. Neither is a patient's ability to fixate on and track an object. The AAN allows that patients in vegetative states can occasionally track objects visually, and the Multi-Society Task Force requires such fixation to be sustained and tracking to be "consistent and reproducible" in order to consider a patient beyond PVS. As a result of this requirement of consistency and reproducibility, the AAN recommends neurologists perform at least two examinations before applying the PVS diagnosis to a patient.

Some vegetative patients exhibit emotions, such as smiling, frowning, laughing, or weeping, but these displays should show "no consistent relation to an appropriate stimulation," instructed Jennett. Experts are also divided as to whether PVS patients can swallow. The AAN indicates a possibility of swallowing, but the Multi-Society Task Force expects most PVS patients to be able to swallow. Yet Dr. James Bernat, a member of the AAN and a recognized expert in brain damage including PVS and MCS, argues that swallowing represents a higher order of brain function than reflex and concludes it is not possible for vegetative patients to swallow.[4]

Lastly, and most significantly as it relates to Terri Schiavo, neurologists haven't reached a consensus on whether PVS patients feel pain. While the AAN and the Multi-Society Task Force maintain PVS patients lose the capacity to experience pain, neurologists in the trenches who responded to an AAN questionnaire in 1990 indicated otherwise. Eleven percent believed PVS patients might experience pain or suffer, and 31 percent responded they were uncertain. In another survey of more than three hundred neurologists and nursing home directors, 13 percent believed vegetative patients might have some awareness, and 30 percent thought they might experience pain.

Overall, Jennett concluded, there's a lot of ambiguity in dealing with PVS. "The theoretical possibility that a patient who is believed to be vegetative might retain some awareness without behavioral evidence of this can never be completely ruled out," he wrote. "The question of what vegetative patients actually experience is likely to remain a matter of debate for some time."[5]

Due to its highly subjective and moving-target nature, there remains a lot of controversy both within the medical community and among the public at large about the clinical diagnosis of PVS. While some neurologists consider it "well-recognized," others pan it as "not well established." Be that as it may, it is a common diagnosis. Based on her discussions with neurologists, Schindler attorney Pat Anderson was left with the less-than-charitable impression that PVS is a "garbage can diagnosis."

TERRI SCHIAVO acquired the PVS label soon after her brain injury. By the time she was released from Humana Hospital–Northside in May 1990, she had made the transition from closed-eye unconsciousness to a wakeful unconsciousness. According to her medical records, a neurological consultation was done the following month, which assessed her as being in a persistent vegetative state. Two days prior to that assessment on June 27, 1990, however, the doctor who supervised Terri's rehabilitative therapy over the first year after her collapse noted some evidence of responsiveness in Terri. On her chart, Dr. David Baras indicated Terri had started to show some vocalization while at College Harbor Nursing Home to the extent that she would say "no." She also occasionally exhibited "some voluntary movement on command of eyes and mouth, as reported by her husband and mother." A physical exam revealed she "easily startled to her name or when the bedrail fell down." Most significant, Baras noted that Terri "responds to pain with extremity movement and moaning," which suggests, even early on, she didn't meet the criteria of the AAN and Multi-Society Task Force for the diagnosis of PVS.

On July 24, 1990, results of an MRI (magnetic resonance imaging) showed Terri suffered "profound atrophy with a very atrophic appearing cortex, mild white matter disease." As Baras interpreted for the malpractice jury, her brain had shrunk and a lot of the tissue matter on the top of the brain, as well as the brain stem, had been damaged. Three days later Terri flunked her first barium swallow test. Still, in medical notes written in Terri's chart, Baras echoed the optimism conveyed by therapists and recommended intensive physical, occupational, speech, and recreational therapy with a goal of "advancing her level of awareness and consciousness."

"She could follow some—a one-step command, although that was inconsistent. Nevertheless that information was very important," he told the medical malpractice jury, adding that this indicated to him "that there may be some type of brain function that is returning that would allow her to even have maybe further progress."

Under Baras's care at Bayfront Medical Center in St. Petersburg, where he was the medical director, Terri subsequently underwent two months of intensive rehabilitative therapy. By early- to mid-July 1990, the physical therapist, occupational therapist, and Dr. Baras reported "purposeful movement" in Terri's upper right extremity in that she was flexing her right elbow—not as a reflex but voluntarily. There was no consistency noted with this behavior, however. She was also moving her head toward sound, and her eyes opened to voice and stimulation and displayed some tracking ability. She continued to respond to pain by moaning. Nevertheless, Baras told the jury that because her neurological status showed "little change as far as being able to respond consistently to a stimulus," he determined that Terri remained in PVS. She was discharged from Bayfront on August 25, 1990.

Terri spent the next three months at home with her parents and Michael Schiavo before going to California for experimental surgery, during which electrodes were implanted in her brain for stimulation. Throughout the first month of stimulation, Dr. Eugene Alcazaran noted "increased alertness" in Terri and recorded she turned her head toward voices and away from tactile stimulation and displayed some visual tracking ability. Over the next three months at Mediplex Rehabilitation Center in Bradenton, Florida, physical, recreational, and speech therapists noted that Terri appeared to "focus on several pictures of family for about ten seconds" after commands such as sticking out her tongue, blinking her eyes and nodding, and moving her head away from tactile stimuli. She still responded to pain by moaning, according to her medical records. Heterotopic ossification was developing in her knees, so the full-body nuclear imaging bone scan was performed, as noted in chapter 3.

On the one-year anniversary of Terri's collapse, February 25, 1991, Alcazaran recorded: "Random voicing. Responsiveness—no change. Auditory and tactile stimulation. Step down therapies to appropriate levels."

Terri had hit the magic one-year threshold at which point the AAN and the Multi-Society Task Force deemed the vegetative state to be permanent and "irreversible." Two weeks later, according to her medical records, her general responsiveness tested two points higher, and a nurse reported witnessing her lift her head off her pillow and straining her neck to look at something to her right. She was also observed "humming" for about five minutes. Her monthly physical therapy summary reported she inconsistently followed two-step commands and occasionally responded to requests to verbalize, swallow, and move her arms.

By this time, Michael Schiavo was charting his wife's rehabilitative progress in a diary, which the Schindlers later introduced into the court file. On April 14, 1991, Schiavo described Terri holding her head up, keeping her legs together, and responding to every noise she heard. She also tasted extracts and swallowed. He reported her having crying spells during occupational therapy and thwarting the therapists' efforts. Days later, according to Terri's medical records, Dr. Alcazaran concluded further physical, occupational, speech, and recreational therapy wouldn't "facilitate any more meaningful progress." A week later Dr. James Carnahan concurred with Alcazaran, declaring, "No improvement or change seen by myself over the last four months. No benefit presently seen to therapy plan." Exactly thirteen months after her unexplained collapse, on April 25, 1991, Terri was transferred to the long-term care unit of Mediplex, where she received primarily maintenance care and just one physical therapy session a month.

"Looking back 15 years, if you read her records . . . they were initially very optimistic," summarized medical examiner Jon Thogmartin in the autopsy report. "Maybe she's tracking. Maybe she's trying to communicate. Then you watch the optimistic notes fall and become fewer and fewer. It's very sad to watch."

ALTHOUGH THE doctors lost hope in Terri's recovery, her medical records and her husband's diary reflect continued signs of perceived responsiveness and continued hope on the part of others, including Michael Schiavo. A nurse reported Terri squeezed his hand on command. Schiavo recorded her following his fingers back and forth with her eyes for about three minutes. One remarkable diary passage described Terri lifting her head off and away from the back of her wheelchair. "I asked her if she wanted to get up," he wrote. "She nodded. I asked her a minute later; she did the same motion." By early May 1991 Michael wrote that Terri wouldn't let the speech therapist near her during a session: "She kept pulling her head away from Harriet's hands." Schiavo also reportedly witnessed Terri start to "move her whole body around in bed."

June 1991 progress notes indicate Terri was vocalizing while prone during physical therapy and occasionally saying "stop" to nurses during different procedures. Because Michael Schiavo had expressed concern over Terri's increased "jumpiness" at that time, the brain stimulator was turned off. In September 1991 Terri was discharged to Sabal Palms Health Care Center, and any notion of further aggressive, rehabilitative therapy was abandoned. As Pat Anderson noted, "She was warehoused" and "put on the shelf." Terri failed a second swallow test on August 13, 1991, and a third on June 23, 1992, and six months later Dr. Baras testified to the malpractice jury that her massive brain damage was irreversible. The PVS label stuck.

Months later, after the malpractice award was collected and the ensuing fallout with the Schindlers, staff at Sabal Palm were ordered by Michael Schiavo, according to caregiver Carolyn Johnson, to cease Terri's routine range-of-motion therapy. Nurse and former Schiavo girlfriend Trudy Capone registered her concern that Michael was isolating Terri and keeping her in the dark, because he required the blinds be kept closed in her room. Similar sworn statements were made by registered nurse Carla Sauer Iyer and nursing assistant Heidi Law at Palm Garden of Largo Convalescent Center over subsequent years. These reports were presented in chapter 5. Over the years leading up to the trial in 2000, the notations in Terri's medical chart reflecting any developmental progress all but disappeared. In her sworn affidavit, Iyer reported any such signs of progress were intentionally excised from the medical chart.

"Terri's medical condition was systematically distorted and misrepresented," Iyer asserted. "When I worked with her, she was alert and oriented. Terri spoke on a regular basis in my presence, saying such things as 'mommy' and 'help me.' 'Help me' was, in fact, one of her most frequent utterances. I heard her say it hundreds of times." Iyer further claimed that when Terri was in pain, she would attempt to say the word *pain,* but it would come out more like *pay.*

"When I came into her room and said, 'Hi, Terri,' she would always recognize my voice and her name and would turn her head all the way toward me, saying "Haaaiii." Iyer claimed she made "numerous entries" into the nursing notes in Terri's chart, stating verbatim what Terri said and her various behaviors. She'd write whole pages about Terri's responsiveness because she "felt strongly" it was her duty to report on her patient's condition.

"But by my next on-duty shift [I found] the notes would be deleted from her chart," said Iyer, adding that Michael Schiavo always demanded to see Terri's chart as soon as he arrived and would take it into her room with him and close the door.

Among the progress notes Iyer claimed to have recorded in Terri's chart, and later found they were removed, were her surreptitious feedings of Terri with a baby bottle. According to Iyer, Terri was taking thickened liquids like puddings and Jell-O and was not aspirating. Terri would also "chuckle," "giggle," or "laugh" in response to Iyer's reading something humorous in the newspaper. Like Schiavo had recorded in his diary years earlier, Iyer asserted Terri could move her whole body, upper and lower.

Certified nursing assistant Heidi Law and her co-worker at Palm Garden, Olga, used to affectionately call Terri "Fancy Pants," because she was "so particular about certain things." Law observed that Terri "just adored her baths, and was so happy afterward when she was all clean, smelling sweet from the lotion her mother provided, and wearing soft nightgowns her mother laundered for her." She also liked having her hair combed, according to Law. But Terri definitely did not like the taste of the teeth-cleaning swabs or the mouthwash used at Palm Garden.

"You would always tell when Terri had a bowel movement," Law wrote in a sworn affidavit, "as she seemed agitated and would sort of 'scoot' to get away from it."

Law claimed that Terri exhibited more interest in Olga because she always followed Olga with her eyes. She described Terri as initially clamming up around her but gradually relaxing and becoming more cooperative and less resistant to her over time.

"At least three times during any shift where I took care of Terri, I made sure to give Terri a wet washcloth filled with ice chips, to keep her mouth moistened," Law wrote in her affidavit. "I personally saw her swallow the ice water and never saw her gag. . . . On three or four occasions I personally fed Terri small mouthfuls of Jell-O, which she was able to swallow and enjoyed immensely."

Law similarly reported hearing Terri say "mommy," "momma," and "help me" a number of times. But those notes never made it into Terri's chart, according to Law, who also suspected they were being thrown out without being read. She said she often spotted her notes in the trash can next to the nurses' station.

"I discussed this situation with other personnel at Palm Garden, particularly with Olga, and another [certified nursing assistant] named Ewan Morris," Law stated in her affidavit. "We all discussed the fact that we could be fired for reporting that Terri was responsive, and especially for giving her treatment. The advice among the staff was 'Don't do nothin', don't see nothin', and don't say nothin'.'"

Terri's medical records provide a couple of other isolated nurses' notes documenting instances of perceived responsiveness. The November 11, 1997, assessment by recreational therapist Marie Piarade described Terri interacting with people in her room: "Resident enjoys listening to other people converse; loves to hear jokes and laughs; appears to enjoy music entertainment . . . demonstrates occasional responses, i.e. eye contact, laughter, but not consistent." Piarade makes a similar comment on February 11, 1998.

Other short notations by nurses over the years include:

Nov. 13, 1997	Med given for cramps, moaning loudly . . . menses continues, Darvocet given via G-tube.
Feb. 3, 1998	Moaning and upper body movement noted. Medicated for cramps/pain.
Sept. 26, 1998	Opens eyes when spoken to. Moaning type noises made at times.
Oct. 15, 1999	Sometimes looks at you when you talk to her.
July 5, 2000	Pain—crying out, grimacing during her menstrual cycle.
Aug. 30, 2000	Discomfort as evidenced by moaning, grimacing

"The first signs of recovery are often observed by family, nurses or therapists," PVS expert Jennett observed. "Claims by them to have noticed meaningful responses must always be investigated carefully with a willingness to revise the diagnosis, although these often prove to have been based on wishful thinking about improvement because of overoptimistic interpretation of reflex activity by those close to the patient." It is not likely the multiple observations of Terri's responding to pain and discomfort, and the associated medication of that pain and discomfort by her health-care professionals, amounts to "wishful thinking."

On the other hand, the Schindlers' accounts of Terri's perceived responsiveness were consistently chalked up to "wishful thinking" or a fabricated ploy to influence their court case. As the family described, Terri had different responses for different members of her family. While she consistently "lit up like a Christmas tree" and "squealed" with pleasure in her mother's presence, she had more of a teasing relationship with her father. Another video captures a brief "conversation" Bob Schindler had with his daughter during one of her neurological evaluations. The video shows him holding a panel of Christmas lights, which is a tool used to test a patient's visual tracking ability.

"You know she has a lazy eye. I don't know if you're aware of that or not," Schindler tells the neurologist conducting the examination off camera. "She wore glasses her whole life because her one eye rolls in on her." As he speaks, Terri closes her eyes. Her head is positioned on the pillow facing her father. "Doesn't it? You have one eye that rolls in on you?" Bob asks Terri, leaning in closer to her face. Her eyes open and appear to fix on him. She appears to laugh and smile. Her father, in turn, laughs. "Do you remember that? We used to laugh at that. You used to get mommy all upset. You'd take your eye and let it roll to the side?" As Schindler leans closer to Terri, her eyes close briefly and open, her pupils look up in the direction of his face. "And she'd say, 'Terri what are you doing?'" Terri again emits an apparent laugh. As her father continues to egg her on by repeating how her mother used to get upset and exclaim, "Terri, don't do that!" Terri lets out a loud sustained moan that sounds distinctly more pained than her prior, apparent laughter. The clip ends as Terri's forceful moan drowns out her father's teasing voice.

Numerous relatives, friends, and attorneys claim to have witnessed Terri's interactions with family members. Attorney David Gibbs said he was "blown away" by how "alive" Terri Schiavo was. "Anything that any of your listeners saw on a video clip, multiply that times ten or more," he relayed to the audience of Dr. James Kennedy's *Truths That Transform* radio program. "Terri Schiavo was very much alive. She was as alive as you and I."

"When you walked into her room," Gibbs described, "she immediately recognized different people. Her responses for her mother or her father were completely different. She would communicate. She would jabber back and forth. I watched her dozens of times respond back to her mother. Her mother would say, 'Terri, say "I,"' And Terri would say, 'I.' And the mother would say, 'Say, "love,"' and Terri would say, 'love.' And then she would say, 'Say, "you,"' and Terri would never say the 'you.' But I watched Terri interact with her mom, try to say those words dozens and dozens of times on command. She would laugh and get excited every time her family would come in the room. She would cry every time her mother would leave."[6]

Others outside the family who got to know Terri also maintain she was responsive. Monsignor Thaddeus Malanowski, a Roman Catholic priest of fifty-four years and a retired brigadier general, accompanied the Schindlers to visit Terri at the hospice every Saturday for almost three years. In a sworn affidavit, Father Malanowski described praying with Terri and taking care of her spiritual needs as a person baptized in the Roman Catholic Church.

"While praying and anointing her, I have been impressed with Terri's attentiveness. She does not laugh or cry when I am praying. She listens carefully and quietly to my words, and appears to be very peaceful at the conclusion of the sacrament," Malanowski testified. Similarly, nursing assistant Heidi Law described in her court affidavit that Terri would become quiet while the priest prayed with her. She couldn't bow her head because of her "stiff neck," Law noted, "but she would still try." She would also close her eyes during the prayer, and open them after he uttered the traditional "amen." In his court affidavit, Malanowski described two incidents that he felt reflected Terri's "function of the intellect and the will."

"On one particular Sunday, I said, 'Terri, I come here every week praying for you in English. Today, I'm going to pray for you in Polish!' Terri began to laugh at this remark, understanding that I was teasing her," Malanowski said. "Again, on St. Patrick's Day, I told her that her parents and I were going to sing for her. When we sang our rendition of 'When Irish Eyes Are Smiling,' Terri laughed after listening intently."

Michael Schiavo dismissed Terri's perceived smiling, laughing, and crying as evidence of cognition, pointing out that nurses had reported hearing Terri laughing in her room while she was alone. "I've seen Terri do that before. She does it for me also when nobody else is in the room. So it's not surprising to me," he said in reference to the video of Terri with her mother. When asked whether the video gave him hope, he responded it did not. "I had a lot of hope for Terri, especially in the beginning. But when doctor after doctor after doctor tells you there is no more hope; this is going to be your life," he said without finishing his thought.

SCHINDLER ATTORNEY Pam Campbell also heard the chorus of doctors chanting PVS. In the months leading up to the 2000 trial on Schiavo's original petition to remove the feeding tube, she reportedly tried to find a physician who would be willing to contradict the PVS diagnosis. Campbell was representing the Schindlers pro bono, and without the benefit of a budget to conduct depositions, her efforts to find a countering expert witness proved futile. She agreed to stipulate to the PVS. For their part, the Schindlers did not know how vital it was to prevent Terri from acquiring the PVS label from a court. They had faith in the judicial system and didn't understand the politics involved in the case. They were under the impression this was a private, family matter, and they assumed once they got into a courtroom, common sense would prevail. They believed the case hinged on Terri's wishes, and the judge would reach the same conclusion as the independent guardian ad litem, namely, that Michael Schiavo's credibility as a witness of Terri's oral expressions of her end-of-life wishes was compromised by his financial stake in her death. In retrospect, the PVS stipulation may have been an unrecoverable error. (This will be explored in depth in chapter 13.)

"You will hear a lot of medical testimony concerning the persistent vegetative state that Theresa Schiavo currently exists in. We do not doubt she's in a permanent vegetative state," Campbell stated in her opening remarks but then appeared to reveal her own misunderstanding of this state of consciousness by contradicting herself. "However, a lot goes to the cognitive activity and brain activity of Theresa Schiavo. In reading through some of the medical records, you will hear testimony about her no recognition. However, you will hear testimony from our side there is recognition. She does recognize her mother."

Despite the AAN recommendation that "observations of family members, caregivers, and professional staff participating in the daily care" of patients should be factored into the evaluation for PVS, the doctors' opinions carried the day in the trial proceedings, and all other observations charted through the years in Terri's medical records were written off. Longtime-nurse-turned-columnist Barbara Stock commented that this lack of respect for nurses was par for the course.

"In the news we hear that nurses are desperately needed, but why should we bother?" she wrote in a March 26, 2005, Internet column. "Apparently we are just ignorant bedpan slingers of no importance to the courts. We don't even have the intelligence to know when a patient is responding to us. We do not know if a patient is in pain. How long does your doctor spend with you at the bedside when you are in the hospital? . . . Who is it that you see all the time? You see the nurse. Who knows what is going on? The nurse."[7]

In fact, Dr. Gambone, Terri's treating physician hired by Michael Schiavo in February 1998, testified he only saw Terri "at least every other month." His visitations later dwindled to ten minutes every four months, according to court transcripts. During those visits, he reported he witnessed no signs of awareness on Terri's part and determined she was in PVS. He described waving his hand in front of her eyes and not eliciting any kind of blinking response. Gambone, who is board certified in internal medicine and geriatric medicine, whose patients are mostly eighty to eighty-five years old, further testified he usually read nurses' notes on Terri when he visited Palm Garden of Largo Convalescent Center, but he did not review the notes of the recreational therapist. For that reason, he was unfamiliar with Marie Piarade's notes describing Terri's laughing at jokes made by visitors. He'd also never visited Terri in the company of her family and was unaware of her perceived responsiveness to them. When confronted with the information by attorney Campbell, Gambone stressed "consistency" was what mattered, and without it, Terri's responses amounted to "random" rather than "purposeful" acts.

"If you said nine out ten times she turned to me, that would have some meaning," he testified.

Gambone also attributed Terri's documented moaning amid pain and discomfort as "a brain stem response," which supported his diagnosis of PVS. His testimony concurred with the earlier testimony of neurologist Dr. James Barnhill.

As a consulting neurologist for other physicians, Barnhill testified he encountered elderly patients once a week at the community hospital where he worked. These patients had suffered from severe strokes, cerebral hemorrhages, ruptured aneurysms, head injuries, and Alzheimer's. He indicated he consulted with families about the pros and cons of inserting a feeding tube or allowing the elderly patients to die.

"What we basically go on is the guideline from the family, hopefully conveying to us what the patient would want under those circumstances," Barnhill testified.

During his introduction to the court, Felos prompted Barnhill to divulge that he had served as an expert witness a half dozen times in similar trials over the past sixteen years. Specifically, Barnhill revealed he had testified for Felos in favor of removing the feeding tube from eighty-nine-year-old stroke victim Estelle Browning in Felos's prior high-profile right-to-die case. Felos and Barnhill later teamed up to conduct what Schindler attorney Anderson derisively called "death cruises." The two taught a continuing education course titled Geriatrics: End of Life Issues over a ten-night Panama Canal cruise aboard Holland America's MS *Rotterdam* in early 2002. Among the objectives of the cruise conference listed in their promotional literature were discussions of "the legal and philosophical underpinnings for removing or refusing unwanted medical treatment" and how to equip participants to "manage inertia and resistance among health care professionals." The right-to-die duo have been scheduled to teach a course on Advance Directives and End of Life Care and Neurology for a five-night Bahamas cruise in January 2006 aboard Holland America's MS *Westerdam*.

On the basis of two visits with Terri in March 1998 and January 2000, with the latter lasting ten minutes according to court transcripts, Barnhill declared Terri was in a permanent vegetative state. He later testified that once the persistent vegetative state was considered permanent, a DNR "is appropriate." He did not specify whether the DNR needed to have been signed by the patient prior to incapacitation. It may be he was of the same mind as Gambone, who put a DNR not signed by Terri in her chart in 1998 per the instructions of Michael Schiavo.

Barnhill conveyed that two prior neurological assessments of Terri performed by other doctors over the years, the fact that Terri was referenced as being in a chronic vegetative state throughout her medical chart, and her 1996 CAT (Computer-Aided Tomography) scan (also called a CT scan) aided him in making his own determination. Barnhill spent a large part of his testimony showing the graphic comparison between Terri's 1996 CT scan and a CT scan of his own brain. The comparison was striking.

"The significance," he told the court, referencing Terri's scan, "is there is almost no brain tissue in here. . . . There is very little inside this skull other than spinal fluid." And he summarized, "In my opinion, you could not have this scan, this appearance of a scan, and have anything other than a persistent vegetative state."

In his book, PVS expert Bryan Jennett states, "There is . . . no radiological appearance that is diagnostic for the vegetative state." In contrast, he indicates developments in functional MRI (fMRI) make it a more useful diagnostic tool for PVS.[8]

Radiologist William Maxfield later disputed Barnhill's conclusions in a sworn affidavit filed with the court. "CT or MRI brain studies, even with contrast, show only anatomy and not function," he argued. "In order to accurately diagnose the condition known as persistent vegetative state (PVS) from a radiological standpoint, functional brain imaging studies must be done on the patient. . . . It is incredible to me that functional imaging of the brain has not been obtained."

Maxfield further disputed Barnhill's interpretation of Terri's CT scan. "My review of the CT images of May 5, 1996 shows that there is a marked enlargement of the ventricles but there is significant cortical tissue in both cerebral hemispheres," he stated. "In my imaging practice I see patients with ventricles this large or larger with only minimal to moderate neurological disorders."

Radiologist Thomas Boyle similarly derided Barnhill and other neurologists' interpretations of Terri's CT scan on his popular weblog, CodeBlueBlog.com. "I've watched a steady stream of neurologists, bioethicists, and neurologists/bioethicists from Columbia, Cornell, and NYU interviewed all week on Fox and CNN and MSNBC," Boyle wrote in a March 29, 2005, posting. "They all said about the same thing, that Terri's CT scan was 'the worst they'd ever seen' or 'as bad as they've ever seen.' Here is the problem with these experts: they don't interpret CT scans of the brain. RADIOLOGISTS DO." Boyle further emphasized that while a neurologist might look at the CT scan of the brain of one of his patients, that is entirely different from "interpreting CT's of the brain *de novo,* for a living, every day, without knowing the diagnosis and most times without a good history."

"The neurologist doesn't get sued for making a mistake on an opinion of a CT of the brain," Boyle further stressed, "the radiologist does." To back up his contention, Boyle offered $100,000 on a $25,000 wager for any neurologist (and $125,000 for any neurologist/bioethicist) involved in Terri Schiavo's case—including the television pundits—who could accurately single out PVS patients from functioning patients with better than 60 percent accuracy on CT scans.

"If the neurologist can be right 6 out of 10 times he wins the $100,000," Boyle challenged. As of the time of this writing, there's been no word of any takers.[9]

Boyle also maintains comparing Terri's CT scan to a healthy adult's CT scan is disingenuous, at best, unless the comparison subject was eighty or ninety years old. In such an elderly person's CT scan, he argued, you would see "similar atrophy" and a brain more closely resembling Terri's.

"I have seen many walking, talking, fairly coherent people with worse cerebral/cortical atrophy," Boyle continued. "Therefore, this [CT scan] is in no way prima facie evidence that Terri Schiavo's mental abilities or capabilities are completely eradicated. I cannot believe such testimony has been given on the basis of this scan."[10]

In addition to placing great importance on his interpretation of Terri's CT scan, Barnhill admitted his review of nurses' notes consisted only of looking at the "minimal data set dated Feb. 11, 1998," presumably given to him by Felos, that only went back "six months to a year, if that." Thus Barnhill did not see the majority of notations in Terri's chart that recorded perceived instances of responsiveness, which occurred before she was transferred to a nursing home at the end of 1991 and aggressive physical and rehabilitative therapy ceased. However, in reacting to the retelling of some of the responses noted, Barnhill testified that smiling, grimacing, crying, laughing, moaning, and turning one's head toward sound are all reflex activities performed in the brain stem that do not represent cognitive function. When asked how he would explain the numerous suggestions of cognition witnessed by caregivers and Schindler family members and friends, Barnhill chalked them up to wishful thinking.

"My experience has been, in many cases, that people tend to see or interpret things based on their own expectations and beliefs and wants. If you want to see it, you are more likely to see it," he testified. Logic dictates the opposite would also be true.

With no testimony to contradict Barnhill's lone neurological assessment, and the dismissal of nurses' and therapists' notes as "hearsay," the 2000 trial proceedings drew to a close. Two weeks later a local group of physicians, nurses, pharmacists, attorneys, clergy, and their spouses opposed to physician-assisted death and euthanasia filed a motion to intervene in the case. Dr. Jay Carpenter, on behalf of Professionals for Excellence in Health Care, essentially argued more consideration needed to be given to the observations of Terri's parents and nursing staff who, he said, had the "undeniable advantage of round-the-clock observation of the patient" as opposed to the short observation periods of the treating and consulting physicians.

"There is tremendous 'discrepancy' between parents and health-care professionals with respect to the interpretation of purposeful behaviors seen in 'PVS' patients," the former chief of staff for Morton Plant/Mease Hospital in Clearwater, Florida, wrote in the petition to intervene. Carpenter cited a 1993 study that found parents in 92 percent of the cases studied claimed their PVS children could recognize voices. Another 62 percent believed their children could convey their likes and dislikes. "Physicians are not omnipotent," the doctor self-referentially noted. The medical group also found fault with the PVS diagnosis in general, as demonstrated by its use of quotation marks around the term in the petition.

"The 'persistent vegetative state' diagnosis fails to carry any information about etiology, and is 'levied' upon non-communicative patients only after all treatment has failed," Carpenter asserted in an attached affidavit. "There is no physical test or assessment tool that can tell us, with great certainty, exactly what the brain is capable of, whether conscious or unconscious, and whether 'cognitive behavior' is taking place." Carpenter also recommended giving Terri a swallowing test to see if she had acquired the ability to take food and water orally since her last test, which was performed nearly eight years earlier. Carpenter asserted that removing the feeding tube without first conducting such a test amounted to "murder."

On February 10, 2000, Judge Greer ruled to deny the group's intervention. The next day he ordered Terri's feeding tube be removed, finding "beyond all doubt that Theresa Marie Schiavo is in a persistent vegetative state" and that she had no hope of ever "regaining consciousness and therefore capacity." Greer dismissed the footage offered into evidence of Terri purportedly responding to her mother, and he attributed the associated testimony of Mary Schindler as wishful thinking.

"The overwhelming credible evidence is that Terri Schiavo has been totally unresponsive since lapsing into the coma almost ten years ago," Greer wrote in his ten-page ruling. "Her movements are reflexive and predicated on brain stem activity alone, [and] she suffers from severe structural brain damage and to a large extent her brain has been replaced by spinal fluid." Terri did not want to live under these circumstances, he concluded.

Thus the ruling became "the law in the case," as Felos repeatedly reminded reporters over subsequent years, that Terri was in a persistent vegetative state and wished to die. Now there was a court order for her death. The right-to-die train had left the station, and Terri Schiavo was on board whether she wanted to be or not.

8

Dueling Doctors

THE MEDIA COVERAGE OF Judge George Greer's February 11, 2000, ruling prompted more medical experts with varying specialties to come forward over the next year to dispute the PVS diagnosis and urge new diagnostic testing be done. Like Jay Carpenter, Drs. John Young and James Avery accompanied the Schindlers on their visits at the nursing home in the weeks after the court ruling. They did so without the permission of Michael Schiavo, however, and later testified they were unaware his approval was required. And he granted permission to no subsequent physicians who came forward to examine Terri, including the investigator with the Advocacy Center for Disabled Persons who was investigating allegations of abuse and neglect. (This will be discussed further in chapter 15.)

During a March 2, 2000, court hearing, Young, who earned his medical degree in the British West Indies, testified he had observed Mary Schindler putting holy water on her finger and applying it to the inner part of Terri's lips around the tongue. "I then watched her throat and watched her tongue action and watched her swallow," he said. He recommended Terri be given a new swallowing test before her scheduled feeding-tube removal based on his observation that she handled her own saliva and sinus secretions, which experts estimate amounts to one and a half liters of fluid a day. Similarly, Avery, who is board certified in internal medicine and pulmonary medicine, noted in his sworn affidavit: "There was no dribbling, choking, or gagging. This raises the possibility that she may be able to swallow and take food and water orally, obviating the need for the gravity-flow feeding tube." Avery added, "Her actions are indications of cognitive behavior, not reflexes."

But Judge Greer was not swayed. He agreed with Michael Schiavo and denied the petition seeking a swallowing test. According to her medical records, Terri was last given a formal swallowing test at the HCA Medical Center Hospital on June 23, 1992. Michael Schiavo, however, repeatedly asserted there were more recent tests over the years, but he has never offered any documentation.

With the swallowing issue set aside, Judge Greer scheduled the removal of the feeding tube, and Terri was transferred quietly to hospice. At the same time, Michael secured a court authorization on March 28, 2000, to prevent the Schindler family from taking photographs and audio or video recordings of Terri, and outside Terri's room he posted a security guard who was paid out of her guardianship funds. Schiavo explained that he did this for Terri's privacy, which indeed remained one of her reserved rights as an incapacitated ward. After the appellate process was exhausted and the U.S. Supreme Court refused to review the case, Terri's gastric feeding tube was removed for the first time on April 24, 2001.

About this time Pat Anderson joined the case. The constitutional theory buff and Stetson Law School graduate had spent the past two decades working in media law for the outside attorney of the *St. Petersburg Times.* The native of Pinellas County was no stranger to difficult cases. Ten years earlier she had tried a defamation case for five weeks that was based on stories that had won the Pulitzer Prize for investigative reporting. "That was a corker," she recalls with her customary enthusiasm for a good fight. Little did she know that defending Terri Schiavo's right to life would trump that experience and exact a huge personal toll. Her obsession with the case for the better part of four years caused her to have trouble scheduling her own wedding. Two marriage licenses were applied for and issued but expired before she could catch a spare moment to get married. She also missed out on a lot of memorable moments with a grandson who was born right after she took the case. After working pro bono for the first sixty days, Anderson continued to serve the cause for half her normal hourly rate. "It has ruined me financially," she confessed without regret. Perhaps the greater injury Anderson suffered as a result of the outcome of the case was that she lost her faith in the judicial system. As a result she altered her practice to minimize litigation and now primarily focuses on real estate law.

Sixty hours into Terri's "death process," as Felos called it, Pinellas–Pasco Circuit Court Judge Frank Quesada ordered the feeding tube reinserted to give the Schindler family an opportunity to pursue a lawsuit against Michael Schiavo based on testimony from Cindy Shook suggesting he perjured himself in the 2000 trial. During this initial reprieve seven medical experts came forward to dispute Terri was in PVS and to urge new diagnostic tests to prove or disprove their claims. Michael Schiavo refused to allow these physicians to see Terri. Their comments and recommendations, offered in sworn affidavits and filed with the court, were based on a review of medical records, court documents, footage of Terri shown at the 2000 trial, and their experiences in treating brain-injured patients. This group of doctors included and commented:

Neurologist Jacob Green: "There is clear reactivity and an emotional responsitivity to the person who comes into her room as shown on the videotape. This reactivity shows a significant amount of brain damage, but it is my opinion based on reasonable medical probability that she is not . . . in a persistent vegetative state."

Internist Richard Neubauer, specialist practicing hyperbaric medicine: "I have treated patients who were in conditions similar to Ms. Schiavo's and who improved with hyberbaric oxygen therapy. . . . In my opinion, to forego treatment of this patient and deny her nutrition and hydration amounts to murder."

William Hammesfahr, pioneer of vasodialator drugs to treat brain injuries: "It is my opinion that the CAT scan readings or MRI readings of Ms. Schiavo's brain were misrepresented to the Court during the trial in January 2000. There is significant brain tissue in Ms. Schiavo's case. It is not true that her cerebellum has been replaced by spinal fluid. She has viable brain tissue in her cerebellum space, not just scar tissue or spinal fluid."

Neuropsychologist Alexander Gimon, formerly on Harvard University faculty: "Mrs. Schiavo is clearly able to respond cognitively to environmental stimuli. She interacts verbally and motorically with her mother and with doctors giving verbal instructions. It is clear on its face that she has brain matter for these functions, but has been deprived of appropriate therapy and stimulation."

Neuroradiologist William Maxfield: "I cannot agree with the diagnosis of persistent vegetative state. In the records provided to me I find no imaging procedures to evaluate brain function, such as SPECT or PET brain scans. CT or MRI brain studies, even with contrast, show only anatomy and not function. . . . It is incredible to me that functional imaging of the brain has not been obtained."

Retired Miami neurologist William Russell: "Undoubtedly she is more aware of her surroundings than former President Reagan [who was battling Alzheimer's at the time]."

After Greer refused to hear any of the new testimony by Shook or the seven medical experts, the Second District Court of Appeal on October 17, 2001, mandated that Greer hold an evidentiary hearing to determine whether "new treatment offers sufficient promise of increased cognitive function in Mrs. Schiavo's cerebral cortex—significantly improving the quality of Mrs. Schiavo's life—so that she herself would elect to undergo this treatment and would reverse the prior decision to withdraw life-prolonging procedures." The evidentiary hearing was scheduled for October 11, 2002. In the months leading up to the six-day hearing, it was decided that five board-certified expert physicians, preferably neurologists, would weigh in on Terri's condition. Two doctors would be solicited by Felos, two by Anderson, and the swing vote would come from a neutral medical expert to be appointed by Greer since the parties could not agree on an independent fifth expert.

In July 2002 the expert witnesses convened for a pretrial hearing to determine which diagnostic tests Terri would undergo. Functional MRIs and PET (positron emission tomography) scans, which show the perfusion of blood in the brain and delineate which areas of the brain are functioning, are standard diagnostic tools used by neurologists to evaluate the extent of brain damage and confirm PVS. Terri's medical records reflected she last had an MRI on July 24, 1990—four months after her brain injury. There was no record of her ever undergoing a functional MRI (fMRI) or PET scan. The Schindlers listed MRI and PET scan on a list of twenty-five diagnostic tests they sought for Terri. According to Dr. David Stevens, executive director of the seventeen-thousand-member Christian Medical Association, some studies conducted in early 2005 have shown that PET scans have allowed researchers to gauge the amount of brain activity in patients thought to be in PVS.

Judge Greer ruled in favor of Felos and Schiavo's preference to restrict new testing to an EEG, an ultrasound of the carotid artery, a new CT scan, and a SPECT (single photon emission computed tomography) scan. As their rationale for objecting to an MRI, Felos's expert witnesses cited an FDA alert regarding a danger to patients with electrical implants to undergo that test. Thus the medical experts began their examinations of Terri.

WHILE THE debate raged over Terri Schiavo's neurological status, the American neurological and neuroscientific community was expanding its understanding of the brain. AAN neurologists coined a new clinical entity, the minimally conscious state (MCS), to apply to a subgroup of patients with severe alteration in consciousness but who have neurologic findings that don't meet the criteria for vegetative state (VS). The prevalence of adult and pediatric MCS cases was estimated in early 2002 to be between 112,000 and 280,000.

"These patients demonstrate discernible behavioral evidence of consciousness but remain unable to reproduce this behavior consistently," AAN neurologist J. T. Giacino and his colleagues wrote in a February 2002 article in *Neurology*. The authors represented the Aspen Neurobehavioral Conference Workgroup and outlined new diagnostic criteria for MCS in the article. The MCS diagnosis required "clearly discernible evidence of self or environmental awareness" be demonstrated "on a reproducible or sustained basis" by one or more of the following behaviors:

- following simple commands
- gestural or verbal yes/no responses (regardless of accuracy)
- intelligible verbalization
- purposeful behavior, including movements or affective behaviors that occur in contingent relation to relevant environmental stimuli and are not due to reflexive activity

The authors provided examples of the last behavior, which included appropriate smiling or crying, vocalizations or gestures that occur in direct response to linguistic content of questions, and pursuit eye movement or sustained fixation that occurs in direct response to moving or salient stimuli. The distinction between the MCS diagnosis and the PVS diagnosis criteria appears largely to rely on the "reproducible and sustained basis" requirement. Discernible evidence of self or environment only observed on one occasion, for instance, would necessarily result in a PVS versus MCS diagnosis unless that discernible evidence was "sustained," which isn't defined. Is visual tracking for ten seconds considered "sustained"? Or must it last a minute or more? That determination was left up to the diagnostician.

The Aspen Workgroup recommended "extended assessment" to determine whether a simple response, like a finger movement or an eye blink that is observed infrequently, occurs in response to a specific environmental event or on a coincidental basis. In other words, the amount of time spent assessing these behaviors exhibited by a patient was key to making the fine-line determination as to whether that patient was in PVS or MCS.[1] According to PVS co-creator Fred Plum, "Responsiveness can vary from time to time according to metabolic or toxic factors, drugs or fatigue."[2]

One of the Aspen Workgroup participant-authors, neurologist Ronald Cranford, was selected by Felos to evaluate Terri Schiavo and testify at the evidentiary hearing. In apparent contradiction to the Aspen Workgroup's recommendation of "extended assessment," Cranford admittedly assessed Terri for a period of forty-two minutes, during which he determined she was in "irreversible" PVS. He would later make this claim with "105 percent" certainty. Cranford, the former chairman of the AAN's Ethics and Humanities Subcommittee, also disregarded AAN's recommendation of "repeated" or "multiple" examinations for PVS diagnoses.

In contrast, Dr. William Hammesfahr, one of the two medical experts who testified on behalf of the Schindlers, spent three hours with Terri over multiple visits. "Examining patients with brain injuries takes a long time," Hammesfahr testified. "They don't process the way the rest of us do. So you can't go through examinations very rapidly. You have to give them time and do different parts of the exam very slowly and very frequently, repetitively while you try to identify how their body is working and what can be done about it. . . . When you give them a command, they may not respond to that command right away. So you have to observe them quite a while to see if they do respond because there is a consistent delay." Hammesfahr and others criticized Cranford for what they described as his "rapid-fire" multiple commands of Terri, which they argued made it impossible for her to respond.

More concerning to the Schindlers, however, was Cranford's record as a right-to-die activist. (This will be more fully developed in chapter 10.) As a medical ethicist with a "special interest" in physician-assisted suicide and euthanasia, the University of Minnesota Medical School professor is a familiar face at right-to-die trials across the country. He has testified in favor of death in eight major right-to-die cases that have climbed the judicial ladder to the U.S. Supreme Court, including *Cruzan v. Director, Missouri Department of Health* (1990), where he testified he would even consider spoon-feeding to be "medical treatment."

"He is a 'right-to-die' proponent. He believes there are people who have lives not worthy to be lived, and those lives should be ended," David Stevens with the Christian Medical Association told Cybercast News Service, "and that colors him and his medical opinions. And examples of that are overstating the case to assure that people's feeding tubes are removed."[3]

While Cranford claimed a perfect record for the cases in which he has testified that were heard by the U.S. Supreme Court, he does have one prominent misdiagnosis on his résumé. In 1979 he diagnosed police Sgt. David Mack, who was shot in the line of duty, as "definitely . . . in a persistent vegetative state . . . never [to] regain cognitive, sapient functioning." Twenty-two months later Mack started waking up and eventually regained nearly all his mental ability. On CNN's *NewsNight,* with host Aaron Brown, Cranford pointed out the distinction with the Terri Schiavo case was that, unlike Mack's CT scan, which didn't show any change, Terri's CT scan showed, in his view, "irreversible atrophy." Later he admitted he couldn't rule out MCS.

"You cannot look at that CAT scan and say this is PVS versus MCS, but you can look at it and say there's irreversibility. It's extensive destruction, and it may be PVS. It could be MCS, but it's irreversible. There's just no cerebral cortex left," he asserted.[4] While the distinction between PVS and MCS may not matter to Cranford, it would have made a world of difference to Terri, given that Florida law doesn't provide for the removal of feeding tubes from minimally conscious patients.

At the evidentiary hearing, Cranford testified he had examined or observed "hundreds" of patients in a vegetative state. He said that typically there's no more brain to shrink after five or ten years in a vegetative state. Claiming that he had reviewed "thousands and thousands of CAT scans," Cranford called Terri's brain shrinkage "as bad as you could get."

From his clinical perspective, Cranford explained his PVS diagnosis by stating that Terri lacked consistent visual fixation and completely lacked visual tracking, although he admitted that during one of three trials she successfully tracked a multicolored balloon. In the videotape of Cranford's examination, he moves a shiny balloon from side to side. Terri tracks the balloon with her eyes and moves her head from side to side to keep it within her line of sight. Her response surprises Cranford, who exclaims, "Oh, you do see that, don't you? You do follow that a bit, don't you?" Later in the examination Cranford became even more animated in reaction to Terri. "It's got to be in your field of gaze, doesn't it? You've got to see it first, then you can follow it a little bit. There we go! That's good! That's good!" However, Cranford testified Terri would have to exhibit sustained visual pursuit for more than five minutes in order to demonstrate consciousness. Recall that the Multi-Society Task Force's diagnostic guidelines failed to define "sustained."

Cranford similarly testified that Terri failed to exhibit "consistent and reproducible" responses to her mother, according to the gold standard adopted by the Multi-Society Task Force. The standard, however, is more encompassing of patients than the definition of PVS laid out in Florida statute 765.101 (12): "A permanent and irreversible condition of unconsciousness in which there is: (a) The absence of voluntary action or cognitive behavior of any kind. [And] (b) An inability to communicate or interact purposefully with the environment." This statute sets forth the conditions for the legal refusal or removal of life-prolonging medical procedures from a patient. (This statute, which changed after Michael Schiavo filed his petition to remove Terri's feeding tube in 1998, will be examined in chapter 12.)

Cranford further testified that Terri's startled responses to clapping and other loud noises were "reflexes," along with her smiles, grimacing, and moaning. He said it was "extraordinarily rare" for PVS patients to speak but described the hypothetical utterance of "no" by a person in PVS as a reflex. "Stop that," on the other hand, Cranford said would require a higher level of thinking.

Neurologist Dr. Melvin Greer, a professor at the University of Florida College of Medicine and a former president of AAN, whose testimony was also solicited by Felos, similarly concluded Terri Schiavo was in PVS. Dr. Greer also interpreted Terri's 1996 CT scan as showing "profound atrophy of the brain," where the tissue had shrunken and spinal fluid was filling the crevices and essentially dominating the space. Greer testified he saw no change between the 1996 and the 2002 CT scans. "There is no treatment available that can help this unfortunate young woman," he stated.

Dr. Hammesfahr, a neurologist in private practice in Clearwater, Florida, solicited by the Schindlers, offered testimony that Terri wasn't in PVS and might benefit from therapy that utilized vasodilators, which work to increase the blood flow to the brain. Hammesfahr claimed he had treated between two thousand and three thousand stroke victims and about one hundred patients diagnosed with anoxic encephalopathy, or brain damage due to lack of oxygen, which was the nature of Terri's injury. Hammesfahr holds a U.S. patent for his pioneering technique, which employs the use of a special type of ultrasound and new medications that have proven more successful than those used in vasodilatation in the treatment of brain injury over the past fifty years. While he was unable to offer statistics or any success rate for his vasodilatation therapy, he testified that his therapy had resulted in improvement in his patients' cognitive function. He pointed out a few patients who were present in the courtroom, including the daughter of a partially paralyzed man he treated eight years after the man had suffered a stroke. Following months of therapy, the man was able to walk again, Hammesfahr said.

Based on his examination of Terri, Hammesfahr described her as "alert and responsive to her environment." He said she responded to specific people best and tried to please others by doing activities for which she got verbal praise. According to Hammesfahr, Terri was able to differentiate voices, respond to music, and differentiate music from stray sounds. While she ignored one tape recording of live piano music, she verbalized during the other and appeared to interact with the music. She stopped making noise when the music stopped. Additionally, Hammesfahr determined Terri had voluntary control over multiple extremities, although her motor abilities were difficult to assess because of severe contractures; she could swallow and likely eat; she felt pain; and she was partially blind.

Radiologist Dr. William Maxfield served as the second expert for the Schindlers. Maxfield has a background in both nuclear medicine and radiology and practiced hyperbaric medicine for twenty years. He uses hyperbaric oxygen therapy to treat brain disorders and multiple other conditions, including stroke, cerebral palsy, MS, and emphysema. As Maxfield explained, high pressure inside a hyperbaric chamber pushes oxygen into the fluids and tissues of the body, increasing oxygenation by as much as 1,200 percent. Since oxygen is fuel to the brain, increased oxygen increases its fuel. The technique has been used for over a century and is more widely used outside of the United States. While Medicare authorizes eleven uses for hyperbaric medicine, Maxfield testified, Russia has seventy-three approved uses for the therapy. Based on his review of the current literature, Maxfield told the court that studies in Mexico were conducted where hyperbaric therapy was combined with stem cells to cause regeneration of brain and spinal cord. Researchers reported individuals who had total paralysis of their legs for up to three years were walking after therapy. Maxfield testified he believed Terri Schiavo could benefit from hyperbaric therapy.

"I've seen improvement in more hypoxic episodes where the brain stem is much worse than what this is," he said, referencing Terri's July 2002 CT scan. "When I was in medical school, we were taught that brain tissue never regenerated. But the experimental animal data and also the current clinical data is now telling us that that is not true."

Maxfield testified he'd interpreted some twenty thousand nuclear imaging scans and thousands of CT scans. According to his interpretation of Terri's CT scans and the SPECT scan, there was functioning brain tissue remaining in all parts of her brain, with the highest degree of functioning, or least amount of damage, sustained in the frontal areas and the cerebellum—the areas that deal with awareness and cognition. He found the least degree of functioning, or most damage, in the occipital areas in the back of the brain, which indicated some degree of blindness. The amount of damage to the cerebral cortex and the motor areas fell somewhere in between, but the scans indicated some function in those areas. Interestingly, Maxfield testified the 2002 CT scan showed no more loss of brain tissue from the 1996 CT scan.

"Would you have expected a person with this SPECT scan to have some awareness?" Pat Anderson asked Maxfield during her direct examination.

"Yes, I would," Maxfield replied. In fact, following his clinical evaluation of Terri performed over four days, Maxfield concluded Terri was not in a persistent vegetative state but was aware, responded to her mother and piano music, had the ability to visually track a balloon and lights, and could swallow.

Dr. Peter Bambakidis, a neurologist with the Cleveland Clinic Foundation, provided the swing vote in the 2002 evidentiary trial. He served as the neutral, court-appointed medical expert. Considering that Bambakidis had never testified in a trial before, it's unclear how Judge Greer received Bambakidis's name. Although he's licensed to practice medicine in Minnesota, Bambakidis said he didn't have a professional relationship with University of Minnesota professor Ronald Cranford or any other physician associated with the case. He also said he didn't have any "preexisting social relationships" with any of the parties or attorneys in the case. During cross-examination, Schindler attorney Anderson asked Bambakidis how he came to be a witness at this trial.

"That's a good question. I know that the judge telephoned me and asked me if I would be interested in serving as an independent expert to the court in this particular matter. I gave it some thought and said that I would and sent him the information that he requested, the CV, etc.," Bambakidis replied. "I believe his comment was that they wanted somebody who worked for the Cleveland Clinic."

"Who is they?" asked Anderson.

"I don't know. You would have to ask the judge," he answered. Judge Greer did not volunteer the information. Requests for interviews with Judge Greer were declined on the basis that it was "not appropriate" for him to offer public statements while the case was still open. (The case remained open at the time of this writing.)

Bambakidis revealed during cross examination that he'd had roughly ten conversations with Schiavo attorney George Felos prior to his taking the witness stand, that Felos had sent him medical records and other materials for him to use in his independent review of Terri, had given him guidance the morning he was scheduled to testify, and had also provided miscellaneous administrative support, such as providing directions from the airport to Terri's hospice. Bambakidis reported that Felos had initially contacted him after he had agreed to serve as expert witness on the case.

After his plane from Ohio was delayed three hours, Bambakidis said he met Felos and Michael Schiavo in the lobby of hospice and obtained a history on Terri from Schiavo before his thirty-minute examination. The prior arrangement was for the Schindlers to also be there for his examination. Due to Bambakidis's flight delay, however, they were not present when he arrived. He testified he made no attempt to contact them to supplement his understanding of Terri's history that evening or anytime thereafter.

In a September 16, 2003, press release, supporters of the Terri Schindler-Schiavo Foundation raised suspicions that Bambakidis may not have been the neutral, independent witness he was presented to be. According to the release, supporters determined Bambakidis's brother Gust managed the Ohio chapter of the American Hellenic Education Progressive Association (AHEPA).[5] Marketing materials promoting seminars conducted by Felos indicate he served as a governor for the Greek-American organization. A *St. Petersburg Times* article reporting the tragic death of Felos's father in 1995 indicated Felos inherited his affinity for AHEPA. According to the article, James George Felos, a first-generation American whose parents emigrated from Greece, had "held fast to his roots" by supporting AHEPA. The article ended with a request from the family that donations be made to AHEPA.[6]

Bambakidis recently indicated it wasn't appropriate for him to give interviews about the case, "out of respect to those involved." He then ventured a comment to his local paper: "My sense is that this poor woman became a pawn in a family squabble and was exploited in an unseemly fashion."[7]

Under direct examination from Felos, Bambakidis interpreted Terri's 2002 CT scan as "markedly abnormal" in that it showed a "very, very prominent enlargement of the fluid spaces within the brain. The reason that that fluid is there is because there's been such profound loss of tissue. It's become filled in by that fluid." He elaborated, "The ventricles . . . enlarge accommodating to the fact that that normal brain cortex has become lost. It's not there anymore." Bambakidis further described that the cerebral cortex was "very, very vital" to personhood.

"Those aspects of human existence involving awareness of one's self, awareness of those around us, our ability to communicate, our ability to experience pleasure on a conscious level, and our ability to suffer as well is a function of the cerebral cortex," said Bambakidis. "It's frightening to think that such a relatively small area of the brain has such an important role in what makes us—I don't mean [to be] pejorative. I was going to say totally human."

After acknowledging he wasn't an expert in CT interpretation, Bambakidis testified his clinical findings were typical for individuals in a vegetative state. Specifically, Bambakidis noted that Terri exhibited the "classic decorticate posturing," with her head leaning and turned slightly to the right and her upper extremities severely contractured or flexed, seen in patients whose "cortex is not there any longer." Bambakidis said he was unable to elicit a response from Terri by clapping his hands, calling her name, and applying noxious stimuli to her feet and ankles. Bambakidis also concurred with Drs. Cranford and Greer that Terri's swallowing, moaning, and smiling were random reflexes governed by the brain stem, not voluntary, purposeful behaviors.

In testifying about the electrical activity measured in Terri's brain by the EEG, Bambakidis called the amplitude "abnormally low" and pointed out the frequencies and the amplitudes didn't change spontaneously the way they should and didn't respond to stimuli.

Under cross-examination from Pat Anderson, Bambakidis conceded the footage of Terri apparently responding to her mother and seeming to smile and verbalize in her presence was a "concern" for him, and he testified this assignment required "soul searching" on his part because of the ramifications of his diagnosis. In the end, he said he weighed the totality of the evidence, including the assessments of the doctors that came before him, in reaching his conclusion.

WITH THE swing vote coming down on the side of PVS, Judge Greer rendered a decision affirming his original ruling that Terri remained in PVS, although in his November 22, 2002, order, Greer stated his decision was not based on "a simple head count" but rather that he had "considered all factors." In his latest order it was clear Greer was persuaded by Cranford that consistency of behavior or response was the relevant indicator, even though such was required neither by Florida statute nor the AAN.

"At first blush, the video of Terri Schiavo appearing to smile and look lovingly at her mother seemed to represent cognition," Greer wrote. "This was also true for how she followed the Mickey Mouse balloon held by her father. The court has carefully viewed the videotapes as requested by counsel and does find that these actions were neither *consistent* nor reproducible. . . . She clearly does not *consistently* respond to her mother."

Greer calculated that Dr. Hammesfahr and Mary Schindler had collectively given Terri 111 commands and asked her 72 questions over the course of several hours of the videotaped examination. "The court saw few actions that could be considered response to either those commands or those questions," Greer wrote. Then, in what some consider to be an extraordinary move on Greer's part, he raised the bar even higher for Terri than Cranford had and determined Terri's responses needed to be more than "consistent." They needed to be "constant" in order for her to not be ruled in PVS. "The court finds that based on the credible evidence, cognitive function would manifest itself in a constant response to stimuli," Greer declared.

With the PVS determination behind him, Greer then addressed the specific instructions of the appellate mandate and assessed the two treatment options put forth by Hammesfahr and Maxfield.

"It is clear from the evidence that these therapies are experimental insofar as the medical community is concerned with regard to patients like Terri Schiavo, which is borne out by the total absence of supporting case studies or medical literature," he said in the order. "The mandate requires something more than a belief, hope of 'some' improvement. It requires . . . that the treatment offers such sufficient promise of increased cognitive function in Mrs. Schiavo's cerebral cortex so as to significantly improve her quality of life." Hammesfahr and Maxfield themselves freely admitted their therapies came with no guarantees. Anderson viewed the requirement of "significantly improve[d] . . . quality of life" as unreasonable. In her analysis, the appellate court had "stacked the deck" against Terri. (This will be discussed in chapter 13.) Greer again ordered the feeding tube removed, scheduling the "withdrawal of life support" for 3:00 p.m. on January 3, 2003. The ensuing appellate process delayed that until October 15, 2003.

ON THE eve of the PEG-tube removal, the Schindler family staged a press conference to announce they had sneaked a camera inside the hospice in violation of Schiavo's court order and had made a five-minute videotape of Terri. They released copies to the media hoping the footage would prompt Florida Governor Jeb Bush and the Department of Children and Families to intervene and take custody of their daughter.

"I went in with the camera because I expected Terri to be dying very shortly, and I wanted to bring the truth out," Bob Schindler explained at a press conference. When asked whether he was prepared to go to jail for contempt of court he responded, "What happens, happens. But if there's anything regarding Terri that could help her, that is not going to injure anyone or do anyone harm, then I'm [supportive of it.]" The Schindlers said they believed they were violating Terri's privacy in order to save her life.

"I think Michael Schiavo and his attorney were scared to death to get Terri in a wheelchair and out in the pubic," said Bobby Schindler. "That's why they stopped all videos from being taken, all pictures from being taken and they warehoused Terri in a hospice room for the last five years and didn't let her outside. They were scared to death to allow Terri outside because their whole public media campaign was to, as best they can, describe my sister as a nonperson."

In the secret footage, Mary Schindler again kisses Terri on the cheek and playfully plants kisses elsewhere on her face. Her nuzzling elicits an apparent smile and laughter from her daughter. Later she asks Terri to say "mom," and Terri seems to respond, making noise and apparently attempting to form the words with her mouth. As she struggles to produce the word, her eyebrow furrows and her smile is replaced by a grimace.

"She gets frustrated, you can hear it in her voice," Mary Schindler explained. "But that's her best effort to say, 'I'm in here and I'm trying to talk to you.'"[8]

Somehow, as was often the case over the decade-long court battle, Michael Schiavo and his attorneys learned about the impending video release ahead of time. Guardianship attorney Bushnell faxed a letter to Schindler attorney Anderson threatening to prevent the family from visiting Terri and seeking "other remedies from the court, as appropriate" if the tape were released. The letter did not sway the Schindlers.

The clandestine video enraged Michael Schiavo, who said Terri would be "mortified." "She was very, very particular about the way she looked, very proud when she walked out the door," echoed Scott Schiavo. "She would be so upset to have the world seeing her that way, and Michael knew that."[9] Brian Schiavo called the Schindlers' dissemination of this latest footage of Terri "extremely offensive" and said it "would have killed" Terri if she knew about it. "All that footage that's out there? All that was done against court order. I don't know why the Schindlers and their attorneys weren't sanctioned for that, other than Judge Greer didn't want to take it out on the 'poor parents,'" he said. "But they used that to create problems. All they did was put it out there for the public to look at."

Not all the footage made public over the years was illicitly obtained, however. Following the evidentiary hearing, Anderson introduced the videotaped examinations of Terri by neurologists into evidence in February 2003. Once that happened, the video clips culled from those tapes became public record. Clips of Terri apparently interacting with her parents were posted on the Schindler family's Web site in 2003 in an effort to demonstrate to the world that Terri was no vegetable.

The footage created a groundswell, and by March 5, 2005, some thirty-three physicians from across the country—including neurologists, speech-language pathologists, a brain surgeon, and medical doctors—had provided the Schindlers with sworn affidavits disputing the PVS diagnosis and urging new testing and/or therapy for Terri. Several offered their services in either evaluating or treating Terri. Many felt she might improve. These affidavits were submitted to the court and added to the case file. The testimony included the following statements.

Speech-language pathologist Sara Green Mele, Rehabilitation Institute of Chicago: “Mrs. Schiavo is clearly aware of her environment and interacts with it, albeit inconsistently. She is able to comprehend spoken language, and can, at least inconsistently follow simple one-step commands.”

Psychiatrist Ralph Ankenman worked with brain-injured patients at Madison County Hospital in London, Ohio: “I have been successfully using a new and experimental treatment with my patients, which I believe should be considered for the treatment of Terri Schiavo.” As Ankenman described, the treatment involved Namenda, which works to modify an amino acid receptor in the brain and cure dissociation in the brain. “The long-duration lack of speech seen after injury trauma is not always due to destruction of brain structures. Sometimes it is due to a state of brain dysfunction that is reversible.”

Neurologist Beatrice Engstrand: “It is clear that she is more than reflexive, . . . I believe she is at least minimally conscious.”

Developmental psychiatrist Alyse Eytan: “It appears that Ms. Schiavo responds to certain stimuli. Even if those responses are random at times, I believe that more advanced interventions with multisensory stimulation for a lengthy period of time would be beneficial.”

Harry Goldsmith, general surgeon working all over the world assisting in the treatment of brain and spinal cord conditions: “I have been able to increase cerebral blood flow and biological agents into the brain of patients. Generally, if we are able to increase the blood flow to her brain, she might show improvement. An increase in blood flow allows for an increase in oxygen, neurotransmitters, etc.”

Carolyn Heron, physical, medical and rehabilitation doctor (PMR): “Ms. Schiavo does show appropriate facial response to stimuli. She also sits up independently. These behaviors are not consistent with someone in a vegetative state. There she is at least in a minimally conscious state (MCS). I believe she is better than minimally conscious.”

David Hopper, clinical director of Traumatic Brain Injury Unit at the University Medical Center of Southern Nevada: “Often a neurologist diagnoses PVS upon admission and there is no follow-up evaluation which leads to failure to update/change the diagnosis. There is a high misdiagnosis of PVS due to lack of proper cognitive and detailed neurological assessment. I strongly recommend that Terri Schiavo receive further testing regarding her current level of cognitive functioning."

Neurologist Lawrence Huntoon: "These behaviors indicate awareness of the environment, and this type of behavior distinguishes minimally conscious state (MCS) from persistent vegetative state (PVS)." Huntoon cited apparent evidence Terri responded to her mother and had sustained visual pursuit.

Speech-language pathologist Pamela Hyena: "There seems to be a lot of communicating going on with Ms. Schiavo." Hyena suggested Terri might be taught to communicate using an "eye gaze communication board."

Psychotherapist and speech-language pathologist Jill Joyce: "Based on my observations and experience, it is my opinion that Ms. Schiavo would be able to learn how to swallow if given the proper therapy. . . . I have seen . . . patients that were diagnosed as being in a persistent vegetative state . . . come back to a cognitive state when given proper therapy."

Neuroscientist and neurologist Philip Kennedy: "I strongly recommend that she be allowed the opportunity to be examined through the use of a functional MRI (fMRI). . . . There are newer technologies since what was available in 2002 that will allow us to determine if Terri Schiavo can be assessed for signs of cortical function."

Speech-language pathologist Kyle Lakes: "There is a relatively new swallowing therapy called VitalStim. It is an electro-therapy used to restrengthen the throat muscles. It trains the throat muscles to function again by using small electrical currents to stimulate the muscles responsible for swallowing. The success rate for VitalStim has been huge."

Ricardo Senno, specialist in brain-injury medicine and former medical director of the Rehabilitation Institute of Chicago's Brain Injury Medicine and Rehabilitation Program: "I have developed rehabilitation programs for patients just like Terri Schiavo. Because of continued advances in medical testing and treatment, even within the past several years I believe, from a medical point of view, Ms. Schiavo deserves another evaluation."

Stanley Terman, member of National Board of Medical Examiners and American Board of Psychiatry and Neurology: "My clinical position is that all living beings should be given every opportunity to express themselves and should therefore be asked in the most diligent, careful, and patient way." Terman recommended an MRI be done and requested an opportunity to interview Terri Schiavo.

On his own, the Reverend Robert Johansen, a Catholic priest with the Diocese of Kalamazoo, Michigan, spent ten days on the telephone in early March 2005 recruiting and interviewing neurologists who were willing to offer court affidavits. In a March 16, 2005, article published in *National Review Online,* Johansen said that he had "commitments from over thirty other [neurologists] who are willing to testify that Terri should have new and additional testing, and new examinations by unbiased neurologists."[10]

Meanwhile, the onslaught of doctors' affidavits failed to impress either the trial or appellate courts. That included the eleventh-hour testimony of neurologists William Cheshire Jr., of the Mayo Clinic in Jacksonville, Florida, and Joseph Fins of New York Presbyterian Hospital/Weill Cornell Medical Center, who served as part of an advance team for Governor Bush's prospective intervention by the state's Department of Children and Families (DCF). DCF is statutorily mandated to protect vulnerable citizens from neglect, abuse, or exploitation. The agency had the authority—and attempted to exercise that authority—to intervene in the case and take custody of Terri. While it was weighing whether to do so, agency officials solicited opinions from Drs. Cheshire and Fins. Both reported to DCF that they believed Terri might have been misdiagnosed and that she was more likely in a minimally conscious state rather than in PVS.

Cheshire filed an affidavit on March 23, 2005, summarizing his findings after a ninety-minute visit with Terri, his review of her medical records, and his viewing of the videotaped examinations performed by his colleagues during the evidentiary hearing. By then Terri was into her sixth day of dehydration. Given the timing, Cheshire's affidavit, in which he urged Terri's immediate transfer from the hospice to a hospital for restoration of nutrition and hydration, was explosive.

"There is a greater likelihood that Terri is in a minimally conscious state than a persistent vegetative state," he wrote. "This distinction makes an enormous difference in making ethical decisions on Terri's behalf." The DCF volunteer primarily focused on the fact that "pain issues" kept surfacing throughout Terri's medical records. He noted the definition of PVS published by AAN precluded patients in PVS from having the capacity of experiencing pain or suffering. Cheshire specifically referenced what he called a "remarkable moment" in the videotaped examination by Hammesfahr:

> At 2:44 p.m., Dr. Hammesfahr had just turned Terri onto her right side to examine her back with a painful sharp stimulus (a sharp piece of wood), to which Terri had responded with signs of discomfort. Well after he ceased applying the stimulus and had returned Terri to a comfortable position, he says to her parents, "So, we're going to have to roll her over . . . ' Immediately, Terri cries. She vocalizes a crying sound, "Ugh, ha, ha, ha," presses her

> eyebrows together, and sadly grimaces. It is important to note that, at that moment, no one is touching Terri or causing actual pain. Rather, she appears to comprehend the meaning of Dr. Hammesfahr's comment and signals her *anticipation* of pain. This response suggests some degree of language processing and interpretation at the level of the cerebral cortex. It also suggests that she may be aware of pain beyond what could be explained by simple reflex withdrawal.

Cheshire concluded, "If Terri is consciously aware of pain, and therefore is capable of suffering, then her diagnosis of PVS may be tragically mistaken." The neurologist listed other behaviors Terri demonstrated that he believed cast a reasonable doubt on the prior diagnosis of PVS. These included:

- her behavior was frequently context-specific
- she fixated her gaze on colorful objects or human faces for some fifteen seconds
- she demonstrated emotional expressivity by her use of single syllable vocalizations such as "ah," making cooing sounds, or by expressing guttural sounds of annoyance or moaning appropriate to the context of stimulation
- she inconsistently followed commands such as closing her eyes and lifting her leg during Hammesfahr's examination

"To enter the room of Terri Schiavo is nothing like entering the room of a patient who is comatose or brain-dead or in some neurological sense no longer there," Cheshire wrote. "The visitor has the distinct sense of the presence of a living human being who seems at some level to be aware of some things around her. As I looked at Terri, and she gazed directly back at me, I asked myself whether, if I were her attending physician, I could in good conscience withdraw her feeding and hydration. No, I could not. I could not withdraw life support if I were asked. I could not withhold life-sustaining nutrition and hydration from this beautiful lady whose face brightens in the presence of others."

Cheshire's determination is significant, because it represented a complete change of course for him. At the top of his report he disclosed he approached this case with the belief that it can be ethically permissible to discontinue artificially provided nutrition and hydration for persons in a permanent vegetative state. "Having now reviewed the relevant facts, having met and observed Ms. Schiavo in person, and having reflected deeply on the moral and ethical issues," he stated, "I have changed my mind in regard to this particular case."

According to Cheshire, the case of Terri Schiavo "differs fundamentally from end-of-life scenarios where it is appropriate to withdraw life-sustaining medical interventions that no longer benefit or are burdensome to patients." That is because Terri's feeding tube was neither a burden, nor painful, nor infected, nor eroding her stomach lining or causing any medical complications. And as Cheshire pointed out, Terri could not be considered medically terminal. She would not die but for the withdrawal of food and water.

MORE THAN two months after Terri Schiavo's death, Pinellas–Pasco County medical examiner Jon Thogmartin confirmed that she "died from marked dehydration" as a result of the removal of her feeding tube. He estimated Terri Schiavo would likely have lived another decade otherwise. Thogmartin couldn't provide an answer for the question of PVS, although the media were largely persuaded he had and variously reported the autopsy "backed Schiavo" in his longtime assertion of PVS. (Examples of this and other media misinformation will be provided in chapter 16.)

Thogmartin and consulting neuropathologist Dr. Stephen Nelson stated in the autopsy report that PVS is a clinical diagnosis made through physical examination of a living patient—not a pathological diagnosis made postmortem. Still, Nelson reported that pathological and anatomical findings, such as her shrunken brain and dilated ventricles, were "consistent" with the PVS diagnosis reached in the courts. He pointed out that Terri's brain weighed 615 grams, which is less than half of the expected tabular weight for an adult her age. He also pointed out that Terri's brain weighed less than her famous vegetative predecessor, Karen Ann Quinlan.

At the June 15, 2005, press conference held to announce the autopsy findings, Nelson went further in lending support to the court's diagnosis of PVS. He emphasized the pathological findings were "very consistent" with PVS and resisted this author's suggestion that perhaps they might also be consistent with MCS.

"Can you pathologically tell the difference between a person who was in PVS versus MCS?" I asked.

"No. There are no published studies on pathological correlations to the clinical diagnosis of MCS," Nelson responded.

"So you can't rule it out?" I persisted.

"I can't rule out the possibility she was in a MCS, but there's nothing in the pathological findings that is inconsistent with PVS," he said somewhat defensively, as though it were important to him to confirm the PVS diagnosis. Later he made the point that PVS was a "well-recognized, well-established" clinical diagnosis.

The significance of Nelson's admission that his pathological findings could be just as consistent with MCS as PVS was lost on the approximately three dozen other members of the media gathered.

In a critique of the autopsy posted on her weblog, ErosColoredGlasses .blogspot.com, physician and scientist Dr. Sherry Eros called it "medically reprehensible" for Nelson to have stated to the press that the autopsy results are either "consistent with" or "not inconsistent with" a PVS diagnosis without emphasizing "that it is illegitimate to use postmortem findings to retroactively make the clinical diagnosis of PVS." Eros further questioned the relevance of findings that are "consistent" with PVS.

"When the scientific and medical data are equally consistent with both x and non-x, as in the Schiavo case, then it is utterly meaningless to suggest . . . that it supports or establishes one or the other as true," she wrote. "It is only when the physician or the ME can use data to 'rule out' something, by finding that the data is 'not consistent with' such a diagnosis, or cause of death, that something meaningful has been said." Eros further derisively equated Nelson's phrase "very consistent" with the nonsensical "very pregnant."[11]

While deferring all the PVS questions to Nelson during the press conference, Thogmartin didn't steer completely clear of the political ramifications of his autopsy. "This damage was irreversible, and no amount of therapy or treatment would have regenerated the massive loss of neurons," he said in reference to the "profound atrophy" of Terri's brain. The statement was an endorsement of Schiavo's often-repeated contention and justification for not pursuing the therapy at Shands Hospital or any other aggressive rehabilitative therapy after Mediplex.

"From the first pleading that we filed in this case in 1998, we stated in the pleadings that Terri suffered massive and profound and irreversible brain damage," attorney Felos told reporters at his June 15, 2005, press conference. "For years, the treating physicians, the doctors, the responsible physicians, Mr. Schiavo, the courts, have said over and over again that there was no rehabilitation therapy or other therapy that could improve Mrs. Schiavo's condition. That was also found by the medical examiner."

Thogmartin's comment, however, was perceived by some to have been carefully crafted to lend support to Schiavo's claim. Specifically, critics called his reference to "regenerat[ing] the massive loss of neurons" a straw-man argument in that therapy is never intended to regenerate lost neurons but rather to nourish and retrain surviving neurons to pick up the slack.

In questioning the notion of "irreversible" brain damage, broadcast columnist Lionel Waxman in a postautopsy commentary on Terri Schiavo cited a 1999 study in which researchers at Carnegie Mellon University and the University of Pittsburgh discovered tremendous plasticity in the adult brain whereby it spontaneously "healed" or reorganized itself. Functional MRI scans done on the brains of two middle-aged stroke victims showed the brain function associated with language shifted away from the stroke-damaged area of the brain to the corresponding area on the undamaged side of the brain. This reorganization was observed in as few as three days and up to nine months after the brain damage.

"The new findings demonstrate extremely rapid adaptation in adult patients," researcher Keith Thulborn of the University of Pittsburgh Medical Center told the newswire. "While no one looks forward to a stroke, there is some comfort in knowing that we all carry around a set of thinking spare parts that know how to install themselves if the need arises."[12]

Critics additionally point out that while a severely shrunken brain would appear to connote total loss of function to the uninitiated, the intentional removal of significant amounts of brain matter is actually done as treatment for brain disorders. Hemispherectomy, which is the surgical removal of one of the two cerebral hemispheres of the brain, has a long neurosurgical history dating back to 1928, according to the Cleveland Clinic. A recent review of hemispherectomies performed at the Cleveland Clinic Pediatric Epilespy Surgery Center between January 1997 and December 2001 for the purpose of curing intractable seizures concluded that the treatment is a "successful and safe technique."[13]

A glaring omission in the autopsy report, noted by Eros, is the absence of discussion about how much the brain shrinkage is attributable to the dehydration process. In other words, in the same way Thogmartin was careful to point out that Terri's post-resuscitation potassium level, which he asserted was directly affected by the resuscitative efforts, isn't a reliable measure of her pre-arrest potassium level, the weight of Terri's brain after thirteen days of dehydration isn't a reliable measure of the weight of her brain prior to the removal of the feeding tube. As Eros cited, neurologists at the University of Münster, Germany, found dehydration significantly changes brain volume. Specifically, they reported in an article published in *Neurology* that "lack of fluid intake for 16 hours decreased brain volume by .55 percent."[14] Applying this rate of shrinkage to Terri's time element of thirteen days, which is admittedly an unscientific extrapolation of the data, suggests a minimum of 11 percent of the shrinkage of Terri's brain is attributable to the dehydration episode.

"The brain, no less than the rest of the body, is composed largely of water. Common sense dictates that there will be significant weight loss in all organs under circumstances of extreme long-term dehydration," Eros observed, adding that Karen Ann Quinlan died naturally of pneumonia and not by long-term dehydration.

Hammesfahr also criticized the perceived spin of the autopsy report. He emphasized that the medical examiners' findings detracted from the PVS diagnosis. Namely, large areas of Terri's brain were "relatively preserved," in the words of Nelson, and the critical areas were among those "relatively preserved." Nelson's analysis of Terri's brain tissue confirmed Maxfield's interpretation of the CT and SPECT scans that the frontal areas of the brain, the areas that deal with awareness and cognition, remained relatively intact.

"In fact, the relay areas from the frontal and front temporal regions of the brain, to the spinal cord and the brain stem, by way of the basal ganglia, were preserved," said Hammesfahr, adding that this explained Terri's "evident response" to her family members and others.

Jerri Lynn Ward, a Texas attorney who specializes in medical ethics, similarly noted the preservation of the critical areas. "The frontal temporal and temporal poles and insular-cortex demonstrated relative preservation," Ward said, reading from the autopsy report, during an interview on Joseph Farah's WorldNetDaily *RadioActive* radio talk show. "What this tells us is that her cortex retained function and that her brain was more normal in the area that controls higher-level thinking. . . . It's possible Terri was aware of everything being done to her—yet could do little to make people aware that she was there," Ward added.[15]

"As meaningless as this term 'relative preservation' may be, the preservation of these brain regions makes the autopsy 'consistent with' consciousness," echoed Eros. "This includes anything ranging from a minimally conscious state to some variant of the 'locked-in syndrome.'"

Hammesfahr also added, "Dr. Maxfield and myself both emphasized that she was a woman trapped in her body, similar to a child with cerebral palsy, and that was born out by the autopsy, showing greater injury in the motor and visual centers of the brain."

Perhaps the most striking postmortem finding in Thogmartin's autopsy is that he described Terri's occipital lobes, or vision centers, as "dead" and declared she was blind. Felos was quick to seize upon this finding as vindication, although he avoided using that precise word. "One of the most, I think, startling conclusions, not startling in the fact but helpful that it's been made, is his finding that Terri was blind," he said. "We have been saying for years and years and years the expert testimony showed that Terri's eye movements and apparent response to visual stimuli was a reflexive action. It was the result of a brain stem activity, which is consistent in PVS patients. She had no critical sight, and that was a finding by the medical examiner as well." Felos added, "So Mr. Schiavo was pleased to hear the hard science and evidence of those findings."

In their examinations, Hammesfahr and Maxfield both noted Terri appeared to suffer some degree of blindness. But they testified, along with countless other neurologists, physicians, and clinicians over fifteen years, that Terri exhibited some visual tracking and fixation. Even Cranford, who testified for Felos, admitted in court that Terri successfully tracked the multicolored balloon in the first of his three trials. The clinical evidence, therefore, suggested Terri retained some visual capacity at least up until her death. Perhaps the dehydration process may also factor into this finding. But it was not addressed by the autopsy report.

"Obviously, the pathologist's comments that she could not see were not borne out by reality, and thus his assessment must represent sampling error," suggested Hammesfahr. "Ultimately, based on the clinical evidence and the autopsy results, an aware woman was killed."

"Terri was dehydrated to death before our eyes. The moral shame of what happened is not erased because of Terri's level of disability," the Schindler family said in a statement released responding to the autopsy report. "No one would say that 'blind people' or 'brain-injured' people should be put to death. That would be an irresponsible and heartless position to take. Tragically, that is what happened to Terri. As a society, it seems that we have lost our compassion for the disabled."

9

At Death's Door for 1,815 Days

IN THE WEEKS FOLLOWING Judge Greer's original death order in February 2000, Michael Schiavo transferred his ward to Hospice Woodside, which is owned and operated by the Hospice of the Florida Suncoast. The move helped to seal her fate. Hospice patients, by definition, are on their deathbeds, and the end is expected within six months. Hospice staff leaders, workers, and volunteers are geared toward affording their patients a "good death." Countless Americans can testify that since hospice became prominent in the 1980s by virtue of Medicare coverage in 1983 and Medicaid in 1985, millions have benefited from hospice expertise in pain management and the emphasis on the emotional, psychological, psychosocial, and spiritual aspects of dying in their last days. For untold numbers of patients, if not for hospice, there would be no one to hold their hand as they take their last breaths.

Hospice operates according to Florida Statute 400.6605 and Chapter 58A-2 of the Florida Administrative Code. It is therefore statutorily required to provide services only to the terminally ill or to those patients whose medical prognosis establishes a life expectancy of six months or less, assuming the illness runs its normal course. The hospice approach to medical treatment recognizes that the impending death of an individual warrants a change in focus from curative care to palliative care, which is simply providing for the reduction or abatement of pain and suffering and allaying fears associated with dying.

The Florida regulations governing nursing-home care are more extensive than those governing hospice. While nursing-home patients must be seen by a physician at least once a month for the first ninety days after admission and bimonthly thereafter, there are no such requirements for hospice patients. While state regulations mandate a certain proportion of nursing staff to the patient population, the nursing-staff requirements are much more lax at hospice. At nursing homes, patients are required to have care plans that are reassessed every three months. At the time of Terri's transfer, a hospice was not required to have care plans for its patients. That became a requirement later that year. Some nursing homes object to withholding treatment or otherwise following advance directives in a manner that hastens death, either on moral grounds or out of fear of litigation. That is largely not the case at hospice.

The Department of Children and Families (DCF) requires hospice patients be certified by two physicians as terminally ill upon their admission. Terri Schiavo was not terminally ill, however. Even medical examiner Jon Thogmartin estimated she would likely have lived another ten years. Terri's treating physician Dr. Victor Gambone testified during the 2002 evidentiary hearing that Terri was fairly healthy in most every respect, but she was brain injured and diagnosed in PVS. While PVS is considered a permanent, or terminal condition, it's an exercise in semantics to characterize a patient with a terminal condition as terminally ill.

But that is precisely what was done. Gambone testified in court that Terri's transfer "definitely was not my decision" and that he placed Terri in hospice because Michael Schiavo had so instructed him. He insisted he did not sign the paperwork certifying she was terminal. In fact, the Internet news site *Empire Journal* reported the initial certification report on file for Terri's April 2000 transfer listed her "terminal condition" as "vegetative state" but was not signed. Instead, the file indicates there was "verbal confirmation" given on March 3, 2000, by Gambone with written certification on April 11, 2000, by Hospice medical director William Moore.[1] According to nurse activist and Schindler supporter Cheryl Ford, Terri's medical chart contained the following notation dated April 11, 2000: "Based on the patient's diagnosis and current condition, I expect this patient has a limited life expectancy of (six) months or less, if disease continues to take its usual course, and hereby certify patient as eligible for hospice." Ford said the statement bears signatures in the names of Gambone and Moore.

The day before Gambone's "verbal confirmation" certifying Terri's eligibility for hospice, Kevin Mort, the administrator at Palm Garden of Largo

Convalescent Center, where Terri had been residing, testified in a hearing before Judge Greer that the publicity of the case was causing disruptions at his facility. He described two occasions in which random visitors had walked into the nursing home with intentions of praying over Terri and sprinkling holy water. Mort also complained about the level of media attention being paid to Palm Garden, and in response to questioning by Felos, revealed that the Schindlers had met with a television crew at the nursing home on February 23, 2000, and on another occasion had accompanied a spiritual group seeking to perform a healing. This created conflicts for Mort, who had explicit instructions from Michael Schiavo to bar any visitors whom he hadn't approved. In his testimony, the administrator also alluded to a phone call from an individual threatening violence. Greer stopped him from divulging the details of that conversation due to its hearsay nature.

"My concern is, if that's going to continue, I do not know if we can continue to ensure her safety and the safety of the other residents in the facility," Mort told the court. "This is a highly emotional issue on both sides, I understand that. But the facility is being caught in the middle on this." The rationalization for transferring Terri to hospice was thus laid out.

The Schindlers lodged their objection to Terri's relocation to hospice in a motion to have her transferred to a registered nursing home, arguing the placement in hospice was "inappropriate," given that she wasn't terminally ill. They emphasized she would receive minimal medical treatment, as compared to the nursing-home environment, and feared the "conditions of care . . . could result in her demise." Specifically, they expressed concern the "facility may administer medications which may, in essence, hasten [her] death."

The motion was denied. And Terri remained at hospice.

During a meeting at hospice in January 2001, staff members discussed whether it was appropriate for Terri Schiavo to be there, and some suggested she should be discharged immediately. The conclusion reached, however, was that once the court order to remove her feeding tube was carried out, her death would be imminent and, therefore, with respect to the standing court order, Terri could be considered terminal.

At the time she took up residence at Hospice Woodside, the average length of a patient's stay was 78 days. Terri stayed there 1,815 days, give or take a few days in which she was hospitalized for treatment of an infection, before the court order to dehydrate her to death was carried out.

The Hospice of the Florida Suncoast is said to be the largest community-based, nonprofit hospice in the world, with revenues of more than $81 million in 2003, as reported by the *Empire Journal*.[2] It was originally incorporated in

1977 as the Elisabeth Kübler Ross Hospice, Inc., in honor of the psychiatrist and prolific author of the seminal book *On Death and Dying*. According to its Web site, the hospice is the only licensed hospice and health and human services system in Pinellas County, Florida. A staff of approximately one thousand people and an army of some three thousand volunteers serve roughly eighteen hundred patients daily. Program services are delivered through seven different nonprofit divisions. More than half of the patients served live in their own homes or those of their relatives.

Hospice's residential program at Woodside offers fifty-four beds and twenty-four-hour care in a homelike setting, according to company literature. For patients who can afford to pay, the annual fee is said to be approximately eighty thousand dollars. The agency reportedly provides nearly ten million dollars' worth of uncompensated care annually due to the fund-raising efforts of its foundation. Hospice Woodside Villas opened in 1997 for the terminally ill who have limited financial resources. Terri Schiavo resided in the Villas and was allowed to stay for free after 2002, when she was declared indigent, according to guardianship attorney Bushnell.

Judge Greer authorized Michael Schiavo's establishment of a "qualified under 65 disabled trust" on July 2, 2002, and all the remaining assets in Terri's guardianship were liquidated and transferred to the trust. Bushnell told the Associated Press that Medicaid picked up Terri's medical costs for the last couple of years of her life, which is a normal practice under pooled disabled trusts.[3] Hospice officials say the agency never received any Medicare or Medicaid reimbursement for Terri Schiavo's inpatient care. If they had, a case could be made for Medicaid and Medicare fraud. Under longstanding federal rules, Medicare and Medicaid beneficiaries must be certified as terminally ill by two doctors. Title 18, section 1861(dd) of the Social Security Act sets forth the provisions for hospice care, which, like the Florida statute, spells out the distinction between curative and palliative care offered to patients. In 1995 Medicare covered 65 percent of hospice services, according to statistics compiled by the National Hospice Organization.

In the late 1990s federal auditors with the inspector general's office of the Department of Health began cracking down on hospice facilities across the country for treating patients who weren't on the brink of death and getting reimbursed by Medicare for them. The program was called Operation Restore Trust. A federal audit performed at the Hospice of the Florida Suncoast in April 1995 suggested the agency frequently disregarded its stated corporate purpose, outlined in its articles of incorporation, which is to "provide a service for patients medically diagnosed as terminally ill." The audit found 364 patients who had been in hospice care for more than 210 days. Of those, 176 were found not to be terminal and therefore not eligible for reimbursement from Medicare. For another 118 of those cases, auditors were unable to conclude from the patients' medical records whether they had a terminal illness. As a result, the federal government initiated collection proceedings to recover $14.8 million from the agency in Medicare overbilling.

The Reverend Barry Howe, chairman of the Hospice of the Florida Suncoast board of directors in 1996, responded to a draft of the audit report in a letter to the regional inspector and offered different statistics. Howe stated that over the first six months of 1996, the average length of stay was ninety-eight days, and the median length of stay was forty days. He stressed his agency had met the published requirements of eligibility for hospice care in 100 percent of the cases reviewed by the auditor.

"No regulations exist mandating additional documentation in the Hospice record to support the certification decision as contrasted with the provision of services," Howe argued. He then made the case that Medicare dollars could be saved if the "terminal" requirement were to be expanded or scrapped.

"Research has shown that Medicare saves more than $1.50 for every dollar spent on hospice care. If you succeed in restricting use of hospice care to the period after there is no possibility that the patient will survive more than six months, the inevitable result will be that many more Medicare beneficiaries will receive more expensive, less appropriate care until they die or are referred to hospice care days or hours before death," he warned. "This outcome would reverse years of progress made by this hospice and others around the country."

"Many people come to us on death's door," Hospice of the Florida Suncoast chief executive Mary Labyak added in an interview with the *Wall Street Journal*. "There is overwhelming evidence that these people needed hospice care. We've reviewed every case, and we feel we would prevail in nearly all of them."[4] The *Empire Journal* reported Hospice of the Florida Suncoast spokesman Michael Bell recently said the matter had been resolved, but the 2004 annual report of HHS, released on December 31, 2004, indicated the collection action was still active.[5]

During a public forum exploring end-of-life issues at the Sunshine Senior Center in St. Petersburg in 1998, Hospice of the Florida Suncoast board member Martha Lenderman discussed the scrutiny her facility endures under the federal government over the "few terminally ill patients who live too long." She suggested one plan to avoid the scrutiny was to provide more uncompensated care. But she added there was fear that the federal government would perceive such a strategy as "an illegal inducement."

The Hospice of the Florida Suncoast was named in two class-action lawsuits filed in 2003 by former employee and donor Fluffy Cazalas on behalf of all donors. The first lawsuit alleged $7.6 million in contributions raised by the nonprofit agency were funneled into its for-profit subsidiary, a software company named Suncoast Solutions, without disclosure to the contributors of the diversion of funds. Cazalas worked in the IT department for two and a half years. She was brought in for the implementation of and training for a Suncoast Solutions software application distributed to approximately one hundred hospice facilities around the country. Cazalas claimed that she and others were paid by the nonprofit hospice but were working for the for-profit subsidiary. A second suit claimed the software company disseminated private and confidential patient and employee data, including names, identifiers, social security numbers, and sensitive information pertaining to HIV during the development of the software program. Specifically, according to Cazalas, the help screens within the application contained screen shots of actual records of patients at the Hospice of the Florida Suncoast. A memo documenting a meeting between Cazalas and a hospice supervisor, in which the supervisor apparently admits to using actual patient data and pledged the practice would stop, is posted on the Hospice Patients Alliance Web site.

The plaintiff further alleged in-kind donations to the Hospice of the Florida Suncoast had been diverted or utilized by individuals for personal gain. The *St. Petersburg Times* reported a couple who bequeathed almost all of their assets to Hospice of the Florida Suncoast—including their Clearwater home, as a gesture of gratitude as well as to help pay for the care of other terminally ill patients—may not have had their last wishes honored. Pinellas County property records showed the Hospice of the Florida Suncoast sold the property to one of its employees for ten thousand dollars less than its appraised value. According to the paper, Hospice of the Florida Suncoast officials initially denied a bargain had been made and asserted that the home sold for "close to or above its appraised value." When faced with evidence to the contrary in the appraisal, Hospice of the Florida Suncoast president Labyak still defended the sale by noting the agency saved money on the transaction because no agent's commission was involved. Then-board chairwoman Lenderman assured the newspaper that sales of future homes donated to Hospice of the Florida Suncoast would be monitored more closely.[6]

"There's definitely a lot of corruption there. It's not a good place at all," commented whistleblower Cazalas, who says she "feared for her safety" after the initial filing of the lawsuits, when she became the target of unknown assailants. "They rigged my car so that two tires blew at the same time while I was driving. There were multiple car chases where they would come after me, trying to run me off the road. They had someone following me with a video camera as an intimidation tactic." According to Cazalas, a trace of the license plate of her video-camera stalker revealed he was a private investigator who told her attorneys he had been hired by the hospice. Cazalas said statements from a mechanic regarding the tampering of her car and the information from the private investigator were turned over to the FBI. As for the lawsuits, they have all either been settled out of court or are on the verge of being settled, reported Cazalas.

"Things have changed so much in hospice since I started ten and a half years ago," Geraldyne Habermehl, manager of Hospice of the Sunrise Shore in Alpena, Michigan, commented to the *Washington Post* in 1998. "It was pure hospice then. Now it's dog-eat-dog, dirty, competitive fighting. It was a service before. Now it's a money deal." The newspaper exposed tactics employed by for-profit hospices in competing over the dying, including paying salespeople to recruit patients. The U.S. inspector general issued a "special fraud alert" warning that some hospices were suspected of paying kickbacks to nursing homes in order to "influence the referral of patients."[7]

Former Hospice of the Florida Suncoast nurse Christina Brundage lamented witnessing a similar transformation at the nonprofit agency during her tenure from 1995 to 2000. "In 1995, they were very patient oriented and nurse oriented. It was the nicest atmosphere that I've ever worked in. It changed in those five years and became much more money oriented," she said. "I remember one time hearing Mary Labyak at a monthly meeting saying, 'We have to corner the market.' And to me that was a turning point, when you start talking about dying as 'cornering the market.' And they began finding ways to try to get people into hospice under means other than terminal. So they had a palliative care program and were going into hospitals and trying to come up with patients there."

As she reflected, Brundage revealed those five years she worked at Hospice of the Florida Suncoast were the happiest of her life. She felt she was finally truly fulfilling her calling as a nurse. She described it as "the best job" she ever had. And that's saying a lot, given aspects about the agency's atmosphere she says she couldn't stomach as a devout Christian, like the predominance of New Age believers and required seminars on therapeutic touch and other nontraditional, more mystical practices.

"It had a cult atmosphere. It wasn't just you went to your job. They put a high price on loyalty and also on never talking to the media or anybody. They wanted to control every piece of information that came out—even if it was good," she added. "The organization thinks it's God and is heavy-handed with its employees."

Former employee Julie Wells vouched for that. She filed a lawsuit claiming Hospice of the Florida Suncoast fired her in retaliation for her complaints about some of its practices, including the release of patients' family names and identifiers without consent. Another nurse, who was fired during Terri Schiavo's last days, claimed her release was because she expressed support for keeping Terri alive.

"She's not physically ill, other than being brain damaged," Cybercast News Service quoted Nora Wagner as telling WPTF radio reporter Sarina Fazan on March 23, 2005. The nurse of thirty years, who had worked at the Hospice of the Florida Suncoast for two years as a contract employee, said she got into a "healthy debate" with her co-workers over the course of Terri's slow dehydration.

"They think it should be over," Wagner said. "They think she wouldn't . . . want to live like this, and they're just in agreement the tube should come out, that the husband is the guardian, and he should have the say." Wagner said her employment agency called her shortly after the debate and told her the hospice officials were upset with her comments and didn't want her back.

Other hospice workers were reportedly as conflicted as Wagner but did not speak up for fear of losing their jobs. One woman reportedly called Cazalas in tears after Terri's death. "She had an opportunity to actually see Terri's medical records and she called me crying and saying, 'They lied to us.' She saw in the records the notes from nurses about Terri's responsiveness," said Cazalas.

During her radio interview, Wagner emphasized Terri had been well cared for by the hospice staff, saying it was remarkable she didn't have bedsores or scars of healed bedsores despite having been bedridden for fifteen years.[8] Michael Schiavo and his attorney consistently pointed to this excellent care to refute the Schindler family's repeated complaints of neglect and abuse.

The Schindlers don't dispute Terri received quality maintenance care from her caregivers, but they have strenuously objected to the complete lack of rehabilitative and physical therapy since late 1991 that resulted in her severe contractures, discomfort, and physical deterioration. The Schindlers also battled with Hospice of the Florida Suncoast administrators over incidents they perceived as reflecting a desire on the part of the hospice to hasten Terri's death. Letters in Terri's medical records indicate the Schindlers' chronic frustration over Terri's suffering from repeated virus- and flu-like infections that lingered several months, during which the couple "pleaded" and "begged" for a doctor's examination or a chest x-ray.

"Your action of denying Terri a routine chest x-ray to determine if Terri may have contracted pneumonia, speaks volumes," Bob Schindler wrote in a March 18, 2003, letter to administrator Pat Sargent. "It appears you are being instructed to make critical medical decisions based on instructions from a person who is medically unqualified," he added in reference to guardian-husband Michael Schiavo. "I am confident we mutually share the same esteem for the medical profession and the ethics contained within such a highly regarded vocation. Therefore, Mary and I implore you to provide the routine medical care we are requesting for Terri."

Another bone of contention concerned the temperature in Terri's room. In November 2002 the parents reported consistently finding the thermostat set at 64 degrees Fahrenheit and finding Terri coughing and cold to the touch. They say they would ease the thermostat up only to find it back down in the 60s upon their return.

Bedridden patients are highly susceptible to pneumonia. And after a volley of letters, Schindler attorney Pat Anderson raised the issue in a court petition. The Hospice of the Florida Suncoast responded to the concern by placing a lockbox over the thermostat to keep the temperature set at 75 degrees.

Correspondence to industry watchdog Ron Panzer, with the Hospice Patients Alliance, purportedly from Hospice of the Florida Suncoast staff displayed a sense of hurt and anger among the nurses and aides over criticism waged at them due to the controversy surrounding the case. "The staff at Woodside and Mary Labyak showed nothing but compassion for all sides. Now, in appreciation for five years of compassionate and loving care for Terri, we are enduring bomb threats, safety issues and police stationed at the Hospice. How dare any of you judge us," one nurse's e-mail read.

At a press conference announcing Terri's death, attorney George Felos complimented the hospice workers, calling them "angels of mercy." He said, "It was just unbelievable to see the incredible amount of compassion, warmth and love and caring and skill which they used throughout this entire process to help Mrs. Schiavo have a death with dignity."

But according to former nurse Christina Brundage, most of her colleagues possess a "sheep" mentality in terms of following orders, which she said explains why few caregivers publicly expressed objection over the dehydration death of Terri. Still, Brundage applauded her fellow hospice nurses who go into patient homes, and she stressed they do their jobs well and provide excellent care with a lot of heart and soul. She said they were well trained to treat every symptom and to try to make patients feel as good as possible so they can live their lives—what time they had left—as normally as possible. Brundage said the training included comprehensive instruction on pain management.

"We were always told, you're not taking care of a patient, you're taking care of a family," she said. That care includes bringing in equipment the family can't afford, including a hospital bed, attending to pain and whatever symptoms the patient has, and talking to the family and the patient, sounding them out on how they perceive the situation and coaching them on what to expect.

The modern hospice movement embodied the ethos espoused by its founder, Dame Cicely Saunders, who urged a middle path between two undesirable approaches in caring for the terminally ill: aggressive, high-tech curative care and death by euthanasia. The principle doctrine of hospice, which Brundage learned in her training, was "death should neither be hastened nor postponed." Hospice, therefore, is seen as the cornerstone of "death with dignity," in which patients have control over the quality of life they experience while they're dying. Such self-determination is the foundation upon which Derek Humphry builds his promotion of "assisted dying" and euthanasia, however, as a Hastings Center Report pointed out. In Humphry's view, the ultimate expression of self-determination is "self-deliverance," or "assisted dying."

"Many terminally ill patients use the outstanding and caring programs of hospice. Then, quietly with the assistance of a compassionate physician who has provided them with the appropriate medicines, they privately end their own lives at the time of their choosing," Humphry's successor at the Hemlock Society, John Pridonhoff, asserted. The passage of the Hemlock-backed Death with Dignity Act in Oregon ushered in a new level of collaboration between hospice and Hemlock, reports the Hastings Center.[9] Former Florida Hemlock Society president Mary Hudson pinpoints 1992 as a pivotal year for her state.

"I've known hospice nurses to quit in 1992 when it was decided that hospice could abandon tube feedings in patients who wanted it to be stopped. Several nurses just quit because they didn't think it was right. I don't know how those particular individuals feel now, but I think you'll find that hospice nurses are on board, as are the doctors," said Hudson.

A former hospice nurse herself, Hudson explained the reasoning behind the shift in attitudes. "There are some people who see something terrible coming: ALS, Alzheimer's, MS, or Parkinson's," she continued. "There's going to be ten years of constant downhill, being a burden to yourself and others, and lower quality of life, and patients don't want it. And I don't consider that suicide." She contrasted suicide, which she defined as a "permanent solution to a temporary problem" with "rational, hastened death" as a "permanent solution to a permanent problem."

Former nurse Christina Brundage also witnessed hospice's embrace of hastened death. She wrote an open letter about an "illegal euthanasia" she had recently observed in a different hospice facility, and it was posted on the Hospice Patients Alliance Web site. She described her continued visitation of a terminally ill patient (she called him "Joe") as a friend after his condition deteriorated to the extent he required the support of stronger male nurses and ceased to be her patient. Joe's wife had admitted him into a hospice facility after "sheet burn" developed to a severe level in need of medical attention. Although he had eaten a healthy breakfast of scrambled egg and a full glass of Carnation Instant Breakfast without difficulty the morning of his admission, once situated, the hospice staff forbade Joe's wife to feed him or bring him any food or water "because of the danger of aspiration." The wife called Brundage alarmed that her husband was also not being given his antibiotics and his fever was escalating. Brundage paid a visit to Joe's facility, where she asked the charge nurse why her friend wasn't receiving antibiotics, food, or water. "She said it was their policy," wrote Brundage. "She said she was just following routine practice to deny food, water, and antibiotics." Instead, Joe was getting twenty milligrams of liquid morphine every eight hours.

"The next day," Brundage wrote, "the same charge nurse came in and when Ellen asked if he couldn't have some water, the charge nurse said, 'You don't seem to be comfortable about his dying.' She used the word *dying* three times right in front of him. She said she would have someone else come and talk to her because, 'You're not getting it.'" Two days later Joe slipped into a coma. The staff responded to his rapid breathing, cold extremities, and minimal urine output by administering morphine. The doctor's order was for two to six milligrams "PRN," or as needed. Joe died that night.

"I think we did a really wonderful job at hospice. But if people start thinking we're bumping them off, it's going to change all that wonderful feeling to suspicion," Brundage concluded. "As a movement it's got noble goals. But it's been taken over by the George Soros mentality I think. It's sad because people dying don't need the extra stress of wondering if people are going to hasten their death."

"The killing of patients in hospice is extremely common; however, the industry never talks about it," says hospice watchdog Ron Panzer. "Hospice nurses and doctors know it goes on, and if they deny it, they're lying." On his Web site Panzer offers testimony from four families who witnessed the hastening of death of a loved one similar to that described by Brundage. In 1999 coroners in Volusia County, Florida, ruled nineteen patient deaths in hospice and ICU units were suspicious and reportedly due to morphine overdoses. After prosecutors refused to press charges, a specially appointed commission investigated the matter and ruled the deaths were due to natural causes.

Panzer expressed his concern about the role played by hospice in a quality-of-life era: "The practice of enrolling chronically disabled patients into hospice endangers all disabled citizens of the United States and directly violates their Constitutional rights to life, liberty, and the pursuit of happiness. The disabled are not so much afraid of getting anthrax or being shot; they are afraid that society will toss them away like a used tissue and kill them. The disabled are terrorized by those holier-than-thou self-proclaimed bioethicists who have no morality and no sense of humanity."

MARY LABYAK'S affiliation with the Hospice of the Florida Suncoast dates back to its founding in 1977 when she began as a patient volunteer. She stepped up to chief executive officer in 1983 and has held that position ever since. Florida Department of State Division of Corporation records reveal Labyak also served on the board of directors at the hospice between 1991 and 1999. She is also a leader in the national hospice industry, having served as chairperson of the National Hospice Organization (NHO), now known as National Hospice and Palliative Care Organization (NHCPO), and a national director and treasurer of NHCPO. On its Web site, NHPCO explains many hospice care programs added palliative care to their names in recent years to better reflect the range of care and services they provide. NHPCO is the largest nonprofit membership organization, representing hospice and palliative care programs and professionals in the United States.

On the day Terri Schiavo's feeding tube was removed for the second time and while Florida legislators and Governor Jeb Bush were scrambling to intervene, the NHPCO issued a press release on October 15, 2003, to "clarify the role of Hospice" in the controversy and to deflect criticism over its being caught in the middle: "Hospice provides pain and symptom management and a range of psychosocial services and spiritual support to patients and their families through the duration of life-limiting illness. Hospice does not make decisions for patients or families, nor sit in judgment of their choices. . . . Neither the specific hospice or NHPCO is involved in the legal proceedings associated with the patient or the decision to remove the feeding tube." The statement also took the opportunity to advocate advance directives. As debate over Terri Schiavo continued to escalate, NHPCO posted a set of "talking points" on its Web site, presumably to help affiliates properly handle media inquiries into the Terri Schiavo saga. The suggestions include:

> **Theme:** Hospice not involved in legal issues
> **Message:** Neither the specific hospice provider nor NHPCO is involved in the legal proceedings or feeding decisions associated with this case.
> **Supporting Point:** Hospice does not make decisions for patients or families, nor sit in judgment of their choices.

In a press release posted on its Web site, the Hospice of the Florida Suncoast includes the praise it received from the Robert Wood Johnson Foundation, which cited the agency in 2002 as an "island of hope in a sea of mediocrity" in the foundation's first nationwide report card on care at the end of life.

"Our community," observed Mary Labyak in response to the honor, "is unique in that care partners from all walks of life—including health and human service providers, health care organizations and community volunteers—have worked together for twenty-five years to provide comfort and compassion to those at the end of life and their families."

Over the decades the agency has amassed considerable political clout. The list of names of those who have served on the agency's board of directors or its community advisory board over the years is a veritable who's who of politicians and other Tampa Bay–area movers and shakers, including Congressman Michael Bilirakis, his son and state representative Gus Bilirakis, longtime county commissioner Barbara Sheen Todd, Circuit Court Judge John Lenderman, his sister and former state social services supervisor Martha Lenderman, former Pinellas County Sheriff-turned state representative Everett Rice, Clearwater cardiologist Lofty Basta, and prominent right-to-die attorney George Felos, who sat on the board for nine years (according to his promotional literature).

According to the Florida Department of State Division of Corporations, the records filed indicating Felos's departure from the board are dated March 26, 2001. In addition, Felos served as chairman of the board of directors from 1996 through March 8, 1999. Panzer speculated Felos's presence on the board of directors in the years leading up to and at the time of Terri's transfer likely enabled some rule bending in terms of the Hospice of the Florida Suncoast's charter and its statutory mandate. (Repeated requests for interviews with Felos were declined, and numerous calls to Hospice of the Florida Suncoast were not returned.)

Felos also provides pro bono legal help to Hospice of the Florida Suncoast patients and their families. His affiliation with the hospice began in 1991, when he became a patient volunteer. As he describes in *Litigation as Spiritual Practice,* the hospice movement first appeared in the late 1960s and 1970s as an alternative to overzealous doctors who viewed death as "the enemy"; hospice was about "retrieving death from the profane and returning it to the sacred." The same force that created hospice now propels the right-to-die movement, he said. Over the years at Hospice of the Florida Suncoast, he claims he acquired a respect for the "profound mystical process" that is death.

"The volunteer sits with a dying patient once or twice a week, giving the caregiver time for relief. I found that work very satisfying," he remarked in an interview with *GreekNews.* "When somebody walks into my office, and they say their spouse is dying and they have to make an end-of-life medical choice, I don't care what their status or persona is; when you meet people like that, you are relating to them in a very core way. . . . When you're invited into someone's home and are there to help them through a profound mystical process like death, it's an honor and a privilege. Just the feeling that you've helped somebody through that process is very rewarding."

His positive outlook on death was put to the test in August 1995 with the sudden, tragic death of his father and law partner. According to news accounts, James George Felos died at age seventy-three from injuries he sustained in a fluke car accident in his own driveway. Florida Highway Patrol records cited by the *St. Petersburg Times* indicate he was standing outside his car in the driveway of his Palm Harbor home while his wife backed past him in her car. Jean Felos had left the passenger door open on her car, and as she passed her husband's car, her door hit that car and bent backward, pinning him between the two cars. Mrs. Felos reportedly panicked and hit the accelerator instead of the brake, causing her car to quickly back into the street, dragging her husband along with her. She then backed over her husband, according to troopers interviewed by the paper.[10]

George Felos has contemplated his own death. In his book he describes a bizarre experience he had in which he believes his mental powers caused the airliner he was traveling in to nearly crash. He writes that his idle thought: "I wonder what it would be like to die right now?" accompanied with visualization was met by the plane losing its trajectory and slowly dipping nose-down into a free fall, as if it had run out of fuel—just as he pictured in his mind. As he became conscious of the unsettled passengers around him, he shifted his thoughts and the plane stabilized. Twenty minutes later the pilot announced the aircraft's autopilot program had mysteriously ceased to function. "At that instant a clear, distinctly independent and slightly stern voice said to me, 'Be careful what you think. You are more powerful than you realize.' In quick succession I was startled, humbled and blessed by God's admonishment," he writes.[11]

Raised in the Greek Orthodox Church, the divorced father of a teenaged son described his spirituality as a syncretistic mix of Christianity, Buddhism, Hinduism, and Native American ceremonial practices. He is a diligent yoga practitioner and instructor who frequently invites friends over to his home to chant "I am that I am . . . I am that I am . . ." while he plays a tune on his harmonium, according to the *St. Petersburg Times.*

"We're not the body. We're not the mind. We're not our thoughts. We're not our emotions," said Felos. "In essence, we're spiritual beings."[12]

"We are made in the image of God," he wrote in his book. "This does not refer to having two arms, two legs, and a head. It means that in some way we naturally possess the attributes and qualities of the Universal Consciousness."[13] As such, Felos believes he has the ability to "soul speak" to people in vegetative states. He describes employing the skill to discern his first right-to-die client's wishes. At the age of eighty-nine, Estelle Browning suffered a stroke in 1986 and lay in a nursing home for more than a year before Felos met her. Although she had signed an advance directive about a year prior to the stroke specifically indicating she did not want to be kept on life support—including a feeding tube—if death were imminent, the nursing home refused to withdraw the nasogastric tube because she was not terminal. Browning's only surviving relative and former housemate hired Felos to petition the court to remove the feeding tube. Felos expressed initial discomfort over the prospective life-and-death decision.

"We would never absolutely know if Mrs. Browning indeed retained, underneath that impaired exterior, cognizance of her dilemma. Did I want the responsibility of implementing a choice that perhaps was no longer hers?" he writes. The bedside encounter that followed apparently eased his qualms:

> I stared as far into her eyes as I could, hoping to sense some glimmer of understanding, some hint of awareness. The deeper I dove, the darker became

> the blue, until the blue became black of some bottomless lake. "Mrs. Browning, do you want to die? . . . Do you want to die?"—I near shouted as I continued to peer into her pools of strikingly beautiful but incognizant blue. It felt so eerie. Her eyes were wide open and crystal clear, but instead of the warmth of lucidity, they burned with the ice of expressionlessness. . . . As I continued to stay beside Mrs. Browning at her nursing home bed, I felt my mind relax and my weight sink into the ground. I began to feel light-headed as I became more reposed. Although feeling like I could drift to sleep, I also experienced a sense of heightened awareness. As Mrs. Browning lay motionless before my gaze, I suddenly heard a loud, deep moan and scream and wondered if the nursing home personnel heard it and would respond to the unfortunate resident. In the next moment, as this cry of pain and torment continued, I realized it was Mrs. Browning. I felt the mid-section of my body open and noticed a strange quality to the light in the room. I sensed her soul in agony. As she screamed I heard her say, in confusion, "Why am I still here . . . why am I still here?" My soul touched hers and in some way I communicated that she was still locked to her body. I promised I would do everything in my power to gain the release her soul cried for. With that the screaming immediately stopped. I felt like I was back in my head again, the room resumed its normal appearance, and Mrs. Browning, as she had throughout this experience, lay silent.

Felos acknowledges his experience with Browning was "highly subjective" and that a persuasive argument could be made that it was the product of a "willing imagination" serving a need to justify the petition to remove her feeding tube, which would result in her death.

"My communication with Mrs. Browning was real, and of course you must choose for yourself whether or not to believe it—and it really doesn't matter to me if you do or don't," he concludes.[14]

Curiously, Felos determined Browning was "more than vegetative" because "she appeared able at times to interact with her environment in a rudimentary way" and medical records and nursing home aides reported she occasionally smiled and "made infrequent utterances 'in an attempt to communicate.'" Yet when the Schindlers, physical therapists, and various nursing home aides attributed the same behaviors to Terri Schiavo in her medical records and publicly, Felos never entertained the possibility that she, like Browning, was "more than vegetative." And he repeatedly declined to answer reporters' questions as to whether he was able to "soul speak" to Terri.

10

Right to Die vs. Not Dead Yet

As a teenager, Terri Schiavo viewed a made-for-television movie about the plight of Karen Ann Quinlan. The New Jersey resident was only twenty-one years old when a mix of alcohol and drugs caused her to cease breathing for at least two fifteen-minute intervals on the night of April 15, 1975. Friends attempted mouth-to-mouth resuscitation but could not revive her. By the time Quinlan arrived at Newton Memorial Hospital, her temperature had soared to 100 degrees, her pupils were unreactive, and she was unresponsive even to deep pain. The young woman was hooked up to a respirator that sustained her breathing until her father won permission a year later from the New Jersey Supreme Court to have it disconnected. She died naturally nearly nine years later from pneumonia.

Quinlan represented a landmark legal case in the right-to-die movement. Expert witnesses—including Dr. Fred Plum, who had helped coin the phrase "persistent vegetative state" four years earlier—testified before the court that severe brain damage had left Quinlan in that paradoxical "wakeful unconscious" state without any cognitive function. Court testimony indicated she was emaciated by the time of the trial, having lost forty pounds, and was undergoing a "continuing deteriorative process." She grimaced and made "stereotyped cries and sounds" associated with brain-stem function characteristic of the vegetative state. Still in its infancy, PVS was even less understood than it is today. As a result of her diagnosis, physicians gave Quinlan no more than a year to live. Subsequently, the court ruled in favor of terminating her life support—the respirator and a feeding tube—over the objections of her doctors and the state attorney, who claimed interests in defending the right of the physician to administer medical treatment according to his best judgment as well as the preservation of the sanctity of human life.

"We have no hesitancy in deciding," the New Jersey Supreme Court judges declared, "that no external compelling interest of the state could compel Karen to endure the unendurable, only to vegetate a few measurable months with no realistic possibility of returning to any semblance of cognitive or sapient life. We perceive no thread of logic distinguishing between such a choice on Karen's part and a similar choice which, under the evidence in this case, could be made by a competent patient terminally ill, riddled by cancer and suffering great pain; such a patient would not be resuscitated or put on a respirator . . . not be kept against his will on a respirator."

The state high court also found Quinlan's unwritten right of privacy implied in the Fourteenth Amendment to the Constitution encompassed a decision to decline medical treatment. After admitting it could not discern Quinlan's supposed choice to live or die from the testimony describing conversations she had with friends prior to her brain injury, the court concluded Quinlan's right of privacy could be asserted on her behalf by her father, who had been appointed guardian.

Terri Schiavo's childhood friend Diane Meyer testified she had watched a compelling movie about Quinlan in 1982, which was six years after Quinlan's respirator and feeding tube were removed and three years before her death. Meyer said that the movie prompted her to tell Terri a cruel joke about Quinlan in which she derogatively referred to the woman as a "vegetable." This sparked a sharp rebuke from Terri: "Where there's life, there's hope." The irony that Terri Schiavo would find herself similarly diagnosed as vegetative less than a decade later and would also have her life support removed in accordance with wishes expressed by her guardian is profound.

Unbeknownst to her, Terri Marie Schiavo joined the company of Karen Ann Quinlan and Nancy Beth Cruzan. This trio of women in their twenties, each beset by severe brain injury, collectively advanced the right of Americans to refuse medical treatment deemed burdensome and/or demeaning in order to hasten or usher death in the manner and at the time of their choosing—summarized as the right to die. In *Cruzan v. Director, Missouri Department of Health,* the question of whether to terminate artificial life support dealt solely with the removal of a feeding tube, which was pertinent in the case of Terri Schiavo. *Cruzan* was the first right-to-die case to be heard by the U.S. Supreme Court.

Late on the night of January 11, 1983, twenty-five-year-old Nancy Cruzan flipped her car on a curvy country road in the Ozarks of southwest Missouri. She was thrown thirty-five feet from the vehicle and landed face down in a ditch alongside the road. Paramedics who reached Cruzan estimated she had not been breathing for six to twenty minutes. They declared her "Code Blue. Clinical Save." She was revived, put on a respirator, and transported to the hospital. In the ensuing weeks Cruzan recovered her ability to breathe on her own, and the respirator was unplugged. A nasogastric feeding tube, which ran up her nose and down her throat, was removed, and its long-term cousin, the PEG tube, was surgically implanted in her stomach.

"I signed the consent form to begin the artificial feeding," Joe Cruzan, Nancy's father, said during a *Frontline* interview on PBS. "Looking back on it, I would like to have let her go that night because Nancy died—our Nancy died that night. We've got her body left, but she has no dignity whatsoever there, and she was a very, very proud, independent person. And you would see what was left there and you wondered why. Why? What's the purpose in this?"[1]

Months later Cruzan was moved to the Missouri Rehabilitation Center in Mount Vernon. After four years of regular visits to the rehabilitation center, Joe and Joyce Cruzan asked that their daughter's feeding tube be removed. But the medical staff refused, partly due to personal and professional conflicts with the idea, partly out of fear of litigation. The couple was told they needed a court order, so they contacted the American Civil Liberties Union, retained a lawyer, and petitioned the Jasper County Circuit Court. Organizations like the American Medical Association, American Association of Neurological Surgeons, American College of Surgeons, and the Missouri State Medical Society weighed in on the case on the side of the parents. Meanwhile, the National Right to Life Committee, the International Task Force on Euthanasia and Assisted Suicide, and disabilities-rights groups backed the state of Missouri, which took the customary position of defending the preservation of life.[2]

After a three-day hearing, the trial court ruled in favor of the parents, finding Cruzan's fundamental right of liberty under the state and federal constitutions permitted her to refuse or direct the withholding or withdrawal of "artificial death-prolonging procedures" and that Cruzan's comment to a former housemate prior to her incapacitation that she did not want to live as a "vegetable" was indicative of a current wish to die.

The state supreme court reversed the decision, however. While recognizing the right to refuse treatment as embodied in the common-law doctrine of informed consent, the state high court questioned its applicability to the Cruzan case. The judges also disagreed that the state and federal constitutions embodied a right to refuse medical treatment, and they were further swayed that Missouri living will statutes favored the preservation of life in the absence of "clear and convincing evidence" of a patient's wishes.

On June 25, 1990, the U.S. Supreme Court affirmed the appellate court. Chief Justice William Rehnquist wrote in the Court's opinion that the parents' wishes were outweighed by the state's interest in the preservation and protection of human life. The justices concluded Missouri was entitled to guard against potential abuses by surrogates who may not act to protect the patient, and the appellate court's "clear and convincing evidence" standard was appropriate in cases involving life-and-death decisions. The Court additionally opined the state should not be called upon to make judgments about the "quality" of a particular individual's life. The High Court recognized the common-law doctrine of informed consent as greatly encompassing the right of a competent individual to refuse medical treatment, stating, "For the purposes of this case, we assumed that the United States Constitution would grant a competent person a constitutionally protected right to refuse lifesaving hydration and nutrition." While the ruling did not help Cruzan, it did fuel the right-to-die movement.

On December 14, 1990, the case went back before the state judge, who newly applied the "clear and convincing standard" and ordered the feeding tube removed. Nancy Cruzan died in the hospice unit of the hospital 12 days later. Joe Cruzan calculated it was 1,206 days since their initial request to remove the feeding tube.

"There have been times that, you know, I've thought, 'How can you murder your own child?'" he said in the PBS interview nearly two years later. "Our decision was based on what we felt that Nancy would want and that's all we have to justify. What—if the decision's wrong, if we're playing God, then I'll have to live with that, and I'm willing to."[3]

More than a decade later, Florida Probate Judge George Greer applied the "clear and convincing evidence" standard to *Schiavo v. Schindler*, the adversary action over the feeding tube within *In re Guardianship of Schiavo*, and also came up with a right-to-die ruling. But while the U.S. Supreme Court justices specifically found that Cruzan's observations about not wanting to live as a vegetable did not necessarily equate with a desire to have artificial hydration and nutrition removed, Greer made the mental leap to the conclusion that Terri's wishes were to have her feeding tube removed and to die of dehydration. (This ruling will be examined in depth in chapter 13.) What also distinguishes *Schiavo* from *Cruzan* is the fact that Terri's wishes were disputed among her family members.

From *Quinlan* to *Cruzan*, the right to die evolved from the removal of a respirator from a patient deemed terminal, using the "substituted judgment" of the guardian, to removal of a feeding tube from a nonterminal vegetative patient, according to the "specific intent" principle, in which her undisputed, pre-incapacitation oral expressions were tested against a "clear and convincing evidence" standard. The right-to-die cause further advanced in *Schiavo* to the removal of a feeding tube plus orally administered fluids from a nonterminal patient whose medical condition was widely disputed and whose wishes were hotly contested but measured against a "clear and convincing evidence" standard amid overtures of a "best interest" standard.

It is interesting to note that the medical community in particular, and American society in general, underwent a transformation in values over the thirty years between *Quinlan* and *Schiavo* so that, whereas the physicians refused to honor the parents' request to withdraw Quinlan's respirator in 1975 and Cruzan's feeding tube in 1987, doctors were encouraging Michael Schiavo to remove his wife's feeding tube by 1998 and were dismissive, and in some instances derisive, of the Schindler family's efforts to keep her alive in recent years. In the minds of many, the notion of the sanctity of life—that all human life is a gift from God and therefore is intrinsically sacred—is now viewed as anachronistic in an age where the right of self-determination pervades all aspects of life, including death.

Fox News judicial analyst and author Judge Andrew Napolitano blames the watershed U.S. Supreme Court abortion ruling in *Roe v. Wade* for the metamorphosis in America's mind-set about the right to die. "We look at death differently. We have become a culture of death," Napolitano stated in an interview on the cable network program *The O'Reilly Factor.* "Since *Roe v. Wade* and the cases and the legislation that have followed it, it has become too easy for judges to say, 'Oh, she wanted to die. Let her die.'"[4]

Indeed, the stratagems and talking points employed in the abortion movement were recycled for the euthanasia and right-to-die causes. While pre-1973 abortion proponents argued abortions took place in dark alleys, and therefore it was incumbent upon government to erect safeguards, right-to-die proponents similarly maintained legalization of physician-assisted suicide and euthanasia was needed to standardize the underground practice and protect physicians from prosecution. But the promotion of death as public policy in America can be traced back nearly a century before *Roe v. Wade.*

In 1900 the fundamental Judeo-Christian principle of the sanctity of life, and the associated Commandment "Thou shalt not kill," reflected in the original framework of American society, was eschewed as "unreasonable dogma" by physician William Duncan McKim, who perceived it as a barrier to "saving civilization" from drunkards, criminals, and people with disabilities, as author Ian Dowbiggin describes in *A Merciful End: The Euthanasia Movement in Modern America.* McKim and others who pushed for a "natural right to a natural death" sowed the seeds for an organized euthanasia movement that came to the fore in the 1930s amid the philosophies of eugenics, positivism, social Darwinism, and scientific naturalism.[5] Dowbiggin found the same forces that promoted eugenics were also behind birth control and abortion.

By the time the Reverend Charles Potter founded the Euthanasia Society of America (ESA) in New York in 1938, the American Eugenics Society had succeeded in passing eugenic sterilization laws in forty-one states. According to Dowbiggin, who culled his information from the files, minutes, and records of the ESA and its leadership, Potter believed the legalization of euthanasia would be the crowning glory to a life already dedicated to eugenics, birth control, world peace, the emancipation of women, and the defeat of Christian fundamentalism. Dowbiggin wrote that Potter viewed people with disabilities as needing to be "mercifully executed by [the] lethal chamber" and believed "social cowardice" explained their continued existence. Undeterred by the mounting backlash over the secret Nazi euthanasia program administered to more than two hundred thousand individuals with disabilities in Germany, ESA boldly drafted legislation in 1943, with the help of birth-control activist Jean Burnett Tompkins, to legalize involuntary euthanasia for "idiots, imbeciles, and congenital monstrosities."[6] American psychiatrist and ESA president Dr. Foster Kennedy suggested it was morally acceptable to "kill with kindness."

Not surprisingly, the ESA created a furor among the disabled and their advocates, who would thereafter eye proponents of the right to die with suspicion and distrust. In truth, certain elements of the modern-day right-to-die movement espouse positions not too dissimilar from their eugenic predecessor. In 1998 Derek Humphry, who founded the pro-euthanasia organization Hemlock Society, promoted what he called "a duty to die" while complaining that America's elderly were "putting a strain on the health care system." Humphry suggested physician-assisted suicide could solve the "economic toll" of the dying experience.[7] Humphry also addressed the emotional toll of death by suggesting elderly couples should have the right to commit double suicide to avoid bereavement after one spouse became terminally ill.[8] Although Humphry proposed *voluntary* euthanasia—as opposed to involuntary—his ideas were perceived by disability rights advocates to connote a "dangerous" bias in favor of the able in society over the disabled or infirm. Such a bias spawned the Nazi killings, they pointed out.

The duty concept wasn't an original idea. A year earlier, John Hardwig of the department of philosophy at the University of Tennessee posed the question: Is there a duty to die? "We like to think of modern medicine as all triumph with no dark side at all. Our medicine saves many lives and enables most of us to live longer," Hardwig wrote in an article published in a report of the Hastings Center. "The costs—and these are not merely monetary—of prolonging our lives when we are no longer able to care for ourselves are often staggering. If further medical advances wipe out many of today's 'killer diseases'—cancers, heart attacks, strokes, ALS, AIDS, and the rest—then one day most of us will survive long enough to become demented or debilitated. These developments could generate a fairly widespread duty to die."

It is no coincidence the rhetoric sounds the same, according to Rita Marker, head of the International Task Force on Euthanasia and Assisted Suicide. "All of the major right-to-die organizations have their roots in attempts to legalize not only assisted suicide, but also euthanasia," she wrote in an article published in *Philanthropy Magazine* in 2001. "Like Eliza Doolittle, they have become respectable over time and no longer wear euthanasia advocacy on their sleeves," she added with a reference to the poor-street-vendor-turned-high-society-heroine in the musical *My Fair Lady*.

Marker proceeded to point out the best funded of the modern-day movement, Choice in Dying, which recently closed its doors, was really a reincarnation of the controversial ESA. According to New York State corporate records, the ESA changed its name to Society for the Right to Die in 1975, then to National Council on Death and Dying in 1991, and finally to Choice in Dying in 1992. In 2000 Choice began "evolving into a new organization" called Partnership for Caring. The mission of the organization, however, as outlined in its articles of incorporation filed with the state, was never amended during the name changes. Marker quoted the corporate purpose on record with the state in 2001: "To disseminate information to the public by all lawful means of the nature, purpose, and need of euthanasia, and to foster its general adoption. By the term 'euthanasia' is to be understood the lawful termination of human life by painless means for the purpose of avoiding unnecessary suffering and under adequate safeguards."[9]

In 1968 Florida lawmaker Dr. Walter W. Sackett proposed the first right-to-die bill based on a living will document that had been created by ESA in 1949 and was reintroduced in 1967 by human rights lawyer Luis Kutner.[10] The proposed legislation provided for the removal of care from severely retarded persons in state hospitals. The *San Francisco Examiner* reported that Sackett estimated "$5 billion could be saved over the next half century if the state's mongoloids were permitted merely to succumb to pneumonia." The report caught the attention of the National Association for Retarded Children, which moved to block it and vowed continued resistance for any future measures. Although the bill was defeated, Choice in Dying listed the introduction of this legislation in 1968 among its legal achievements under a section titled "A Historical Perspective" on its Web site.[11]

"Today when mercy killing is discussed, it is couched in euphemisms—words of gentleness or the language of rights. Titles of euthanasia advocacy groups contain words like 'compassion,' 'choice,' and 'dignity,'" Marker continued, asserting that the descriptors "right to die" and "death with dignity" applied to the modern-day movement are also euphemisms. As Marker and attorney Wesley Smith described in an article posted on the International Task Force's Web site, language has always been a tool for the physician-assisted suicide and euthanasia proponents. Back in 1939 ESA treasurer Charles Nixdorff took issue with a *New York Times* article reporting on the society's proposed euthanasia legislation for its use of the words *killing* and *death*. He requested the paper describe euthanasia as "merciful release."[12] It didn't. The bill failed miserably.

"Euthanasia proponents have learned a lot about public relations in the six decades since the Euthanasia Society of America made that first attempt to gain legislative approval for mercy killing. One lesson they have heeded is that all social engineering is preceded by verbal engineering," Marker and Smith observed.[13]

Derek Humphry is an expert on verbal engineering. In 1980 he founded the Hemlock Society in Santa Monica, California, with the goal of achieving "assisted dying" in America. On his Web site, he explained his choice of wording: "I have struggled for twenty years to popularize the term 'self-deliverance,' but it is an uphill battle with a news media which is in love with the words 'assisted suicide' and 'suicide.' They are headline grabbers. Also, we have to face the fact that the law calls all forms of self-destruction 'suicide.' Additionally, all medical journals today refer to 'assisted suicide' in their papers."

Whatever it's called, Humphry says suicide is justified under the following conditions:

1. Advanced terminal illness that is causing unbearable suffering—combined physical and psychic—to the individual despite good medical care. This is the most common reason to seek an early end.

(And as Oregon research has shown, being a burden to others is an additional factor.)

2. Total loss of quality of life due to protracted, incurable medical conditions.
3. Grave physical handicap, which is so restricting that the individual cannot, even after due consideration, counseling and re-training, tolerate such a limited existence. This is a fairly rare reason for suicide—most impaired people cope remarkably well with their afflictions—but there are some disabled who would, at a certain point, rather die.[14]

While suicide is no longer a crime in any state, there are laws and policies in place to prevent suicide and suicide assistance. Physician-assisted suicide is only legal in Oregon.

"You cannot ask to be killed. Punishments for this are usually 'life' and for assisted suicide, fines or up to fourteen years in prison," Humphry wrote in an essay posted on his Web site. "It is this catch-all prohibition which ERGO [Euthanasia Research and Guidelines Organization] and other right-to-die groups wish to change. In a caring society, under the rule of law, we claim that there must be exceptions for the hopelessly ill after all other avenues have been exhausted." While many modern-day right-to-die organizations publicly advocate physician-assisted suicide but draw the line at euthanasia, Hemlock lobbies for both.

"Physician-assisted suicide [drinking a lethal medication prescribed by a physician] is not as efficient as voluntary euthanasia [allowing a physician to give you a lethal injection]. Even using the best barbiturates, the oral route takes much longer—up to eleven hours in a few cases—which is a terrible strain on family present," Humphry explains.[15] Over the past two decades, Humphry has published multiple how-to suicide guides, starting with *Let Me Die Before I Wake* in 1981. His blockbuster follow-up in 1991, *Final Exit,* sold 540,000 copies within eighteen months, and subsequent sales have surpassed one million.

University of Pennsylvania bioethicist Art Caplan summed up concerns over physician-assisted suicide in a series of ominous and somewhat prophetic questions he posed in 1998: "Who will say who is terminally ill and on what basis? Who will assess the competency of those requesting to die? How long will they have to wait? How will police and insurance companies be able to distinguish between murder and assisted suicide? And will . . . insurance companies give rebates to those who offer to end their lives cheaply?"

Stung by adverse publicity surrounding the suicide of his second wife, Humphry resigned as executive director of the Hemlock Society in 1992 and launched the Oregon-based ERGO to craft public-policy initiatives seeking to legalize euthanasia in America. For Humphry, that's a process advanced by increments: "We have to go stage by stage, with the living will, with the power of attorney, with the withdrawal of [medical treatment]," he said in an interview in *National Right to Life News.* "Your side would call that the 'slippery slope.' . . . We would say, proceed with caution, learning as we go along how to handle this very sensitive situation."[16] True to his road map, the past twenty years have seen the widespread adoption of living wills, beginning in 1983 with the passage of the Natural Death Act in California and eventually spreading to all fifty states plus the District of Columbia. Following on the heels of these advance-directive laws, came the evolution in life support eligible for withdrawal from respirators to feeding tubes.

The "assisted dying" of infants sparked debate in 1983 after a whistleblower called attention to the demise of "Baby Doe." An Indiana couple had acquiesced to the recommendation of doctors to allow their Down's syndrome baby to be starved to death. Years later, Walter Owens, the physician in attendance during the baby's death, testified before the U.S. Civil Rights Commission. "In an ideal society, one might say we should consider only the welfare of the child," said Owens. "But this is not an ideal world and we do not have unlimited resources. Money which is spent, and we're talking of many times—$400,000 or $500,000 or even one million dollars spent on these children—that is money that is not available for the education of normal children."[17]

Owens likely took a cue from Australian ethicist Peter Singer, who compared significantly disabled children with pigs and dogs in an infamous guest editorial published in *Pediatrics* in 1984. Disability advocate Thomas Nerney, president of the Center for Self-Determination, gives credit to Richard John Neuhaus, director of the Rockford Institute Center on Religion and Society, for publicly announcing in April 1988 what many would only privately admit was "the return of eugenics" in America. "Thousands of medical ethicists and bioethicists, as they are called, professionally guide the unthinkable on its passage through the debatable, on its way to becoming the justifiable until it is finally established as the unexceptional," Neuhaus wrote in his provocative essay. "Those who pause too long to ponder troubling questions along the way are likely to be told that 'the profession has already passed that point.' In truth, the profession is usually huffing and puffing to catch up with what is already being done without its moral blessing."[18]

Former Surgeon General C. Everett Koop famously and prophetically quipped at the time, "We have 'Baby Does' now. It won't be long before we have 'Granny Does.'"

Baby Doe shared newspaper headlines with another proposed death-by-dehydration-and-starvation case in 1983. After suffering a miscarriage and spousal abandonment, twenty-five-year-old Elizabeth Bouvia checked herself into Riverside General Hospital in the Los Angeles area in 1983 and demanded assistance in her plan to starve herself to death. Paralyzed from birth, the cerebral palsy sufferer wanted intravenous morphine and comfort care to ease the pain of her suicide. When the hospital refused, Bouvia turned to the American Civil Liberties Union for pro-bono legal aid. She was referred to attorney Richard Scott, a founding member of the Hemlock Society, according to the *Los Angeles Times*.[19] The ACLU sued on behalf of Bouvia, seeking to get a court order to force the hospital to assist in her death. The lower court refused, but the appellate court reversed the trial court's ruling and argued Bouvia's assisted death didn't amount to suicide.

It took three years for Bouvia to win the right to starve to death. But by then she no longer found the idea attractive. Although she wanted to die, she told the newspaper a morphine regimen she had begun would make the process of starvation "unbearable." "As time goes on, starvation gets to be less and less an option for me. Back in 1983, it was a good option," she said. "I never wanted to die, but I don't want to live like this." Meanwhile, Bouvia's attorney, who reportedly battled depression for most of his life, shot himself to death.[20]

THE BOUVIA case made an impression on the right-to-die movement. Daniel Callahan, then director of the Hastings Center, observed that year, "Denial of nutrition, may, in the long run, become the only effective way to make certain that a large number of biologically tenacious patients actually die." The problem was, he noted, providing food and fluids was still considered basic care. And a "deep-seated revulsion" existed over the prospects of withholding or withdrawing nutrition and hydration. Callahan's words rang true a short decade later, as they helped shape a more nuanced right-to-die movement that promoted a "third path" to death—not wholly natural, not suicide, but something in between.[21]

Elizabeth Bouvia also caught the attention of the disabled community, and her case provided a stepping-off point for the disability rights movement. Advocates feared the quadriplegic was playing into the hands of the euthanasia proponents who historically pointed the finger at the disabled as likely candidates.

"Why do courts conclude that petitions for assisted death by persons with severe but non-terminal disabilities do not implicate suicide?" queried disability rights advocate Diane Coleman before she answered her own question. "This trend is rooted in pervasive and largely unconscious societal prejudices against people with disabilities."[22]

At the time of the Bouvia case, Coleman was an organizer of American Disabled for Attendant Programs Today (ADAPT), a disability rights group that used civil disobedience tactics to convey its message. Coleman has had a neuromuscular disability since birth. Doctors told her parents she wouldn't live past the age of twelve. When she turned nine, they changed their minds. She has used a motorize wheelchair since she was eleven years old. When she became a lawyer, she applied her acumen to fighting for the civil rights of her largely forgotten disabled peers. Looking back over the legal history of the right-to-die movement, Coleman says the *Cruzan* opinion, which declared a feeding tube should be considered the same as any medical treatment, sounded alarms among the disabled.

"When food and water got put on the table as something that could be taken away, no pun intended, that made a lot of people very concerned," she said. "The difference between food and water and any other medical treatment is that, without it, anybody would die, whereas for other medical treatment that's not the case. Other medical treatment is tied to the medical condition the patient has."

An ounce of humor and a ton of determination have made the grassroots disability group she helped form in response to Jack Kevorkian–assisted suicides a force to be reckoned with. Coleman came up with the group's name, Not Dead Yet, which is a reference to a scene from *Monty Python and the Holy Grail*, and she eventually became its president. Since 1996 the group has staged approximately a dozen protests, filed ten amicus curiae briefs, testified in Congress three times, and written countless conference briefs for state legislators. Not Dead Yet mobilized sixteen other national disability rights organizations to file an amicus brief in *Schiavo v. Schindler*.

"One thing about *Schiavo* that sunk in for me," said Coleman, "they won't let her eat orally. They won't even try to wean her from the feeding tube. They won't let people drip water into her mouth even though she swallows her own saliva. . . . A lot of people were shocked by that. But a lot of people couldn't see the relevance. They were more focused on, 'Well, I know I wouldn't want to live like that.' So therefore, whatever it takes."

The adult daughter of S. C. Lewis (she prefers to go by initials to protect her daughter's privacy) suffered severe brain injury as an infant after receiving the DTP vaccine. Lewis spent the past four years working to support the efforts of the Schindler family to keep their daughter alive. To her, Terri's plight touched a nerve.

"Terri exemplifies a programmed bias against disability," Lewis said, echoing Coleman. "What's going on with Terri is an extension of something I see every day when I'm out with my daughter. We walk into the grocery store or a public area, and without anybody saying a word, sometimes it gets so noisy I can't even stand it." The noise Lewis "hears" is the visually expressed annoyance and anger over the fact she has brought her daughter out in public. She uses the analogy of pecking chickens. "A chicken gets injured and the other chickens peck it to death. What's going on with human nature is not much different from the pecking chickens. You become a victim of something and you continue to get re-victimized. It's ugly out there," she said. "Terri was discriminated against based on her cognitive ability. If you have a healthy person, who was not brain-injured, who for some reason has trouble swallowing and needs a feeding tube for food and fluids, you wouldn't pull their tube."

To the estimated 125,000 adults and 10,000 children in America fitted with feeding tubes, they're no big deal, advocates say. It's just another piece of adaptive equipment. Life goes on, or at least it should. Lewis estimated at least 25 percent of her daughter's classmates can't feed themselves, and more than two dozen are on feeding tubes. She wonders whether they'll be next, and she's not alone. Many in the disability community view Terri Schiavo as evidence of a new eugenics movement.

"I think this is a global agenda to eliminate people who are, in somebody else's opinion, considered a drain or a burden on resources, to set public policy, and change the way these things are looked at so that people consider death as a solution," Lewis concluded. "And they keep expanding the list of candidates for death. If parents of profoundly retarded kids had any clue what was going on, they'd be rioting in the streets. And yet they're not."

In fact, the voice of objection over Terri Schiavo from the disability community overall was muted. That's largely because the community doesn't speak with one voice. Lewis likens the fractious disability rights movement to the early days of the civil rights movement, when not all African Americans supported the push for advancement by the NAACP and the Southern Christian Leadership Conference. There are disabled right-to-life proponents like Joni Eareckson Tada, who declared, "Nobody is ever better dead than disabled, especially if there might be a question that that person might not know the Lord Jesus Christ."[23]

And there are disabled right-to-die advocates like Coleman: "If Terri had clear and convincing evidence of her wishes, or if she had selected Michael Schiavo as her guardian, we wouldn't have been involved. . . . We figure if the person selects the person they trust, then that's what they want. The trust might be misplaced but, hey, we're not going to second-guess that."

The disparate voices within the disabled community also stem from the wide spectrum of disability. Some of those on the end with physical disability but no cognitive impairment see themselves as distinct from individuals on the other end of the spectrum with cognitive impairment.

"We're independent, we're working, living in the community," Karen Hwang, a thirty-seven-year-old quadriplegic told *Washington Post* reporter Ceci Connolly. "Just to have somebody say we are vulnerable, that's patronizing and insulting. For some people, the big fear is being kept alive in this persistent vegetative state," she added. "I'm one of them."[24] Fear appears to motivate both sides of the right-to-die movement.

IN THE 1990s the general public became engaged in the right-to-die movement after the Hemlock Society spearheaded twin ballot initiatives to legalize physician-assisted suicide in Washington and California in 1991 and 1992. After voters said no, Derek Humphry's ERGO conducted a survey to determine "if euphemisms allow people to come to grips with brutal facts which, stated another way, would be repugnant to them." After the results indicated strong support for the language "to die with dignity," the Oregon referendum was retooled. By 1993 Hemlock's Death with Dignity Act met with voter approval, albeit by the slimmest of margins (51–49 percent). The referendum permits doctors to prescribe lethal overdoses of drugs for the purpose of assisting a patient to commit suicide. Oregon's state Medicaid program picks up the tab. But the implementation of the law was held up in the courts for years. Humphry declared victory for ERGO: "The euphemisms won."[25]

The 1990s also saw the rising profile of Dr. Jack Kevorkian and his self-described death equipment. His string of assisted suicides, and one incident of euthanasia in Michigan in 1999, which resulted in a second-degree murder conviction, helped stratify the right-to-die movement. Kevorkian and the Hemlock Society pose one end of the spectrum actively promoting assisted-suicide and euthanasia.

"There are forty-three organizations around the world trying to legalize the right of patients to hasten their deaths. Dr. Kevorkian was one very important spoke in the wheel, but the wheel will not go flat if anything happens to him," Hemlock's national director Faye Girsh commented after Kevorkian's conviction.[26]

A more moderate group of doctors supports physician-assisted suicide but in a more sensitive way than that exhibited by Kevorkian. This group—which includes Drs. Timothy Quill, Marcia Angel, and Barbara Coombs Lee, the executive director of the Oregon-based Compassion in Dying, who now promotes the California Compassionate Choices Act of 2005, which would give the state an "assisted dying" law like the one in Oregon—sought to distance itself from Kevorkian.

"This trial was much more about Dr. Kevorkian's idiosyncratic behavior than about making good decisions about end-of-life care," Quill told the *Detroit Free Press*. "I think people are beginning to see Kevorkian is . . . way out on his own."[27] In 1991 the Rochester, New York, physician confessed in the *New England Journal of Medicine* that he prescribed a lethal dose of sleeping pills to a woman (he referred to her as Diane) suffering from acute leukemia. As Quill described, it took time for him to warm up to the idea when confronted with the hospice patient's wish to commit suicide to end her suffering. Diane first refused treatment for the leukemia. He eventually referred her to the Hemlock Society and then prescribed the barbiturates and explained how much was needed to commit suicide.

"I was setting her free to get the most out of the time she had left and to maintain dignity and control on her own terms until death," Quill explained in the article. A New York prosecutor sought an indictment against Quill, but the grand jury failed to cooperate. Then Quill decided to challenge New York's ban on assisted suicide, in *Vacco v. Quill*, which went all the way to the U.S. Supreme Court.

"Are we better off with an open system subject to regulation? Or are we better off with a secret system as we currently have, where you have to hedge your intentions and where when people get help, they get helped in secret?" he argued in court. New York Attorney General Dennis Vacco replied: "The central thesis of our entire argument is that broad sections of Americans will be subjected to abuse if this becomes a constitutionally protected right."[28]

The *New England Journal of Medicine*'s executive editor, Dr. Marcia Angel, added an editorial to Quill's article in which she described the experience of her eighty-one-year-old father, who shot himself rather than linger with advanced cancer. "If physician-assisted suicide had been available, I have no doubt that my father would have chosen it," she stressed. Instead her mother found her husband's body the next morning in a pool of blood.[29]

All the while Hemlock and others were making headway on the assisted-suicide front. The more nuanced "third path" to dignified death prophesied by Callahan in 1983 had evolved into a movement unto itself as others began promoting this form of "voluntary passive euthanasia" (as MCS Workgroup member Dr. James Bernat described it) as a viable alternative to physician-assisted suicide. With the hospice community on board, the third-path movement gained significant momentum. One pillar of the third path to dignified death was removal of treatment. Another pillar was palliative care.

"There is an alternative to physician-assisted suicide. That option is hospice, declared Jennifer Morales of the National Hospice Organization. "When terminally ill patients are given proper medical and supportive care, the desire for assistance with suicide generally disappears." Hospice leaders have been working over the years to make their alternative available to a wider range of patients, not just those who are terminal. The key is changing the Medicare requirement.

Longtime hospice physician and cofounder of the Missoula Demonstration Project, Ira Byock, also voiced his support for this new thrust in 1995. "Patient refusal of nutrition and hydration (PRNH) is hardly new, indeed, virtually all hospice clinicians remember people who came to a point in their illness when they could be described as having 'lost their will to live' and who recognized that continued eating and drinking was having an undesired, life-prolonging effect," Byock wrote in the *American Journal Hospice and Palliative Care*. Like Daniel Callahan before him, Byock questioned how the general public would react. While acknowledging PRNH was commonly practiced at hospices, Byock suggested that for the uninitiated, any promotion of PRNH might be perceived as "self-absorbed hair splitting." In other words, he suspected the distinction between this third path to death and physician-assisted suicide might be lost on the medical community, the general public, and the courts. Byock considered the position of Quill, Angel, and Coombs to be "radical" and just a few notches below the actions of Kevorkian.

"The practice of a physician or nurse responding to a patient's request for assistance in suicide by discussing the option of refusing to eat or drink appears to stretch the 'fine line' of ethical practice to the point of disappearing," Byock observed but then later made the case for why PRNH offered a good solution. "Unlike physician-assisted suicide, refusing to eat or drink is a purely personal act. While it may require information, the decision obviates the need for physicians, nurses, or other agents of society to participate. After adequate discussion, and in the context of continued caring, at some point the patient's choice becomes 'none of our business.'"[30]

But what if, during that "continued caring," measures were taken that hasten death? In fact, a corollary debate to PRNH would be the ramifications of aggressive palliative care, or the administering of sedatives at dosages that risk death. The concept is called "double effect," whereby morphine or other opiates administered by physicians to ease the pain of the dying process have the double effect of accelerating or shortening the process. In other words, the pain-killers used to kill the pain kill the patient. The widespread acceptance and endorsement of this concept would lead assisted suicide and euthanasia critics to view *palliative care* as a new euphemism that serves to obfuscate along the lines of the *right to die* and *death with dignity.* Proponents of legalizing euthanasia and physician-assisted suicide themselves use the argument that the line between hastening death with pain-killers, combined with the removal of life support and assisting in a suicide, is "transparently false." Third-path proponents see a distinction, however. Rutgers Law School Professor Norman Cantor explained the fine line between the two was that suicide involves initiation of a self-destructive action, while refusal of treatment involves letting a fatal affliction follow its natural course.[31] That assumes only the terminally ill will travel the third path.

In 1997 first Congress then the U.S. Supreme Court wrestled with the ethical hairsplitting. With near unanimity Congress passed the Assisted Suicide Funding Restriction Act, which sought to ensure no federal taxpayer dollars would fund physician-assisted suicide in Oregon or elsewhere. The legislation allowed for two notable exceptions, however, which indirectly endorsed the passive euthanasia practices of withholding or withdrawing life-sustaining medical treatment and the accompanying pain management that leads to death. The third path gained Congress's approval.

Next the Supreme Court weighed in on the prickly issue when it rendered decisions in twin assisted-dying cases sponsored by Compassion in Dying. Four physicians who occasionally treated terminally ill or suffering patients sued the state of Washington, and three gravely ill patients sued the state of New York. Both argued that the states' bans on assisted suicide were unconstitutional. The physicians (including Quill) and patients asserted a liberty interest protected by the Fourteenth Amendment's due process clause extended to a personal choice by a mentally competent, terminally ill adult to commit physician-assisted suicide. The nation's High Court dismissed the argument, however, declaring the asserted right to assistance in committing suicide was not a fundamental liberty interest protected by the due process clause.

"This asserted right has no place in our nation's traditions, given the country's consistent, almost universal, and continuing rejection of the right, even for terminally ill, mentally competent adults. To hold for the respondents, the Court would have to reverse centuries of legal doctrine and practice, and strike down the considered policy choice of almost every state," read the majority opinion delivered by Chief Justice William H. Rehnquist in *Washington v. Glucksberg*. The justices further held the "constitutionally protected right to refuse lifesaving hydration and nutrition," as it was discussed in *Cruzan*, was "grounded in the nation's history and traditions, given the common law rule that forced medication was a battery, and the long legal tradition protecting the decision to refuse unwanted medical treatment."

In the majority opinion delivered in *Vacco v. Quill*, the chief justice asserted, "This court disagrees with the Second Circuit's submission that ending or refusing lifesaving medical treatment is nothing more nor less than assisted suicide. The distinction between letting a patient die and making that patient die is important, logical, rational, and well established."

Excerpts from the transcript of oral arguments in *Washington v. Glucksberg* on January 8, 1997, reveal how the justices arrived at a decision to split the difference.

ASSOCIATE JUSTICE RUTH BADER GINSBURG: In the Cruzan case, the court recognized a liberty interest and yet it upheld restrictive legislation. . . . So couldn't one take the same approach here, there is a liberty interest, but because of the risks and dangers involved, considerable state regulation is permissible?

ASSOCIATE JUSTICE SANDRA DAY O'CONNOR: What are the state interests you would argue support the law here in the event that a liberty interest is recognized?

WILLIAM L. WILLIAMS (senior assistant attorney general of Washington, presenting his case in support of upholding his state's ban on assisted suicide): There are three important state interests that are involved. The first one is life, which includes the state's interest in . . . preventing suicide. And, in the hierarchy of constitutional value, certainly the protection of life is the highest. . . . The second one is to prevent abuse and undue influence, and certainly the risk is higher in the physician-assisted suicide context than it is in the refusal of treatment context. And third, there is a strong interest in regulating the medical profession. Precisely because physicians have the capacity to injure or perhaps cause the death of their patients, the state has an important interest in maintaining a clear line between physicians as healers and curers and physicians as instruments of death of their patients. . . .

CHIEF JUSTICE WILLIAM H. REHNQUIST: It would be very difficult to assume a liberty interest [in refusing medical treatment] and rule in your favor in this case, would it not? Because if we assume a liberty interest, but nonetheless say that, even assuming a liberty interest, a state can prohibit it entirely, that would be rather a conundrum.

ASSOCIATE JUSTICE ANTONIN SCALIA: I suppose that proclaiming a liberty interest is cost-free so long as you can proclaim them and then say, however, they can be outweighed by various social policies adopted by the states. We can say there's a liberty interest in murdering people, however, it's outweighed by the state's interest in preserving the lives of its citizens. I guess we could do that, couldn't we?[32]

The rulings on the twin cases reaffirmed a patient's constitutional liberty interest in rejecting life-sustaining medical intervention while upholding the states' statutes baring assisted suicide. The combined effect was to leave the matter to the states to craft their own laws on physician-assisted suicide and the regulation of palliative care, or end-of-life medical treatment. "Throughout the nation, Americans are engaged in an earnest and profound debate about the morality, legality, and practicality of physician-assisted suicide," Rehnquist wrote. "Our holding permits this debate to continue, as it should in a democratic society."

While on one level the ruling was a blow to the right-to-die movement for those pushing for legalization of physician-assisted suicide, or active euthanasia, on another level it furthered the cause of others by affirming the "passive euthanasia" alternative. The justices gave tacit approval to the "double effect" by concluding that death hastened by increased palliative measures does not constitute prohibited conduct as long as the intent is to relieve pain and suffering. Warren Professor of Catholic Studies and research professor of law at the University of Tulsa Russell Hittinger summed up the High Court ruling with this headline ASSISTED SUICIDE: NO AND YES, BUT MAINLY YES.[33] The U.S. Supreme Court had validated the third path to dignified death.

WHILE THE right-to-die forces were advancing the cause, skirmish by skirmish, at the national level, attorney George Felos was making his own strides on the Florida front. Felos was a founding member of the National Legal Advisors Committee with Choice in Dying. When asked on live television by Fox News's anchorman Steve Dooce if he was a member of the Hemlock

Society, Felos said that he "has been a guest speaker for the Hemlock Society" but failed to answer the question.

The self-described crusader for an individual's right to die says he has taken on about ten such cases over the past decade, earning him the reputation as "the person you want to see when you want to let someone die," according to the *St. Petersburg Times.*[34] The talent agency Felos relies on to schedule speaking engagements, seminars, and end-of-life debates bills him as "America's foremost right-to-die expert" who "overcame the Congress and both Governor Bush and President Bush." Schindler supporters noted in an August 2004 press release that the online booking site Eagles Talent Connection, Inc., a prominent speakers and entertainers bureau, offered the speaking services of Felos on "The Terri Schiavo Saga" for fees ranging from ten thousand to fifteen thousand dollars.[35] (The site no longer lists Felos.) But Felos insists *Schiavo* wasn't part of an agenda.

"This case is not about a movement or a philosophy. It's about carrying out Terri Schiavo's wishes. Her wishes, as found by the court . . . and as affirmed by the court on appeal, is that she did not want to be kept alive artificially," Felos said in 2002. "What I'm an advocate for and I believe in is that individuals have a right to control their own body and the right to choose what medical treatment they want and what medical treatment they don't want. . . . If you've made the decision that medical treatment is no longer a benefit for you and you don't want it, then you do have the legal and constitutional right to refuse it. And I'm an advocate of allowing people to enforce that right."

Felos says he actively opposes euthanasia because it "is contrary to law." He believes public support for euthanasia and assisted suicide stems from "our inadequate end-of-life health care system." He also blames opposition to the right to die on fear of death.

"This case has a lot more to do with the fear of death than the sanctity of life," he said of the Schiavo case in an interview with the Associated Press on the day Terri died.[36]

Felos, who admits to having a "fascination with death and dying" and isn't bothered by the nickname "death attorney," is working to help Floridians overcome their fear in a variety of ways. As mentioned in an earlier chapter, he teams up with the neurologist he solicited to testify in the 2000 trial, James Barnhill, to lead Geriatrics and End of Life Issues cruises, which offer continuing education credits to internists, family physicians, geriatricians, neurologists, and other professionals who confront end-of-life issues with patients and clients.

After Felos's death-cruise partner Barnhill's expert testimony in the 2000 trial was challenged, and the appellate court mandated an evidentiary hearing to further explore Terri's medical condition, the "death attorney" called on "Dr. Humane Death" to serve as an expert witness. Neurologist Ronald Cranford is a familiar face at right-to-die trials across the country. As a medical ethicist who promotes physician-assisted suicide and "passive euthanasia"—terminating respirators, dialysis machines, feeding tubes, and administering narcotics—the University of Minnesota Medical School professor estimates the cases in which he has terminated care number in the hundreds.[37]

In addition, Cranford was the featured speaker at the 1992 national conference of the pro-euthanasia Hemlock Society, which recently changed its name to End-of-Life Choices. He joined the board of directors of the Choice in Dying Society, an organization created when the Society for the Right to Die—the 1975 reincarnation of ESA before it morphed into Choice in Dying in 1992—merged with Concern for Dying in 1991. As Rita Marker described in her *Philanthropy* article, Choice in Dying recruited Cranford and eleven other physicians in 1989 to write a report that was ultimately published in the *New England Journal of Medicine* and echoed on the front pages of newspapers across the country. The report concluded it was morally acceptable for doctors to give patients information about suicide and the necessary drugs to accomplish death. While acknowledging that assisting suicide was "the same as killing the patient," Cranford enthused: "We broke new ground and we were very aware we were doing it. We felt it was an opportunity to make a statement that's very controversial and stand by it."[38]

Cranford again courted controversy in 1991 when, in a twist of medical ethics, he and his colleagues at Hennepin County Medical Center in Minneapolis, Minnesota, went to court to unplug an eighty-seven-year-old woman's respirator over the objections of her husband of fifty-four years. Doctors asked a judge to replace the husband as guardian because he was holding out for a miracle when the situation was futile, in their professional opinions.

Cranford headed the neurological intensive care unit where Helga Wanglie was diagnosed as in a persistent vegetative state after a respiratory attack cut off oxygen to her brain. He said his medical center was "the first hospital to have the guts to go to court and say doctors should not be forced to give futile medical treatment."[39]

Doctors had first tried to convince retired lawyer Oliver Wanglie to disconnect his wife's life support. Hennepin ethics consultant Dr. Steven Miles said that of the 1.7 million people who die in nursing homes and hospitals each year, about 1.3 million of those are preceded by the decision to withhold or withdraw life support. Cranford said families rarely fail to heed doctors' advice to remove life support.[40] But Wanglie, a devout Lutheran, refused.

"It's the doctors' job to sustain life, not to snuff it out," a defiant Wanglie told the Associated Press at the time. "You recall what Hitler did in Germany? He killed off the elderly people, sick people, like they were weeds."[41] The judge ruled in Wanglie's favor, and Helga died three days later of natural causes. Wanglie said he believed his wife would be proud of him. "We felt that when she was ready to go, that the good Lord would call her," Wanglie said. "She placed a high value on human life. . . . We were flatly opposed to euthanasia."[42]

The ruling angered Cranford, who called the case a question of economics: "Society will have to look at whether it should support spending $800,000 for the care of someone in a persistent vegetative state when there are 37 million people in this country who are under- or uninsured and without adequate medical care." Cranford's statement overlooked the fact that Wanglie's private insurance company footed the bill in this case.[43]

One of Cranford's former medical students at Hennepin observed his professor's name "sends a shiver down my spine" and asserted that Cranford had an obsession with death. "We would do rounds and present cases," he said. "If the case was a middle-aged person with a stroke, Cranford would talk about death and dying. If the case was a young woman with the new onset of MS, Cranford would talk about death and dying. Brain tumor? Death and dying. Parkinson's disease? Death and dying."

Cranford's views have not changed over the years since the Wanglie case. In 1997 he wrote an opinion piece in the *Minneapolis Star Tribune* titled WHEN A FEEDING TUBE BORDERS ON BARBARIC. "Just a few decades ago cases of brain death, vegetative state, and locked-in syndrome were rare," he wrote. "These days, medicine's 'therapeutic triumphs' have made these neurologic conditions rather frequent. For all its power to restore life and health, we now realize, modern medicine also has great potential for prolonging a dehumanizing existence for the patient." Cranford suggested the antidote for this "dehumanizing existence" was physician-assisted suicide.

"Many onlookers are dismayed by doctors' fear of giving families responsibility in these cases; our failure to appreciate that families suffer a great deal too in making decisions; our archaic responses to pain and suffering; our failure to accept death as a reality and an inevitable outcome of life; our inability to be realistic and humane in treating irreversibly ill people. All of this has shaken the public's confidence in the medical profession." Cranford went on to blame right-to-lifers and disability groups for discouraging families from making the choice for euthanasia.[44]

During cross-examination at the evidentiary hearing in November 2002 Schindler attorney Pat Anderson probed Cranford's earlier literary work in an attempt to demonstrate a bias on his part against Terri. He affirmed he was still of the mind to view unconscious patients as nonpersons from a constitutional standpoint. He coauthored a law review article published in the *American Journal of Law and Medicine* in 1992 titled "Consciousness: The Most Critical Moral Constitutional Standard for Human Personhood."

Ironically, Felos instructed readers of his book that the "credibility of experts" in a valuation contest in the courtroom is "often the decisive factor" and warned litigants against using an expert with an "apparent conflict of interest."[45] "While perhaps not in bed together," to use Felos's words, "it sure looked like heavy petting" between the two right-to-die activists in the minds of many observers.[46] In somewhat of a "pot calling the kettle black," Felos charged Dr. Jay Carpenter, the first medical expert to challenge the PVS ruling in a petition before the court, as having a "strong bias" in that he admitted he considered the removal of nutrition and hydration without first conducting a swallow test and administering oral food and fluids was tantamount to "murder."

Meanwhile, in his book Felos characterizes feeding tubes as "an instrument to cruelly perpetuate a painful, degrading, and horrific existence." And in an apparent adoption of the adage, "The best defense is a good offense," Felos repeatedly lobbed accusations that the Schindlers were puppets for the "fanatic" and "fundamentalist" right-to-life organizations without being candid about his and Cranford's ties to right-to-die organizations. During a press conference in August 2003, Felos scolded reporters for failing to investigate the nature of the role of pro-life groups' support for the Schindlers.

"I haven't heard any of the press ask the tough questions of the other side. Where are you getting the money? What money have you received? Who's funding this effort? Where is the money that you collected from your Web site going? And who are the organizations that are funding this effort?" Felos demanded. As he likely predicted, the local press dutifully raised the questions and filed a report soon after the press conference.

Even more predictably, say the Schindlers, the local press largely failed to pose those same questions to Felos. When one reporter asked, the Schiavo attorneys conceded they "had been contacted by some groups" but would neither name them nor discuss whether they had accepted their backing.

Felos would later admit the ACLU was underwriting Schiavo's litigation expenses. But a point that gets lost in this tit-for-tat debate, however, is that framing this case as a right-to-life cause puts the cart before the horse. Specifically, the right-to-life, anti-euthanasia, and disability rights organizations joined the family's fight *after* Judge George Greer branded the case as "right to die."

11

"Transforming the Culture of Dying"

AFTER THE SUPREME COURT left the door ajar for physician-assisted suicide on a state-by-state basis and validated the third-path alternative, the now-stratified right-to-die/death-with-dignity movement mobilized with unprecedented scope. The movement gained the backing of a consortium of large, private foundations like George Soros's Open Society Institute (OSI) through its Project on Death in America (PDIA), the Robert Wood Johnson Foundation (RWJF), the Greenwall Foundation, and more than a dozen others.

"Few people realize the vital role private foundations play in promoting societal change. More often than not, major shifts in public attitudes and public policy come not from grass-roots clamor but rather from the hard work of a committed few activists with the ideas and the donors who fund them," observed euthanasia foe Rita Marker of the International Task Force on Euthanasia and Assisted Suicide. "Without the money that is the mother's milk of public advocacy, those inspired to agitate for change would not get very far. The assisted suicide/euthanasia movement typifies this phenomenon."

For its part, the Greenwall Foundation "takes no stand on any issues which it funds" but merely seeks to bring out information about issues, foundation president William Stubing told Marker. That's also the case for Greenwall's grantee, Choice in Dying, which considered itself a "broker of unbiased information about both sides [of issues]."[1] More broad-minded than its eugenic predecessor, Choice in Dying placed emphasis in its literature on the promotion of advance directives and hospice-style palliative care, as do Soros's Project on Death in America and the Robert Wood Johnson Foundation. Prominent opponent of physician-assisted suicide Dr. Kathleen Foley is director of PDIA and coauthor of *The Case Against Physician-Assisted Suicide* (2001). RWJF's position on physician-assisted suicide and euthanasia is neutral. Spokeswoman Andrea Daitz describes the nonpartisan, nonprofit foundation's stance as similar to that of the Greenwall Foundation. "We support projects to further research in the end-of-life field," said Daitz. "We don't support a position on the outcomes."

In late 2003 the *Boston Globe* reported PDIA and RWJF were phasing out a decade-long campaign into which the foundations had poured more than $200 million into end-of-life initiatives and research. "I worry that people will think pulling out means it didn't work, it wasn't a success, it's not glamorous, it's not sexy," Foley told the newspaper. On the contrary, the pulling out symbolized just the opposite: the steady stream of funds dating back nine years for PDIA and nearly fifteen years for RWJF has resulted in a massive transformation in how the medical community in particular and American society as a whole views and deals with death. America evolved from a "death-denying" society, in the words of Hastings Center director Daniel Callahan, to a death-embracing culture by the time Terri Schiavo died of dehydration as a result of the removal of her feeding tube without her explicit permission. And although she didn't benefit, pain management and the practice of palliative care received a huge boost from PDIA, RWJF, and other foundations.

"What's good that's come out of it is that now pain is accepted as the fifth vital sign, which is something that never was before," said Laura Schmidt-Pizzarello, a medical writer who was dying of pancreatic cancer at the time. "I think that was really a major coup."[2]

Billionaire financier, philanthropist, political activist, and George W. Bush–basher George Soros survived the Nazi occupation of his homeland in Budapest, Hungary, emigrating first to London, where he obtained a degree from the London School of Economics, and ultimately to the United States in 1956. He founded an international investment fund, Quantum, through which he accumulated a personal fortune estimated at more than $7 billion. He remains chairman of that fund as well as of his New York–based Open Society Institute, which provides oversight to a network of philanthropic organizations active in more than fifty countries and working to help "shape public policy to promote democratic governance, human rights and economic, legal and social reform," according to the institute's literature.

That goal is also applied here in America. Cybercast News Service reported OSI tax records show a recipient of OSI's beneficence in the United States was the American Civil Liberties Union and its state affiliates, who received $4.41 million.[3] As was demonstrated in the Elizabeth Bouvia case, later in the 1997 case of a Florida AIDS patient, and most recently in the Terri Schiavo case, the organization promotes physician-assisted suicide and the right to die. Soros, who once told a biographer he wanted to be the "conscience of the world," doled out $400 million to that end last year alone. He also spent $27 million of his own money to defeat President Bush in the 2004 election.[4] Soros describes himself as an agnostic and admits at times his self-regard borders on "God-like."[5]

The Project on Death in America was one of Soros's first U.S.-based philanthropic initiatives. In launching it in October 1994, Soros said he chose the "problem of dying" because of his personal experiences with his parents' deaths. In a November 30, 1994, speech given for the Ming Fisher lecture series at Columbia Presbyterian Medical Center, a transcript of which is posted on his Web site, Soros described the 1963 death of his father, who died at home of a terminal illness.

"I was there when he died, yet I let him die alone. I could see him, but I wasn't at his bedside," said Soros. "I just didn't know that it might make a difference." Soros told the audience he then read Elisabeth Kübler-Ross's *On Death and Dying* and was better prepared for the more recent passing of his mother.

"She had joined the Hemlock Society and had at hand a means of doing away with herself. I asked her if she needed my help; I offered it, although I wasn't particularly keen to do it," he said. "At the point of decision, however, she did not want to take her own life, and I'm glad she didn't. Her decision gave the family a chance to rally around and be there as she prepared to die." Soros said that his mother's death was a "very positive experience" for the family. He then pledged to spend fifteen million dollars over the next three years to "promote a better understanding of the experiences of dying and bereavement and by doing so help transform the culture surrounding death." By 2003 PDIA had invested forty-five million dollars in that effort.[6]

Since its 1972 bequest from industrialist Robert Wood Johnson, the foundation that bears his name has distributed more than three billion dollars in grants. Based in Princeton, New Jersey, it is the largest philanthropy devoted exclusively to health and health care in the country. Of particular concern to the foundation, according to its promotional literature, is assuring that all Americans have access to quality health care at a reasonable cost;

improving the way services are organized and provided to people with chronic health conditions; and reducing the personal, social, and economic harm caused by substance abuse. Grantees have included hospitals, medical and public schools, hospices, professional associations, research organizations, state governmental agencies, and community groups. The personal experiences with death of the leadership at the foundation prompted a meeting in 1985 to discuss how to change dying in America.

Between them, Soros's PDIA, which distributed $48 million in grants, and the RWJF, which invested more than $148 million, succeeded in changing textbooks, curricula, certification, and accreditation criteria at medical and nursing schools; institutionalizing palliative (or end-of-life) care at hospitals, nursing homes, and hospices; changing state laws and policies to pave the way for widespread use of the third path to death; and changing the public perception about death through a massive multimedia campaign that recruited fifteen different newspapers, Public Broadcasting System television, and National Public Radio. The money trail of this end-of-life care campaign, exhaustively researched by the pro-life Christian education ministry LifeTree, Inc., and graphically presented on its Web site, tracks the evolution of the effort beginning in 1989.[7]

In 1989 RWJF launched a twenty-eight-million-dollar study of dying in America. Touted as the largest study of its kind ever undertaken, the five-year effort involved nearly ten thousand critically ill patients in five leading medical institutions: Beth Israel Hospital in Boston; Cleveland's MetroHealth Medical Center; Duke University Medical Center; Marshfield Medical Center in Marshfield, Wisconsin; and the UCLA School of Medicine. Among the findings that came out of the 1995 Study to Understand Prognosis and Preferences for Outcomes and Risks of Treatments (SUPPORT):

- Efforts to prolong life too often merely prolonged dying.
- Almost 40 percent of patients studied spent at least ten days in intensive care, where aggressive treatment is the norm.
- Pain was common: according to their families, half the patients able to communicate in their last three days of life had serious pain.
- Only 3 to 4 percent of advance directives are followed.
- Inadequate communication between medical professionals and patients resulted in discrepancies between patients' desires and their actual treatment.
- Almost half the physicians didn't know their patients' preference regarding resuscitation.

The study was summarized in a press release issued by the foundation: "Too often, patients die alone, in pain, and hooked up to machines; the health care system doesn't know when or how to stop treatment of dying patients; and the tools experts said would improve care for these patients didn't work." The findings were published in the *Journal of the American Medical Association* and interpreted in an article by medical ethicist Daniel Callahan in a special supplement to the *Hastings Center Report*. Following Callahan's lead, in 1996 RWJF devised and executed a massive three-pronged strategy called the Last Acts initiative to raise awareness and influence change in attitudes and laws. The ambitious and wide-ranging goals consisted of the following:

1. Improving communication and decision making at the end of life
2. Changing the culture of health-care institutions
3. Changing American culture and the public's attitudes toward death

Within this three-pronged attack, seventeen projects were developed, and eleven task forces and resource committees were formed to tackle the challenges. "Last Acts will be much more than platitudes about a good death," RWJF president Steven Schroeder pledged at a Last Acts conference in October 1997, according to a report of the conference. "It will push for specific reforms across the board—reforms that, if successful, will involve millions of Americans."

THE SUPPORT study served as a recruiting tool for the foundation, which succeeded initially in enlisting the participation of approximately 120 national health and consumer groups across the country in its Last Acts campaign. The coalition later spanned more than 900 organizations and included such health-care giants as the American Medical Association, the American Nurses Association, the American Hospital Association, and the American Association for Retired People. On the roster of leading participants was Choice in Dying, the organization to which George Felos acknowledges an affiliation. In early 2000 Choice in Dying reorganized into Partnership for Caring. By August of that year RWJF tapped Partnership for Caring to be the national program office of Last Acts, awarding the right-to-die organization a one-million-dollar grant. Partnership for Caring later merged with Last Acts in January 2004, and the resulting entity was named Last Acts Partnership. Hospice of the Florida Suncoast president and board member Mary Labyak served as corporate secretary and treasurer for Partnership for Caring, according to industry watchdog Hospice Patients Alliance. Last Acts Partnership now represents the largest coalition of hospice industry lobbyists in the world. Over the past decade, with the support of the one-million-dollar grant from RWJF, the modern incarnation of the eugenic Euthanasia Society of America (ESA) wove itself into the modern hospice movement under the leadership of Labyak and others.

RWJF also doled out grants totaling $420,680 through the Last Acts initiative to the National Hospice and Palliative Care Organization (NHPCO), where Labyak was national director and treasurer. NHPCO developed and coordinated a project to assess the impact of various treatment strategies on the quality of hospice and palliative care programs in order to produce clinical guidelines that would be the model for accreditation of palliative care services across the country. Beginning in 1999, the Hospice of the Florida Suncoast served as one of six experts and grantees for this project. The point person listed for the Hospice of the Florida Suncoast was Kathy Egan, vice president of the Hospice Institute, a research, education, and consulting arm of the nonprofit corporation. PDIA also designated a two-hundred-thousand-dollar grant to help NHPCO strengthen its organizational infrastructure and expand its reach into "diverse communities." Yet while many foot soldiers in NHPCO support physician-assisted suicide, the organization as a whole opposes it.

RWJF designated Hospice of the Florida Suncoast as one of three regional resource centers across the country for an initiative of the Last Acts campaign called Rallying Points. Through their Rallying Points role, Hospice of the Florida Suncoast served as a mentor to regional community coalitions working to improve care for the dying. The Midwest Bioethics Center in Kansas City (which became the Center for Practical Bioethics) and Ira Byock's Missoula Demonstration Project (subsequently renamed Life's End Institute) were designated as the other two regional centers.

Byock was also selected to serve as program director for a twelve-million-dollar RWJF initiative called Promoting Excellence in End-of-Life Care, which tackled the expansion of palliative care in difficult clinical contexts. Byock hopes to be able to undo the "medicalized misery that dying has become." He is also past president of the American Academy of Hospice and Palliative Medicine, an organization that promotes physician-assisted suicide and euthanasia only as a last resort to alleviate a patient's suffering.

"Euthanasia and/or physician-assisted suicide (PAS) may well become legalized in our society," the academy predicts in its position statement. "Were such legalization to occur, the Academy would promote many precautions to their use as well as intense efforts to alleviate suffering and obviate any perceived need for PAS or euthanasia. In the practice of palliative care, the appropriate response to the request for physician-assisted suicide is to increase care with the intent to relieve suffering, not to deliberately cause death. Within hospice and palliative care programs in this context, the Academy would promote an approach of non-interference and, above all, non-abandonment of the patient and family."

The Hospice Institute was named as the agency for licensing and training hospices around the country in implementing Byock's Missoula-VITAS Quality of Life Index (MVQOLI). According to Byock's Web site, the instrument produces a quality of life profile for each patient that is then used "both as an assessment tool to inform care planning and as an outcome measure." The index involves twenty-five items that assess five dimensions of a person's subjective experience—symptoms, functional status, interpersonal relations, emotional well-being, and transcendence. Within each dimension the scale runs from minus thirty to plus thirty. According to Byock, dimensions that are below zero diminish quality of life and dimensions that are above zero augment quality of life.

Quality of life represents the nexus between proponents and opponents of the right to die and assisted suicide. To advocates, the concept provides sound justification for refusing or withholding medical treatment deemed invasive and dehumanizing while acknowledging doing so means imminent death. To critics, the highly subjective quality-of-life valuation provides the intersection at which competent, well-intentioned palliative care specialists—or ill-intentioned eugenic forces—turn down the proverbial slippery slope toward involuntary euthanasia. While the licensing and uniform adoption of the MVQOLI appears as a move toward standardizing a protocol, thereby decreasing its subjectivity, the assessment of another person's quality of life remains subjective.

In his closing arguments in the 2002 evidentiary hearing, Felos stated, "Your Honor, I think that there are many, many of us, in fact, the overwhelming majority of people would agree that there are fates worse than death. I believe the overwhelming majority of people would say if I were in such a horribly impaired condition as Terri Schiavo I'd rather not have cognizance of it than be cognizant of it. Can you imagine the agony and torture? Could we even conceive of the torture and agony if Terri Schiavo had cognition of her condition? Thank God. Thank God she doesn't."

"Terri fits into the category of people mentioned for whom protections are extremely limited," Bob Schindler wrote in a commentary about his daughter's plight titled "Dehumanizing the Disabled." "Our society is now conditioned to evaluate people based on their 'quality of life.' The truth is Terri was sentenced to death for the 'crime' of being disabled and dependent."

In a joint statement issued in October 2003, national disability rights groups took issue with the "better off dead" attitude, expressing itself through the Terri Schiavo case: "In this matter of living as a disabled person, those of us who live with a disability are the experts—not husbands, not parents, not doctors, not ethicists. We know that life with a disability is worth living."

By caring for her brain-damaged daughter, S. C. Lewis came to view quality of life as having less to do with one's internal world, inside one's body, than outside. "Quality of life has more to do with your surroundings than just what you physically are able to do. It mostly has to do with how you're treated. If you took a perfectly healthy person and shoved them in a dark closet, and slipped them some yucky food under the door a couple of times a day, they'd have a pretty miserable quality of life," she observed. "Then if you take somebody who has profound brain injury and has quadriplegia and you play nice music, take them out by the pool, let them hear the birds and feel the wind rustling through their hair, let them eat great food, give them a way to communicate and maybe even give them a full body massage a couple of times a week, they're going to have a pretty good quality of life."

David Stevens of the Christian Medical Association believes the "quality of life" concept smacks of atheism and agnosticism. "Unfortunately," he observed in a radio interview with Dr. D. James Kennedy of the Coral Ridge Ministries, "in our legal system, as well as our health-care system, certain groups of people are defined out of personhood. You're not a person if you don't have the quality of life where your happiness supersedes the pain and suffering you have." He added, "That's a very secular way of approaching people's worth. Not seeing them made in the image of God. Not seeing them as having value within themselves because the essence of God is in them."[8]

Neurologist and medical ethicist Ronald Cranford testified in the evidentiary hearing that people in vegetative states lose their personhood in terms of constitutional rights. Bioethicist Bill Allen with the University of Florida College of Medicine didn't add Cranford's qualifier while answering the question of personhood posed by MSNBC anchor Joe Scarborough on March 29, 2005:

SCARBOROUGH: Do you think [Terri Schiavo] is a person still?

ALLEN: Well, I think she has lost the distinguishing feature, or she has lost the physiological ability for awareness, self-awareness, which is the distinguishing feature of human being or, if you will, even the divine image.

SCARBOROUGH: So, she is not a person anymore because she doesn't have awareness?

ALLEN: If she doesn't have awareness, which is the case in persistent vegetative state, yes.[9]

"Personhood theory would reduce some of us into killable and harvestable people," warned attorney Wesley Smith, senior fellow at the Discovery Institute. Smith called attention to the conclusion in 1997 of several doctors writing for the International Forum for Transplant Ethics that people diagnosed as being in a persistent vegetative state should be redefined as dead for purposes of organ procurement. And he raised this issue with bioethicist Allen.

SMITH: If Terri is not a person, should her organs be procured with consent?

ALLEN: Yes, I think there should be consent to harvest her organs, just as we allow people to say what they want done with their assets.

"Know this," concluded Smith, "there is a direct line from the Terri Schiavo dehydration to the potential for . . . stunning human strip-mining . . . becoming a reality."[10] Supporting Smith's conclusion is the fact that, at the same time, the condition of persistent vegetative state was being newly defined in Florida's advance-directive statute and procedures for making "anatomical gifts" were expanded to give surrogates "more opportunities . . . to consider this alternative" for the decedent. (This will be discussed in the next chapter.)

IN 1995 Soros's PDIA teamed up with RWJF, the Nathan Cummings Foundation, the Rockefeller Family Office, and the Commonwealth Fund—a total of twenty different organizations—to form a consortium to be known as Grantmakers Concerned with Care at the End of Life. According to PDIA's progress report, the coalition organized conferences and shared information in order to inform funders about the major social, economic, and medical issues in end-of-life care and to encourage them to address those issues in their grant making. PDIA's recommended targets for grant making by the consortium included:

- Support collaborations of hospice programs, hospitals, and academic medical centers.

- Fund initiatives to introduce or expand palliative care services in nursing homes and assisted living facilities to help avoid hospitalization and enable residents to be cared for in comfortable and familiar surroundings.
- Support palliative care programs for indigent patients, patients without family caregiving support, or patients without health insurance.
- Fund pediatric palliative care within routine healthcare settings rather than in hospice settings only. Many parents won't consider palliative care if it means foregoing potentially curative therapies.
- Support grassroots coalitions to educate policymakers about . . . the limitations of the Medicare Hospice Benefit and suggested improvements.
- Support national organizations that are already working to examine and transform public policy affecting end-of-life care.
- Support community outreach and education about advance-care planning. Living wills, advance directives, and healthcare proxies are essential tools that enable people to make informed choices about end-of-life care.

Soros's PDIA set its sights on the culture of medicine in hospitals and nursing homes, where almost 70 percent of Americans die. The foundation created the Faculty Scholars Program, which provided $13.4 million to outstanding clinical and academic leaders in medicine and nursing who were in a position to change the medical culture from the inside out. Five to eight scholars were chosen each year to receive two-year awards of up to $76,500 per year. All scholars conducted a clinical, research, educational, or advocacy project for the period of their award. The University of Minnesota's Dr. Steven Miles, who along with Ronald Cranford and his colleagues on the ethics committee at Hennepin County Medical Center went to court to pull Helga Wanglie's respirator, was named among the first group of scholars. In its initial report, PDIA touted the eighty-seven faculty scholars selected over the program's nine-year history as "among the most prominent and active leaders of palliative care" today. PDIA noted, however, that of the more than one hundred thousand medical school faculty members in the United States, fewer than one hundred specialize in palliative care. PDIA announced intentions to foster palliative care faculty in the nation's medical schools and to support the establishment of a university chair in palliative medicine.

Similarly, RWJF awarded $832,000 to Stanford University and $998,000 to the Massachusetts General Hospital to provide in-depth training to medical school faculty so they would be equipped to teach end-of-life care to their students. Training doctors to focus on patient care in dying would take time and require a revolutionary approach to medicine. Since the advent of major advances in medical technology in the 1950s, physicians have been programmed to be "conqueror" of death, and when a patient dies, death is considered a failure. It would take considerable reprogramming to return physicians to the pre-medical-high-technology mind-set of accepting death. (That's not to say terminal or other patients haven't been aided in dying quietly behind closed doors, despite the revolution in medical technology.)

"Assisted suicide does occur and it is certainly not a rare phenomenon," Dr. Sidney H. Wanzer, director of the Health Services Center at Harvard Law School, told the *New York Times* in 1989. "As to how frequently," he said, "I'm just not sure." The *Times* article then addressed how AIDS had created a sense of urgency among euthanasia and assisted-suicide proponents. One such crusader, Marty James, a Los Angeles man who said he had helped at least a dozen friends kill themselves before AIDS killed them, said, "The public would be surprised at how helpful doctors are willing to be."[11]

A *Journal of the American Medical Association* survey, cited by the *Lakeland Ledger* in 1998, found 25 percent of doctors have been asked to end the life of a terminally ill patient. The American Society of Internal Medicine found that one in five doctors obliged such requests.[12] Medical ethicist Curtis Harris sided with the majority who would refuse. "If you have nothing to live for and you're at peace with dying, then you may decide to die," the president of the American Academy of Medical Ethics told the *Times,* but he added, "It's not the physician's role to be the killer. If we take on that role, we lose one of the major ethical and moral tenets of our profession."

There is evidence the efforts of PDIA and others to "transform the culture of dying" have paid off. While the American Medical Association declared itself against physician-assisted suicide, it adopted new principles for end-of-life care that emphasized pain relief and following patients' wishes for "dignified deaths."

"What has been shocking to me," Schindler attorney Pat Anderson said, summarizing her years spent litigating the Schiavo case, "is the shift in attitude of the medical profession. Some lives are not worth living, according to these guys. It's a dollars-and-cents attitude. 'They're never going to get any better. Why should we expend scarce health resources on them? They need to die. They're taking up valuable space.' It's horrible. Absolutely horrible."

On May 30, 1999, Harris held a special ceremony for thirty graduating students from the University of Oklahoma College of Medicine. What made it special was the recitation of the traditional Hippocratic oath, a treatise attributed to "the great physician," as Plato hailed the fifth-century Greek named Hippocrates. After the *Roe v. Wade* U.S. Supreme Court ruling, OU, like most medical schools, had revised the oath to exclude prohibitions on abortion and euthanasia.

"I will neither give a deadly drug to anyone if asked for it, nor will I make a suggestion to this effect. Similarly, I will not give to a woman an abortive remedy," reads the oath to which graduating medical students have historically sworn allegiance since 1181. Like the Commandment "Thou shalt not kill," this edict has been largely discarded as anachronistic in a modern, AIDS-afflicted era where the population is aging dramatically and living longer amid the marvels of medicine.

IN SEPTEMBER 1997 RWJF next set its sights on reforming state governmental policy. A short three months after the U.S. Supreme Court's decision to turn the matter of physician-assisted suicide over to the states, the foundation designated a grant of $149,486 to the National Conference of State Legislatures (NCSL) in Washington DC to draft guidelines for state legislators to follow in crafting new end-of-life legislation. Working in tandem with the Center to Improve Care of the Dying, the NCSL produced and distributed 10,500 copies of its guidebook *State Initiatives in End-of-Life Care: Policy Guide for State Legislatures* to all legislators, their medical commissions, law libraries, medical educators, and the general public, according to the RWJF's grant results report filed in June 1999. Key legislators received special mailings that included audiotapes from NCSL's first of two national conferences. The guidebook—which was reviewed by the National Hospice Organization (where Mary Labyak served as chairperson), the University of Wisconsin, the Midwest Bioethics Center, the American Bar Association, and sixteen other national organizations—addresses the following questions:

- What do model laws legalizing assisted suicide look like?
- What can states do to remove barriers to effective pain management?
- What types of health-care services are available to the dying, and what are their deficiencies?
- How can advance-care planning be improved?
- How have state task forces been effective in advancing discussions about end-of-life care?
- Who pays for end-of-life care?

"According to the Institute of Medicine's Committee on Care at the End of Life, most end-of-life services are financed through public sources," states the NCSL guidebook. "About three-fourths of those who die each year are 65 or older, so are covered by Medicare at the time they die. In addition, Medicaid, a jointly financed federal and state program, covers about 13 percent of Medicare beneficiaries, as well as younger persons who are poor. These two programs thus pay for a large percentage of the total expenditures on end-of-life care." Over subsequent pages the authors make the case that promoting greater access to hospice care over hospitalization or nursing-home care shifts the cost burden from the states to the federal government. It then highlights the barriers to expanding hospice access, with the chief one being the Medicare requirement that hospice patients have a prognosis of six months or less to live. A proposed remedy within the states' authority was to expand the Medicaid hospice eligibility beyond the six-month survival criteria.

Discussion of economics in the realm of end-of-life care decisions harkens back to 1968 with the Choice in Dying–backed bill floated by Florida legislator Walter W. Sackett to remove care from severely mentally retarded patients at state facilities. Once again the economies of physician-assisted suicide looked attractive to Florida lawmakers as they braced for an estimated 5.4 million people over the age of sixty-five to populate the state by 2025, which amounted to 26 percent of the projected population. A 1995 analysis by the legislature's Elder Affairs and Long Term Care commission estimated the state's Medicaid costs in 2010 will range from eight billion dollars to twenty billion dollars.[13]

The NCSL guidebook devoted eight of its forty-four pages to addressing the physician-assisted suicide debate, taking an evenhanded approach at providing both sides of the argument. It concluded: "All parties, however, agree that state legislators can echo and implement the Supreme Court's support for palliative care. Enacting pain management laws and researching financial options for patients at the end of life can have a tremendous effect on the future. Expanding hospice-type models of care can help ensure that people die painlessly and at home or in home-like settings, not in the hospital. Making advance directives and advance care planning part of every dying patient's experience might guarantee that Americans will be informed of their options at the end of life and that their wishes will be followed."[14]

By early 1998 RWJF had pumped $11.25 million into twenty-one community-state partnerships established to "remove policy and practice barriers that impede good end-of-life care." Four more partnerships were added by 2003. With the NCSL's guidebook and an average grant of $450,000, these community-state coalitions went to work in Alabama, California, Connecticut, the District of Columbia, Florida, Hawaii, Iowa, Kansas, Kentucky, Maine, Michigan, Minnesota, Nevada, New Hampshire, New Jersey, North Carolina, North Dakota, Oklahoma, Rhode Island, Utah, and West Virginia. The grant program office was set up at the Midwest Bioethics Center in Kansas City, a community-based ethics center established in 1984 that changed its name to the Center for Practical Bioethics.

According to RWJF's Last Acts grant reports, Florida was among the earliest states to establish an end-of-life community-state partnership. Sometime in 1996 or 1997 the RWJF grant of $449,960 was awarded to Florida Hospices and Palliative Care, a network of all hospices in the state, which established the Florida Partnership for End-of-Life Care. Samira Beckwith, president of Florida Hospices and Palliative Care and a former chairperson of the National Hospice and Palliative Care Organization (NHPCO), became the point person. In the words of John Carney of the Center for Practical Bioethics, the state hospice "spearheaded" the RWJF end-of-life care community-state partnership in Florida. Additionally, Gema Hernandez, former secretary of the Florida Department of Elder Affairs, joined the national advisory committee for Last Acts's community-state partnerships program. With money secured and the statewide infrastructure already in place, the Florida hospice industry next needed a foot in the door with the Florida legislature in order to carry out the RWJF mission of changing the law governing end-of-life care. (This will be detailed in the next chapter.)

The Last Acts community-state partnerships model was inspired by a prominent former secretary of Florida's Health and Social Services Agency, Jim Towey, whose nonprofit Florida Commission on Aging with Dignity launched its own campaign, Project 2010 AD, in 1996. The Democrat who had been appointed to the cabinet in 1993 by Governor Lawton Chiles but was ousted from his position in 1996 by Senate Republicans who refused to confirm his nomination became the first to sound the alarm about the impending deluge of seventy-six million baby boomers expected to retire by 2029 and move to the Sunshine State. Like billionaire Soros, Towey was motivated to devote himself to the "problem of dying" after the agonizing death of his father, Edward Towey, who died of a heart attack. Towey observed his father's final days and concluded more needed to be done for people approaching death. "Nursing home patients are cut off from light, and they are very lonely," Towey told his alma mater's campus newspaper, *Florida State Times.*

Subsequently the Florida Commission on Aging with Dignity received a $398,690 grant from the RWJF, $85,000 from the Claude and Mildred Pepper Foundation, and $87,926 from the Weinberg Foundation for an eighteen-month project to conduct a series of forums around the state to raise awareness. Beyond the money, Towey's nonprofit organization had significant political clout. The commission's advisory board included Lawton Chiles, Jeb Bush (who had yet to be elected governor and was at the time chairman of a conservative, grass-roots policy institute called the Foundation for Florida's Future), Archbishop John Favalora, and Rabbi Solomon Schiff. Towey's stature as a health-care expert and accomplished politician, a political missionary of sorts—not to mention his ties to Jeb Bush—ultimately prompted President George W. Bush to tap him to head the White House's Faith-Based Initiatives program, where he continues to serve as director.

"I'm basically a salesman," Towey explained in describing Project 2010 AD. "I'm using my contacts to bring people together so we can show people how important this problem is to all of us."[15] What happens to a state with more elders and fewer Medicare and Medicaid dollars? Are the boomers considering long-term care insurance and completing advance directives? Are they saving enough to live to be ninety? How can Florida care compassionately and cost effectively for aging people with a spectrum of needs? What tax policies might encourage adult children to care for their parents? These questions framed Towey's task at hand, according to a *Palm Beach Post* editorial announcing the formation of this commission.[16]

But first and foremost, the commission's agenda was to promote better palliative care to end suffering—a goal Towey shared with the RWJF. Towey is a Roman Catholic who once flirted with the idea of becoming a priest, and he learned a lot about death and dying through twelve years of working with Mother Teresa of Calcutta as legal counsel. "What amazed me was that, in this impoverished country, the dying in her home were cared for with such personal attention and tenderness. Their hands were held, their pain was treated. Dying was not handled as simply a medical moment but as the spiritual experience that it was," he wrote in an open letter posted on the commission's Web site. "Then I came back home to the United States. Care here was miserable. I saw people dying in pain and alone. Their last days weren't comfortable or peaceful, and often their last wishes were ignored."

Observing Mother Teresa's "commitment to the God-given dignity of those entrusted to her care" helped to shape Towey's impressions of dying and led to the creation of an innovative living will called the Five Wishes. Thanks to the networking power of Last Acts, more than four hundred organizations throughout the country distributed the Five Wishes. A toll-free hot line was also set up in June 1997 to help distribute some one hundred thousand copies of the advance directive. Towey announced the benchmark at the Last Acts leadership conference in October 1997, where he was a guest speaker. Then, in May 1998, gubernatorial candidate and commission advisory board member Jeb Bush took the opportunity of a debate sponsored by the commission to voice his support for the Five Wishes.

At the unveiling of Towey's Commission on Aging with Dignity in December 1996, representatives from members of the Last Acts Initiatives coalition—the Florida Medical Association, the Florida Health Care Association, the Florida Nurses Association, and Florida Hospice—joined him in calling for a third path between pain and poison at the end of life. As Towey described, a third path "leaves patients free of chronic pain, allows patients to choose treatment that must be carried out by doctors and family members, and promotes hospice care and other services that allow terminally ill patients to be cared for in their homes or a home-like environment"—essentially the planks in the platform developed by Last Acts in response to the 1995 SUPPORT study.

Towey expressly opposed physician-assisted suicide and warned that, because of its large elderly population and "fraying safety net for the poor and disabled," Florida was vulnerable to the quick fix of assisted suicide. In the wake of Oregon's Death with Dignity referendum, Towey was concerned about society's drift toward euthanasia: "I saw how much easier it would be to kill [the poor and elderly] than to care for them," he told the *National Catholic Reporter* in reference to his experience in India. "The minute the economy starts to sputter, who's going to get squeezed? The poor and the elderly. They always do."[17]

"We don't want to see Dr. Kevorkian's van cross this state's border," Towey stated on another occasion. "Florida can do better for its sick and suffering than that. We are our brother's keeper, not our brother's killer." While an overt criticism of the then-popular physician-assisted suicides carried out by Jack Kevorkian, the statement also subtly took aim at ongoing efforts by the Hemlock Society to make assisted suicide legal in Florida.

But in an era of partnership-building, fueled by foundation money, among entities along the stratified right-to-die spectrum all working to "transform the culture of dying," it wouldn't be long before the Mother Teresa disciple would shake hands with Hemlock Society founder Derek Humphry.

12

Statutory Serendipity or Set-up?

WANTED: Terminally ill patients and cooperative doctors to serve as plaintiffs in a lawsuit challenging the state's assisted-suicide law. Candidates must be credible, articulate, and want to die.

IN THE SUMMER OF 1994 the Florida Hemlock Society ran a front-page article in its newsletter, seeking to recruit participants in what would be a meticulously orchestrated test case for legalized assisted suicide.[1] Up to fifty patients and a dozen physicians responded and were evaluated by Hemlock organizers. Should the Florida courts give their blessing, the doctors needed to be willing to provide the prospective plaintiffs with a self-administered injection of a lethal concoction of drugs. The society turned to the ACLU to provide a lawyer for the right-to-die cause. The case raised the question of whether an 1869 state statute banning assisted suicide violated the privacy amendment in Florida's state constitution.

After eliminating older candidates and those deemed depressed or suicidal, Hemlock Society organizers focused on two cancer patients and thirty-five-year-old AIDS sufferer Charles Hall as their plaintiffs. A former Pizza Hut manager from Citrus County, Hall maintained he most likely had been infected with the AIDS virus through a blood transfusion fifteen years earlier in Texas, where he underwent back surgery. By the time the case came to trial in West Palm Beach, Florida, both cancer plaintiffs had died and AIDS had taken a marked toll on Hall. He had hepatitis and arthritis, was wheelchair-bound and legally blind, suffered from chronic pain, could only swallow liquids, and had shrunk from 170 pounds to a slight 100 pounds.

He wrapped tape around his wedding ring to keep it from slipping off his gaunt finger. His daily regimen included forty pills to ease his symptoms.

Hemlock paired Hall with seventy-four-year-old Cambridge University–educated Dr. Cecil McIver. The retired Jupiter, Florida, doctor agreed to be on call for the lethal injection. Hall acknowledged to the press the doctor-patient relationship was borne out of and framed by the cause and not the disease. "I'm not ready to die, but when I am, I want to go with the aid of a kindhearted man like Dr. McIver," Hall told the *Fort Lauderdale Sun-Sentinel*. "I know he's not my regular doctor, but I trust him as much as I do my own treating physician."[2]

With the ACLU's recommendation of one of its board members, attorney Robert Rivas, to serve as legal counsel, Hemlock had all the parts in place for a right-to-die trial that was two years in the making—two years and a lot of money. The ACLU and the Hemlock Society spent a hundred thousand dollars on the effort by the time the first ruling was rendered in the case. But it was money well spent, as Charles Hall became the first person in state history to be granted the right to commit suicide with the assistance of his doctor. But he had that right for only a matter of minutes, before the appellate process put Circuit Court Senior Judge Joseph Davis's historic ruling on hold.

Davis, a retired judge from Seminole County who was brought in to hear the case because all the Palm Beach County judges were said to have full schedules, ruled on January 31, 1997, that Florida had no interest in causing "the prolongation of Mr. Hall's pain and suffering." Still, Hall passed up the opportunity for legal assisted dying, telling the Associated Press, "I'm far from ready to die" and that he hoped death would come peacefully and naturally.

Choice in Dying executive director Karen Orloff Kaplan commented to the local paper at the time that meticulous planning went into the orchestration of the case. "Challenging the law is a much more careful process than it seems on the surface," she said. "These groups know they can't afford to be seen as radical or way out, on the other side of the law."

The Reverend Ralph Mero—a Unitarian Universalist minister in Boston and former executive director for the right-to-die group Compassion in Dying, which sponsored the court cases in New York and Washington that led to the June 1997 twin assisted-suicide rulings by the U.S. Supreme Court—confirmed the orchestration by the Hemlock Society and the ACLU was par for the course. "This is a standard process for developing American constitutional provisions," he said. "All of these cases are not only important in terms of law, but in their education of both the general public and the press."[3]

Jim Towey warned that Davis's decision set a "chilling precedent" and contended that legalized assisted-suicide was ripe for abuse in that he perceived the very old, mentally ill, and people with disabilities "might be pressured into choosing death."[4] "It's ethical and moral at some point to withhold medical care," he clarified, "but I don't think Florida wants to start down the path of assisted suicide."[5]

Meanwhile, the Florida Hemlock Society launched a phone campaign, hoping to capitalize on the ruling. The society contacted all 160 state lawmakers in its quest for a sponsor of legislation similar to what had been passed into law in Oregon. While the organization managed to drum up a half-dozen lawmakers willing to cosponsor the bill, none would agree to file it, reported the *Tampa Tribune*.[6]

On July 17, 1997, the state Supreme Court, in a five-to-one decision, reversed the trial court ruling and said "no" to assisted suicide. The court found the state's interest in preserving life, preventing suicide, and upholding the integrity of the medical profession outweighed Hall's privacy rights. The state high court also took a page from the nation's High Court in drawing a distinction between the refusal of medical treatment and the right to commit physician-assisted suicide. And like William H. Rehnquist and his colleagues had done a month prior, the Florida Supreme Court turned the matter over to legislators to further hash out, according to the consensus of public opinion. Hall died eight months later due to complications from AIDS.

WHILE THE Hemlock Society was busy laying the groundwork for the Hall case, and Choice in Dying was closely watching and eagerly awaiting the outcome, a founding member of that right-to-die organization's National Legal Advisors Committee was working steadily to advance the cause on the other coast of Florida, in Pinellas County. George Felos worked on a string of right-to-die cases after *In re Guardianship of Browning*. On December 13, 1995, he received a call from Schiavo guardianship attorney Deborah Bushnell seeking "assistance with analysis of life-prolonging procedures statute." The thirty-minute phone call was listed in an itemized petition Bushnell filed requesting reimbursement of fees out of Terri's medical trust fund. She charged Terri $82.50 for the call.[7]

During that conversation, Felos would have informed Bushnell that the advance-directive statute she was referencing, F.S. Chapter 765, as enacted in 1992, defined "life-prolonging procedures" as "any medical procedure, treatment, or intervention which utilizes mechanical or other artificial means to sustain, restore, or supplant a spontaneous vital function; and when applied to a patient in a terminal condition, serves only to prolong the process of dying." The statute defined "terminal condition" as one caused by "injury, disease, or illness from which there is no reasonable probability of recovery and which, without treatment, can be expected to cause death." Felos would have further informed Bushnell that in order to remove "life-prolonging procedures" from Terri Schiavo, two physicians would be required to certify her as terminal.

Michael Schiavo and Felos met in early 1996, according to Schiavo's court testimony, and began planning a strategy to seek the court's permission to remove Terri's feeding tube. Bushnell subsequently phoned Schiavo about "associating George Felos to handle removal of life support issue." According to a fee petition dated September 30, 1997, she charged Terri's guardianship fund $54 for placing that call. On March 5, 1997, Schiavo signed a contract authorizing Felos to "represent him in connection with the withdrawal and/or refusal of medical treatment." The agreement held that Felos would be paid $195 an hour plus costs, which would be "borne by the client." As was discussed in chapter 4, Terri's medical trust fund paid Felos's fees which, when combined with the other Schiavo attorneys' bills and guardian ad litem fees, ate up the lion's share of the monies earmarked for her medical and rehabilitative treatment.

In early April 1997 Bushnell petitioned the court for authorization to hire Felos "in connection with the issue of withdrawal and/or refusal of medical treatment for the ward" and to pay his fees and costs out of Terri's guardianship funds. On April 18, Judge Mark Shames returned the order stamped "Not Signed," with a handwritten notation on the bottom that read, "Does not appear that notice has . . . been given to parents and/or other interested persons." It's unclear from this notation whether Shames specifically recollected having consulted with the Schindlers on the case years earlier, before the attorney became a circuit court judge. The Schindlers met with Shames in 1993 when they were searching for an attorney to file their first petition to remove Michael Schiavo as guardian in the wake of the controversial urinary tract infection incident. The couple did not retain Shames's services, however, because they couldn't afford his fees. They later questioned the ethics of his taking the case as a sitting judge, having had prior contact with one of the parties. Pat Anderson, however, doubted he even remembered meeting the Schindlers.

According to Bushnell's fee petition, Shames's unsigned order sparked a series of calls, beginning on May 5, between Schiavo and Bushnell and the judge's office. Bushnell noted she took a thirty-minute "telephone call from Mike Schiavo re handling timing of petition for attorney fee for George Felos and request that I contact judge with additional information." Bushnell promptly placed a "telephone call to Judge Shames's office re corresponding with judge re issue of attorney fees to evaluate issue of removal of life support for ward." She drafted a follow-up letter that day to the judge, which she attached to a renewed petition filed with the court on May 14, 1997. In her letter, Bushnell assured the judge that Felos would personally inform the Schindlers, and they would not be surprised by a sudden ruling from his court.

"The guardian is aware that the issue of withdrawal or refusal of medical treatment for the ward is a difficult issue . . . and that the ward's parents will need to be involved," Bushnell wrote. "It is anticipated that the parents will initially be approached gently and informally by Attorney Felos regarding this issue, that Hospice will be involved, and that counseling will be provided to the guardian and the parents to assist with the decision-making process."

Felos's next move was shrewd, Anderson noted. While all other Florida right-to-die cases had involved the state or a hospital as the opposing party, the right-to-die attorney "baited" Bob Schindler, in her words, into becoming his adversary instead. The difference? The state or hospital would have unlimited resources to throw at the case; Bob Schindler had none. In a letter dated August 20, 1997, Felos informed the Schindlers that the court had authorized Michael Schiavo to employ him "in connection with the issue of withdrawal and/or refusal of medical treatment for your daughter Theresa."

In an apparent attempt to soften the blow of his bombshell letter, Felos stated: "At this point in my representation, I am in the process of obtaining information about Theresa's past treatment and her prognosis. In addition, I am also trying to gather information regarding what Theresa's wishes would be in this situation, if she were able to express them. Determination of patient intent while the patient was competent often proves very helpful in reaching a medical treatment decision after the patient becomes incapacitated." Felos requested a meeting with the couple and then recommended they seek the services of a mental health counselor at the Hospice of the Florida Suncoast, where he was chairman of the board at the time.

"I felt sick at my stomach," Bob Schindler told WorldNetDaily, describing his reaction to the letter. "I couldn't believe it. It was like being sucker punched right in the gut. I never ever thought Michael would go that far."

Schindler said he was not taken in for a minute but immediately understood a "final determination" had been made and Terri's life was on the line. He phoned Felos to see if there wasn't "a bit of wiggle room." Felos reportedly responded that matters had gone too far and there could be no turning back. The Schindlers immediately set about looking for an attorney who would take the case pro bono. They found Pam Campbell.[8]

Another Felos move perceived as shrewd on the part of Schindler supporters was his petitioning the court to transfer the case from the St. Petersburg division to Clearwater, ostensibly to be closer to his and Bushnell's Dunedin offices. Judge Shames granted the transfer on December 19, 1997. The transfer ensured Judge David Seth Walker, whose pro-life religious views were well known, would not be hearing the case. In fact, Walker would later state "You feed goldfish" during his adjudication of an identical case on March 21, 2002, in which he ordered the feeding tube connected to thirty-two-year-old David Bryer, who was diagnosed in PVS, *not* be removed. "This Court must give deference to human life, no matter its state. The lack of medical ["probability"] of neurological improvement is insufficient to command its termination. We must feed David Bryer," Walker wrote in his opinion.[9]

While Felos had committed himself to pursue the withdrawal of "medical treatment," Florida statutes did not provide for the specific removal of artificial nutrition and hydration, that is, feeding tubes. Without the benefit of state statutory law, he likely expected he could argue for the removal on the basis of state case law, which included the 1990 Florida Supreme Court ruling in *In re Guardianship of Browning*. The court concluded, "A competent person has the constitutional right to choose or refuse medical treatment, and that right extends to all relevant decisions concerning one's health." Although the elderly stroke victim died before the case advanced to the state's high court, the ruling would have authorized the removal of Estelle Browning's feeding tube even though she was not terminally ill. The lower courts had refused to apply her written advance directive, which specified the removal of artificial nutrition and hydration, but that removal was predicated on her death being "imminent," which it was not. The high court justices based their opinion on the "fundamental right" of everyone to sole control of his or her person.

"The right involved here is one of self-determination that cannot be qualified by the condition of the patient," the opinion read, according to Felos's summary in his book. The justices also fell in line with the ethical hairsplitting of the June 1990 U.S. Supreme Court ruling in *Cruzan* and found "no significant legal distinction between supplying food and water through a tube and other forms of medical treatment."[10] In his book, Felos goes on to describe that the Florida legislature "eventually" brought the state's advance-directive statute up to date with the law handed down by the state supreme court. He downplayed the fortuitous timing of this, however. While the advance directive law was revised in 1992 to incorporate the outcome of *Browning*, it would not be until 1999 that feeding tubes were added to the definition of life-prolonging procedures eligible for removal. This would prove important to *Schiavo* because, unlike Browning, Terri Schiavo had no advance directive. A specific protocol was established in the advance-directive law for handling patients without advance directives and would be applied to Terri's case. Before *Browning*, the Florida Supreme Court determined the right of privacy provided in article 1, section 23 of the state constitution gave both competent and incompetent persons the right to forego life-prolonging procedures in *John F. Kennedy Memorial Hospital v. Bludworth* and *Corbett v. D'Alessandro*.

Through *In re Guardianship of Browning* Felos scored a significant win for the right-to-die movement in Florida, which was struggling in the legislative arena. While *Browning* was pending before the Florida Supreme Court, Representative Jim King (R-Jacksonville) cosponsored a bill during the 1989 legislative session that would have allowed the attending physician and another doctor to remove feeding tubes from patients with terminal conditions if they determined such sustenance was a life-prolonging procedure. Years earlier, King had written Florida's Death with Dignity Act, which laid the foundation for the current advance-directive law and served as a national model. The deaths of his parents from prolonged illnesses in nursing homes had inspired him to craft the legislation. He considered it his "legacy." The 1989 bill had the backing of the Florida Medical Association, Florida Nurses Association, Florida Hospice, the Florida Council on Aging, and the Silver-Haired Legislature. Opposition from the Florida Catholic Conference and Florida Right to Life was customarily stiff.

In the end, Governor Bob Martinez vetoed the landmark legislation out of concern it was jumping the gun and should wait for the state supreme court ruling on *Browning*. Martinez also indicated he was "concerned about the complexity of the human condition in the circumstances covered by the legislation as well as the medical, ethical, social, and technological advances which relate to this subject."

The Florida Right to Life president at the time, Ken Connor, who would later serve as counsel to Jeb Bush in the Schiavo case, applauded Martinez' veto. "I think the governor's action was very courageous and will go a long way toward protecting the rights of the elderly," Connor said. "The euthanasia juggernaut has been derailed, but it will be back."[11]

"With the executive and legislative branches of government closed to change, right-to-die advocates were left with the judiciary,"[12] Felos commented in his book. Along came Michael Schiavo with just the case right-to-die advocates were looking for.

ON MAY 11, 1998, Felos and Michael Schiavo filed the original petition to remove Terri's feeding tube. In the petition, Felos outlined that Terri had an irreversible medical condition such that she was dependent on artificial provision of nutrition and hydration through a gastric feeding tube. He added that, prior to her incapacity, she had "specifically expressed her desire not to remain alive should she be in an irreversible condition . . . and not to have her life maintained by artificial means should she be in such condition." Felos cited the privacy-rights provisions in the Florida Constitution and the Fourteenth Amendment to the U.S. Constitution as well as Chapter 765 of the Florida statutes as justification for why Terri was "entitled to have artificial sustenance discontinued."

In preparation for the filing, Felos had collected sworn affidavits from newly hired treating physician Victor Gambone and consulting physician—and "death cruise" partner—James Barnhill. Sticking to the wording of the advance-directive statute, both stated Terri was not competent to make medical-treatment decisions, they were unaware of any advance directive that would prohibit the removal or withholding of life-prolonging procedures, and her condition was "terminal." Neither affidavit specified the nature of her terminal condition, defined in the state statute at the time as a condition that "without treatment, is expected to cause death." In his petition, Felos argued Terri's inability to intake fluid and nutrition naturally was a terminal condition. He also dabbled in semantics and characterized her as "terminally ill."

Neither Terri's brain injury nor her inability to swallow was sufficient to cause her death, however. The malpractice trial had determined she had a life expectancy of more than fifty years. Fitting Terri into this terminal-condition scenario, therefore, was predicated on defining artificial hydration and nutrition as "treatment." Assuming she hadn't developed the ability to take food and fluids orally since her last swallow test in 1992, removal of this "treatment" would indeed induce death. While the Florida Supreme Court found "no significant legal distinction" between artificial feeding and other artificial life support in *Browning*, the statutory definition of life-prolonging medical treatment still did not include feeding tubes, despite Representative King's valiant efforts over the years.

The petition sought a finding from Judge Greer that "there is clear and convincing evidence of the Ward's intent to forego artificial provision of sustenance in her current condition" and an order authorizing Schiavo to proceed with the discontinuance. Felos hedged his bets and also posed a Plan B: "In the event this court does not find clear and convincing evidence of the Ward's intent, make a finding it is in the best interest of the Ward that artificial life support be discontinued, and thereupon, enter an order authorizing the guardian to proceed with the discontinuance of said life support." The best-interest standard deals with the assessment of a person's quality of life and whether the benefits of treatment outweigh the burdens. While there was a national trend afoot moving courts from a specific-intent standard and a substituted-judgment standard to a best-interest standard in regard to determining an incapacitated patient's wishes, Florida statutes did not yet do so.

WITHIN DAYS of Felos's May 11, 1998, petition, the state House Elder Affairs and Long Term Care committee voted unanimously to pass HB 3387. The measure, sponsored by Representative Lois Frankel (D-West Palm Beach), designated memory-disorder clinics in Palm Beach and Leon counties to serve Alzheimer's sufferers. Seemingly tacked onto the bill at the last minute was a provision that created a twenty-two-member panel at the Pepper Institute on Aging and Public Policy at Florida State University to conduct a study of end-of-life care. As the bill describes, the panel would include representatives from hospice, nursing homes, assisted-living facilities, hospitals, physicians, nurses, government officials, and consumers. The Panel for the Study of End-of-Life Care was directed to submit an interim report to the governor, president of the senate, and speaker of the house in six months, by January 31, 1999, and a final report within the year, by August 1, 1999. The measure was filed with the secretary of state on May 29, 1998, and became law without the governor's approval on May 30, 1998. Samira Beckwith and Mary Labyak would be the first named panelists in the interim report. Thus the Florida Hospice network now had a presence in the Florida legislature. In fact, the RWJF-sponsored community-state partnership had more than a presence, but rather, it was given carte blanche authority to change Florida law.

The analysis of HB 3387 does not indicate where the proposal for the panel came from. Charlie Liem, current staff director for the Elder Affairs and

Long Term Care Committee, was working in the Department of Elder Affairs at the time, and he recalled that the genesis of the panel was Jim Towey and his Commission on Aging with Dignity. "He had just gotten a lot of attention and so a number of the legislators established a panel which would look at [Towey's] recommendations and findings, plus get input from particularly the nursing home folks on how to handle the issue," Liem said. "I just vaguely remember a lot of interest about how we ought to modify state statutes to accommodate progression in medical care and the new thinking on how you ought to handle palliative care with people who are dying."

The *Tampa Tribune* reported nine months earlier, in September 1997, that Towey met with state Representative Bob Brooks (R-Winter Park), chairman of the house Elder Affairs and Long Term Care Committee, to discuss ideas for new end-of-life care legislation.[13] This was at about the same time that the RWJF commissioned the National Conference of State Legislators to lay the groundwork for the community-state partnerships aimed at changing state laws.

The Tampa paper also reported an unlikely alliance had formed over those same months between Towey and the pro-euthanasia Hemlock Society. According to the paper, the idea came about during a debate Towey set up in Florida between Hemlock founder Derek Humphry and national hospice and fellow Last Acts leader Ira Byock. Looking back, former Florida Hemlock Society president Mary Hudson recently described the partnership as one formed on either side of a "barbed-wire" fence. The partners stood intransigently on opposite ends of the assisted suicide and euthanasia spectrum. But Towey declared they still had "a lot in common."

"We both want patients to have more control over their care. We both want better pain management. We're both opposed to the overly medicalized deaths people suffer in hospitals," Towey explained to the *Tribune*. Another link between these two death-with-dignity forces was their advocacy of the third path. According to the paper, Towey met with Hudson to work out the details of their nascent alliance.[14] By then, the Hemlock Society had abandoned efforts to pass assisted-suicide legislation in Florida. A blurb under "Recent Developments in Physician-Assisted Suicide—October 1997" posted on the Web site of Willamette College of Law in Oregon reported the Hemlock Society had abandoned efforts to push a physician-assisted-suicide law in Florida after it failed to find a legislator to sponsor the bill. "Instead, Hemlock has joined forces with the Florida Commission for Aging with Dignity (which opposes physician-assisted suicide) to seek passage of legislation to improve end-of-life care," the notice stated.[15]

Hudson was in the process of drafting a legislative bill on pain treatment titled Florida's Pain Management Bill when she met with Towey. The proposed legislation sought protection from civil liability for physicians who prescribed high doses of drugs that had the double effect of killing the patient's pain and the patient. "People are suffering needlessly and requesting aid in dying," read the letter of introduction attached to the draft measure sent by Hudson to lawmakers for their consideration in the 1998 and 1999 legislative sessions.

A *Tampa Tribune* editorial at the time predicted this influential duo would make an impact on dying: "Towey and Mary Bennett Hudson, Hemlock's Florida president, haven't worked out the details of a specific bill, but they know they want to convince lawmakers that death deserves more attention than it has gotten in the past," the commentary read. "Their combined political strength has the potential to help all Floridians die more peacefully."[16]

Bob Brooks, a former infectious-disease specialist who was subsequently appointed secretary of the Department of Health by Governor Bush, served as the End-of-Life Panel's chairman. Department of Elder Affairs Secretary Bentley Lipscomb served as deputy chair until December 1998, when he was replaced by newly appointed secretary Dr. Gema Hernandez, who was also a national advisor for RWJF's community-state partnerships program. Brooks worked with Pepper Institute executive director Melissa Hardy to staff the panel. Like so many other leaders in the death-with-dignity movement, Hardy was inspired by the death of her mother, who was resuscitated in contravention to her will and died what death-with-dignity proponents call a "medicalized death" in the hospital. Hardy's eye-opening experience put the Pepper Institute on the same path to reform as Towey's commission.

Sponsor RWJF charged its statewide panel to focus on three goals:

1. Build clinical capacity to deliver quality end-of-life care.
2. Empower individuals, families, and communities to advocate for quality end-of-life care.
3. Help reform public policies to support quality end-of-life care.

According to instructions laid out by the legislature, Florida's twenty-two-member End-of-Life Panel was composed of:

Two persons representing hospice organizations and one hospice consumer appointed by the Florida Hospice Association

Three persons representing nursing homes and assisted living facilities
Three persons representing hospitals
One person each appointed by the Florida Medical Association, the Board of Medicine, the Board of Osteopathic Medicine, the Florida Bar, and the Florida Nurses Association
One member appointed by the president of the Senate
One member appointed by the speaker of the House
One person representing Towey's Commission on Aging with Dignity
Two persons appointed by the Pepper Institute
One person representing the Health Quality Assurance Division of the Agency for Health Care Administration
The Secretary of Elder Affairs and one consumer representative appointed by the secretary.

Accordingly, the panel consisted of Samira Beckwith, Mary Labyak, Jack Gordon, LuMarie Polivka-West, Dr. Howard Tuch, Marshall Seiden, Dr. Susan White, Belita Moreton, Joan Fullbright, Dr. Alvin Smith, Dr. Gary Winchester, Dr. Robert Panzer, Kenneth Rubin, Cathy Emmett, Senator Ron Klein (D-Delray Beach), Representative Bob Brooks, Jim Towey, Dr. Marie Cowart, Dr. Leo Sandon, Marshall Kelley, E. Bentley Lipscomb, and Stan Godleski.

Although the panel was lauded by Brooks and Hardy for its heterogeneous composition, the panelists' background information provided in the January 31, 1999, interim report revealed that, in terms of ideology, the participants were more of one mind than a hodgepodge of disparate views. Specifically, the consumer representative appointed by Lipscomb, Stan Godleski, worked in the hospice industry, serving as vice chair of the board of trustees of Hospice of Southeast Florida. Godleski was also a former state director of AARP, which backed Representative King's 1989 legislation to pull feeding tubes from terminal patients. Likewise, Cathy Emmett's Florida Nurses Association backed King's 1989 effort. Emmett was also a board member of the Florida Bioethics Network, which placed a singular priority on patient self-determination. The appointed representative of the Florida Medical Association, Dr. Alvin Smith, was also a member of Towey's Commission on Aging with Dignity.

The cross-pollination of professional experiences suggested several of the panelists shared the goals of Last Acts—changing laws to foster and institutionalize palliative care and the third path to dignified death, expanding access to hospice and minimizing death at hospitals, and promoting widespread use, recognition, enforcement, and liability protection for carrying out advance directives. This was not unexpected, given that the End-of-Life Panel doubled as the Last Acts community-state partnership in Florida.

The panel deviated from its legislative mandate and elected to solicit input from seventeen nonvoting advisors, whom it invited to join in the discussions at the meetings. While this board of advisors included Dr. D. Mike McCarron of the Florida Catholic Conference, the addition of other bioethicists, hospice representatives, and right-to-die proponents further skewed the collective thinking. Among the advisors was Kenneth Goodman, the director of the bioethics program at the University of Miami. Goodman served as the keynote speaker at the Florida State Guardianship Association's 2005 conference at which Michael Schiavo was awarded Guardian of the Year. "Frankly, what he said his wife wanted is what most reasonable people want," the *Orlando Sentinel* quoted him as saying. "It's primitive to believe that human consciousness is not important. What most of us value about life is cognition and communication and interaction. We don't value simply not being dead."[17]

Another advisor who played an active role on the panel was right-to-die advocate Dr. Lofty Basta. Panel chair Brooks recruited the Clearwater cardiologist and founder of Project GRACE (Guidelines for Resuscitation and Care at End-of-Life). Basta brought along another member of his organization's executive committee, the Reverend Celillon Alteme. Vice president at Project GRACE was Mary Labyak, and in exchange for Basta's participation on the panel, Brooks joined Project GRACE as an advisor. Basta later served on the community board of advisors for Labyak's Hospice of the Florida Suncoast.

According to the minutes of panel meetings, bioethicist Bill Allen with the University of Florida College of Medicine was invited to address the group on September 15, 1998. As discussed in the previous chapter, Allen expressed the opinion on MSNBC's *Scarborough Country* that Terri Schiavo was no longer a person after her brain injury.

Project GRACE is a statewide effort under the auspices of the American College of Cardiology's Florida Chapter to establish guidelines for end-of-life care. According to its Web site, the group is "dedicated to changing the death-defying, technology-driven approach to end-of-life care to a holistic, compassionate one that respects human dignity and the individual's best interests and personal wishes." Lofty Basta wrote about his participation in Florida's End-of-Life panel, and Brooks penned an article describing his recruitment of Project GRACE in a special supplement to the journal *Clinical Cardiology* in February 2000.

With his reference to the "medicalization of dying" echoing Towey's sentiment, his goal of "transforming America's death-denying medical culture," and his citation of RWJF's SUPPORT statistics, Basta could almost be accused of working from Last Acts talking points.[18] But Basta arrived at his right-to-die advocacy through his own brush with death. In 1987 the successful cardiologist who formerly viewed himself as a "mighty healer" was diagnosed with prostate cancer. He said his experience as a patient was humbling and taught him how invaluable it was to have the right to say "no" to treatment. He shared this epiphany in a book, *Graceful Exit: Life and Death on Your Own Terms*. Like Towey, Basta also developed his own version of an advance directive form.

In response to the legislative mandate to include clergy on the End-of-Life panel, the Pepper Institute appointed Florida State University professor of religion Dr. Leo Sandon. According to his background information provided in the interim report, the ordained minister writes a regular religion column for the *Tallahassee Democrat* and has an academic interest in "ethical issues of an aging society," but he was not an active religious leader of a congregation or ministry. Indeed, "clergy proved to be a very difficult group to engage," according to the Last Acts grant report.

Noticeably absent in the legislature's mandate for the composition of the panel was any representation of pro-life and disability rights organizations, like Florida Right to Life and Not Dead Yet. Thus critics of Terri Schiavo's death accuse the lawmakers of stacking the deck on the panel charged with the important task of dictating end-of-life law that would impact all Floridians. Melissa Hardy attempted to remedy this somewhat with the addition of D. Mike McCarron of the Florida Catholic Conference on the advisory board.

Still, Brooks and Hardy believed the panel was "an innovative and effective approach to the formulation of End-of-Life (EOL) policy recommendations." Brooks and Hardy wrote an assessment of the panel, published in the *Journal of Palliative Medicine,* stating: "Crucial to the success of the panel were the dimensions of the deliberative process embraced by the panel. This process supported an impressive level of mutual respect, trust, and openness among the panel members that, with only minor exceptions, allowed the members of the panel to rise above the parochial political battles that have often preempted serious debate on controversial EOL issues."[19]

Over its thirteen-month existence the panel hosted seven public hearings throughout the state to gauge Floridians' sentiments on the issues. To advertise each hearing, Brooks submitted an opinion piece in local papers that described some of the horror stories to which the panel hoped to write a new ending:

- "In Orlando, an elderly woman became seriously ill while visiting a restaurant. An emergency-medical team resuscitated her and rushed her to a local hospital, where she underwent open-heart surgery. She lingered in the intensive-care unit for a week, unresponsive, before finally dying. She was 81 and had not wished to have extraordinary measures used to prolong her life."
- "In Cape Coral, a son and his wife struggled to provide comfort and care in their home to his elderly mother, who had Alzheimer's disease. Before dementia overcame her, the elderly woman and her son obtained a living will to ensure that she would not be kept alive against her wishes. But after a home-health aide found the woman not breathing, emergency-medical technicians arrived to resuscitate her. The son explained that his mother filled out a living will. Not enough, the medical workers said—they could officially recognize only a state-approved 'Do Not Resuscitate' order. Distraught, the son apparently fetched a revolver and ordered the emergency-medical technicians to leave his mother alone. Arrested before he could say good-bye to his dying mother, the son now faces felony charges."[20]

IN ADDITION to the public forums, the panel held ten formal meetings, during which members and advisors gradually hashed out recommendations for the legislature. Likely due to Towey's influence, combined with Brooks's adamant opposition to assisted suicide, the panel refused to address the issue: "Nothing in this recommendation should be taken to promote or condone physician-assisted suicide or euthanasia," the final report declared. Similar language made its way into the associated statute, Chapter 765, which was revised as a result of the panel's recommendations. Instead, the primary goals of the panel were to improve pain management of individuals on their deathbed; provide more training of health-care professionals on death and dying issues and the importance of honoring advance directives; creating a standardized do-not-resuscitate form so that it would be portable and easily recognized by EMT, hospital, and nursing home and hospice personnel; and providing protection from civil liability for those medical personnel who honored advance directives.

Minutes of the work group and panel meetings show an additional chief concern among panelists and advisors, which repeatedly surfaced at the public forums, was the need to better define or eliminate the "terminal" requirement for life-prolonging procedures to be refused or withdrawn and to lower the requirement of having two physicians certify a patient as terminal to one physician's certification.

"We're finding that many health-care professionals—doctors and nurses—and family members don't agree when someone is terminal," said panel member and state senator Ron Klein.[21] Panel discussion revealed many physicians were hesitant to make the terminal diagnosis because it automatically resulted in lost care and coverage.

The confusion and hesitancy behind the terminal diagnosis motivated other panelists like Alvin Smith and Broward County attorney Kenneth Rubin, who represented the Florida Bar on the panel, to urge "terminal" be scrapped altogether. "Why do I have to be terminal in order to have my medical wishes respected if I'm eighty years old, have led a good life, and recorded those decisions when I was still competent?" Bob Brooks asked rhetorically.

Klein concurred. "I think the public testimony showed us that the terminal illness language was more of an impediment than a protection. If removing it eases their burden, I think it's the direction all states should go," said Klein's legislative aide, Kelly Skidmore.[22]

"Terminal is almost impossible to define," agreed panel member Jack Gordon, the longtime head of the Hospice Foundation of America. "We are all terminal. It's just a question of when, and the when is not definable."[23]

Twenty-one of twenty-two panelists voted to remove the terminal requirement from Chapter 765, which critics argued would have effectively made the advance-directive process a back door, of sorts, to assisted suicide. Jim Towey was the lone dissenter. "We shouldn't be making this dramatic change until we have heard more from the disabled, the poor, the elderly," he argued. "Those groups aren't worried about getting too much care. They are worried about getting any care at all."[24]

On January 31, 1999, the End-of-Life Panel released its interim report, outlining a total of twenty-four recommendations. Four dealt with advance directives, nine addressed palliative care and pain management, and eleven regarded the financing and general regulation of end-of-life care. The key recommendations were to drop the "terminally ill" requirement, reduce the certification requirement from two physicians to one in the presence of an advance directive, standardize the DNR and make it portable, protect provider actions taken in accordance with advance directives, and expand access to and education about palliative care and pain management. Additionally, the panel unanimously endorsed the following goals:

- The right to refuse treatment and the patient's right to make decisions about his or her care and his or her surrogate's right to carry out the patient's wishes when he or she is no longer capable of decision making.
- The right to die without aggressive curative treatment does not equal an obligation to die at any age or with any disability. This right is about supporting an individual's right to make choices along the life continuum in the context of their values, their beliefs, and their situations.

WHILE THESE objectives reference the "right to die" and the "right to refuse treatment" in general terms, no specifications were provided as to what treatment the panelists' viewed to be eligible for removal. Specifically, feeding tubes, or artificial nutrition and hydration, were not mentioned in the panel's recommendations. Likewise, there were no recommendations related to the vegetative state. The likely reason for this was that these issues were not raised by the general public at the open forums, according to the minutes of the hearings.

With the panel's recommendations in hand, the legislative members of the panel went back to Tallahassee to work within their respective committees to craft legislative proposals. Senator Klein returned to the senate's Health, Aging and Long-Term Care Committee, which consisted of Charlie Clary (R-Destin), Mandy Dawson-White (D-Fort Lauderdale), Howard Foreman (D-Fort Lauderdale), Jack Latvala (R-Palm Harbor), William "Doc" Myers (R-Stuart), and Burt Saunders (R-Naples).

Representative Brooks, who was appointed secretary of the Department of Health on January 1, 1999, handed the panel's recommendations to the house Elder Affairs and Long-Term Care Committee. Representative Nancy Argenziano (R-Crystal River) sponsored the resulting legislative proposal. Among her cosponsors was Representative Gus Bilirakis (R-Palm Harbor), who is a past member of both the Hernando–Pasco County Hospice and the Hospice of the Florida Suncoast boards of directors. The other committee members and cosponsors were David Bitner (R-Port Charlotte), Elaine Bloom (D-Miami Beach), Heather Fiorentino (R-New Port Richey), Sally Heyman (D-North Miami Beach), Suzanne Jacobs (D-Delray Beach), Suzanne Kosmas (D-New Smyrna Beach), Curt Levine (D-Boca Raton), Ken Littlefield (R-Wesley Chapel), Alzo Reddick (D-Orlando), and Eleanor Sobel (D-Hollywood).

Both the subsequent Senate and House committee bills went beyond the recommendations spelled out in the End-of-Life Panel's interim report and redefined "life-prolonging procedure" to specifically include "artificially provided sustenance and hydration." While the summary of the House bill claimed the End-of-Life Panel specifically recommended the feeding-tube provision, the Senate bill linked the provision to the general goals unanimously endorsed by the panel of "the right to refuse treatment" and "the right to die without aggressive curative treatment." This lone revision, which proved fatal for Terri Schiavo, meant feeding tubes could now be pulled from patients pursuant to the conditions laid out in the advance-directive law. Under the cover of the End-of-Life Panel, the 1999 legislature succeeded in quietly accomplishing what Representative Jim King and others had been struggling to achieve for a decade.

During the floor debate, lawmakers were more focused on a raging fight over the proposed removal of the terminal requirement. The Florida Catholic Conference and Governor Bush balked at the panel's recommendation to scrap the term. Legislators reportedly scrambled to strike a compromise in the final hours of the session and wound up putting the terminal requirement back in the measure but modifying it per the Senate bill. As a result of the compromise, the legislators made very specific changes to Chapter 765. In addition to the terminal requirement, two other conditions were added as triggers for the advance-directive protocol: an "end-stage condition" (such as advanced Alzheimer's) and "persistent vegetative state." The compromise was seen as necessary protection for the disabled and other vulnerable citizens. While Towey hailed the eleventh-hour about-face, Mary Labyak and Kenneth Rubin were nonplused. "A panel is convened, people worked hard, and I feel that their recommendations were not followed," Rubin told *Broward Daily Business Review.*

"This is a step, not as big a step as [we] had hoped to make," said Melissa Hardy. "Whether it's going to be enough is still a question mark."[25]

THE LEGISLATURE followed through on the panel's recommendation to reduce the requirement of two physicians to one for determining terminal condition, end-stage condition, or persistent vegetative state in an advance directive or surrogate scenario. But lacking an advance directive, two physicians' opinions were still required. The lawmakers also approved a process for creating a standardized version of the DNR order, adopted the panel's recommendation on improving access to and education about palliative care, provided civil liability protection for those who honor DNRs, and authorized the state's pharmacist licensing board to implement a new pain management certification that required pharmacists to undertake regular, continuing education to maintain certification.

Other noteworthy features of the 1999 legislation were that the designation of anatomical gifts were added to the advance-directive process, and physicians or facilities who refused to execute advance directives would have to transfer such patients to a facility that would comply. The cost of the transfer would be borne by the uncooperative facility.

In a striking departure from the panel, the legislation created a special section in Chapter 765 that introduced the notion of "best interest" of the patient. Both the House and Senate bills sought to establish a procedure for discontinuing life-prolonging procedures for a person in a persistent vegetative state who had neither an advance directive nor designated a health-care proxy prior to incapacitation. Under this new section of the law, life support could be removed from the so-called unbefriended if a guardian deemed it was in the patient's best interest. Recall that the only requirements for court-appointed guardians are that they be residents over the age of eighteen with no criminal background and no financial interest in the ward—although this last criterion was effectively waived for Michael Schiavo.

George Felos later expounded on this change in statute in his closing arguments during the 2002 evidentiary hearing: "Until a very recent amendment to Chapter 765, in order to remove artificial life support if there were no written directives, Your Honor, or written designation of a proxy, you must—you are required to have clear and convincing evidence of the patient's intent." He added, "[Chapter] 765 was amended to add 765.404 which was a special statute, section of the statute, on persistent vegetative state. And they said, when there is no advanced directive and we have no evidence as to what the intent of the patient is, then under certain circumstances artificial life support can be removed from a patient in a persistent vegetative state if it's in the best interest of the patient." Felos went on to define this best-interest standard as being based on the consensus of public opinion that "most of us in this situation would choose not to be kept alive artificially."

The combination of this new best-interest standard and the feeding tube being defined as medical treatment held potentially ominous consequences for the tens of thousands of guardianship cases across the state. As a result, feeding tubes could be pulled from patients in terminal or end-stage conditions or in PVS who had neither written nor oral advance directives, so long as their court-appointed guardian, in consultation with the attending physician and the "medical ethics committee" of the facility where the patient resided, or else the Florida Bioethics Network, concluded it "is in the best interests of the patient."

"Let me tell you the dirty little secret that I've discovered in litigating this case and looking into medical literature," said Schindler attorney Pat Anderson. "Old people in nursing homes in America have their feeding tubes disconnected. They're starved to death every day of the week. There's no court intervention because there's no family member to oppose it. Now, a lot of times it's the family member who wants to inherit who thinks it's way too inconvenient to have Aunt Minerva hang around for too much longer."

More than just a threat to the elderly, S. C. Lewis, the mother of an adult disabled daughter, believed "best interest" was code for the prejudice people have about disability. "When they adopted this 'best interest' standard, you no longer have to know what the patient's wishes are," she said. "Anybody can be killed by a proxy's refusing medical treatment on their behalf."

By April 29, 1999, ninety days after the panel filed its interim report, Governor Bush added his signature to the legislation, and Florida law was changed, effective October 1, 1999. Less than four months later, George Felos stood in court and declared it was "the law in Florida" that artificial provision of sustenance is considered medical treatment. The swift and timely revisions to the Florida statute connected the dots in the May 1998 petition filed by Felos between Terri's condition being terminal and the proposed discontinuance of her artificial hydration and nutrition. But even more fortuitous for Felos, the statute newly defined Terri's diagnosed PVS condition. Additionally, the brand-new section to the statute created to establish the best-interest standard supported Felos's fallback position of finding the discontinuance in Terri's best interest in the event the court would not consider the Schiavos' testimony clear and convincing evidence of her wishes.

Was it statutory serendipity or a set-up? Where did those very specific changes to Chapter 765—passed out of the legislative committees—that were tailor-made for *Schiavo v. Schindler* come from? Kelly Skidmore, legislative aide to bill sponsor Klein, described the bill-drafting process as very collaborative and could not recall where the feeding-tube provision came from. "It could have come from hospice," she ventured. "Just like any piece of legislation, once it has been put into bill drafting, then everybody has the opportunity to say, 'Put this in' or 'Put that in.' . . . It could have come from another member of the legislature who for whatever reason wanted [the provision]—I'm not saying that happened with this particular piece of legislation." For former House majority leader Jim King, who was subsequently elected to the state senate while the legislature was hammering out the changes to 765, it was an opportunity to take care of unfinished business dating back to 1989 regarding the removal of feeding tubes. His chief legislative aide said the removal of feeding tubes was something he would have advocated in 1999. And King was applauded by the Hemlock Society, renamed End-of-Life Choices, for his reluctance to support "Terri's Law," which passed while he was president of the state senate in 2003. He has since called it "the worst vote" he ever made. His biography posted on the Florida government Web site lists him as the current president of the board of directors of Florida Hospice and Palliative Care, which coordinated the creation and management of the End-of-Life Panel. His honors and awards list includes the Hospice Hall of Fame Award.

A common thread of hospice runs from RWJF, through the End-of-Life Panel, through the House legislative committee, through the lawmakers debating the bill on the floor, to the final product of a changed law that benefited Felos in trying *Schiavo v. Schindler.* The hospice links between and among Hospice of the Florida Suncoast president and End-of-Life panelist Mary Labyak, then-chairman of the Hospice of the Florida Suncoast board George Felos, End-of-Life panel member and future Hospice of the Florida Suncoast board member Lofty Basta, and house legislation cosponsor and fellow Hospice of the Florida Suncoast board member Gus Bilirakis prompted Schindler supporters to call the provision redefining artificial sustenance as medical treatment the "Schiavo Amendment."

Interestingly, the Hemlock Society subsequently drafted Felos to be the guest speaker on October 6, 2001, to serve as their expert on the 1999 law at a Hemlock-sponsored event to help Sarasota seniors update their living wills. Likewise, Choice in Dying sent out eight thousand letters to alert its members to the changes in the law.

"The euthanasia movement is fueling this whole case. They're trying to get legalized physician-assisted suicide approved in Florida," Bob Schindler speculated in 2002. "And Terri's a pawn." Was Terri Schiavo another Charles Hall? Brian Schiavo says his brother Michael is neither a member of the Hemlock Society nor was he recruited by them or any other right-to-die organization. Brian Schiavo says he even tried to recruit the Hemlock Society to help defray the cost of litigation, but the organization steered clear of the case.

"We had nothing to do with litigation of any kind. Our position through the entire [Terri Schiavo case] was that this is why advance directives are critically important to have completed so that this sort of public spectacle doesn't happen to you," said Hemlock spokesman Christian Abeyta.

"Everybody has lost sight about what this whole court case is about," Brian Schiavo lamented in an interview with the *Salt Lake City Deseret News*. "And that's what the frustrating part is, because it's about Terri. This whole thing is about Terri."[26]

13

"Judicial Homicide" or Rule of Law?

IN WRAPPING UP HER opening arguments in the original trial over Michael Schiavo's petition to remove his wife's feeding tube, Schindler attorney Pam Campbell wished Judge George Greer "good luck." The politically savvy lawyer offered this goodwill gesture because the trial marked Greer's first in probate court after having spent the prior two years in the Family Law Division. Greer took his first seat on the bench in the Pinellas–Pasco County Sixth Judicial Circuit Court in January 1993 and was initially assigned to the Juvenile Division. He then spent more than three years in the Probate, Guardianship, and Trust Division before being assigned to Family Law.

The Clearwater Bar Association March 1998 newsletter reported that Greer was "experiencing a strong learning curve" in Family Law.[1] That was a polite way of addressing the raging controversy swirling around one of his recent rulings, which had fatal consequences. On February 26, 1998, forty-four-year-old Helene Ball McGee petitioned his court for a protective injunction against her husband, whom she said had forced himself on her sexually, burned her belongings, and accused her of being "possessed by the devil."

"He wrote a letter stating he wants to change my name to Celene because Helene is from hell and must be destroyed," McGee wrote in her petition. "I am afraid he will act on these threats and try to kill me because my name is Helene." Because she told the court clerk he had never physically abused her,

Greer denied the petition. Two weeks later the husband stabbed the woman to death, and Greer got his first taste of public protest, when her co-workers rallied outside the courthouse outraged by his handling of the case.

"She was terrified," one of her co-workers told the *St. Petersburg Times.* "She told me, 'Maybe he's going to have to kill me before I can get a restraining order.'"[2] The paper reported that records indicated Pinellas County sheriff's deputies were called out to the McGees' home twice for domestic-violence incidents, during which the husband was found to have burned his wife's collection of angels, crosses, and other religious items in the fireplace, along with thirty pairs of her shoes.

Greer defended his ruling, asserting that hindsight is 20/20. "I have read, reread, and reread it," he said of the woman's petition. "I saw no violence. I saw no real fear of imminent violence."[3]

"As a judge, there's always the fear that you're going to miss something and somebody is going to get hurt," Greer recently told the local paper looking back on the incident. "It happens in all cases. When you make those kinds of decisions, there's very little you can do to be 100 percent certain because you never have 100 percent of the facts."[4]

"Now this same gender-biased judge, with utter disdain for women, is the same judge in charge of the Terri Schindler Schiavo case," retired Lee County Sheriff John McDougall railed in an open letter, drawing attention to the McGee killing posted on various Internet sites in March 2005.

With the Terri Schiavo case, Greer faced an avalanche of criticism and received scores of threatening e-mails and letters that prompted the sixty-three-year-old jurist to travel with a sheriff's deputy escort. The FBI arrested one San Francisco woman for writing on an America Online message board, "If [Terri] dies, I will kill Michael Schiavo and the judge."[5] Agents similarly arrested a man in Fairview, North Carolina, on charges of sending an e-mail threat allegedly offering a $250,000 bounty for Michael Schiavo's death and $50,000 for Judge Greer.

Over the course of his seven-year tenure on *In re Guardianship of Schiavo,* Greer rendered numerous controversial orders, the discussion of which could fill a book. This chapter will highlight the decisions that sparked the most debate and prompted some, including attorney Ken Connor, to characterize the outcome of the adjudication by Greer and the Second District Court of Appeals and the refusal of the Florida Supreme Court to review the case as "judicial homicide."

"As one who is concerned about protecting innocent life and who recognizes that the law's first responsibility is to protect innocent life, you have to look at what has gone on heretofore and shake your head in dismay at the way in which the legal system has operated," Connor, who served as legal counsel to Governor Bush, remarked in a radio interview with talk journalist John Sipos in April 2004. "What has happened in the lower courts, in my view, in a very real sense represents a black eye to our justice system."[6]

GEORGE GREER donned his black robe after a successful career in local politics. Born in Brooklyn, New York, but raised in Dunedin, Florida, Greer graduated from Clearwater High School and then attended St. Petersburg Junior College and Florida State University, where his housemate was future Doors lead singer Jim Morrison. In an uncalculated move that would later prove beneficial to his political career, Greer also attended FSU's archrival, the University of Florida, where he earned his law degree. The young lawyer practiced zoning and land-use real estate law and worked as a volunteer on various judicial campaigns. At the age of forty-six he set his sights on the county commission and wrested a seat away from the board's lone Democrat. The Republican became a fixture on the commission over eight years, also serving as the chairman of the commission.

Like a magnet to controversy, Greer was publicly criticized in 1991 for being one of five commissioners who took a $4,130 trip to Grand Cayman Island to study water desalination plants.[7] Before that there was the Coopers Point land coup, in which the proverbial "I've got swamp land in Florida to sell you" took place. The late 1980s scandal involved Clearwater city environmental manager Michael Kenton, who spent years lobbying the state to buy 136 acres of environmentally sensitive land, known as Cooper's Point in Pinellas County, for use as a city park. When the state offered a reported $37,500 for half of the 25 developable acres, Kenton approached the city with a proposal to buy. He failed to disclose, however, he owned a 15 percent stake in the transaction. Kenton partnered with a prominent land developer, the Sembler Company, and bought the property for $1 million. Sembler then hired Kenton as its environmental consultant for $50,000 due to his "expertise in getting developments through the city's red tape," and Kenton resigned from his city job.

Little more than two months later the *St. Petersburg Times* caught wind of a scheme to sell the same parcel of land to the city of Clearwater for $2.6 million. Publicity initially killed the deal. At that point, Greer and his fellow county commissioners decided to bail Kenton out by putting up $1.3 million, or 65 percent of the purchase price of $1.95 million, in order to enable the deal to still go through with the city. Clearwater wound up with the deed after shelling out the other $650,000, leaving many wondering what was in it for the county.[8] The *Times* editorial board questioned the role Greer played in the arrangement, noting that his close friend, who would run his judicial campaign a couple years later, was the attorney Sembler hired to orchestrate the deal. The paper pointed out attorney Timothy Johnson had "an amazing record of having his clients' proposals win official approval."

"[There's] a lot of smoke surrounding [this] major land deal. It would behoove the County Commission to be satisfied there is no fire here before approving the Cooper's Point purchase," the editorial board wrote. "We are speaking of principles in public land purchase programs."[9]

Friends and colleagues describe Greer as impenetrably calm, detailed, articulate, and a "hands-on everyday politician." An "everyday politician" who counts Pinellas County's heaviest hitters among his close friends, including political consultant Mary Repper and former chamber of commerce chief Ed Armstrong. Greer has a reputation for being vindictive, and it's said he "never forgets." Upon a request for an interview with the judge, public information officer Ron Stuart said that Greer would not be commenting on the case so long as it remained open, deeming it "inappropriate." The case is still open at the time of this writing. Greer has taken the opportunity of several interviews with the *St. Petersburg Times* to comment, however.

"The really difficult part of this job," he complained in a March 6, 2005, article, "is that you can't defend yourself." Greer is legally blind and has a soft voice and a mild manner.

"I don't think he has any real enemies," David Kurland, a lawyer and former roommate, said of his longtime friend. "He has a political streak in him. He understands political survival." Former commission colleagues observed that Greer avoided the spotlight. "I cannot believe that in his worst nightmare he could have imagined a case more heart-wrenchingly political," fellow longtime commissioner and Hospice of the Florida Suncoast community advisory board member Barbara Sheen Todd said of Greer's presiding on the Schiavo case.[10]

Schindler attorney Pat Anderson offers a countering assessment. "He's a politician," she said. "He loved the spotlight, talking to reporters, schmoozing. Yeah people who say he hated the spotlight, they either have another George Greer in mind or they just don't know him. He was delighted." Anderson also said when she was deciding whether to take the case back in 2001, she was told that Greer "never got reversed."

In re Guardianship of Schiavo was said to have affected the self-described "compassionate conservative" jurist at a personal level. In the days leading up to the final removal of the feeding tube on March 18, the pastor of Greer's Calvary Baptist Church sent a letter to Greer, reported WorldNetDaily, counseling him about Terri's prospective death as a result of his order. "You must know that in all likelihood it is this case which will define your career and this case that you will remember in the waning days of life. I hope you can find a way to side with the angels and become an answer to the prayers of thousands," Pastor William Rice wrote.[11] Following an exchange of letters, Greer reportedly withdrew his membership from the church. The *St. Petersburg Times* reported the Southern Baptist said he had unrelated problems with the church, but was also unhappy about coverage of the Schiavo case in the Florida Baptist Witness, the news journal of the Florida Baptist State Convention. Rice had written a column published in the news journal challenging the removal of Terri's feeding tube. In his letter to Greer, Rice took issue with comments Greer made in the March 6, 2005 *St. Petersburg Times* article about his relationship to the church.[12]

"There are no Ten Commandments out there," Greer said while pointing to his outer office. "My oath is to follow the law, and if I can't follow the law, I need to step down."[13]

"RULE OF TERRI"

"THIS 'RULE of law' business really sets my teeth on edge," said Pat Anderson. "I know what the Florida statutes provide, and I know how they were disregarded in this case." Instead, Anderson believed what she called the "Rule of Terri" governed *Schiavo:* "If it will help her to die, then we definitely observe every nicety in the rule or the statute or the case law. If it will impede her death, we will ignore it completely."

"My pleading binders are three feet high. I put fifty to seventy affidavits in front of [Greer]," she said, referencing the affidavits from medical experts disputing the PVS diagnosis; the testimony from Cindy Shook, Trudy Capone, and Fran Casler that Michael Schiavo wasn't telling the truth about knowing Terri's wishes; the sworn statements by Carla Sauer Iyer, Heidi Law, and Carolyn Johnson alleging neglect and abuse of Terri by Michael Schiavo in his capacity as her guardian; and more. "In the whole time I was on the case, I was only able to put Dr. [William] Hammesfahr and Dr. [William] Maxfield on the stand live. And that was only because the [Second District Court of Appeals] ordered it. So when people talk to me about the rule of law, I'm not really impressed. That tells me that they don't know the case, they haven't looked into it."

Within weeks of Judge Greer's original ruling, the sworn affidavits from medical experts disputing the PVS diagnosis began to trickle in. Greer refused to hear them. He also declined to hear the testimony of former Schiavo girlfriend Cindy Shook whose testimony surfaced on April 24, 2001, after Terri's feeding tube was removed for the first time. Greer ruled her testimony missed the one-year deadline on newly discovered evidence. After failing to arouse Greer's attention, the Schindlers took Shook's testimony to civil court. Sixty hours into Terri's first dehydration and starvation ordeal, her parents sued Michael Schiavo in the general civil division of the circuit court claiming that he had "engaged in an intentional . . . deceptive, and intolerable course of conduct that amounts to perjury, fraud on the court." After Circuit Court Judge Frank Quesada ordered Terri's feeding tube reinserted, the suit landed before a three-judge panel of the Second District Court of Appeals on July 11, 2001. The panel, led by Judge Christopher Altenbernd, determined the Schindlers' suit in the civil division of the trial court was really an attempted end run around Greer, ordered the Schindlers to take their case back to Greer, and ordered him to hear the new testimony.

"We conclude that a final order entered in a guardianship adversary proceeding, requiring the guardian to discontinue life-prolonging procedures is the type of order that may be challenged by an interested party at any time prior to death of the ward," Altenbernd wrote in the unanimous opinion. In other words, the judges established a new legal standard by determining wards in life-and-death guardianship cases should be given the same protection as death-row inmates.

In Anderson's view, the Rule of Terri also revealed itself in the months leading up to the evidentiary hearing mandated by the appellate court, when Greer denied the Schindlers' request to have Terri undergo twenty-five different diagnostic tests for purposes of evaluation ahead of the unprecedented court proceedings. Greer favored Michael Schiavo's petition seeking to severely limit the diagnostic testing. Florida statute 765, which outlines the conditions under which life-prolonging procedures can be withheld or withdrawn, specifies the condition of vegetative state must be determined and diagnosed as permanent.

Greer also authorized the payment of the expert witnesses solicited by George Felos to come out of Terri's guardianship but refused to extend the same arrangement to the expert witnesses on the Schindler side. Specifically, $8,444.21 was disbursed to Dr. Peter Bambakidis and the Cleveland Clinic, $7,715 was disbursed to Dr. Melvin Greer's Family Clinical Practice at the University of Florida, and Dr. Ronald Cranford and his travel agency were reimbursed $2,477.16. Greer did authorize Drs. William Maxfield and William Hammesfahr to be paid deposition fees in the amount of $500 and $1,000, respectively.

After the hearing, and upon Pat Anderson's discovery of the full-body nuclear imaging bone-scan report, Greer ruled in favor of Michael Schiavo not to investigate the matter. He also rebuffed Anderson's entreaties to compel Michael Schiavo to appear for a deposition, even though he ruled Anderson could depose both Schiavo and his fiancée. Schiavo dodged several appointments to give sworn testimony in regard to Anderson's 2002 motion to remove him as guardian.

As another aspect of the Rule of Terri, the Schindlers pointed to Greer's consistent denials over the years to permit Terri to have swallowing therapy and a test to see if she could receive food and fluids orally. According to Terri's medical records, her last swallow test was on June 23, 1992. Dr. Jay Carpenter with Professionals for Excellence in Health Care testified that he observed Terri over a forty-five-minute period handling her saliva and sinus secretions properly, which indicated to him she might be able to swallow. He argued pulling the feeding tube without first giving Terri therapy amounted to "murder." Speech-language pathologist Sara Green Mele with the Rehabilitation Institute of Chicago testified that Terri had "a good or excellent prognosis for being able to be taken off her feeding tube." Mele successfully weaned four cognitively disabled patients off of feeding tubes in the month prior to evaluating Terri.

In a March 2, 2000, hearing, Dr. James Barnhill testified that, since the 1992 swallow test, annual examinations by a speech pathologist indicated Terri had a high risk of aspiration, and so he concurred with treating physician Dr. Victor Gambone "there was no point in doing another swallowing study." Barnhill further testified Terri had uninhibited bite-reflex activity, which would create a problem in oral feeding, and he predicted attempted oral nutrition would result in aspiration with insufficient nutrition passing to her stomach to maintain her. Caregivers Carla Sauer Iyer and Heidi Law claimed they occasionally fed Terri thickened liquids like Jell-O, and she did not aspirate. Felos argued their testimony was fabricated, and Greer subsequently found it not credible. "The court does not feel that another medical procedure merely to specify what portion of insufficiency would result from the removal of the feeding tube warrants the granting of this [swallow test]," Greer ruled on March 7, 2000.

In his report to Governor Jeb Bush, guardian ad litem Jay Wolfson, who was appointed by Chief Circuit Court Judge David Demers pursuant to

"Terri's Law," which was passed by the legislature in October 2003, stated there was "feasibility and value in swallowing tests and swallowing therapy being administered" to Terri. He put a qualification on it, however, suggesting Schiavo and the Schindlers needed to agree in advance how they would use the results of the test. Nevertheless, Greer held firm to his 2000 ruling and denied subsequent requests for swallow tests and therapy.

After Terri's death, Pinellas-Pasco chief medical examiner Jon Thogmartin weighed in on the swallow-test controversy. He called the reported Jell-O feedings "extremely dangerous." On the basis of the three swallow tests in 1991 and 1992 and the subsequent evaluations by the speech pathologist, Thogmartin concluded Terri could not swallow. His pathological findings showed her throat muscles had atrophied. "The removal of the feeding tube would have resulted in her death, whether she was fed and hydrated by mouth or not," he declared at the June 15, 2005, press conference to release his report, explaining that she would have aspirated any fluid and eventually choked to death. His postmortem findings showed evidence of aspiration in the lungs, but he wasn't sure how much of that was due to the dehydration she suffered.

In responding to the autopsy, the Schindlers stressed that Terri's inability to swallow was the result of muscle atrophy. "Terri was denied therapy for twelve years, and muscles atrophy when they are not used. We will never know if therapy would have helped," the family said in a statement. In petitions and civil lawsuits filed over twelve years, the Schindlers consistently raised the issue of the cessation in Terri's therapy that occurred in late 1991, according to her medical records, when she was transferred from an aggressive rehabilitation center to the first of two nursing homes, before finally coming to reside at hospice for her last five years.

MOTIONS TO RECUSE

THE RULE of Terri prompted the Schindlers to file five motions to disqualify Judge Greer over the years, beginning with a motion filed April 12, 2001. In an affidavit filed in support of the motion, Bob Schindler stated he feared Greer harbored a "bias or prejudice" toward him and his family. One example of this alleged bias he cited was the fact that Greer had refused to allow testimony from Bobby Schindler during the 2000 trial about conversations he had with Terri shortly before her collapse "to the effect that she was unhappy in her marriage and was planning to divorce Mr. Schiavo." In opposition to the motion, Felos countered, "A party's dissatisfaction with a judge's rulings is legally insufficient to constitute grounds to disqualify the judge." Likewise, Greer found the motion "legally insufficient" and denied it. Greer found the subsequent motions equally "not legally sufficient." During a November 5, 2003, hearing on another motion to disqualify, Anderson described a phone conversation Greer had with an unidentified woman who apparently shared the details with Anderson.

"When she brought up the issue of Michael Schiavo's living with another woman and perhaps giving him an ulterior motive in these proceedings, you replied, 'Everybody sins; let he who is without sin cast the first stone,'" Anderson said, according to a transcript of the hearing. "There are other remarks, Judge, but I think it's clear that you've gone too far in discussing the merits [of this case]. I know you've put a lot of work in this case."

Greer admitted to taking the phone call but maintained he simply directed the person to "please read the orders." He added, "Miss Anderson, I can't control the media any more than you can."

"Judge, I don't want to get crossways with you on this, but I really think, because of your pattern of rulings, the perception of bias in the public mind is there, and frankly, I feel the bias," Anderson persisted. "I feel that if Terri called you from Hospice, you'd try to talk her into giving up and dying. I feel that you're committed to her death."

Two months earlier Anderson based another motion to disqualify on the grounds of ex parte communications. In that motion, Anderson cited conversations Greer reportedly had with Florida deputy attorney general John Carassas and with longtime friend and Pinellas County Sheriff Everett Rice at a baseball game regarding the case. Greer reportedly expressed outrage to Carassas over a letter Governor Jeb Bush had faxed him urging the appointment of a guardian ad litem.

Rice later applauded Greer for not disqualifying himself from the case: "I think one of the most telling things about Judge Greer's integrity is that he could have dumped this case many times. He would not shirk his responsibility and he would not dump it on a fellow judge."[14] But Greer's former colleague and fellow Cayman Island traveler Charles Rainey told the *Miami Herald* he believed Greer should have recused himself.[15]

GUARDIANSHIP OVERVIEW

GREER'S OVERSIGHT of Terri's guardianship also drew criticism. As was discussed in chapter 5, wards of guardianship retain reserved rights, regardless of incapacitation. Statute 744.3215 lists those rights, which include the rights:

- To be restored to capacity at the earliest possible time.
- To receive necessary service and rehabilitation.
- To be treated humanely, with dignity and respect, and to be protected against abuse, neglect, and exploitation.
- To receive prudent financial management for his or her property.
- To receive visitors and communicate with others.
- To counsel.

The Schindlers argued in multiple actions before Greer that Michael Schiavo proved himself unqualified to serve as Terri's guardian based on his alleged violations of the rights listed above. In addition to demanding resumed therapy, the family argued Schiavo's openly adulterous relationship with Jodi Centonze, with whom he has lived for ten years and has fathered two children, denied Terri her right to be treated with dignity and respect. They repeatedly filed petitions seeking a divorce for Terri, which were denied.

The family also argued that spending the lion's share of Terri's medical-care trust fund monies on paying Michael Schiavo's attorneys who were fighting for her death amounted to mismanagement of her property. Their complaints fell on deaf ears in Greer's court as he proceeded to authorize endless expenditures from her guardianship fund, including the cost of her cremation and burial. In 1998 the court-appointed guardian ad litem Richard Pearse suggested Michael Schiavo had a serious conflict of interest, which was grounds to disqualify him as guardian, according to the provisions in state statute. Pearse registered concern that the medical malpractice award money, which amounted to $713,828.85 at that time, hurt Michael Schiavo's lone testimony that Terri didn't want to live under her circumstances.

"His credibility is necessarily adversely affected by the obvious financial benefit to him of being the ward's sole heir at law in the event of her death while still married to him. Her death also permits him to get on with his own life," Pearse wrote in his report, which recommended Greer deny Schiavo's petition to remove the feeding tube.

George Felos responded to this conflict-of-interest claim in his original May 11, 1998, petition, arguing the malpractice award posed a conflict of interest no matter which side of the family is in charge. "There is likelihood in the foreseeable future that [Michael Schiavo] may remarry. If such an event occurred subsequent to the ward's death, petitioner would inherit the ward's estate and the ward's parents would not inherit any portion of the ward's estate," he wrote. "If [Michael Schiavo] remarried prior to the ward's death, upon a divorce, the ward's parents would inherit the entire estate of the ward. Hypothetically then, either [Michael Schiavo] or the ward's parents could substantially gain financially by asserting their respective positions regarding discontinuance of the ward's artificial life support."

The Schindlers' subsequent petitioning to remove Michael Schiavo as guardian, including the November 15, 2002, petition, sought the appointment of one of Terri's siblings, who would not inherit anything upon Terri's death. The petition was never heard.

Among the Schindlers' claims of Schiavo's abuse, neglect, and exploitation of his ward, which state statutes provide wards the right to be protected from, were the restrictions he placed on Terri's visitation. Bobby Schindler and Suzanne Vitadamo were bumped from Schiavo's approved-visitors list in 2001 reportedly because they had inquired at Hospice Woodside whether it was possible to orally feed Terri after her feeding tube was removed. The following year Schiavo barred Terri's parents from visiting for forty-nine days as a result of their release of the clandestine video. Also dropped from the list was Father Thaddeus Malanowski, who provided spiritual ministry to Terri on a weekly basis for close to three years. The family complained Schiavo was "keeping Terri isolated from those willing and desirous of comforting her" and called his behavior an "abuse" of his power as guardian. Greer was apparently not concerned. Guardianship advocates see such tight control of wards exerted on the part of their guardians as par for the course in a system rife with abuse and lacking any serious court oversight.

In the minds of judges, advocates complained, guardians could do no wrong. That appeared to be the case with Greer, who allowed Schiavo to consistently file his mandatory annual guardianship plans late. The outcome of Greer's granting four consecutive extensions to Michael Schiavo on the deadline to file was that he submitted his annual reports for 2002 and 2003 in June 2004. Guardianship plans are progressive plans, which according to the guardianship statute, detail the "plan for provision of medical, mental health, and rehabilitative services in the coming year." Without these plans in place, Greer would have no idea about the welfare of the ward—whether she was being properly cared for in a nursing home or locked in a closet without food, for example.

Under Florida law, the court must review the annual guardianship report to ensure it meets the needs of the ward. Court approval of the plan "constitutes authority for the guardian to act in the forthcoming year." Greer served on a sixteen-member state Committee for Guardianship Monitoring, which has a mission to "be proactive to discover and respond to disputes and issues" to ensure the court fulfills "its legal obligation to protect and preserve the interests of the ward, and thereby promote confidence in the judicial process." Guardianship-reform advocates questioned his commitment to that mission.

GUARDIAN AD LITEM

BEYOND ALLOWING retrospective annual reports, guardianship advocate and Pasco County Clerk of the Circuit Court Jed Pittman believed Greer committed a more serious error: "He should have appointed a guardian ad litem for her." Florida Statute 744.3215 gives wards the right to counsel. Greer did appoint Pearse to give a recommendation on Michael Schiavo's motion to remove the feeding tube in the summer of 1998. After Pearse filed his report on December 30, 1998, recommending Greer deny the motion, George Felos countered Pearse's report with a charge of bias. Pearse then petitioned the court that his term be extended or Greer appoint another guardian ad litem to represent Terri. But six months before the 2000 trial, Greer discharged Pearse and never appointed a replacement. He also disregarded Pearse's recommendation.

As former Schindler attorney Jeff Eckert explained, a guardian ad litem was critically needed during the 2000 trial proceedings to challenge Michael Schiavo's testimony regarding his alleged end-of-life conversations with Terri. "If an attorney had represented her, they would have objected to that testimony because it comes under . . . a well-known law called the Dead Man's Statute. You can't testify about what a dead person or incompetent person testifies to if you have a financial stake. The financial stake in this case was $700,000," Eckert said during an interview on CNN's *TalkBack Live*.[16]

Jay Wolfson, who served as guardian ad litem for thirty days in late 2003, also recommended in his report to Governor Bush that Terri should have a permanent guardian ad litem. "During the more than nine years of adversarial relationships involving Theresa, no permanent Guardian Ad Litem has been appointed to stand exclusively in her shoes," he wrote. "As long as controversy and an adversarial legal relationship exists in Theresa's case, a Guardian Ad Litem should be appointed to represent her exclusive interests." Judge David Demers subsequently rejected the Schindlers' request to reappoint Wolfson after his thirty-day term expired, citing the pending court decision over the constitutionality of "Terri's Law."

In a January 24, 2001, opinion written by Christopher Altenbernd, again on behalf of the unanimous three-judge panel, the Second District Court of Appeals ran interference for Greer, in a sense, by affirming Greer's "discretionary decision" to act as Terri's guardian ad litem instead of keeping one appointed to the case. "Because Michael Schiavo and the Schindlers could not agree on the proper decision, and the inheritance issue created the appearance of conflict," Altenbernd wrote, "under these circumstances, the two parties, as adversaries, present their evidence to the trial court. The trial court determines whether the evidence is sufficient to allow it to make the decision for the ward to discontinue life support. In this context, the trial court essentially serves as the ward's guardian. Although we do not rule out the occasional need for a guardian in this type of proceeding, a guardian ad litem would tend to duplicate the function of the judge, would add little of value to this process, and might cause the process to be influenced by hearsay or matters outside the record."

Anderson could not accept Altenbernd's reasoning. She called it a "totally insane" holding by the appellate court to essentially write Florida Statute 744.3215 "off the books." "That particular ruling opens the floodgates to mass killing in Florida," she said, "and really in other states in the union to the extent that Florida's Terri Schiavo experience has blazed new trails for euthanasia advocates. The case law, the history of the case here, will provide support that a brain-injured, innocent, defenseless, vulnerable adult can be put to death without having their own lawyer because it would be too expensive, would result in 'hearsay,' would be 'duplicative' . . . and so forth and so on."

Not only was the appellate court opinion contrary to Florida Statute 744.3215, according to Anderson, but it also conflicts with Florida Statute 744.309 (b), which states, "no judge shall act as guardian . . . except when he or she is related to the ward by blood, marriage, or adoption or has maintained a close relationship with the ward or the ward's family and serves without compensation." Schindler attorney Joseph Magri ran this objection to the appellate ruling and its conflicts with Florida statutes straight up to the Florida Supreme Court, which declined to hear the case.

"What is shocking about this is that if you're a convicted felon under a death sentence in Florida, there is a mandatory requirement that the Supreme Court review the decision . . . and yet in this case the Supreme Court declined to review any appeal arising out of the Terri Schindler Schiavo case. So the net effect means that convicted capital felons have greater protection than an innocent person such as Terri Schiavo," said attorney Ken Connor. "If Terri Schiavo dies pursuant to court order, this will be a judicial homicide."

Felos consistently defended Greer's decision to not appoint a permanent guardian ad litem for Terri. "Petitioner's characterization of Judge Greer as a 'proxy,' . . . does not change the identical role he played here: the neutral arbiter of factual and legal disputes," he wrote in a March 24, 2005, pleading to the U.S. Supreme Court. "The claim that Judge Greer violated Chapters 744 and 765 of the Florida Statutes by allegedly acting as Mrs. Schiavo's 'guardian' and/or 'proxy' cannot, as the district court concluded, withstand scrutiny. Chapter 744 merely precludes a judge from acting as a guardian except under certain familial circumstances, and has no application here: Mr. Schiavo, not Judge Greer, is Mrs. Schiavo's guardian." Felos further argued in favor of Greer's not appointing separate counsel for Terri. "Mrs. Schiavo had a guardian (Mr. Schiavo) who was legally obligated to represent her interests, and who was represented by counsel, who in turn represented her interests."

Judge Greer consistently quoted Altenbernd's opinion in future rulings to justify his decisions over the next four years to not appoint a guardian ad litem or allow Terri access to her own counsel.

NO TERRI VISIT

In serving as Terri's proxy for seven years, many question why Judge Greer never met his ward. Ten days before the start of the 2000 trial, the Schindlers filed a motion requesting Greer visit Terri at Palm Garden of Largo Convalescent Center. Pamela Campbell argued that, because it was a bench trial, and Schiavo and Felos had disputed guardian ad litem Richard Pearse's input, it was increasingly apparent the case rested solely on Greer's shoulders. She felt he should "personally visit with the ward . . . in order to have a current and clearer perspective so as to make a more informed opinion as to the issues at hand." At a hearing on the matter, however, Felos argued that since both parties had agreed Terri was in PVS and her condition wasn't in dispute, observing her was unnecessary. Greer agreed with Felos.

Bronx Supreme Court Justice Douglas McKeon believed it was a no-brainer to go to the bedside of incapacitated witnesses. In a one-week period in Aril 2005, McKeon made three nighttime visits to the Children's Hospital of Montefiore Medical Center, where a thirteen-year-old boy had been declared brain dead after a tooth infection spread to his brain. His mother was reluctant to authorize removal of life support and filed a petition to block hospital administrators. After conferring with hospital administrators and doctors, the judge arranged for an outside doctor to examine Teron Francis and confirm the hospital's assessment. Once that happened, the mother was satisfied it was time to take her son off of the respirator.

"When you come right down to it, there is no greater decision that confronts a judge than a decision involving whether somebody lives or dies," McKeon said. "It seems to me that your whole being has to go into making that decision. You have to feel that you have done everything humanly possible to learn the facts and to do the right thing. And there may not be any legal rationale for what I'm about to say, but I think you have to look at that person. You have to be in their presence. You have to stand by their side."

When asked whether he was concerned about being accused of judicial activism, McKeon responded, "I don't think that's judicial activism. I just think that's your obligation. . . . These are helpless human beings who can't speak for themselves. You have to become involved. I don't think you can be detached."

TERRI'S WISHES

GREER'S MOST controversial rulings serve as bookends to the contentious court battle over Terri Schiavo, from his original "death order" to a ruling in the last days that amounted to "ordering the commission of a felony" in the minds of some. In 2000 Greer earned condemnation for discrediting and dismissing nearly all of the Schindler testimony as "clearly biased" and "slanted" while finding nearly all of the Schiavo testimony "credible" and "candid." Greer specifically discarded the testimony of Terri's mother, sister, and childhood girlfriend Diane Meyer on the basis of "fuzzy math." Not realizing Karen Ann Quinlan didn't die immediately after her respirator was unplugged in 1976, Greer estimated Terri would only have been eleven or twelve when she reportedly watched television programs about Quinlan. Meyer asserted the movie she viewed was in 1982, when Terri as a nineteen-year-old reportedly stated, "Where there's life, there's hope" following Meyer's crude joke.[17] Attorneys only discovered computational error on Greer's part in early 2005. Their revelation went nowhere, as Greer rejected Schindler attorney David Gibbs's motion that "this mistake of fact should reverse the court's determination of the credibility of the witness, Diane Christine Meyer." Greer wrote in his March 9, 2005, ruling, "Her applicable testimony regarding the conversations about Karen Ann Quinlan was in the present tense. Since the subject was the removal of the life support that occurred in the 1970s, her testimony that the conversations occurred in 1982 was not credible." He added, "Moreover, although the witness appeared credible at first, as her testimony progressed it became clear to the court that she was not an unbiased witness. . . . Based on this review, the error regarding Karen Ann Quinlan's death date does not change the court's conclusion that there was clear and convincing evidence supporting its decision on what Theresa Marie Schiavo would have chosen."

At the heart of the credibility issue were Terri's wishes. As George Felos stated in his opening arguments, "The major issue in this case is what Terri's intent was." That's a good question, said Bush attorney Ken Connor in 2004, while he was preparing to depose Michael Schiavo as part of his defense of the constitutionality of Terri's Law. "We'd like to know, for instance, why Mr. Schiavo, when he was seeking to recover millions of dollars in connection with the underlying medical malpractice case, didn't tell the jury that Terri's wishes were to starve and dehydrate under these circumstances," he said.[18]

Despite the questions surrounding Michael Schiavo's credibility, Greer defended his delay and ruled his belated recollection that Terri said she wouldn't want to live dependent on artificial means, and similar testimony by his brother and sister-in-law, rose to the level of "clear and convincing evidence." Critics argued the judge failed or misapplied the standard established by *Cruzan* and, as a result, that his ruling was dangerous. "That standard is vital to the survival of hundreds of thousands of people with severe disabilities in guardianship because, as numerous studies prove, guardians too often value the life of their ward far less than the ward values his or her own life," explained disability rights advocate Diane Coleman.

Even attorney George Felos believed there was a chance his client's testimony might not pass this stringent test, and so he offered an alternative in his 1998 petition for Greer to find that discontinuance of artificial nutrition and hydration was in Terri's "best interest."

When the late John Paul II delivered a statement on March 20, 2004, equating the withdrawal of food and fluids from the incapacitated with "euthanasia by omission," attorney Pat Anderson seized the opportunity to argue that removal of Terri's feeding tube would violate the practicing Catholic's religious beliefs. "I feel the duty to reaffirm strongly that the intrinsic value and personal dignity of every human being do not change, no matter what the concrete circumstances of his or her life. A man, even if seriously ill or disabled in the exercise of his highest functions, is and always will be a man, and he will never become a 'vegetable' or an 'animal,'" the pontiff declared.[19] After an international symposium at the Vatican on life-sustaining treatments and the vegetative state, John Paul II proclaimed the administration of food and water, even when provided by artificial means, is not a medical act or a life-prolonging medical procedure, but rather a natural means of preserving life. He stated its use should always be considered "ordinary and proportionate, and as such morally obligatory for Catholics."

"Terri has now changed her mind about dying," Anderson wrote in a motion in July 2004, based on the papal statement. "As a practicing Catholic at the time of her collapse, who was raised in the Church and who received twelve years of religious schooling and instruction, Terri does not want to commit a sin of the gravest proportions by foregoing treatment to effect her own death." Anderson and volunteer co-counselors bolstered the motion with a memorandum of law filed September 2, 2004, in which the attorneys argued that all Catholics are obliged to submit to doctrines of faith or morals proclaimed by the pope, as successor to Peter and vicar of Christ on earth.

In reply, Felos argued that Terri's "religious beliefs [were] irrelevant since she left specific oral advance directives that were clear and convincing evidence of her intention to terminate [the] medical treatment," and that Anderson's motion failed to demonstrate the pope's speech constituted a substantial change in church policy.

Citing the fact that the Schindlers had already argued the pope's 1980 *Declaration of Euthanasia* in their appeal to the Second District Court of Appeal, Greer ruled, "Nothing has changed. There is nothing new presented regarding Terri Schiavo's religious attitude, and there is still no religious advisor to assist this or any other court in weighing her desire to comply with this or any other papal pronouncement."

Attorney Gibbs and the volunteer co-counselors promptly appealed Greer's ruling: "The record contains minimal testimony in the 2000 trial about Mrs. Schiavo's religious beliefs and practices. The nine sworn affidavits appended to [Anderson's July 2004] motion and memorandum of law present a substantial amount of new factual information on this subject, and the finding that there is nothing new presented is simply contrary to the record."

"When the trial court ruled in February 2000 that Mrs. Schiavo would elect not to be kept alive by life-prolonging procedures, the Roman Catholic Church had not made a clear and explicit statement on what constitutes a 'life-prolonging medical procedure.' . . . Indeed, no Roman Pontiff had ever addressed the issue," the attorneys wrote in the appeal. "Whatever her decision was before the Pope spoke, Mrs. Schiavo would now decide to continue the provision of her food and water by artificial means."

The Second District Court of Appeal, without opinion, denied the appeal on December 29, 2004.

TERRI IN PVS

THE OTHER hotly contested aspect of the 2000 ruling—and a pillar of the whole case—was the determination that Terri was in persistent vegetative state. "At first blush, the video of Terri Schiavo appearing to smile and look lovingly at her mother seemed to represent cognition," Judge Greer wrote in his ten-page ruling. "The court has carefully viewed the videotapes as requested by counsel and does find that these actions were neither consistent nor reproducible. . . . She clearly does not consistently respond to her mother."

As was discussed in chapter 8, Florida Statute 765 defines PVS as "a permanent and irreversible condition of unconsciousness in which there is the absence of voluntary or cognitive behavior *of any kind*. Greer apparently took his cue from Ronald Cranford who repeatedly relied on a requirement of consistency with perceived behavioral responses in his determination that Terri was in PVS. But in his order Greer actually raised the bar even higher for Terri and declared her responses needed to be "constant" in order for her to avoid the PVS label: "The court finds that based on the credible evidence, cognitive function would manifest itself in a *constant* response to stimuli."

"That new definition is broad enough that those who are seeking to do so can drive a hearse through it," Rita Marker, with the International Task Force on Euthanasia and Assisted Suicide, wrote in an amicus curiae brief later filed in the case. "The trial court's new standard would lead to inconsistent and overly broad determinations of what is or is not a 'permanent vegetative state' and potentially subject thousands of people with severe cognitive disabilities to third-party enforcement of their 'right' to die," agreed Max Lapertosa, who composed another amici curiae brief filed on behalf of Not Dead Yet and sixteen other national disability rights organizations.

On January 24, 2001, the three-judge panel of the Second District Court of Appeals affirmed Greer's ruling: "We have carefully reviewed the record. The trial court made a difficult decision after considering all of the evidence and the applicable law. We conclude that the trial court's decision is supported by competent, substantial evidence and that it correctly applies the law."

Greer and Felos would thereafter assert they were "affirmed" in the face of criticism or the suggestion of impropriety. But a common public misperception is that when a court case reaches the appellate level, it means a new set of eyes retries the case. This is not the case. The standard of appellate review holds that as long as there is competent, substantial evidence to support a court's findings of fact, the appellate court will affirm. Findings of fact are given great deference on appeal because the appellate court does not have the opportunity to observe the demeanor of the witnesses. Only legal errors get reviewed de novo.

"An appeal is not a new trial. No new evidence is introduced. A reviewing court presumes the trial judge was correct in his decision and may only upend the lower court if it misapplied the law or had no evidence to support its factual conclusions," Felos explained in his book. "Facts that can be interpreted two ways provide no grounds for reversal. If the salient fact in an auto injury case is whether the light was red or green at the time of the accident, and one witness says it was red and three others saw it as green, an appellate court has no legal authority to overturn a trial judge's conclusion it was red. That is why appeals that challenge the factual findings of lower courts have a very slim chance of success."[20]

Over the years the Schindlers amassed a sizable number of affidavits from medical experts who disputed the PVS finding based on their review of Terri's medical records and the taped neurological examinations from 2002. Because of the high misdiagnosis rate—43 percent—and the advent of MCS, or minimally conscious state, some forty medical specialists filed affidavits in court demanding new diagnostic testing before authorities proceed with the removal of the feeding tube. In the eleventh hour in March 2005, Department of Children and Families investigator Dr. William Cheshire Jr. visited with Terri for ninety minutes in addition to reviewing her medical records and the taped neurological examinations. He concluded: "There is a greater likelihood that Terri is in a minimally conscious state than a persistent vegetative state. This distinction makes an enormous difference in making ethical decisions on Terri's behalf."

Greer responded in a ruling that the distinction did not matter to the extent that it was found "by clear and convincing evidence" that Terri "did not want to live under such burdensome conditions and that she would refuse medical-treatment assistance." Rather than being muffled, the chorus of dissent grew louder as Greer rebuffed the attempted intervention by the state social services agency, DCF, and congressional committees. Greer had earlier defied Governor Bush and the Florida legislature by ruling Terri's Law unconstitutional, when Florida law dictated he should have presumed it was constitutional, according to legal analysts.

"I think Judge Greer made the decision back in 2000 that he didn't think Terri should live. We call that the death order. And the mountain of evidence—the plethora, the truckload of evidence—[that came in] as to

Terri's wishes, as to the conflict of interest, as to Terri's medical condition [was ignored]," said Schindler attorney David Gibbs III. "Unfortunately in this case Judge Greer basically dug in and he . . . decided that his original decision in 2000 would stand regardless of what was shown to him, regardless of what the governor wanted, regardless of what the Florida Legislature wanted, then unbelievably . . . regardless of what the Congress, the federal government, the Department of Justice, or the president wanted."[21]

Greer caught flak from both sides of the aisle.

"There were times that we were mad at the judge because he wouldn't follow through with the judgment," Brian Schiavo said. "Always giving [the Schindlers] another opportunity and another opportunity, but after a while it was all frivolous." And Felos often complained about the "delay tactics" of the Schindlers and their "throwing everything but the kitchen sink" into their motions. In an August 26, 2003, press conference he also expressed frustration with Judge Greer for apparently dragging his heels and with "the folly of the judicial system." He added, "I also want to mention we are disappointed that Judge Greer did not set an immediate date for the removal of the artificial feeding tube. There is no practical reason why that hearing could not have been held later this week."

Felos continued, "The snail's pace of this case, as in other cases, eventually frustrates the privacy interests and liberty of the patient. The courts have already found and declared that she did not want to be kept alive artificially in this condition. They've already found that she has a right to remove her feeding tube. Yet as we go on and we have further delays and we have a feeling on the part of the judiciary that time is not of the essence—how these cases often resolve is the patient dies from other causes while artificial life support is in place. And that's a tragedy."

Eventually, by February 2005, Greer had reached the point of no return. In an order dated February 25, he announced, "Five years have passed since the issuance of the February 2000 Order authorizing the removal of Theresa Schiavo's nutrition and hydration and there appears to be no finality in sight to this process. The Court, therefore, is no longer comfortable in continuing to grant stays pending appeals." And he held firm to this resolution.

Gibbs took issue with that ruling, appealing to the Second District Court of Appeals over the fact that Greer modified his 2000 order by ordering the guardian to cause the removal of Terri's "nutrition and hydration" instead of authorizing him to discontinue "artificial life support." This distinction sparked thunderous outrage.

S. C. Lewis exclaimed, "You have to feed disabled people! It's against the law to not feed a disabled person." The mother of a severely brain-disabled daughter took particular offense from Greer's March 8, 2005, order barring oral nutrition and hydration in addition to the removal of Terri's feeding tube. That order paved the way for Terri's thirteen days of "marked dehydration," in the words of medical examiner Jon Thogmartin, who commented he'd never seen such a high sodium–low water content in a person before.

"It's against Florida Statute 825," Lewis added. "Judge Greer ordered the commission of a felony and ordered the Pinellas Park Police Department to comply with the commission of a felony based on evidence they didn't think she could swallow? She hadn't had a swallow test in ten years."

But the ruling caught the attention of U.S. Representative Dave Weldon (R-Florida), who introduced the Incapacitated Person's Legal Protection Act in Congress. (This measure, and the explosive reaction to it, will be explored in chapter 14.) "Of the many rulings that Judge Greer has invoked on Terri Schindler-Schiavo, the most troubling and inhuman was his recent decision to deny food or water to touch her lips should the death order come into effect. When our judicial branch refuses to defend the weakest among us, it has lost its constitutional bearings and deserves to be criticized and given society's highest disapproval," Weldon observed on March 11, 2005, and had his statement posted on the House Web site.

Greer's ruling added momentum to an Internet petition posted for the purposes of impeaching him. The *Empire Journal* reported in March 2005 the online petition had collected more than forty-one thousand electronic signatures. At the same time, Pamela Hennessey, the media volunteer for the Terri Schindler-Schiavo Foundation, filed a formal request with the Florida House of Representatives Judiciary Committee to initiate articles of impeachment against Greer.[22] Apparently that request was reviewed and discarded. "I'm unaware of any official effort to impeach him," said Brenda Ajamian, senior legislative aide to the committee chair, Representative David Simmons (R-Longwood), adding that she'd heard from sources, "Judge Greer acted correctly in all instances." Likewise, the state Judicial Qualifications Commission reported no formal complaints against Greer. Meanwhile, Greer was reelected by a wide margin on August 31, 2004, and his legal peers at several area bar associations awarded him their top honors in support of his handling of *Schiavo* in the wake of her death. On July 15, 2005, the Florida chapter of the American Board of Trial Advocates named Greer and U.S. District Judge James Whittemore recipients of its Jurist of the Year award.

BEYOND GREER . . .

AS THE primary adjudicator in *Guardianship of Schiavo,* Greer is the most visible target for faultfinding. But rulings by other jurists are also candidates for critique. Fellow Sixth Judicial Circuit Court Judge W. Douglas Baird, who is married to a *Tampa Tribune* reporter and is said to socialize with employees of both the *Tribune* and the *St. Petersburg Times,* publicly questioned the constitutionality of Terri's Law before Governor Bush had filed his first pleading defending the law. Baird then ultimately declared it unconstitutional. He also refused to permit the Schindlers to be parties in the case, even though the appellate judges opined they considered the parents of a ward to be interested parties. Baird also protected Michael Schiavo from having to give testimony under oath in a deposition with Ken Connor, who sought evidence on behalf of Governor Bush, disproving Schiavo's claims that Terri wanted to die. Baird agreed with a motion from Felos and the ACLU that argued allowing the governor's attorneys to take their requested seven depositions opened the door to revisiting the already decided guardianship case.

"I think this entire matter has already become more than it should about personalities and less about the law," Baird told the *St. Petersburg Times* shortly after he acquired the case. "I don't think I need to contribute to that."[23]

While grateful the Second District Court of Appeals held Greer's feet to the fire and mandated an evidentiary hearing to revisit the PVS ruling in 2002, Pat Anderson argued in her closing arguments the court "stacked the deck" against the Schindlers. "We conclude that the Schindlers . . . must prove only by a preponderance of the evidence that the initial judgment is no longer equitable," Judge Christopher Altenbernd wrote in the October 17, 2001, mandate. "To meet this burden, they must establish that new treatment offers sufficient promise of increased cognitive function in Mrs. Schiavo's cerebral cortex—significantly improving the quality of Mrs. Schiavo's life—so that she herself would elect to undergo this treatment and would reverse the prior decision to withdraw life-prolonging procedures."

The appellate court further held the evidentiary hearing was "only for the purpose of assessing her current medical condition, the nature of the new medical treatment and their acceptance in the relevant scientific community." In other words, no unproven alternative therapy could be proposed, which is essentially how George Felos and Ronald Cranford characterized the vasodilatation and hyberbaric therapy protocols of William Hammesfahr and William Maxfield.

"Is help available for Terri?" Anderson posed in her closing arguments. "In a way the Second DCA has stacked the deck against it. It has to be new therapy, but it has to be accepted in the literature. Dr. Maxfield testified it probably takes six to eight years from the time that there are research findings to the time that the actual practice has changed."

As predicted by Anderson, Greer subsequently ruled the therapies were "experimental insofar as the medical community is concerned with regard to patients like Terri Schiavo, which is borne out by the total absence of supporting case studies or medical literature."

As was discussed in chapter 10, disability rights activists took issue with the subjective requirement that the new treatment "significantly improve her quality of life." "Ms. Schiavo's fate is intertwined with that of many people with disabilities who must rely on surrogates," wrote Max Lapertosa in an amici curiae brief on behalf of seventeen national disability rights organizations. "If the legal standard of proof in cases involving termination of life support is watered down to the point where Ms. Schiavo's 'quality of life'—as determined by others—justifies her death, then one cannot distinguish Ms. Schiavo from anyone else who is 'incompetent,' including thousands who cannot speak due to developmental or physical disabilities. It is naive to believe such attitudes would not be used to justify the death of people with severe disabilities if the opportunity arose."

Disability advocates were also disappointed the U.S. Supreme Court refused to hear the case. Disappointed, they say, but not surprised. "It was all about the technicalities of constitutional law pertaining to the branches of government," said Diane Coleman with Not Dead Yet, "and not about Terri Schiavo's constitutional right to due process."

The final cog in the wheels of justice in *Schiavo* was U.S. District Judge James Whittemore, who was given jurisdiction to hear the case after the unprecedented action by Congress and President Bush. For those mildly, moderately, or even viscerally opposed to the intervention by the federal executive and legislative branches in a state judicial proceeding, Whittemore's ruling that "Terri Schiavo's life and liberty interests were adequately protected by extensive process provided in the state courts" was vindication that politicians should not have intruded in a "private family matter." As Felos had predicted following oral arguments in Whittemore's Tampa courtroom, "The Constitution is preserved."

Schindler supporters and other legal minds weren't so sure. They view Whittemore's refusal to order a temporary restraining order to restore Terri's feeding tube while he apparently conducted a de novo review of a twelve-year legal battle in little more than twenty-four hours as a one-two punch to Terri Schiavo, the thousands of severely disabled Americans she represented, and the brilliant checks-and-balances scheme crafted by the Founding Fathers to protect the nation from tyranny.

"Judge Whittemore's ruling refusing to feed Terri while a full trial is conducted in federal court flouts the clear intent of Congress in passing the federal Terri's Law," observed Burke Balch, director of the National Right to Life Committee's Robert Powell Center for Medical Ethics. "The senators and representatives who crafted and voted to enact the federal Terri's Law repeatedly emphasized, during its consideration in Congress, that it would be inconceivable that a federal court, directed to conduct a new proceeding fully to determine Terri's rights, would not reinsert the feeding tube for the duration of those proceedings."

Under the rules of the U.S. Senate, unanimous consent was required for the federal Terri's Law. Due to opposition from Senator Carl Levin (D-MI), Congress could not mandate that Terri be fed while a federal judge conducted a de novo review, so this was left to the discretion of Whittemore.

In his review, the Clinton appointee and former public defender rejected Schindler attorney Gibbs's argument that the withholding of nutrition and hydration and denial of rehabilitative therapy constituted a violation of the Americans with Disabilities Act (ADA) and the Rehabilitation Act of 1973. Whittemore stated the ADA only applied to claims of discrimination by a "public entity"—state government—and pointed out that neither Michael Schiavo nor the Hospice of the Florida Suncoast were public entities. Whittemore later declared Judge Greer, who was also named as a defendant in the suit, was not a "state actor." Whittemore found the Rehabilitation Act only applied to the hospice, which receives federal funds, and said the hospice's compliance with Greer's court order did not amount to discrimination.

Responding to Gibbs's argument that the "clear and convincing evidence" standard endorsed by the U.S. Supreme Court in *Cruzan* was not met in this case, Whittemore emphasized the High Court did not "mandate" the use of the standard, and he added that the allegation that the quantum of evidence did not rise to the level of "clear and convincing" amounted to a matter of state law, not federal constitutional law.

"The implications of the judicial death order which was the outcome of this litigation are ominous for all persons with disabilities," argued Gibbs and Catholic University associate dean Robert Destro. "Individuals who are the subject of substituted judgment proceedings are among the most vulnerable of our citizens who cannot speak for themselves. It has taken our nation many years to make good on its commitment to equal justice for persons with profound cognitive disabilities. Unless the State of Florida retains the power to protect the rights of its most vulnerable citizens through due process and equal protection of the laws, the Fourteenth Amendment's guarantees will apply only to those who are capable of defending them on their own."

Whittemore declared the Fourteenth Amendment "inapplicable" because he determined Terri had been granted due process. The federal judge concluded the three guardians ad litem appointed to represent her interests over the course of the litigation maintained her due-process rights. He failed. however, to notice or mention none of the guardians ad litem served during actual trial proceedings. John Pecarek did testify at a hearing in 1993, but he was not made available for cross-examination. Richard Pearse was discharged six months before the pivotal 2000 trial, after Felos charged him with bias. Jay Wolfson similarly was not appointed for the purposes of serving as Terri's counsel during a court proceeding. Contrarily, Wolfson served for all of thirty days, and his recommendations for a swallow test and the permanent appointment of a guardian ad litem were disregarded. "The role of a guardian ad litem in advising the court and the role of an attorney advocating for his client are different roles and one cannot substitute for the other," Gibbs countered.

In addressing the issue of Terri's having legal counsel, Whittemore repeated Altenbernd's opinion that it would be "duplicative." "Throughout the proceedings, the parties, represented by able counsel, advanced what they believed to be Theresa Schiavo's intentions concerning artificial life support," Whittemore wrote in his opinion. "Plaintiffs have not shown how an additional lawyer appointed by the court could have reduced the risk of erroneous rulings."

"For them to say they didn't have ample representation is ridiculous," commented Brian Schiavo. "[Judge Greer] listened to every frivolous motion that came across the bench, and he made judgment on them. Then, finally, he got pissed off when he saw the politics of this."

Whittemore also undercut Altenbernd's validation of Greer's serving as proxy and attributed the notion to the Schindlers. "Plaintiffs' argument effectively ignores the role of the presiding judge as judicial fact-finder and decision-maker under the Florida statutory scheme. By fulfilling his statutory judicial responsibilities, the judge was not transformed into an advocate merely because his rulings are unfavorable to a litigant. Plaintiffs' contention that the statutory scheme followed by Judge Greer deprived Theresa Schiavo of an impartial trial is accordingly without merit," continued Whittemore.

"This massive and intensive judicial . . . scrutiny of a patient's medical condition and intent is unprecedented in the annals of American jurisprudence," concurred Schiavo attorneys in a pleading before the U.S. Supreme Court. "Not only has Mrs. Schiavo's case been given due process, but few, if any, similar cases have been afforded this heightened level of process," the attorneys added, quoting the opinion of the Second District Court of Appeal.

By a two-to-one vote, a panel of the Eleventh Circuit Court of Appeal affirmed Whittemore's rulings. "There is not even a semblance of a due process claim, let alone a substantial showing, as was required for [Whittemore] to grant such relief," wrote the court in its opinion.

For many, Whittemore's ruling and the appellate affirmation ended discussion. They were satisfied the case had been properly handled, Terri had received excessively more than her "day in court."

"This Judge Whittemore reviewed all the evidence that was on the record and decided that there was no additional procedural due process that would affect the ultimate decision in this case, that in fact, the evidence shows that this is what Terri wants," concluded University of Florida law professor Sharon Rush.[24]

For others, Whittemore left the impression this de novo review amounted to more of the same, rather than something brand new. "The statute says 'de novo trial,' That's what it says. That means a complete re-look. You can't do that in an hour-and-thirty-five-minute oral argument." American Center for Law and Justice attorney Jay Sekulow argued on Fox News's *Hannity & Colmes*. "That's not due process. That's a wink and a nod."[25]

"What we asked for in the Congress was a new finding of fact," said Senator Rick Santorum (R-PA). "And this judge in this district ignored it, snubbed his nose at Congress, I think against the law. I think he should be held accountable for it." Likewise Santorum believed Greer's quashing of the House subpoenas also rose to the level of contempt of Congress. Yet no action was ever taken against the jurists.

"**B**Y THE time it was all over with, every point in this case was contested, and that's the kind of case where the presumption in favor of life should be applied. And yet I think there was a general feeling, 'We're sick of these lawyers. We're sick of this case. We've invested a huge amount of judicial labor in the case. It's over. Stop bothering us.' So Terri died on the altar of upholding standards of appellate review," attorney Pat Anderson summarized.

Resolution of the case amounted to upholding standards of appellate review and, once Governor Bush entered the picture, resisting perceived meddling by the legislative and executive branches. As MSNBC political commentator and former Florida congressman Joe Scarborough pointed out, the Eleventh Circuit Court of Appeals "tipped their hand" about this in their opinion. The three-judge panel wrote, "Lawmakers have acted in a manner demonstrably at odds with our Founding Fathers' blueprint for the governance of a free people, our Constitution."

"I have got to tell you, I am shocked that the Eleventh Circuit admitted what this was all about. This entire Terri Schiavo case is all about a fight between the legislative and judicial branch," commented Scarborough. "In my opinion, they are willing to let her die because they don't want to cede power to the United States Congress or the president. . . . This is not about justice. This is about power."[26]

"Sometimes good law is not enough, good medicine is not enough, and all too often good intentions do not suffice. Sometimes, the answer is in the process, not the presumed outcome," wrote Jay Wolfson in the introduction to his guardian ad litem report. In the process that was *Schiavo v. Schindler*, many more questions can be found than answers.

14

Terri's Law

IT'S MIDAFTERNOON IN THE steamy month of September 2003 in Jacksonville, Florida. A bunch of vivacious youngsters swarm into a residential backyard armed with cap guns and Hula-Hoops.

"Hi, Mom. What are you doing? We're going to play cowboys and Indians," they announce.

"Not right here. Can you all play in the front yard?" she replies, putting her hand over her cell phone so that the chattering children will not give away the fact that she isn't dressed in a three-piece suit and sitting in an overstuffed leather chair inside a mahogany-paneled office. The playmates dart away and proceed to begin banging each other with the Hula-Hoops and falling down, pretending to be shot. The mother turns her attention back to her phone.

"Mr. Speaker? As I was saying, I'm so glad you're going to introduce legislation. Somebody needs to do something to save this poor woman. How can you kill someone who's not dying? You must pass a law to save Terri Schiavo."

It's a romantic version of how we would like government to work: hassled housewife of five children, dressed in shorts and flip-flops, standing in her backyard talking to the speaker of the state House of Representatives by phone, encouraging his efforts to craft legislation to address a disabled woman in need. The politician agreed it was important to give it a shot.

"Well, Nancy, we may not be able to save Terri, but it may set a precedent where we can help save other people like Terri," the House Speaker reportedly responded that day.

"Don't say that! You must save her. She cannot be starved to death. We can't do this in Florida," the housewife insisted.

It's romantic and real. Meet Nancy Peek McGowan, whom Schindler attorney Pat Anderson affectionately nicknamed "the hammer." McGowan was the main player from northeast Florida in a small collection of grass-roots volunteers working tirelessly to save Terri Schiavo. This group also included a trio of nurses, including Cheryl Ford and Christina Brundage; S. C. Lewis, the mother of a disabled daughter; a computer guru; PR whiz and media spokesperson Pamela Hennessey; a prominent television broadcaster-turned radio-talk host; a law school pal of Pat Anderson's; and a group of Franciscan brothers from Minnesota. Anderson's Stetson Law School classmate Catherine Peek McEwen was offering her assistance on the case pro bono and had asked her younger sister, Nancy, simply to pray for Terri. But that wasn't enough for McGowan, who decided to take up the cause as her own.

"Terri just kind of drew everyone to herself. And we were all there for one purpose. It was a moral and ethical issue that many of us were just not willing to compromise on. We were all unified in one cause and that was to protect innocent life," McGowan said. "I had this infused passion to try to save Terri because what I saw happening was so wrong and such a violation of human life. It was incomprehensible to me. And I guess I was naive enough to think we were going to save Terri Schiavo."

McGowan is Catholic with a political science degree and comes from a political family. A member of the Republican Woman's Club of Duval Federated and a volunteer for the Justice Coalition, McGowan is accustomed to tackling moral causes while simultaneously making PB&Js for her five children. Her conversation with Speaker Johnnie Byrd (R-Plant City) came about after a chance encounter with Rep. Don Davis (R-Jacksonville) at the beach two weeks earlier.

"Special session coming up, Don. How 'bout we get legislation going to save Terri Schiavo?" McGowan began.

"We could never possibly do that. We don't have the time to muster the votes we need," he responded.

"Well, you should see this petition on the Internet to the governor. People are signing it—they're from all walks of life: Democrats, Republicans, atheists, religious, black, white, poor, and rich. It's just a matter of human rights," she persisted.

McGowan's pitch proved effective, as did the online petition posted by the group's computer guru on a Web site Hennessey donated to the effort. The petition read in part:

> We are requesting that you investigate what the Schindler Family believes are severe abuses conducted against their daughter, Terri Schiavo.
>
> We also request that you review the heavily guarded Department of Children and Families (DCF) sealed investigation report. It contains the agency's findings in response to a formal complaint filed of alleged abuses Terri suffered at the hands of her husband and guardian, Michael Schiavo.
>
> In addition, we ask you to review Terri's court and medical records.

Bob Schindler told WorldNetDaily at the time he was cautiously optimistic about the success of the petition drive, but he had given up on the courts. "Based on our past history with the courts, I've absolutely no confidence in the Florida justice system, the legal system, the injustice system—whatever you want to call it," he said.

After the first wave of five thousand e-mails arrived at the governor's office, Jeb Bush announced he would not intervene in the case. "I'm really limited on what I can do. I think we have to wait and see what the [Florida] Supreme Court says," he said, referencing a pending appeal in the case.[1]

Weeks before she trained her sights on the legislature, McGowan set about recruiting the governor. The housewife who'd never surfed the Internet before swiftly got up to speed and steered into the fast lane of the information superhighway. She began forwarding select analyses of the Terri Schiavo case, which included facts not reported by the media, to the governor and urging his immediate attention. By mid-August McGowan succeeded in getting the ear of the governor when she received a response from him indicating the information was being forwarded to his legal department. The next day, Anderson was contacted by the assistant general counsel for Governor Bush and asked to present a five-page statement to them about the case.

Approximately a week later Bush faxed a letter to Circuit Court Judge George Greer. The letter, contained in the case file, begins: "I appreciate the challenging legal and ethical issues before you in the case of Terri Schiavo. As I have expressed over the course of the past several weeks, our system of government has committed these decisions to the judicial branch, and we must respect that process. Consistent with this principle, I normally would not address a letter to a judge in a pending legal proceeding. However, my office has received over 27,000 e-mails reflecting understandable concern for the well being of Terri Schiavo."

The governor addressed "new rumors" about the guardian's actions related to Terri Schiavo's current care: "It has come to my attention that Mrs. Schiavo has contracted a life-threatening illness, and that she may be denied appropriate treatment. If true, this indicates a decision by her caregivers to initiate an 'exit protocol' that may include withholding treatment from Mrs. Schiavo until her death, which would render this Court's ultimate decision moot. While the issue of Mrs. Schiavo's care is still before the Court, I urge you to ensure that no act of omission or commission be allowed to adversely affect Mrs. Schiavo's health before the Sept. 11 hearing you have set. No one involved should be permitted to circumvent due process or the Court's authority in order to achieve personal objectives in this case."

Terri was, in fact, near death with a white blood cell count of 22,000 and a fever of 102. She was being treated with antibiotics for pneumonia and a urinary tract infection that had developed into sepsis, but Michael Schiavo and George Felos had gone to court seeking permission to stop treating her. Greer agreed to hear the matter and ordered she be treated until the hearing date, but he declined to rule on an emergency basis to allow Schiavo to withhold antibiotics. Anderson noted this was one of the handful of times Greer did not side with Felos. "It is my belief that had [Greer] not gotten the letter from Bush, he would have granted Felos's motion, and Terri would have died then," she said.

Citing a "number of factual disputes regarding Mrs. Schiavo's medical condition, past and current care and therapy, and her prognosis," Bush asked Greer to give "serious consideration" to reappointing a guardian ad litem to independently investigate. He also urged the judge to determine whether "clear and convincing evidence" still existed that Terri wanted to die.

Citing the mandate from the appellate court, Greer announced he was bound to set a date for the feeding-tube removal and declined to appoint a guardian ad litem. For the second time he ordered the tube be removed, this time on October 15, 2003.

Hours after the hearing, Felos and Michael Schiavo held a press conference, during which their anger at Bush was palpable. "I am saddened and angry at Governor Bush's inappropriate attempt to intervene in the case," Felos said, reading a statement from Michael Schiavo. "Bush has deliberately twisted the facts of this case in an apparent effort to kowtow to his right-to-life political supporters. There are no factual disputes remaining in this case. Every factual and legal issue has been examined over and over again by numerous judges and every judge examining the facts and law has ultimately concluded that my wife is entitled to have her medical treatment wishes honored."

The typically soft-spoken Michael Schiavo, who sat next to Felos, appeared incensed. "This isn't his concern and he should stay out of it," Schiavo chimed in.

"It's hard to see how this is not politically motivated," Felos continued. "Apparently twenty days ago, Governor Bush thought trusting the judiciary was sufficient, but in light of political pressure from his political right-to-life constituency he now takes the unprecedented step of trying to intervene in a judicial proceeding. It's just wrong."

Schiavo and his attorney often pointed fingers at the "fanatic" "right-to-lifers" over the years. In truth, prominent pro-life organizations played a role in *Schiavo v. Schindler.* After the 2000 ruling, when Terri was scheduled for the first feeding tube removal, Bob Schindler put out a plea for help to the Life Legal Defense Fund, a small nonprofit in California, which in turn recruited the assistance of the Alliance Defense Fund (ADF), a legal group that works to defend religious liberty, the sanctity of life, and the traditional family. ADF bankrolled a portion of Pat Anderson's litigation expenses.

As the case gathered more momentum, and in measured response to the efforts of End-of-Life Choices, formerly the Hemlock Society, to use the Terri Schiavo case to promote its right-to-die agenda, other organizations like the Family Research Council, Focus on the Family, Concerned Women for America, and the Christian Medical Association mounted a vociferous publicity campaign to combat the right-to-die push. A handful of organizations volunteered their services to the Schindler cause. Chris Ferrara with the Catholic Lawyers Association volunteered to write a pleading, as did Anderson's law school pal, older sister of McGowan, and now-U.S. District Judge Catherine Peek McEwen and Robert Destro, an associate dean of law at the Catholic University of America. The National Right to Life Committee supplied their director of media relations to camp out at Anderson's office and handle the onslaught of journalists' inquiries. The Reverend Patrick Mahoney with the Christian Defense Coalition organized protests.

Arguably, the most recent Schindler attorney, David Gibbs III, is as pro-life as George Felos is pro-death. The devout Baptist's law firm specializes in defending the religious liberties of "Bible-believing organizations." It's an offshoot of his father's Christian ministry, the Christian Law Association, which seeks to spread the gospel of Jesus Christ and help defend constitutionally guaranteed liberties. "I believe that God gives each life a calling,"

Gibbs told the *St. Petersburg Times.* "I believe that I have been called to help other Christians." Gibbs said he covered the case pro bono.

Despite the peripheral assistance of the pro-life groups, the Schindlers' effort to save Terri was a grass-roots mobilization that cut across all ideologies. In response to Michael Schiavo's claim on *Larry King Live* they were being funded by right-wing groups, the Schindlers answered with a press release. In it, Bob Schindler said he could readily document the fact that the family's Web site instead received donations from individuals and no funding from any large organizations. Schindler said their supporters "cut across gender, age, religious affiliation, location, disability, and socioeconomic status." Two days before Terri's death, the *New York Times* reported Schindler authorized a direct-mailing firm to sell a list of their supporters' names. Spokeswoman Pamela Hennessey expressed concern that the family was being exploited and said they did not release any of the names or e-mail addresses gathered at the family's Web site.[2]

IN THE days leading up to October 15, 2003, the Schindlers released the covert videotape they had made in 2001. The footage sparked massive reaction. The e-mails streaming into the Capitol in Tallahassee swelled to 165,000. As the clock ticked down to Terri's second episode of dehydration, the e-mails and faxes reached a crescendo of 5,500 an hour. Felos later likened the correspondence avalanche to a "high-tech lynch mob." As the pressure increased for Governor Bush to exert his executive authority and take custody of Terri, legal scholars submitted analyses supporting his power to act.

"There is probable cause in this case to believe that Ms. Schiavo is a victim of one or more violations of Florida criminal law," wrote Thomas More Law Center's chief counsel and former Kevorkian prosecutor Richard Thompson, along with former federal prosecutors Edward White III and Robert Muise, in a letter to Bush. "Ms. Schiavo's life is at stake. Therefore you should take immediate custody of Ms. Schiavo, provide for her life support needs, including food and hydration . . . direct the Florida Department of Law Enforcement to conduct a full investigation of the facts and circumstances of this case."

Constitutional scholar Herb Titus similarly weighed in: "The chief executive officer of a government is bound by his oath of office to decide matters of constitutional right and power according to the executive's interpretation of the constitution, not according to the judiciary's interpretation. Therefore, if the governor believes that Ms. Schindler-Schiavo has the constitutional right to 'enjoy life' regardless of her present disability, as he stated in filings submitted to the courts, then the governor is duty bound to stop any action taken pursuant to that unconstitutional order that would result in the deprivation of Mrs. Schindler Schiavo's constitutional right to life."

Four days later Governor Bush announced Speaker of the House Johnnie Byrd would introduce HB 35-E (to be known as Terri's Bill) during the special session of the Florida legislature slated for October 20, 2003. Schiavo's guardianship attorney Deborah Bushnell responded to the announcement by faxing a letter to doctors throughout Pinellas County threatening legal action against anyone who defied Greer's court-ordered removal of the feeding tube. Late at night on the first day of the special session, state representatives voted 68–23 in favor of Terri's Bill.

While Speaker Byrd and Representative Davis were revving up legislation to address Terri's plight, Representative John Stargel (R-Lakeland) had been working with pro-life law firms to draft a bill to protect Terri. When the special session was put on the calendar, Stargel's efforts dovetailed with those of Byrd and Davis. Ultimately, Stargel and Davis cosponsored Terri's Bill, which created chapter 2003–418, authorizing the governor "to issue a one-time stay to prevent withholding of nutrition and hydration from a patient" under Terri's specific circumstances and provided that the person who took action in compliance with any such stay would "not be civilly liable" or "subject to regulatory or disciplinary sanctions" and would lapse after fifteen days. Twenty-eight lawmakers did not vote.

"The Legislature's speed was directly proportional to the amount of heat that people from Florida and elsewhere were generating, urging them to step into the gap and stand up on behalf of Terri and others who were similarly situated. I think the people should take heart that their involvement counts and makes a difference," commented attorney Ken Connor.[3]

In comparison, the Senate dragged its feet. But insiders on hand for the debate on the second day of the special session told WorldNetDaily that lawmakers were wrestling with the language of the legislation, conscious that Felos was in the process of filing an injunction to block any executive order from Governor Bush.[4]

Meanwhile, Terri was six days into her dehydration. Pat Anderson accompanied the Schindlers on a visit to hospice. What she saw astounded her. She immediately sent word to the governor's office and McGowan. "They dressed her in clothes to go snow skiing," she said, describing how Terri was wearing a turtleneck sweater and corduroy pants and had two blankets placed on top of her. "I don't know if she'll make it through tonight, Nancy. She's very pale. Her face is sucked in, and she's burning up."

McGowan got on the phone and succeeded in getting a secretary to slip a note with this information into a private meeting of senators convening with then-Senate President Jim King (R-Jacksonville). A short time later the announcement came that the Senate vote was moved up, scheduled for 1:00 p.m. that day. Hours later the senators voted 23–15 in favor of an amended S 12 E, the companion bill to the House measure sponsored by Sen. Daniel Webster (R-Winter Park).

The House promptly approved the bill, 73–24, enacting chapter 2003-418. The governor then signed Executive Order 03–201, which stated in part: "Effective immediately, all medical facilities and personnel providing medical care for Theresa Schiavo, and all those acting in concert or participation with them, are hereby directed to immediately provide nutrition and hydration to Theresa Schiavo by means of a gastronomy tube, or by any other method determined to be appropriate in the reasonable judgment of a licensed physician."

"Like the tens of thousands of Floridians who have raised their voices in support of Terri Schiavo's right to live, I have been deeply moved by these tragic circumstances," Bush declared in a separate statement. "I understand the limitations cited by the judges who have declined to hear the later stages of this case. However, any life or death decision should be made only after careful consideration of all related facts and conditions."

The crowd camped outside Hospice Woodside erupted into cheers upon word of the passage of Terri's Law. "The screaming and crying and singing and praying! It was one of the happiest moments of my life," Christina Brundage told WorldNetDaily, describing the scene.[5] While Suzanne Vitadamo described the day's events as a "miracle," her father revealed: "It's restored my belief in God."

An ambulance was dispatched to the hospice to transport Terri to Morton Plant Hospital in Clearwater for the surgical reinsertion of her feeding tube. With the threat of a lawsuit hanging over their heads, however, doctors waited hours while counsel assessed the level of risk in complying with the executive order. After Circuit Court Judge W. Douglas Baird refused to grant Felos an injunction, an IV line was started and Terri's hydration was restored.

While the unprecedented fast action by the legislature was cause for celebration for the eighty demonstrators gathered outside of Hospice Woodside, it left some lawmakers unsure of themselves. Jim King told the *Tampa Tribune* he was leery of interfering in a case that had been vetted in nearly "every court in the land." He cited "unique and unusual circumstances" as justification for allowing what he considered was a narrowly constructed measure.

Too narrow, the Florida Supreme Court ultimately ruled. "If we are going to err, then let us err on the side of caution," King told the paper. "I just hope to God we've done the right thing."

King later told the *St. Petersburg Times* he and other legislators felt pressured into voting for Terri's Bill by a flood of "phone calls and e-mails" that shut down the state senate phone system and reportedly included "physical and political threats."[6] Although primarily orchestrated by the computer guru and other core Schindler supporters, the communications were deemed by critics to be part of a well-organized national campaign.

"This bill so oversteps our role, it not only sets a dangerous precedent, it turns democracy on its head," complained Rep. Dan Gelber (D-Miami Beach).[7] Senator Tom Lee (R-Brandon) accused Johnnie Byrd of "concocting" the legislation to further his ongoing senate campaign. Byrd denied the claim and stated he was just trying "to do what's right."[8]

While other lawmakers fretted they were attempting to "play God," senate sponsor Daniel Webster felt it was important to "err on the side of life." "There's a woman who can smile, a woman who can respond to her mom and a woman who under current Florida law is alive," he said in an interview on CNN's *Buchanan & Press.* "There's a line right now in the state of Florida, just as there is in every state, that determines whether you're alive or dead. And the legislature is the one that decided what that line would be. And in my opinion, had we not acted, that line would have moved and I wanted to keep it right where it is."[9]

THE HISTORIC move by the legislative and executive branches to override action by the judicial branch of state government prompted a constitutional showdown. George Felos called the emergency measure "odious" and "absurdly unconstitutional." "Terri is the biggest loser here. I mean her personal freedom has been trampled. She was literally absconded from her deathbed in the middle of her dying process," he complained to ABC's *Good Morning America* the following morning.[10]

"Mrs. Schiavo was forced from her hospice bed, was forcibly operated upon, and is now being force-fed through a tube against her will," he wrote in a forty-four-page brief filed with the Florida Supreme Court. "Stripped of her most intimate personal rights, Mrs. Schiavo is more akin to subjects of an absolute dictatorship than citizens of a democratic state." Felos argued that Terri's Law "eradicates Mrs. Schiavo's rights to privacy and due process" and is an "example of legislative and executive overreaching prohibited by the separation of powers enshrined in the Florida constitution."

Making good on its promise to act if the governor intervened, and despite criticism by Not Dead Yet and other civil rights groups that its presence in the case was inconsistent with its mission to protect the Bill of Rights, the American Civil Liberties Union joined the fray as co-counsel on Michael Schiavo's side against the governor and Florida Attorney General Charlie Crist. Howard Simon, executive director of the Florida ACLU, said, "This dangerous abuse of power by the governor and Florida lawmakers should concern everyone who may face difficult and agonizing decisions involving the medical condition of a family member."

Ken Connor defended the legislature's intervention. "It's obvious that the legislature was very disturbed that Terri Schiavo was not afforded the benefit of a guardian ad litem at the time the decision was made to order the withdrawal of food and water in her case," he said. "The legislature saw . . . that the judge effectively said, 'Well it's my role to look out for her best interests.' In effect, he became the de facto guardian making the recommendation and he reviewed his own recommendation and the fact is he was both advocate and adjudicator in that case. The legislature looked at that and said, 'We're not comfortable with that level of protection being afforded somebody who is disabled and in the situation that Terri Schiavo is.'"[11]

Terri's Law was subsequently struck down first by Judge Baird, who ruled it "unjustifiably authorizes the governor to summarily deprive Florida citizens of their constitutional right to privacy," and then by the Florida Supreme Court, which determined it was a violation of the separation of powers. "It is without question an invasion of the authority of the judicial branch for the Legislature to pass a law that allows the executive branch to interfere with the final judicial determination in a case," Chief Justice Barbara Pariente wrote for the court.

The U.S. Supreme Court subsequently refused to hear the case.

ONCE BURNT, twice shy, Florida lawmakers again attempted to intervene in the days leading up to the third—and final—feeding-tube withdrawal on March 18, 2005, but their political will waned. The House passed 78–37 a bill to block the removal of the feeding tube on March 17, 2005, but this time the Senate balked. Nine Republican senators, led by Jim King, delivered the body blow to the measure. "We acted in a Herculean way the last time, and I didn't want to do it again," King explained to the *St. Petersburg Times.*[12]

Daniel Webster again sponsored the legislation to save Terri. He felt confident this measure skirted the constitutional pitfalls found in the original Terri's Law. But despite pressure from Governor Bush, King and his colleagues would not be dissuaded. For the senate president, "one of his key accomplishments" was on the line—Florida's right-to-die law. "I don't want anything on the floor in that Senate that is going to give platforms to people who want to roll back the hands of time for whatever reason," King said several months earlier in explanation of his refusal to take up a bill introduced by Stephen Wise (R-Jacksonville) to make it harder to remove feeding tubes from comatose patients. "As soon as you put something on the floor, as well-intentioned as it may be, anybody can amend it. Then all of a sudden I'm sitting there facing a bill or bills that can dismantle what I consider to be my legacy."

Attorney George Felos was equally concerned about rolling back the progress made. "The fact is that we have a system in Florida that has worked well for the past twelve years," he said in a *Lakeland Ledger* editorial on February 6, 2004. "Because of the notoriety of the Schiavo case, which is one isolated case out of tens of thousands over the years, I think the legislature is politically motivated to look like they are doing something. But I think it makes bad policy and it is not good sense."[13]

ON THE morning of March 18, 2005, the day slated for Terri's tube removal, as the widening demonstration outside Terri's hospice grew more frantic, the U.S. Congress stepped in to rescue Terri. The House Government Reform Committee decided to launch an investigation and issued subpoenas for Michael Schiavo, Terri Schiavo, physicians Victor Gambone and Stanton Tripodis, and Hospice Woodside employee Annie Santamaria. The subpoenas required the recipients to testify at a committee field hearing on March 25, 2005, and produce "all medical and other equipment that provides nutrition and hydration to Theresa Schiavo—in its current and continuing state of operations—and all data, information, and records relating to the functioning of such medical and other equipment." The purpose of the field hearing was to "provide the Committee an opportunity to closely review the role of the federal government in long-term care of incapacitated patients." The doctors and Santamaria were ordered not to remove Terri's feeding tube and to keep her alive until the investigation was complete. Acknowledging that posed a "grave constitutional dilemma" for them, the House committee filed a motion with Judge Greer to postpone the removal of the feeding tube until March 29, 2005.

At the same time the Senate Health Committee requested Terri and Michael Schiavo appear at an official committee hearing to be held ten days later. The subpoenas served only to delay the scheduled 1:00 p.m. tube removal, however, as Greer moved to quash the subpoenas and refused to allow the intervention, stating he saw no "cogent reason" for allowing the committee to overrule years of court rulings.

"What we experienced today in the subpoenas issued by the United States House of Representatives is nothing short of thuggery," fumed Felos. "It was an attempt to intimidate and coerce the treating physicians in this case, the healthcare providers in this case, and Mr. Schiavo."

Days later Greer also thwarted Governor Bush's attempt to take custody of Terri Schiavo through the Department of Children and Families. On the basis of the review performed by neurologist William Cheshire while acting as an investigator for DCF's Adult Protective Services, Bush held an impromptu press conference to announce he was considering taking Terri into protective custody. Cheshire determined Terri might have been misdiagnosed and said it was more likely she was in a minimally conscious state rather than in PVS.

"This new information raises serious concerns and warrants immediate action. Terri is now going on her sixth day without food or water. It is imperative that she be stabilized so that the Adult Protective Services team can fulfill their statutory duty and thoroughly review all of the facts surrounding her case," Bush said. "I'm doing everything within my power to make sure that Terri is afforded at least the same rights that criminals convicted of the most heinous crimes take for granted."

Bush administration officials proceeded to alert administrators at Morton Plant Hospital that Terri might be brought to that facility. This prompted the hospital's lawyers to run to court for marching orders from Greer, and he signed an order forbidding DCF from "taking possession of Theresa Marie Schiavo or removing her" from the hospice. Greer directed every sheriff of the state to enforce his order. The next day Governor Bush dispatched a team of Florida Department of Law Enforcement agents to seize Terri Schiavo, reported the *Miami Herald,* but the agents "stopped short" en route to the hospice.

"The FDLE called to say they were en route to the scene," an official with the city police told the paper. "When the sheriff's department, and our department, told them they could not enforce their order, they backed off. . . . We told them that unless they had the judge with them when they came, they were not going to get in."

"For a brief period, local police, who have officers at the hospice to keep protesters out, prepared for what sources called a 'showdown,'" the *Herald* reported.

Jacob DiPietre, a spokesman for Governor Bush, disputed that characterization. "There was no showdown. We were ready to go. We didn't want to break the law. There was a process in place, and we were following the process. The judge had an order, and we were following the order," DiPietre told the paper.

Apparently, when DCF lawyers filed an appeal to Greer's order at 8:15 a.m., it opened a window of time to take custody of the woman. It took nearly three hours before the judge found out and canceled the automatic stay, shortly before 11:00 a.m. FDLE missed that window, however.[14] And the opportunity was lost.

"I think the governor did what he believed he was authorized to do," McGowan reflected months later. "He didn't plan this like a military operation. That's the job of his legal aides. They decided to send the DCF in front of Greer because, in their mind, 'We're always the squeaky clean, above-board, we-do-things-by-the-law and proper procedure [type of people].' But what they never understood is that the other side never planned to do that."

According to Greer's March 10, 2005, order denying DCF's petition to intervene, the social service agencies bungled the rescue attempt. "DCF's statutorily mandated duty of investigating abuse complaints and of providing protective services does not require intervention in a guardianship," Greer wrote. "In cases of emergency, DCF is empowered to provide emergency services and then petition the court for authority within twenty-four hours. Nowhere in the Act is authority given to DCF to become a party to any guardianship as part of its duty."

THE NEXT week, while Bobby Schindler was pleading the family's case before various federal lawmakers on Capitol Hill, Governor Bush was working the Schindlers' cause from his end, the *Palm Beach Post* reported, based on its review of e-mails from the governor's office. According to the paper, the governor's executive staff exchanged dozens of e-mails with attorneys for Senate Majority Leader Bill Frist (R-TN) and House Majority Leader Tom DeLay (R-TX) in which proposed legislation was drafted and revised in hopes of saving Terri.[15]

Both the House and Senate swiftly passed separate versions of the For the Relief of the Parents of Theresa Marie Schiavo Act and then, in an extraordinary move, convened on Palm Sunday to hammer out a compromise. After the Senate passed a bill unanimously by a voice vote, the House debated the measure late into the night. The act gave the federal court in Tampa jurisdiction to review the facts of the case and determine whether

Terri Schiavo's constitutional rights were violated. "Any parent of Theresa Marie Schiavo shall have standing to bring a suit under this Act," reads the measure. "The District Court shall determine de novo any claim of a violation of any right of Theresa Marie Schiavo within the scope of this Act, notwithstanding any prior State court determination and regardless of whether such a claim has previously been raised, considered, or decided in State court proceedings. The District Court shall entertain and determine the suit without any delay or abstention in favor of State court proceedings, and regardless of whether remedies available in the State courts have been exhausted."

"The Florida courts have brought Terri and the nation to an ugly crossroads by commanding medical professionals sworn to protect life to end Terri's life. This Congress must reinforce the law's commitment to justice and compassion for all Americans, particularly the most vulnerable," argued House Judiciary Committee chairman James Sensenbrenner (R-WI) during the unusual floor debate. "While our federalist structure reserves broad authority to the states, America's federal courts have played a historic role in defending the constitutional rights of all Americans, including the disadvantaged, disabled, and dispossessed. Among the God-given rights protected by the Constitution, no right is more sacred than the right to life."

Florida's House Democrats vehemently opposed the idea of intervening, calling it unconstitutional, an invasion of families' private matters, and the epitome of partisan politics. "What the Congress is designating is that the court system of Florida will lose its long history of jurisdiction of this matter and others like it, and the jurisdiction of the federal court will be substituted," Representative Robert Wexler (D-FL) challenged. "If the Florida courts had found in favor of Terri Schiavo's parents, would we be here this evening? I suspect not. So it is fair to conclude, therefore, that the reason we are here this evening is that the majority is unhappy, objects to the decision rightfully reached by the courts of the state of Florida, and as a result, the majority wishes to undermine over two hundred years of jurisprudence and a long history in this country for respect of our judicial independence as well as the states' court systems and the jurisdictions assigned to it."

"This type of decision happens every single day to thousands across America. Where will we stop if we allow this to go forward? Today it will be Terri Schiavo. Tomorrow it will be someone's brother, or a constituent's uncle," ventured Representative Debbie Wasserman (D-FL). "Do we really want to set the precedent of this great body, the United States Congress, to insert ourselves in the middle of families' private matters all across America?"[16]

Bobby Schindler, on hand for CNN's live coverage of the congressional session, offered his rebuttal on the cable network. "This *is* a family decision. And the family is not making the decision in this case. Michael Schiavo is making the decision. And it astonishes me that Michael tries to portray himself as a loving, caring husband when he has abandoned my sister for the last twelve years," he said. "It absolutely is a family decision, and Terri's family needs to be making the decisions, and they're not given the chance to."

The House passed the bill 203–58 shortly before 1:00 a.m. on Monday, March 20, 2005, three days into Terri Schiavo's final court-ordered dehydration. The "yes" vote included 156 Republicans and 47 Democrats. Fifty-three Democrats and 5 Republicans opposed the measure. President George W. Bush had flown back from his ranch in Crawford, Texas, specifically to be available to sign the bill into law immediately.

"In cases like this one, where there are serious questions and substantial doubts, our society, our laws, and our courts should have a presumption in favor of life," said the president. "This presumption is especially critical for those like Terri Schiavo who live at the mercy of others. I appreciate the bipartisan action by the Members of Congress to pass this bill. I will continue to stand on the side of those defending life for all Americans, including those with disabilities."

Disability rights groups applauded the government mobilization over Terri Schiavo. Some twenty-six national disability rights organizations, led by Not Dead Yet, had been pleading for the country to return to its senses. "A judge's order to terminate the life of a woman with severe disabilities is not a private family matter. Terminating Ms. Schiavo's life support would not be possible without the authority of the courts," said Max Lapertosa, the attorney who represented seventeen of the twenty-six groups who had filed amicus briefs in the case. "This case reflects whether our society and legal system value the lives of people with disabilities equally to those without disabilities."

An angry Michael Schiavo responded with a challenge to both Bush brothers to come visit his wife. "Come down, President Bush," he taunted in an interview with the *St. Petersburg Times.* "Come talk to me. Meet my wife. Talk to my wife and see if you get an answer. Ask her to lift her arm and shake your hand. She won't do it. She won't, because she can't." Schiavo complained that Tom DeLay, whom he described as a "slithering snake," was pandering for votes and didn't care about Terri. "What color are her eyes?" he demanded. "What's her favorite color? They don't have a clue who Terri is. They should all be ashamed of themselves."[17]

"The whole thing was politics. They didn't give a rat's butt about Terri. They only cared about the votes that she represented. That's all that was," echoed Brian Schiavo. "They all thumbed their nose at the system of jurisprudence, and it was absolutely horrendous what they did. It was sickening. And I for one am truly embarrassed to have Jeb Bush as my governor."

The charge of political pandering was common, particularly in light of a one-page memo circulated on the Senate floor that cited the political advantage to Republicans' intervening in the Terri Schiavo case and provided eight talking points in support of the legislation. Brian Dahling, legal counsel to Senator Mel Martinez, admitted he had written the memo and resigned.

Democratic National Committee Chairman Howard Dean said he intended to use the Terri Schiavo case against Republicans in the 2006 and 2008 elections. His top target would be Tom DeLay.[18] "The Schiavo case will probably be the turning point about our ability to make our case to Americans about the incredible invasiveness of Republicans when it comes to making, personal, private decisions," said Dean. Tom DeLay responded, "We, as Congress, have every right to make sure that the constitutional rights of Terri Schiavo are protected, and that's what we're doing."

Senator Chuck Grassley (R-IA) suggested the vote itself defused the pandering claim. "It's hard to say it's politics when you get that kind of consensus in a divided U.S. Senate," he commented to *Time* magazine.[19]

15

Conspiracy Theories

IN THE WAKE OF the failed legislative intervention, a perceptible sense of doom set in on the periphery of the Schindler supporters. The reality that a probate judge could defy Congress and the president stunned many and angered others. "We are living in an oligarchy now," commented Nancy Peek McGowan. "And if we're not careful about who sits on those benches, they're always going to have the last word, and they're going to continue to cause chaos in the United States by their rulings."

But the Schindler family and supporters had grown accustomed to having doors slammed in their faces. As the legal battle over Terri Schiavo's fate wound through the courts over the years, attempts by nursing-home caregivers, hospice insiders, state regulators, and agents of the Florida Department of Law Enforcement to investigate allegations of abuse, neglect, and exploitation on the part of husband-guardian Michael Schiavo were stymied by the heads of those agencies mandated by Florida statute to protect Terri Schiavo from neglect, abuse, and exploitation.

Specifically, complaints filed with the Department of Health, the Agency for Health Care Administration, the Department of Children and Families, the state attorney's office, the Florida Department of Law Enforcement, the attorney general's office, the Pinellas County Sheriff's Office, the Pinellas Park Police Department, and the St. Petersburg Police Department uniformly went nowhere.

"All these agencies were very precisely ordered to see no evil, hear no evil, speak no evil, don't go anywhere near the Schiavo case," said John Sipos, Tampa Bay radio news anchor who switched some years ago to news and public affairs talk. After reporting on the Terri Schiavo case a couple of times and not taking a particular interest in it, he confessed he had an epiphany while interviewing Pat Anderson. As she was talking, he detected tears in her eyes. Something touched him about the level of commitment this aggressive attorney had for Terri Schiavo, and he started to pay closer attention to the facts of the case. When he noticed the systematic resistance on the part of agencies and government officials to talk about Terri Schiavo, he became suspicious.

"From what I was able to learn pretty quickly is that this thing had an incredible stench of collusion to deny this woman her right to live. And it was obvious to me right from the get-go that the only way that this crime could be carried on was that somewhere there was a thumb out there sitting on this case," he observed.

The Department of Children and Families (DCF) received nine reports detailing eighty-nine counts of suspected abuse, neglect, and exploitation of Terri Schiavo over the years, including a seven-hundred-page complaint made on November 2, 2001. The complaint mirrored the allegations contained in the Schindlers' multiple motions and civil lawsuit to remove Michael Schiavo as guardian. Specifically, the complaint argued that, under Florida's guardianship Statute 744, Schiavo's conflict of interest due to his standing to inherit the malpractice award monies made him ineligible to be Terri's guardian. Then, the complaint claimed, his failure to provide continued rehabilitative, occupational, and speech therapy as well as his open adultery, his attempts to end her life by not treating life-threatening infections in 1993 and 1995, his May 1998 petition to remove her feeding tube, and his adding a DNR order to her medical chart should have disqualified him from serving as her guardian. Terri's transfer and continued residence at hospice plus the restrictions placed on visitation and her reported seclusion in her room also factored into the complaint. In addition to the guardianship statute, the complaint also alleged violations of Florida Statutes 825 and 415, which are designed to protect elderly persons and disabled adults from abuse, neglect, and exploitation.

The complainant, who did not wish to be named, claimed to have talked with Mitch Turner, DCF's adult protective investigator assigned to the case, "dozens of times" during a sixty-day review. "It was clear to me that he found credibility in most, if not all, the charges," the complainant told

WorldNetDaily. Turner conducted interviews and requested supplemental records. But after he filed a report of his findings on January 2, 2002, the probe hit a brick wall.

"It went up the ladder. It crashed. The report findings were marked 'Unfounded but with Recommendations,'" the complainant recalled the investigator telling him. When the complainant expressed disbelief at the outcome and asked what "with recommendations" meant, he says the investigator became tight-lipped. "I've said too much. All I can say is keep up the fight," the investigator reportedly said.[1]

After the complainant reported the incident to Pat Anderson, she swiftly issued a subpoena for Turner to testify and share his report with the court. Frank Nagatani, DCF's assistant regional legal counsel, immediately responded with a motion to quash the subpoena, arguing Turner's report and his recollection of his findings were confidential. Nagatani later publicly stated, "DCF is not going to get involved [in the Terri Schiavo case] until this is out of the court." Curiously, someone at DCF mailed a box, containing the hefty complaint, to the complainant in September 2003. The outside of the box was reportedly marked: "You may need this. It was scheduled for destruction."

In addition to DCF, all criminal investigative agencies are also required by the legislature to provide for the detection and correction of abuse, neglect, and exploitation of disabled adults and the elderly. Attorney General Charlie Crist, who was also supplied with documentation of suspected abuse and neglect and urged to convene a grand jury to investigate the allegations, at first denied there were any complaints filed with DCF and then justified taking no action on the matter by similarly explaining it was "in the courts."

Crist's office did take an interest in the case, however, and was said to be keeping an eye on the fund-raising activities of the Schindler family's Web site. Schiavo guardianship attorney Deborah Bushnell uncovered what she believed was evidence of "exploitation" of Terri in the dissemination of video clips of her in exchange for $100 donations, reported WorldNetDaily. Life Legal Defense Foundation (LLDF), a nonprofit, pro-life organization in Napa, California, assembled the video from clips of the neurological examinations, which became public record when Anderson introduced the tapes into the record after the evidentiary hearing. The video was available on the Web site for free, but visitors were encouraged to send $100 donations to LLDF to help defray the cost of litigation. LLDF's Mary Riley told WorldNetDaily the Schindlers hadn't directly authorized the fund-raising, and a promotional letter purportedly bearing Bob Schindler's signature was ghostwritten, but the effort was in keeping with an agreement negotiated between the Schindlers and LLDF in 2001 when LLDF first offered assistance on the case.[2]

Next to scrutinize the case at the behest of the Schindler family was state attorney Bernie McCabe. The Schindler's volunteer spokeswoman Pamela Hennessey filed a complaint on June 3, 2003, on behalf of the family requesting the local prosecutor investigate the case. The twenty-page complaint urged McCabe to look into the nuclear imaging bone scan and caregiver Carla Sauer Iyer's suspicions about the insulin injections as evidence of "possible domestic abuse and attempted murder"; Cindy Shook's testimony as evidence Michael Schiavo gave perjured testimony in 2000; and Schiavo's use of the malpractice-award funds on litigation as evidence of "fraud on the court." Six days later, assistant state attorney Robert Lewis responded to the complaint in a telephone call to Bob Schindler. Lewis reportedly said he concluded there were no crimes to investigate based on the following:

- Schiavo was allowed to change his mind about taking care of Terri for the rest of his life.
- Even if Schiavo had perjured himself in the 1992 trial, the statute of limitations had long since run out.
- The posting of DNRs in the medical charts of patients like Terri is normal.
- Terri's bills were being paid. Therefore, there was no need to look into her finances.
- While the bone scan might show injuries, even if Schiavo caused those injuries prior to or during the time of Terri's collapse, those alleged crimes were also well beyond the statute of limitations.[3]

The statute of limitations was the excuse reportedly offered to special agents with the Florida Department of Law Enforcement (FDLE) by superiors who demanded they close their investigation into the matter. Schindler supporter John Sipos called on a friend, a special agent with FDLE, and, without giving his opinion on the matter, asked him to look into the case. Special Agent Supervisor Mark Dubina and Special Agent Terrell Rhodes subsequently met with Pat Anderson and the Schindlers and reviewed several documents, reports, and video footage provided by Anderson to determine if there was sufficient evidence of a criminal violation regarding Michael Schiavo's battering Terri.

According to a heavily redacted FDLE report filed by Rhodes, the two agents advised Anderson, "Due to the date of the alleged incident, the apparent lack of any real physical evidence, and the jurisdiction of the incident, that the information would be reviewed, but it was doubtful a criminal allegation could be substantiated." According to Sipos, there was more interest on the part of his friend in the other aspects of the case that created what was viewed as potential for "ongoing conspiracy to commit fraud." The agent opened a case file on Michael Schiavo.

"In the self same instant that a case number investigation had been opened by higher ups at FDLE, Dubina was called into his boss's office and directly ordered to shut the case down, not once but twice," said Sipos, who then quoted Dubina's reported reaction: "Never in my more than twenty years of law enforcement have I ever before been directly ordered to shut down a felony criminal probe. Never." The FDLE report bore no hint of the displeasure from higher-ups but offered justification for not pursuing an investigation.

"No indisputable evidence was identified that could justify a case for charging Michael Schiavo with physical domestic abuse," concluded Rhodes in the FDLE report. "It should also be noted that due to the length of time that Terri Schiavo has been in a nonresponsive state (over thirteen years) it would not be possible to prosecute Michael Schiavo of a crime if the allegation could be proven due to the statute of limitations of criminal proceedings under Florida State Statute 775.15."

After the agents' findings were reviewed by three supervisors, including a regional director, the report concluded: "A final decision was made that FDLE would not continue to investigate this allegation based on the previously stated information, but primarily due to the single jurisdictional issue that any criminal violation that might have occurred would have been within the City of St. Petersburg." No mention was made in the report of any interest in pursuing a fraud investigation.

With that door closed, the Schindlers approached the St. Petersburg Police Department, but they were reportedly told the department would not be investigating the case.

Word that the Tallahassee-based Advocacy Center for Persons with Disabilities, the state's federally funded group that monitors the treatment of disabled adults, was attempting to investigate the abuse allegations raised hope for the Schindlers, but that quickly faded. The center is authorized by federal law and the governor's executive order "to investigate incidents of suspected abuse and neglect of individuals with disabilities." After working to gain access to Terri's medical records, the center ultimately dropped its investigation when Michael Schiavo denied permission to examine his wife. The center later sued Michael Schiavo in federal court in October 2003 in an attempt to block the removal of Terri's feeding tube, alleging that doing so may constitute abuse and neglect. U.S. District Court Judge Steven Merryday rejected the argument as a criticism of the established statutory course set out under Florida Statute Chapter 765 and denied the motion.

"One of the terrible ironies of Terri's case is that so many organizations purporting to protect civil and constitutional rights are on the other side," commented Nancy Valko, a representative of the watchdog group Nurses for Life and a vocal supporter of the Schindlers' fight to save Terri. "Just where is the constitutional and civil right to be killed?"[4]

WHY WERE so many elected and appointed officials and state agencies, mandated by Florida Statute 415 to protect elderly and disabled wards, so uniformly aloof about the Terri Schiavo case? That burning question sparked more than a few conspiracy theories among Schindler supporters and observers of the case. One theory follows the money trail of election-campaign contributions to Judge George Greer and concludes something inappropriate was going on. Specifically, Greer amassed a record $162,106 in campaign contributions during his reelection bid in 2004, according to Florida Department of State Election records. In comparison, his rival, Jan Govan, raised all of $27,761. The list of contributors to Greer's judicial campaigns raises the specter of conflict of interest in the minds of some. Specifically, Michael Schiavo's attorneys made donations to Greer's 1998 and/or 2004 campaigns while *In re Guardianship of Schiavo* remained in his hands:

George Felos's law firm, Felos & Felos	$250	May 7, 2004
Deborah Bushnell	$250	March 12, 2004
Hamden Baskin III	$500	March 22, 2004
	$250	May 19, 1998
Steven Nilsson	$250	July 14, 2004
	$100	March 14, 2004
Gyneth Stanley	$150	April 2, 2004
	$200	July 2, 2004
Daniel Grieco	$300	March 22, 2004

The suspicious timing of Felos's contribution was underscored by the *Empire Journal* and by Reverend D. James Kennedy's group, Center for Reclaiming America. Specifically, the donation came May 7, 2004, one day after Pinellas County Circuit Court Judge W. Douglas Baird ruled Terri's Law unconstitutional.

Schindler attorney Pat Anderson called the contributions to judges the "cost of doing business in this county." "A little insurance, don't you know," she said, adding that she was probably the only attorney who didn't participate in the practice. Her name was conspicuously absent from the donor list. But while Anderson takes the contributions from the Schiavo team in stride, Schindler attorney David Gibbs III labeled them a "conflict of interest."

Attorney Dennis Devlaming defended his friend and client, Greer, on the Fox News program *The O'Reilly Factor* and downplayed the perceived conflict of interest. "I think you'll find out that lawyers give contributions to judges, and they appear before those judges. I think the judges with integrity may be grateful for it," said Devlaming. "I've made contributions to judges, and I've lost an awful lot of hearings in front of those judges."[5]

Other Greer contributions that raise eyebrows for observers are two from DCF attorney Nagatani for $50 each on July 8, 2004 and March 14, 2004. Former Pinellas County sheriff-turned-state representative and close friend Everett Rice donated the maximum amount of $500 on June 9, 2004. And deputy attorney general John Carassas gave $100 on July 2, 2004.

Sipos fingers McCabe as the "thumb" on the Terri Schiavo case, preventing investigations into suspicions of abuse. He chalked the resistance up to the "political friendship" between McCabe and Greer and other Pinellas County Republicans like Carassas's boss Crist. "It's common knowledge not only at FDLE, but at all of the other police and regulatory agencies, Pinellas–Pasco State Attorney Bernie McCabe is at the center of demands that criminal probes not be opened, or when opened, they are to be shut down," Sipos asserted.

"I think conversations were had over cocktails. I think that old friendships were called upon," Anderson similarly speculates. "Pinellas is the state's smallest, most densely populated county. Everybody knows everybody. Certainly, George Greer as former county commission chairman would know every player." In fact, the biggest players in local politics count themselves among the close friends of George Greer, including Bernie McCabe and the man said to be the "strongest political force in the county," Ed Armstrong.

"No appointive offices to the city or county are filled without [Armstrong's] okay," said former Clearwater Mayor Gabe Cazares. Greer and Armstrong are so close, the *St. Petersburg Times* reported that, when Armstrong needed a kidney transplant in 2002, Greer volunteered one of his. Armstrong reportedly found another donor.[6] A leading attorney in real estate, land use, and zoning law, Armstrong partners with Timothy Johnson Jr. and Wally Pope at the law firm of Johnson, Blakely, Pope, Bokor, Ruppel, and Burns, one of Clearwater's most prominent firms. As such, their firm serves as legal counsel to the powerful and politically connected Church of Scientology.

Longtime Church of Scientology critic Cazares calls the trio of attorneys the "Pope coalition" and said the law firm's campaign contributions helped fellow real estate attorney George Greer unseat him on the county commission in the 1980s. Cazares speculates the ouster endeared Greer to the Church of Scientology. Florida Department of State Election records show the Pope coalition did not disappoint Greer in his reelection bid in 2004, but each contributed the maximum $500. Given the common practice of law firms making donations to elected officials on behalf of their clients, the question could be posed whether the Pope coalition contributions to Greer represent contributions from the Church of Scientology. Conspiracy theorists worked overtime on the Internet blogosphere trying to place the controversial religious organization behind the scenes of the Terri Schiavo case.

LIKE THE proverbial elephant in the living room, the Church of Scientology dominates the landscape of downtown Clearwater, Florida, which it considers its "spiritual headquarters." Since December 1975, the Church of Scientology has amassed downtown properties worth more than forty-six million dollars, including twenty-one buildings and approximately a dozen vacant lots, for which it is pursuing ambitious development plans. The number of followers living in the community has swollen to twelve thousand, and Scientologists now own more than two hundred small businesses in and around the downtown area. Scientology is officially called Flag Service Organization in Clearwater. Its new fifty-million-dollar Mediterranean Revival Flag Building, nearly completed, occupies an entire city block and dwarfs all other buildings within miles of it. The 1993 IRS ruling granting Scientology tax-exempt status—ending a forty-year battle over the issue—freed the organization to pump the millions it had been spending monthly on litigation into real estate development. Two-thirds of its holdings are tax-exempt, according to the *St. Petersburg Times*. Even with the exemption, however, the church remains the largest taxpayer downtown.

"You can't separate Salt Lake City and the Mormons, and you can't separate Clearwater and Scientology," Scientologist and developer Ray Cassano told the paper.[7]

A private school established in 1998, Clearwater Academy International, became the first of several to use educational concepts promoted by Scientology founder L. Ron Hubbard in its pre-kindergarten through twelfth-grade school. A bronze bust of Hubbard greets students as they stream into the front doors. According to the group's literature, more than two thousand out-of-town visitors come to the area for Scientology training and religious counseling services every year, pumping an estimated $96.7 million into the local community. This economic impact translates into political influence for the Scientologists.

"A lot of the judges and lawyers are with them because they think their power and money will rub off on them," said Cazares. "I think it's horrible. I'm going to do all I can this election year to publicize the fact that they're all indebted to Scientology and we've sold Clearwater."

Scientology spokesman Ben Shaw agrees the church has made friends over its thirty years of existence in Clearwater but laughs at the notion that translates into an ability to control judges. "We have great relations with the city, with the county, state representatives, the police, the fire department, and our neighbors," said Shaw, director of external affairs for the Church of Scientology Flag Service Organization.

But that wasn't the case when the organization first arrived in the quiet Gulf Coast enclave. The secretive church used a front group, United Churches of Florida, to buy the historic Fort Harrison Hotel and the old Bank of Clearwater buildings in late 1975, when the formerly sea-bound Flag Service Organization decided to drop anchor and come ashore. The church's record of going to great lengths to silence critics, such as reporters and former members who speak out against the religious organization, prompt its characterization as a "cult" by some. Cazares described it as a "terrorist organization." His impression stems from having been the target of a multipronged attack by the church for making such public statements as: "I am discomfited by the increasing visibility of security personnel, armed with billy clubs and Mace, employed by the United Churches of Florida. I am unable to understand why this degree of security is required by a religious organization." In addition to filing a million-dollar lawsuit against Cazares, accusing him of libel and slander in 1976, the church also unleashed a sex-smear scandal and attempted to frame him in a sting operation made to look like a hit-and-run accident.

"Dirty tricks are part of their way of doing business and gaining power. They destroy anyone that gets in their way, anyone who opposes them," said the former mayor.

The covert operation to entrap Cazares, engineered by what used to be known as the Guardians Office, was exposed when the FBI raided the organization's Los Angeles and Washington offices in July 1977 and seized 48,149 documents. "The documents revealed that the Church of Scientology came to Clearwater with a written plan to . . . take control of the city," reported *St. Petersburg Times* reporter Charles Stafford in his Pulitzer Prize–winning series in 1980. The fourteen articles described the church's unsettling founding in Clearwater and its "dark side," which included an active program to discredit "enemies" like Cazares and reporters and editors with the *St. Petersburg Times,* which it ranked first on its hit list.[8]

Shaw attributed characterizations of the church as a cult to "ignorance and bigotry or a combination of both." The veteran Scientologist said he was not in Clearwater at the time of the initial conflict with Cazares, but he said his organization had grown up since its Clearwater founding.

"In the 1970s there . . . were people who were doing things that were not our policy and some of them were illegal. We're not proud of that. Nobody is. And we've done a lot of work to clean that out," said Shaw. "If somebody makes an issue out of it now, at the present time, as though it were a significant part of the church, I think it's wrong. I think it's like saying the Republican Party are a bunch of burglars who go out and wiretap their opposing party. It's about as true as that." Still, the Scientologists won't suffer fools.

"We have rabid opponents. If they start an assault on the church or an attack on the church, then we're going to defend ourselves. But it will be done legally. It will be done in a court of law. It will be done in the court of public opinion through the media or whatever means being used, probably, by the person who's taken up the issue against us," said Shaw.

According to the church's Web site, Scientology is "an applied religious philosophy" whose main tenet is, "Man is a spiritual being endowed with abilities well beyond those he normally envisages. He is also able to achieve new states of awareness he may never have dreamed possible." Created by the popular science-fiction writer Hubbard in 1954, Scientology is rooted in Eastern philosophies that focus on man as a spiritual self working toward harmonious integration with his physical world and ultimately the Supreme Being. "Engrams," or pain stored in the body from past traumas, serve as barriers to block an individual's spirit being, or "Thetan," from achieving this harmony. Through what's called an "auditing" process, using a device called an E-meter, sufferers of psychosomatic illnesses can achieve healing or a "clearing" of the stored pain. Counseling packages at the church range from eight thousand to seventy-seven thousand dollars.[9]

In *Litigation as Spiritual Practice,* George Felos describes his own process of clearing blockages caused by past hurts. "The dislodged blocks of my unconscious past were like large cells floating in the psychic space that I could almost see. As they emerged from my dark craggy recesses, they rose upward through my body from the midsection to the chest area and ultimately through my throat into release." He adds, "As these unprocessed experiences entered my throat, I often felt absolute, unimaginable terror—like I was being murdered, hacked to bits. One time I could actually feel a long blade plunging into my chest; another time I could smell the dank, putrid odor of an attacker. Other dark cells brought on indescribably intense grief and its accompanying pain, as if a beloved child of mine were dying in my arms. . . . Paradoxically, cathartic release *is* the experience of the past event, and at the same time it is not."[10]

Similarities between the personal beliefs expressed by Felos, who also purportedly communicated with his son prior to his conception, and the doctrine of Scientology helped fuel the conspiracy theory promulgated on the Internet about the church playing a behind-the-scenes role in the case.

After the 1979 convictions of eleven guardians of the Church of Scientology, including Hubbard's wife, Mary Sue Hubbard, on charges of conspiracy to steal government documents, new leadership moved in. Hubbard protégé David Miscavige took the helm and set to work repairing the damage to the church's public image. Despite its growing acceptance as a civic-minded organization, a recent survey indicates Miscavige still has his work cut out for him. The survey, which was commissioned by the church in 2003, found four out of five Pinellas County residents held an unfavorable opinion about Scientology. Respondents variously used words like "cult," "evil," "scam," and "crooks" to describe the church.[11]

The survey was done in preparation for the trial of a wrongful-death lawsuit filed after the 1995 death of Scientologist Lisa McPherson at the Fort Harrison Hotel. McPherson was involved in a minor car accident, in which she sustained no obvious injuries, but she got out of her car, took off all her clothes, and told a paramedic she "needed help." According to court records, McPherson had a fear of insanity because both her father and brother had committed suicide. That fear is what made the Church of Scientology's auditing process attractive to her. She joined the church at the age of eighteen and stayed with it until her death at the age of thirty-six. She spent between fifty thousand and one hundred thousand dollars on auditing sessions in the two years prior to her death and had just reached the status of "clear" months before, according to court documents.

Emergency officials transported McPherson to Morton Plant Hospital to undergo a psychiatric evaluation. Fellow Scientologists arrived a short time later and explained to doctors that McPherson, as a practicing Scientologist, viewed psychiatry as harmful. They secured her discharge from the hospital and escorted her to the hotel for "rest and relaxation." Instead, McPherson wound up going through the "Introspection Rundown," which is the Scientology protocol for people who have had psychotic breaks.

According to church records and logs kept by Scientologists assigned to watch over her, many of which are posted on a Web site run by the woman's supporters, McPherson spent seventeen days isolated in a closed room, during which she refused to eat, alternatively cried and had violent episodes, soiled herself, and fought with caregivers. She also sustained bruises and bites on her body from cockroaches, according to her autopsy, and lost considerable weight. She was medicated with a sedative prescribed by an unlicensed doctor and given magnesium injections. Finally, when her breathing became labored, Scientologists drove her to a hospital where she was pronounced dead on arrival.

After an unusually long investigation, McCabe charged the Church of Scientology with abuse of a disabled adult and practicing medicine without a license—both felony charges. An integral part of the prosecutor's case was the determination by medical examiner Dr. Joan Wood that McPherson had died of a blood clot in her lungs due to forced bed rest and severe dehydration. She initially believed McPherson had been comatose for twenty-four to forty-eight hours before her death. Wood appeared on *Inside Edition* and discussed her autopsy findings while the church was under investigation. In doing so, she declared herself an enemy, in the eyes of the church. It sued Wood.

"To use one woman's unfortunate death as a means to try to attack and sully her religion is despicable," the church stated in a press release at the time. "That assault was accomplished only through illegal evidence tampering and cover up. We vow to prosecute those illegalities to the full extent of the law." Five years later, after conferring with prominent medical experts hired by the church—including forensics expert Michael Baden—and reviewing additional medical literature, Wood changed the death certificate, labeling the death accidental. She sided with the church's position that McPherson died from a pulmonary embolism that likely resulted from trauma to her leg during the car accident. The revised death certificate scuttled the criminal case and prompted prosecutors to drop the charges against the church.

"While nothing in the review has caused me to believe that the central premises behind the prosecution are erroneous, our ability to establish these necessary facts beyond a reasonable doubt has clearly been compromised," McCabe's assistant Doug Crow wrote in a memorandum recommending the charges be dropped. Crow then asserted pressure was brought to bear on Wood to change her findings. "The church had suggested that, if forced to litigate the issues, the proceedings would reveal information extremely damaging to Wood's office and her career," he wrote. "It is apparent that this unique set of circumstances coalesced to put what Wood characterizes as tremendous pressure upon her and may have impacted the quality of her judgment."[12]

"Joan said herself that she felt pressured by *all* sides, that includes the state and both sides of the civil action," Ben Shaw pointed out. "And what she characterized as pressure is, in fact, paper. She was provided paper by us and by the other party in this whole case. We gave her numerous medical journals and studies that were done. Nobody that I know had any direct contact with her."

A vocal church opponent did a similar about-face during the wrongful-death civil suit over McPherson. After the case crawled through the judicial process in Greer's courtroom and elsewhere for seven years, the about-face sparked a settlement. The *St. Petersburg Times* reported Miscavige later conceded that McPherson would have been better served somewhere other than at the Fort Harrison Hotel after her car accident.[13]

The controversy and associated black eye that the McPherson case represented to McCabe's office remained in the back of many minds as assistant state attorney Robert Lewis conducted his preliminary review of the materials submitted to him purportedly documenting abuse of Terri Schiavo. The last thing the office needed was to get involved in another volatile court case over a disabled young woman.

"I called Bernie McCabe's office when I first got involved in the case and said, 'Look, something's fishy here,'" Pat Anderson recalled. "I was told that they knew all about unwanted medical treatment because of the Lisa McPherson case, and they were not getting involved. It had been judicially determined that Terri wanted to die, that she did not want to remain on life support. Thank you very much for the call. Don't call back."

While dark shadows of the Church of Scientology's past controversy hung over McCabe's office and Terri's hospice ten miles away in Pinellas Park, where Flag Building–style high-tech surveillance cameras and "rooftop snipers" kept watch over the protesters—reportedly arranged by Greer through his connections with former Sheriff Rice—the church held no opinion on the Terri Schiavo matter. "We had no position on the case and no involvement in the case whatsoever," said Shaw, calling the assertions by those in the blogosphere to the contrary "ridiculous and outrageous."

Further dispelling the conspiracy theory, Brian Schiavo said his brother Michael was not a Scientologist. "He's a Christian. He's just a normal guy whose wife dropped dead on him essentially," Brian said.

ON FEBRUARY 23, 2005, DCF changed its mind about steering clear of *In re Guardianship of Schiavo* and filed a petition to intervene in the case. Adult protective investigations supervisor Michael Will explained the agency had received thirty new detailed allegations of abuse, neglect, or exploitation on its hot line between February 18, and February 21. The new information filled a thirty-four-page document. Will sought a sixty-day delay in the removal of Terri's feeding tube while his agency conducted a statutorily mandated investigation.

"Termination of the life of Theresa Marie Schiavo would hamper the investigation into abuse, neglect, and/or exploitation allegations, many of which have previously gone on uninvestigated by the governmental agency charged to conduct such investigations, i.e., DCF," wrote Will. Were the calls to the hot line enough to explain the DCF's about-face?

It's likely the head of DCF, like Bernie McCabe, similarly desired to stay out of the perceived political firestorm that was Terri Schiavo. DCF Secretary Jerry Regier had already had more than his share of controversy. In his first days on the job, after being appointed by Governor Bush in 2002, Regier swiftly came under fire for a Bible-based article he had a written a decade earlier in which he defended "manly" discipline of children and asserted men should have authority over their wives. Jewish groups, including the Anti-Defamation League and the American Jewish Committee, were concerned about Regier's promoting his religious views at his government job and vowed to keep a "close eye" on his activities. Intervening in the Terri Schiavo case on behalf of her right to life might have served as a last straw for the ADL. In December 2004 Regier was replaced by Luci Hadi. The changing of the guard likely factored into the agency's new keen interest in saving Terri Schiavo.

In Diane Coleman's assessment, earlier intervention by DCF might have made all the difference for Terri Schiavo. "If DCF had gone in long ago and pursued an investigation and perhaps sued to oust the guardian and got a different guardian based on neglect, then even if they lost at the lower court level, they could appeal. And when an administrative agency is doing its legal duty according to state statute, the legal presumption and burdens of proof are all in their favor," explained the disability rights advocate. "Getting rid of Michael Schiavo as guardian was key. If that had happened, Terri could have come out of hospice. Everybody could have seen her. She probably could have made her own choice."

Like McCabe and Regier, Charlie Crist, with his eye on the governor's office in 2006, would not have wanted to court controversy. The St. Petersburg native son of first-generation Greek Americans likely perceived that any attempt to interfere with a severely brain-injured woman's court-sanctioned right to die would gain thunderous disapproval.

Anderson believes the aborted FDLE investigation was Crist's doing. "He's from this county, and he and Greer go back a long way," she said. On July 15, 2005, Crist lauded Greer's handling of *In re Guardianship of Schiavo* in his keynote address to the annual convention of the Florida chapter of the American Board of Trial Advocates, where Greer and Whittemore were named jurists of the year.

Pat Anderson offers a final explanation for the hands-off treatment Terri Schiavo received from county and state officials statutorily mandated to protect her: "My assessment from the beginning is that nobody wants to cross a sitting judge." Especially a politically connected judge.

16

Media Misinformation

> Surrounded by stuffed animals and medical equipment in her small hospice room in Pinellas Park, Fla., Theresa Marie Schindler Schiavo died . . .

THE ABOVE PASSAGE IS a provocative lead-in for an obituary and sums up the arguments put forth by Michael Schiavo and George Felos that machines had been needlessly prolonging Terri's death, dehumanizing her with each passing day until she exhibited no more signs of life than the stuffed animals that surrounded her as she breathed her last and slipped peacefully into the afterlife.

But the problem is that this obituary, written by Christine Lagorio, was posted online at CBSNews.com five days before Terri Schiavo actually died. Terri's obituary was the talk of the day on radio airwaves on March 28, 2005. Syndicated radio talk-host Glenn Beck posted the text of the entire report on his Web site, along with a PDF version of how the obituary appeared on the CBS News Web site. Meanwhile talk-host Todd Schnitt pried a statement out of CBS to explain the premature posting.

"All news organizations plan ahead for events that may happen," the CBS statement said. "This story was never posted on our Web site, nor was it ever available via normal site navigation. Unfortunately, it was saved to a portion of the Web site that was accessible by Internet search engines. We removed the story as soon as the error was discovered, and we sincerely regret any confusion that may have resulted."[1]

The significance of this obituary debacle isn't that Web surfers found it early. CBS News was smart to get a head start on what was likely an imminent breaking news story. The real story here is the obvious reliance on one side's perspective and the denial that there were two sides to the story. While it included quotes from Michael Schiavo and his brother, Scott, culled from other press accounts, the eighteen-paragraph story contained no quotes and no reference to the Schindler family. Would Terri's death not affect her parents or siblings? Did her life not matter to them? In fairness to the author, this was a work-in-progress not intended for viewing by the public in its current state. CBS was not alone in shortchanging the Schindlers' side of the story. The Media Research Center found that of thirty-one news reports presented on major networks between March 17 and March 21, 2005, 60 percent concentrated on Michael Schiavo's side of the story, while 40 percent featured the Schindlers' perspective.

"Michael Schiavo, who was at the bedside of his wife Terri when she died . . ." the article later depicts, strangely confident that Terri was not going to die while her siblings were taking their turn at comforting her. This proved an odd foreshadowing of the dispute that would be sparked between a police officer and Bobby Schindler when the end did come. This, combined with the reference to the stuffed animals and the erroneous description of Terri's being surrounded by medical equipment, led Bobby Schindler to conclude, "They staged her death [for purposes of manipulating the media]."

In *Litigation as Spiritual Practice,* Felos prides himself on being a master at manipulating the media: "I was pretty good at trying my case in the media and shaping public opinion."[2] He showcased this skill in August 2003 when he directed reporters to investigate his allegations that "fanatic" "right-wingers" were behind the pressure on the Florida legislature and Governor Bush to intervene.

"I haven't heard any of the press ask the tough questions of the other side. Where are you getting the money? What money have you received? Who's funding your effort?" Felos prodded. And it didn't take long for the local press to dutifully follow his orders and report the answers to those questions.

Perhaps even more noteworthy than the one-sided treatment of the obituary are the egregious factual errors. Specifically, the statement, "the 41-year-old had not enunciated a word . . . since the 1990 heart attack," misses the mark on two levels. For starters, Terri Schiavo did not have a heart attack. She suffered cardiac arrest, which is altogether different. Second, Terri's medical records reflect caregivers in 1991 were accustomed to hearing her say "no" and "stop that" during therapy sessions. Affidavits filed by two nurses who cared for her in the mid-to-late 1990s testified Terri frequently said "mommy" and "momma." She was also heard to utter "pain" and "help me."

The most striking passage in the obituary comes toward the end, where an erroneous account of the events that preceded Terri's collapse are offered. "Terri and Michael had eaten a large meal," the article reads, citing Schiavo's malpractice-trial attorney Gary Fox. "One account says that, after they had finished, Michael rushed to the bathroom upon hearing thumping coming from behind the door. When he opened it, Terri was lying on the floor. 'She had purged, apparently, or vomited, binged, which is what bulimics do,' Fox said."

Where this obscure and false account came from would be interesting to learn. The only truth in it was that Terri had eaten a big meal the night before she collapsed. She had dinner with her parents at a friend's house after attending Mass. Michael Schiavo, however, was at work. His repeated testimony in countless depositions, hearings, trials, and media interviews was that, upon his return home from work, he had crawled into bed beside his wife, awoke to the sound of a thud in the hallway, and found her unconscious on the floor. There was no evidence Terri was bulimic. Michael testified he had never noticed behavior that suggested she had an eating disorder other than her daily consumption of more than a gallon of iced tea. While mistakes can be made by even the most diligent journalists, including this author, critics argued that articles involving life-and-death issues demand a heightened sense of scrutiny and care.

"THE MEDIA'S killing us, and they're killing her, frankly," Bob Schindler lamented at a press conference in October 2003. The family had grown so exasperated with reporters they held the press conference to school them on the pertinent facts in the case and how to report them. Several doctors addressed the journalists in attendance and stressed it was debatable whether Terri was in PVS, despite Judge Greer's court rulings labeling her as such.

"You have to get it through your heads. This girl is not PVS," Bob Schindler pleaded. "She is not a 'plastic plant,' as Mr. Felos says she is," Mary Schindler chimed in. "She is extremely brain-damaged, and she's a human being. She responds to me every time I go in there."

Dr. William Hammesfahr said Terri's eyes fixated on her family and she tried to follow simple commands, such as when doctors ask her to pull against their arm. "This is a case about a judicial system making an error," he said.

Focus on the Family believed the liberal-biased mainstream media promoted and facilitated the judicial error by misreporting the medical facts of the case. The conservative, pro-family organization issued a fact sheet prepared by physician Walt Larimore and bioethics analyst Carrie Gordon Earll to assist the family in correcting the misinformation, or disinformation.

The fact sheet took issue with the blind acceptance in the media that Terri was in PVS and their failure to point out that the condition carries a 43 percent misdiagnosis rate. Plus the media had failed to report that the diagnosis was widely disputed by scores of medical experts who filed affidavits with the court. It also questioned the underreporting of the best evidence in the case supporting Terri's actual medical status, the video of the court-ordered medical evaluation.

"You can see on the tapes how she has a big smile on her face as soon as she sees her mother, like she's opening up a Christmas present," her father remarked. "That's what's so heartbreaking."[3]

While attorney Pat Anderson introduced the videotaped neurological examinations of Terri into evidence shortly after the evidentiary hearing in 2002, CNN ran a report in March 2005 promoting "never-before-seen video." The anchor debriefed a reporter who had spent a couple of hours viewing the tapes and described what she had seen. Perhaps it was "never-before-seen-video," but why was this report more than two years late?

Focus on the Family's analysis also criticized the widespread acceptance that Terri collapsed due to a heart attack or potassium imbalance. Dr. James Barnhill's 2000 trial testimony clearly ruled out heart attack and clearly distinguished the difference between heart attack and cardiac arrest. While Terri was found to have a potassium imbalance, there was no evidence it caused her collapse. This was only the working theory. Incredibly, the Associated Press persisted in declaring a "chemical imbalance caused her heart to stop" after the results of the autopsy and medical examiner Jon Thogmartin specifically stated he believed the chemical imbalance arose from resuscitation efforts and did not reflect her pre-arrest condition.

Perhaps the most worrisome medical misreporting highlighted by the conservative organization was the little reported fact that Terri was not dying of natural causes prior to the removal of her feeding tube. While she lay in hospice, she was not terminally ill but was fairly healthy, according to her treating physician.

Columnist Nat Hentoff called the shoddy and inaccurate reporting of the Terri Schiavo case "the worst case" of "journalistic malpractice" he'd seen in twenty-five years of covering right-to-die cases.[4] An analysis conducted October, 25, 2003, by this author found network news outlets across the board—ABC, CBS, CNN, MSNBC, and NPR—as well as prominent newspapers such as the *Atlanta Journal-Constitution, Baltimore Sun, Cincinnati Enquirer, Miami Herald, New York Times,* and *Washington Post* misreported the facts in the Terri Schiavo case. Specifically, these news outlets repeatedly and erroneously referred to Terri as being "in a coma" or "comatose" and one even asserted she was "brain dead," which subtly endorsed the right-to-die position that Terri's life was pointlessly being maintained wholly through artificial means. The phrase "life support" was also routinely used, which misled media consumers to believe Terri was hooked up to a respirator or ventilator—a "feeding machine" as one columnist imaginatively describes it—instead of simply stating she was dependent on a simple silicone tube, the gastric feeding tube.

Writer and attorney Wesley Smith argued that the basic facts consistently ignored by the mainstream media amounted to a "conspiracy of silence." "It soon became quite clear, however, that increased media attention was not synonymous with increased dissemination of relevant facts," Smith wrote in an October 31, 2003, article in the *Weekly Standard.* "For despite the carpet coverage of the controversy in establishment outlets, the full story *still* isn't being told for the simple reason that most media refuse to report it." Chief among the facts ignored, wrote Smith, was that Michael Schiavo had lived with his fiancée for nearly eight years at that time and had fathered two children by her. "By siring two children with another woman, Michael effectively estranged himself from this marriage. Surely, thinking people would want to know this fact," Smith commented.[5]

The Schindler family additionally faulted the media for never reporting that Terri's alleged wishes did not surface until after Michael Schiavo had announced his engagement to another woman and how all the money that was supposed to be used for Terri's rehabilitation therapy wasn't. "They really gave Michael a free pass on his going back on his word. He testified to a jury that he would use the money for rehabilitation and care, and within six months of the jury's decision he had already tried to kill her. That's troublesome. But, of course, the media just seems to gloss over that," complained Bobby Schindler. "How the media just wants to protect and insulate this guy. It boggles my mind. I think they have a euthanasia agenda. They want to make it as easy as possible to kill these people. Look at the way they're justifying Terri's death! Because her brain damage was at a certain level, it gives us justification for killing her, starving her to death?"

Schindler made his comments in the days after the release of the autopsy report, when it appeared to him that news outlets across the board were spinning the results as vindication for Michael Schiavo and vilifying the

Schindlers. "The autopsy results released yesterday should embarrass all the opportunistic politicians and agenda-driven agitators who meddled in Terri Schiavo's right-to-die case," the *New York Times* preached in a June 16, 2005, editorial. "The medical examiners found Ms. Schiavo's brain 'profoundly atrophied,' only half the normal size, and said that 'no amount of therapy or treatment would have regenerated the massive loss of neurons.' . . . She was completely blind and could not have swallowed food or water safely on her own. Those conclusions underscore how shallow and cynical were the judgments-from-afar by the Senate majority leader, Bill Frist, who is a doctor, and by other Republicans in Congress who contended that Ms. Schiavo looked responsive and that her condition might be amenable to treatment."[6]

Governor Jeb Bush responded with an angry letter in which he said the newspaper's "grotesque and chilling disrespect for the sanctity of life has never been more apparent." He added, "Terri Schiavo was a deeply loved daughter, wife, sister and friend. The fact that her brain was atrophied or that she was blind or could not have been rehabilitated doesn't change that fact."[7]

Medical blogger Dr. Sherry Eros took the *Times*'s editorial to task for regurgitating neuropathologist Stephen Nelson's announcement that the pathological findings were "very consistent" with PVS without also including his qualifying statement that "PVS is a clinical diagnosis arrived at through physical examination of living patients."

"The term 'consistent with' is as close to meaningless as you can get in medical terms," she wrote in her weblog Eros Colored Glasses. "For purposes of understanding the autopsy report, the term 'consistent with' should be considered nothing more than a wild guess or a hunch."

Eros also picked up on the near-jubilation on the part of the mainstream media that the results were perceived to support Michael Schiavo's contentions. At least they perceived them to be that way. She cited examples from AP, the *Washington Post,* MSNBC's Keith Olbermann and Dan Abrams, of news outlets drawing the conclusion Terri was in PVS, despite the fact that the autopsy didn't, and could not shed any light on that question.[8] "What was most striking about the news reports was the smugness and certainty with which the purported scientific 'facts' of the case were misreported," she wrote.

Disability rights advocates were "outraged" by the coverage of the autopsy and the case overall. "As you listened to the television stations or read the *L.A.* and *New York Times,* you too would think the woman was better off dead than disabled," said Joni Eareckson Tada in an interview with radio host Dr. D. James Kennedy. "[But] I am thankful for my quadriplegia. I have been in this wheelchair for thirty-eight years without use of my hands or use of my legs. And God has blessed me so much with this."[9]

Diane Coleman and Stephen Drake find the "better dead than disabled" theme crops up on mainstream media programs time and again. Most recently, the Not Dead Yet activists decried PBS's airing of the documentary *POV: The Self-Made Man* on July 26, 2005, which marked the anniversary of the signing of the ADA. The documentary features videotaped statements of an elderly man who decides to commit suicide rather than face possible disability, medical uncertainty, or complications. "The choice of this particular air date is an affront to people with disabilities in this country," said Coleman in a press release. "It's the fifteenth anniversary of the signing of the ADA, a law that is, for people with disabilities—the nation's largest minority—what the Civil Rights Act of 1964 is for people of color. Not only is it being ignored by PBS, but the network is featuring and promoting a program about a person so terrified of aging and disability that he commits suicide." Drake noted, "Three out of the four credited advisers to the program are longtime assisted suicide/euthanasia advocates. It's being promoted as a tool for adding to the public discourse in regard to assisted suicide, an issue confronting the U.S. Supreme Court and legislators in California."

IN ADDITION to misrepresenting medical facts, many in the media distorted the legal facts. Many took their cue from George Felos, who often made reference to a head count of judges that deliberated over *Guardianship of Schiavo,* which he typically padded with Florida and U.S. Supreme Court jurists asked to review the case but who declined. News outlets drummed home his message to gullible readers and viewers: legions of judges have repeatedly evaluated the evidence and looked at the facts of the case and all were in agreement that Terri was in PVS and wanted to die. By the time of Terri's death, the Associated Press had the tally up to forty judges who "deliberated over the fate of Terri Schiavo," which insinuated all forty had evaluated Terri's wishes. It is unclear whether the AP included the nine U.S. Supreme Court justices who declined to hear the case six times. This author arrived at a total head count of thirty-six.

What's crucial to emphasize, however, is that, of these thirty-six judges who adjudicated various aspects of this multifaceted, complex case over seven years, only four judges specifically addressed the core issues of Terri's wishes and the nature of her medical condition. Of those four judges, due to the standard of appellate review, only one judge—Sixth Judicial Circuit Court Judge George Greer—had access to the witnesses and evaluated the quality of the evidence, reportedly holding it up to the "clear and convincing" standard. The three appellate court judges did not retry the case on either the issue of Terri's wishes or her medical condition. Rather, the judges verified there was evidence presented, and so ruled out the possibility that Greer had abused his discretion. They presumed he had ruled correctly and affirmed his ruling. The three-judge appellate court panel did indicate in its June 6, 2003, opinion that it had "closely examined all the evidence in [the] record" regarding the diagnosis of PVS and "concluded that, if [they] were called upon to review the guardianship court's decision de novo, [they] would still affirm it.

Fourteen of the thirty-six judges, including U.S. District Judge James Whittemore and the Eleventh Circuit Court of Appeals, adjudicated the question of constitutional due process and religious rights violations. Another eleven judges, including the full panel of the Florida Supreme Court, addressed the singular issue of the constitutionality of Terri's Law, the Schindlers' intervention in Michael Schiavo's lawsuit against Governor Bush, and the Florida governor's access to the discovery process and depositions of Michael Schiavo. The remaining seven judges were concerned with issues such as evidence relating to alleged perjury by Michael Schiavo during the 2000 trial, the appointment of a guardian ad litem, and other guardianship issues.

Of course the media weren't alone in this misinformation campaign. "There is the perception possibly that only one judge has been involved in this case. In fact, nineteen judges in the state of Florida have participated in various legal proceedings regarding Terri Schiavo," Robert Wexler said authoritatively during the Palm Sunday House debate. "The court system and the nineteen judges in Florida have been unanimous, unanimous, in stating that from the evidence provided by a standard of clear and convincing evidence, that it is Mrs. Schiavo's wish that she not be required to continue in a persistent vegetative state." Nineteen? Make that four. Again, only one judge evaluated the evidence against a "clear and convincing" standard.

PUBLIC OPINION outside the courtroom matters in high-profile legal battles, as the 165,000 e-mails sent in October 2003 to the Florida Capitol exemplified. Constituents spoke and Florida lawmakers heard them and responded. The lesson learned by observers: Figure out a way to control the community's message, and you will control the outcome. In fact, some polls with leading questions floated after the federal government's intervention misrepresented public opinion as being opposed to Congress's "intrusion" into a "private family matter." For example, a March 23, 2005, CBS News poll determined just 9 percent felt the federal government should decide life-support cases and 75 percent indicated the government should "stay out." "In general, Americans believe the issue of whether a family can remove a patient from life support is not for government at any level to decide," read the news network's interpretation of the poll. The poll question was laid out as follows:

Role of Government in Deciding Life Support Cases:

- Federal government should decide
- State government should decide
- Government should stay out

The way this was posed grossly distorted the reality of what the federal version of Terri's Law sought to accomplish. The poll question implied members of Congress and President Bush attempted to make the decision themselves whether Terri should live or die. In reality, lawmakers gave the Schindlers the opportunity to ask a federal judge to conduct a de novo review of the facts of the case before the trial court's order was carried out.

"I was puzzled by these poll results expressing anger at the government involvement," recalls Pat Anderson. "But then I started thinking about this. To those who don't know anything more about the case than what they've read in a local newspaper, which is going to be some truncated version of a wire story, the government was interfering with a loving husband who was carrying out his wife's wishes. Cast that way, that would make me mad, too. But that's not the facts of the case. People need to understand they were manipulated by the media."

Another case in point is an ABC News poll that found 63 percent supported removal of Terri's feeding tube and 60 percent opposed to the federal Terri's Law. Nearly eight in ten surveyed said they would not want to be kept alive if in a similar condition. The pollsters asked: "As you may know, a woman in Florida named Terri Schiavo suffered brain damage and has been on life support for fifteen years. Doctors say she has no consciousness and her condition is irreversible. . . . If you were in this condition, would you want to be kept alive, or not?"

Again the misleading phrase is "life support." And the loaded question also does not emphasize that Terri is not terminally ill and not in excruciating pain.

A subsequent poll conducted by CNN/USA Gallup more specifically described Terri as "in a persistent vegetative state who was being kept alive through the use of a feeding tube." As a result of the improved wording, the percentage in favor of her death dropped to 52 percent. Most significantly, results of a Zogby poll released the week after Terri's death sharply contrasted with those of the other surveys, most likely because of its careful wording: "If a disabled person is not terminally ill, not in a coma, and not being kept alive by life support, should or should they not be denied food and water?" In response to this question, an overwhelming 80 percent responded they should not be denied food and water. Only 7 percent said people in this condition should be denied. The Zogby poll came too late, however. The ABC, CBS, and CNN/USA Gallup polls, and others made an impression. Former ABC News anchor and NPR political commentator Cokie Roberts declared politicians were "stunned into silence by the polls" on ABC's *Nightline* the day Terri died.[10]

"Frequently cited polls on Terri Schiavo's tragic case illustrated a mass orchestration of public opinion based on profoundly erroneous information," said Robert Knight, director of Concerned Women for America's Culture and Family Institute. Knight, a former *Los Angeles Times* news editor and writer, said in a press release, "It's awful to watch as your fellow Americans are kept in the dark, asked their opinion, and then that manufactured opinion is used as a political hammer."

While politicians grew silent, bloggers continued buzzing as thousands turned to the Internet news sites and weblogs to gather and disseminate *Schiavo* facts. Conspiracy theories notwithstanding, what accurate information did get out about the case was largely disseminated through the Herculean efforts of an active blogosphere that worked to make their voices rise above the din of the uninformed. One Schindler activist, nurse Cheryl Ford, developed a list-serve of some five thousand e-mail addresses of people yearning to stay abreast of the latest developments in the court case. Ford spent so many hours hammering away at the computer, firing off press releases and alerts, she wore out four keyboards in the last year of Terri's life.

The media coverage came full circle after Terri's death when, just as in the early years of the legal tug-of-war, few national media outlets paid any attention to the ramifications. Glenn Beck was the lone voice talking Terri Schiavo on the syndicated radio waves long before the intervention by Governor Bush and Florida lawmakers aroused the slumbering media giants. Once awakened, Schindler supporters feel, the mainstream news outlets did a disservice to the public in its unbalanced reporting of the case. Talk radio and Internet news sites like WorldNetDaily provided the only counterbalance to the local press, perceived by many to be biased in favor of Michael

Schiavo. For example, as Terri lay dehydrating to death, the *St. Petersburg Times* ran a series of profiles painting Judge Greer, Michael Schiavo, and his fiancé Jodi Centonze as the victims. No corresponding profiles were written about the Schindlers. "The *St. Petersburg Times* went so totally overboard in trying to justify its editorial position that I was actually ashamed for them," said former *Times* attorney Pat Anderson. "The *Times* clearly had an ax to grind." Bobby Schindler took particular offense to *Times* editorials urging the Schindlers to "give up" and "let her die."

YET THE media did succeed in defining common ground between the feuding sides of Terri's family. The only issue on which there was agreement between the Schindlers and Schiavos in this sorry saga was the poor job the media was doing in telling the story.

"Once again, you guys do not divulge any of the truth. I'm sorry, but you don't," Michael Schiavo scolded reporters perched before him in August 2003. "Because you don't have the questions. You sit there and listen to the Schindlers, and it's just crazy."

17

"I Kept My Promise"

THE MOOD IN Terri Schiavo's hospice room on the morning of March 18, 2005, was tense but hopeful, as members of the Schindler family, their spiritual adviser Father Frank Pavone, and an attorney from David Gibbs's law firm, Barbara Weller, took turns visiting with her. Faith kept each believing either the federal court, where they had filed a writ of habeas corpus, or members of Congress would succeed in forestalling the scheduled 1:00 p.m. removal of Terri's feeding tube. Any minute now Florida Department of Law Enforcement (FDLE) agents, working on behalf of the Department of Children and Families (DCF), would appear in the doorway with orders to take Terri into protective custody. Or so they believed.

As Weller recalled, Terri was sitting up in her lounge chair, dressed and "looking alert and well." Weller and Suzanne, Terri's sister, were joking with Terri that she was going to fly to Washington DC and testify before Congress. They would go shopping to get her outfitted for the occasion. Best of all, she'd be permitted outside to breathe the fresh air and feel the warm sun on her skin, something they say she'd been prevented from doing for the better part of the last five years.

"At one point, Suzanne called Terri the bionic woman, and I heard Terri laugh out heartily," Weller wrote in a narrative of her last visit. "She laughed so hard that for the first time I noticed the dimples in her cheeks."

As the clock ticked toward 1:00 p.m., the playfulness became tinged with fear. Weller said she leaned over Terri, took her arms, and said, "Terri, if you could only say, 'I want to live' this whole thing could be over today." Weller reportedly begged her to try. According to Weller and Vitadamo, Terri's eyes opened wide, and her expression grew serious.

"She said, 'Ahhhhhh,'" wrote Weller, "Then, seeming to summon up all the strength she had, she virtually screamed, 'Waaaaaaaa.' She yelled so loudly that Michael Vitadamo, Suzanne's husband, and a police officer, who were then standing together outside Terri's door, clearly heard her." Anguish seeped into Terri's face, and she began to cry. Weller and Vitadamo stroked her face and blotted the tears, trying to comfort her. Weller vowed "to tell the world" that Terri Schiavo had tried to say, "I want to live."

Weller and Vitadamo hurriedly filed affidavits with the court, but Judge Greer said they were too late. He dismissed the perceived effort by Terri to communicate that morning as a "stimulus response" to Weller's touching her arms. He likened Terri's verbalization to yanking one's hand away after touching a hot stove. Greer was undeterred by the incident; he had determined in February 2000 that Terri Schiavo wanted to die, and he hadn't changed his mind on the matter. Her feeding tube came out for the final time hours later, triggering thirteen long days of tortured suspense for the Schindlers, the Schiavos, and the watching world. While the Schindlers and others prayed for a miracle to save her life, the Schiavos and others willed that the end of Terri's tragedy would finally come.

"It felt like some peace was happening for Terri," Michael Schiavo told the Associated Press after visiting his wife shortly after her feeding tube was removed. "I felt like she was finally going to get what she wants, and be at peace."[1]

"We really thought right down to the wire that FDLE was going to storm the hospice and take custody of her," reflected Brian Schiavo. "They were going to kidnap Terri and take her out of there. . . . It was a very sad situation. There was a lot of frustration, a lot of anger, a lot of lies."

Among the lies Brian Schiavo cited were the descriptions of Terri given by the Schindlers, their attorneys, and Frank Pavone as dehydration slowly took its toll on her body and death advanced. The Schindlers variously used the words "grotesque," "horrible," and "barbaric" to describe what they witnessed. In stark contrast, Schiavo, George Felos, and right-to-die advocates cast the "death process" as a "painless" and "peaceful" "slipping away."

"Removing somebody's feeding tube is very painless. It is a very easy way to die," Michael Schiavo told Larry King during the October 27, 2003, interview. "[It's] probably the second best way to die; the first being an aneurysm."[2]

"Frankly, when I saw her," Felos told reporters at a press conference outside the hospice, "she looked beautiful. In all the years I've seen Mrs. Schiavo, I've never seen such a look of peace and beauty upon her."

"The look on her face actually is—it looks like a plea for help. It's very sad," Suzanne Vitadamo shared in an interview on *Scarborough Country.*[3] "She is fighting with everything she has. And we'll continue to fight for Terri." Father Pavone described her as looking "very much in distress. . . . She certainly did not look peaceful, as some have claimed."[4]

Which characterization reflected reality?

Dr. David Stevens with the Christian Medical Association witnessed hundreds of cases of fatal dehydration while working in Africa for thirteen years, where the most common cause of death in children is dehydration from gastroenteritis. He describes the dehydration process as follows:

> As dehydration begins, there is extreme thirst, dry mouth, and thick saliva. The patient becomes dizzy, faint . . . has severe cramping in the arms and legs as the sodium and potassium concentrations in the body goes up as fluids go down. . . . The patient experiences severe abdominal cramps, nausea, and dry heaving as the stomach and intestines dry out.
>
> By now the skin and lips are cracking and the tongue is swollen. The nose may bleed as the mucous membranes dry out and break down. The skin loses elasticity, thins, and wrinkles. The hands and feet become cold as the remaining fluids in the circulatory system are shunted to the vital organs in an attempt to stay alive. The person stops urinating and has severe headaches as their brain shrinks from lack of fluids. The patient becomes anxious but then gets progressively more lethargic.
>
> Some patients have hallucinations and seizures as their body chemistry becomes even more imbalanced. This proceeds to coma before death occurs. The final event, as the blood pressure becomes almost undetectable, is a major heart arrhythmia that stops the heart from pumping.

"Contrary to those that try to paint a picture of a gentle process, death by dehydration is a cruel, inhumane and often agonizing death," Stevens concluded in a press release.

"Maybe at the moment of death, and for a couple of days before it, someone is in a coma and maybe isn't in pain," concurred Dr. Joseph Deltito of New York Medical College on CNN's *Nancy Grace.* "But what leads up to that, the seven, eight, nine days that leads up to that, is obviously torture. We have to do better for people than this."[5]

The "exit protocol" prepared by staff at Hospice Woodside on April 19, 2001, and found in Terri's medical chart offers insight into what she was expected to experience after the discontinuation of artificial nutrition and hydration and how the caregivers planned to manage that experience. Handwritten, on Hospice of the Florida Suncoast stationary, and signed by a physician on the Woodside team, the document contained a "brief list of symptoms for which to monitor and the recommended interventions." The list includes dry lips and mouth, compromised skin integrity and possible wounds, inability to clear secretions (blood and thick saliva) from the lungs and resultant respiratory difficulty, and seizures. Naproxen suppositories and two to five milligrams of morphine were recommended if pain or discomfort were "noted."

Pain and discomfort apparently were noted because Terri received five milligrams of morphine sulfate suppositories on March 19, 2005, and again on March 26, 2005, according to the autopsy report. She was also given acetaminophen up to the point of death. Right-to-die activist and neurologist Ronald Cranford maintained the morphine was likely given to Terri "for the benefit of the family" or even to ease the suffering of nurses. He adamantly asserted Terri Schiavo's death was "peaceful." His opinion was predicated on his determination she was in PVS, which dozens of other medical experts disputed. "The death will be peaceful for Terri because she's unconscious," he stated in repeated appearances on the cable news circuit. "She does not feel pain. She's in a vegetative state."

A Washington DC hospice physician speculated during an interview with Fox News's Greta Van Susteren that the morphine amounted to an insurance policy and was administered "to make sure she wasn't in pain." "My sense is, the lack of feeding and hydration itself is probably not painful. But you want to make sure," Carlos Gomez said.[6] The operative word in Dr. Gomez's statement is "probably." In fact, as the *Washington Post* reported, hospice and geriatrics specialists know very little about "the timing and mechanism of death when food and water are withheld from people with severe brain damage who are otherwise in fairly good health." "Nobody has studied it because nobody cares. There is not a National Institute of Advanced Illness," Joanne Lynn with Americans for Better Care of the Dying told the paper.[7]

Right-to-die advocates typically reference two studies in mounting their painless-death argument. Felos summarized them both in a pleading filed with the U.S. Supreme Court on March 24, 2005. The results of a study of conscious patients who had voluntarily undergone terminal dehydration, published in the *Journal of the American Medical Association* in 1994, showed 97 percent said they felt no hunger at all or only initially. Sixty-two percent said they felt no thirst at all or only initially, and all who reported discomfort were treated with palliative measures such as mouth care and narcotics. A 2003 study conducted by hospice nurses who observed the voluntary terminal dehydration of conscious patients, reported in the *New England Journal of Medicine*, concluded: "Most deaths from voluntary refusal of food and fluids were peaceful, with little suffering."

"Symptoms referable to dehydration are few," wrote national hospice leader Ira Byock, "and are readily relieved by simple measures." Both studies revealed the reliance on narcotics or sedation by hospice to render the death "peaceful." Due to the media scrutiny of Terri's case, however, she did not benefit from the full complement of sedation typically available for such a "death process." Certainly, if the double-effect paradigm had been pursued, the Schindlers and critics of Terri's death would have cried foul.

Incidentally, the fact studies have been conducted of voluntary terminal dehydrations indicates it has become a frequent cause of death. "Starving and dehydrating people to death is the de facto health policy in the state of Florida and many other places, too. Terri's case simply ripped the curtain aside and allowed the world to see it. It's nothing new," observed Pat Anderson. "I can tell you, nourishment, hydration is being withheld from all sorts of disabled people who do not have terminal disease," concurred Dr. Deltito on *Nancy Grace*. "Like Pontius Pilate, doctors are washing their hands, believing that they're not really having some sort of stain on them for doing this because it's somehow a natural process if people die by starvation. I think it's barbaric."

David Stevens and others emphasized the inhumanity of death by dehydration by pointing out both federal and Florida law forbids animals to die in this manner. "The biggest ethical issue," Stevens told radio host Dr. D. James Kennedy, "when you take someone off the respirator, when they're dying and it's futile treatment and you're just prolonging suffering during the dying process, you don't also take all the air out of the room. . . . Your goal is not to kill the patient but [to] remove a burdensome treatment. In [Terri's] situation, they gave her nothing by mouth. They would give her no fluids or water. The intent was not to remove a burdensome treatment. The intent was to remove a burdensome patient."[8]

While specialists, academicians, political pundits, and news commentators carried on a public debate over the nature and ethics of death by dehydration, the Schindler family pleaded for mercy. "When I close my eyes at night, all I can see is Terri's face in front of me dying, starving to death," said Mary Schindler at a press conference on day six of the ordeal. "Please, someone out there, stop this cruelty. Stop this insanity. Please let my daughter live."

The demonstrators gathered outside the hospice were also growing more frantic under the watchful eye of rooftop sharpshooters provided by the Pinellas Park Police Department and paid for by hospice at a cost of $98,162.[9] Deputies arrested forty-eight people who, one after the other, attempted to take a cup of water to Terri as part of a public demonstration staged by the Christian Defense Coalition. The crowd, which started as a group of prayerful individuals who came from all over the country to hold vigils and sing, gradually expanded to encompass more bizarre elements, including people wearing costumes, speaking in tongues, banging drums, and playing other musical instruments. One man whiled away the hours by juggling balls. NPR correspondent Ari Shapiro portrayed the story that unfolded amid this motley array as seeming like "some grand, tragic opera, where there was only one possible ending."[10]

"It was very surreal. With all the circus going on outside and trying to concentrate and Terri was dying in the other room," Brian Schiavo described. He stayed with his brother at the hospice most of the time over the final two weeks of Terri Schiavo's life. On the rare occasions that Michael Schiavo left the building, reported People magazine, he slipped out the back into a police van. In view of death threats, friends wondered whether he shouldn't don a bulletproof vest.[11]

The blinds in Terri's room were closed lest some industrious protester or news reporter try to get a peek at the now-dying woman. Day eight proved to be the last time Mary Schindler could endure seeing her daughter in her "ghastly" state for she reportedly vomited afterward. Attorney David Gibbs III accompanied Mrs. Schindler and offered an account of this harrowing visit during a radio interview with Dr. Kennedy.

"What I saw is an image in my mind that will never go away. She looked like a skeleton. Her skin was just stretched around bone. The black under her eyes from her eye sockets was almost to her nose. They put lotion on her to keep her skin from flaking, but because of no hydration she looked sunburned. Her skin was all peeling and red in spots. Her lips were swollen. Her tongue was enlarged and painfully dry," Gibbs said. "I watched Mary Schindler walk in and lean over her daughter. She begins to sob. Then I watched Terri roll over. They were nose-to-nose, eye-to-eye. Both were crying, and Mary was kissing her daughter. I thought to myself, 'In God's name, how have we in the United States of America reached this point?'"[12]

As earlier chapters revealed, a patient's refusal of nutrition and hydration has been promoted and institutionalized as a third path to what's considered a dignified death—it's not suicide, advocates say, but it's not wholly natural either, because it's hastened to some extent by heavy sedation. Tens of thousands of Floridians reportedly have traveled this third path to death in the last thirteen years, since the state's advance-directive law has been in place. Death-with-dignity proponents breathe a sigh of relief that, as a result of evolving advance-directive law, fewer Floridians must suffer the dehumanization of a "medicalized death."

In an age when it's estimated that 85 percent of people who die in America do so as a result of somebody's choice, the third path is seen as a critical vehicle through which to deliver that choice. In the words of former Florida Hemlock Society president Mary Hudson, some ALS sufferers or cancer patients just "want to check out early." And in a state where the population aged eighty-five and older is forecast to increase 91 percent to 524,000 by the year 2010, driving up Medicaid expenditures to $4.6 billion, Florida officials are only too happy to provide choices in dying for the terminally ill.[13] For every brain-injured patient like Terri Schiavo who opts to take the third path to death by filling out an advance directive prior to incapacitation that allows the withholding of life-prolonging medical treatment, the cost savings range from $600,000 to $1,875,000, which is the amount that would have been spent on lifetime care, as estimated by the American Academy of Neurology.

This right to die through the refusal of medical treatment was recognized by the New Jersey Supreme Court back in 1975 as a fundamental right to privacy for the terminally ill. Then in 1990 both the U.S. Supreme Court and the Florida Supreme Court acquiesced to the removal of artificially provided sustenance from those in terminal conditions who've provided "clear and convincing" evidence of their wishes. The high courts drew a distinction between death that results from the removal of life-prolonging treatment and assisted suicide.

But now a Florida court had ordered the removal of artificially provided sustenance from a brain-injured woman who was neither terminally ill nor had an advance directive expressing her wishes to die and whose family was divided over what she would want. A probate judge became the arbiter of Terri Schiavo's life. This resulted in nothing less than her court-ordered death. It didn't matter what her wishes were. It didn't matter what Michael Schiavo and his siblings believed her wishes were. After Judge George Greer's February 2000 ruling, Terri Schiavo was ordered by the court to die. The May 11, 1998, petition, upon which Greer was ruling, reflected the intention of George Felos to get such an order for Terri Schiavo's death one way or another. If not through clear and convincing evidence of her own wishes expressed orally prior to her incapacity, then by the court acting on the best interest of a woman who was in a condition in which "public consensus" holds she would not want to remain alive.

The context in which this best-interest standard, and the option of court-ordered death based on such a standard, poses the greatest threat is the guardianship system, already plagued by a virtual vacuum of court oversight and rampant abuse. Unscrupulous guardians who liquidate the estates of incapacitated people can now simply petition the court to kill their wards so they can move on to the next victim. "[The Terri Schiavo case] has nothing to do with the right to life or the right to die as the public is led to believe," remarked Schindler supporter John Sipos. "It's about guardianship laws being corrupted and the taking of assets of the weak and vulnerable—by friends of Florida's judges."

"Florida has many, many people who live in nursing homes. What are the implications for these people going forward into the future?" queried attorney Ken Connor. "Are we going to respect and protect their lives and treat them as human beings created in God's image? Or are we going to say, 'Well, their quality of life doesn't measure up, their functional capacity is diminished, and so has their human dignity, so out to the garbage heap with them.'"[14]

"We have lost our compassion for the disabled, for the elderly, and [for] people with Alzheimer's," said Bobby Schindler. "We look at people who are disabled and impose our feelings on them and say to ourselves, 'I wouldn't want to live like that.' Well, there's just one problem with that: we're not in that condition. And people who are, many of them, are very content to stay alive and want to be taken care of and kept alive."

Once an incapacitated patient's wishes are left out of the equation, disability rights advocates argue, our society has turned down the slippery slope toward involuntary euthanasia. Whereas *Roe v. Wade* provided a back door to legalized abortion across the country, the 1999 revisions to Florida's advance-directive law as field-tested by *Schiavo v. Schindler* provides a back door to legalized euthanasia.

"People need to understand that the line between life and death is a movable, ephemeral line, and you're not always the one in charge of moving it. Somebody will move it for you and shove you overboard. This is not a case about 'letting' Terri Schiavo die. This was a slow-motion execution that occurred over thirteen days. If she wanted to die, she would not have lasted thirteen days," concluded Anderson. "Euthanasia now as a name and a face."

"Terri Schiavo's case is an in-your-face effort by the right-to-die activists to openly ram the duty to die down the throat of society. It is a precedent-setting case, make no mistake about it," agreed hospice watchdog Ron Panzer, who predicted the case would impact hospice across the country. "Some hospice administrators may be motivated to make a stand against such killings of the disabled. Others will hop right in and join the duty-to-die crowd, using hospice to eliminate the vulnerable, while enriching the hospices and other health-care corporations."

Will Terri's legacy be changed laws? Appellate court judges variously emphasized in their opinions denying the Schindlers relief from Greer's judgment that the judiciary doesn't make the laws upon which it rules. "This case offers a vivid opportunity for the public, whose collective will ultimately decides such matters, to contemplate the confounding issues associated with degenerative illness and catastrophic disability and, thereafter, by a means consistent with government in a republic, to direct their representatives to legislate in accord with their concerted desires, if in conflict with the present state of law," wrote federal district judge Steven Merryday.

Diane Coleman's Not Dead Yet has proposed eight steps for federal and state lawmakers to take "in order to safeguard against involuntary euthanasia." These suggestions include a moratorium on the removal of food and water from people diagnosed in PVS and MCS in the absence of new diagnostic testing, or a written advance directive/power of attorney; providing a due process federal review of contested third-party decisions to withhold treatment in the absence of an advance directive; and state-by-state review of guardianship and health-care decisions laws. A reassessment of the parameters for the right to die is said to already be happening in states across the country, including whether oral expression of wishes represents clear and convincing evidence. Former Florida Hemlock Society president Mary Hudson predicts this Schiavo-inspired backlash will be met with an equal backlash to maintain the status quo. Such opponents of rolling back progress of the right-to-die movement emphasize they have the public-opinion polls on their side.

Bobby Schindler plans to push for Florida and other states to change the law back to define feeding tubes as basic care and not as life-prolonging medical treatment. Through the continued work of a restructured Terri Schindler-Schiavo Foundation, the Schindler family intends to work toward keeping other Terris alive. "Something has to be done to change the laws to make it as difficult as possible to kill somebody," said Bobby Schindler on *Hannity & Colmes*.[15]

Many view Terri Schiavo's legacy as broader acceptance and widespread use of advance directives. Right-to-die advocates speaking out about the case said it underscored the need for written directives and incessantly urged readers and television viewers to fill out their forms now, before it's too late and they lose the ability to ensure their wishes will be carried out. Health and Human Services Secretary Mike Leavitt joined the fray by suggesting the federal government could save large amounts of money if living wills were incorporated in Medicare consultations.

But pro-life advocates criticize the advance-directive forms peddled by End-of-Life Choices, formerly the Hemlock Society, Concern for Dying, and other right-to-die organizations for an orientation toward withholding medical treatment and hastening death. The American Life League calls advance directives, or living wills, a "passport to fatal abuse." The National Right to Life Committee (NRLC) offers its own advance-directive form titled the Will to Live, which is designed to rebuff efforts by health-care providers to hasten death and instead protect the patient's right to treatment and life. "In response to the Schiavo case, many believe they should draw up a living will. This, however, is both unnecessary and dangerous," warned Father Pavone in a press release. "We cannot make treatment decisions today for circumstances of tomorrow that we cannot predict. Whether a medical treatment is morally required depends on those circumstances and therefore cannot be determined in advance."

Further complicating the matter is a report by the NRLC Robert Powell Center for Medical Ethics that indicates laws in all but ten states leave the door open for doctors and hospitals to disregard advance directives. The April 15, 2005, poll found that health-care providers who consider a patient's quality of life too low increasingly were denying life-preserving procedures against the will of the patient and family. In view of this, the smarter alternative, according to experts, is to designate a health-care proxy, power of attorney, or pre-need guardian who can be trusted to make decisions according to one's wishes, as one generally describes them ahead of time.

BUT MAYBE Terri Schiavo wanted to die, as her husband said he belatedly realized in 1997 and has steadfastly asserted ever since. "Who in God's name would subject themselves to what he has gone through for any other reason?" George Felos said of his client. "He always deeply loved her."[16]

"Mike was very upset, crying. It was very, very emotional," Brian Schiavo described of the final days. "He just looked back at the whole thing and said, 'I can't believe this. I'm only doing what she asked me to do, and I'm being made out to be a murderer.'"

While Michael Schiavo remained secluded inside the hospice, Felos handled public relations. "I visited with Terri this afternoon at the hospice," he told reporters on March 28, 2005. "She looked very peaceful. She looked calm. There was music playing in the room. There were flowers in the room. Underneath Terri's arm was a stuffed animal of a tabby cat." He conceded, "Terri's eyes do look more sunken than when I saw her last, and also, her breathing was a little on the rapid side."

The Schindlers and Father Frank Pavone reported Terri had grown "gaunt," there was blood in her eyes, and she was "panting." Weeks later, on Fox News's *Hannity & Colmes*, Bob Schindler characterized what he witnessed his daughter going through as "ghoulish." "I looked in her mouth," Schindler told anchor Sean Hannity, "all I could think of was like a piece of meat in a meat market. And it was like meat that had been out for a while. [The] inside of her mouth [was] like reddish-maroon, because her mouth was all dried. Her lips and everything was cracking from the lack of hydration."[17]

"If the public would watch a starvation-and-dehydration death of a human being who was otherwise healthy, other than the brain damage that my sister had, this whole thing would stop pretty quick," said Bobby Schindler.

Terri's last hours approached. She had entered "the final stages of her death process," as Felos described it. In addition to experiencing periods of rapid breathing, her hands and legs were mottled, which was indicative of her heart's shutting down and ceasing to pump blood into the extremities. Felos and guardianship attorney Deborah Bushnell spent the night at hospice with Michael and Brian Schiavo.

Throughout the night hospice staff shuffled opposing family members in and out of Terri's room so that no Schiavo would face a Schindler. Father Pavone hovered over Terri with her siblings for three to four hours the night before Terri died and then again for the final hour prior to her death. Pavone described the expression on Terri's face as "a combination of dreaded fear and sadness." He recalled, "Her eyes were oscillating back and forth in a way that was just frightening."[18]

According to Pavone's eyewitness account, Terri's last hours were spent in intense prayer. While at least one police officer kept watch and Bobby Schindler stroked Terri's head, Pavone chanted ancient hymns of the Roman Catholic Church in Latin, including the *Victimae Paschali Laudis*, which is the ancient proclamation of the resurrection of Jesus Christ.

"There I saw before my eyes the deadly work of the Culture of Death," wrote Pavone. "I proclaimed the victory of life. 'Life and death were locked in a wondrous struggle,' the hymn declares. 'Life's Captain died, but now lives and reigns forevermore.'"

As they intermittently chanted and observed periods of reflective silence, a beautiful bouquet of roses and lilies on the night table next to Terri's bed caught Pavone's attention. He saw that the vase was filled with water.

"I said to myself, this is absurd. This is absurd. These flowers are being treated better than this woman. She has not had a drop of water for almost two weeks. Why are those flowers there? What type of hypocrisy is this? The flowers were watered. Terri was not," Pavone pondered.

At approximately 8:45 a.m. on March 31, 2005, a hospice staffer informed the Schindlers and Pavone it was time for a medical evaluation and ushered them into the hall. But before they left, Terri's siblings kissed her forehead. "We love you and we're here for you," they whispered. The Schindlers knew Terri's end was near and begged the police officer to be allowed to stay in the room, even though Michael Schiavo was en route.

"I know what's going on here," Bobby Schindler told the officer. "They're staging this. And I don't care about all of that. I just want to be in the room with my sister when she passes away." The Schindlers offered a compromise: allow the security guard to be in the room as a buffer between the Schiavos and Schindlers. The idea was rejected.

At that point the Schindlers and the priest were escorted off the property and Michael Schiavo took over the bedside vigil. Terri died at approximately 9:00 a.m. As George Felos said at the ensuing press conference, Michael was "cradling" Terri, who "died a calm, peaceful, and gentle death." After the Schindlers spent some time with Terri's body under the eyes of a police officer, hospice workers bathed her, and then Michael Schiavo and his attorneys spent more time with her. The medical examiner was notified, and the hospice workers reportedly held a memorial service for their longtime resident.

"There was a gathering of . . . thirty to forty hospice workers who formed a circle around the body, which was now on the medical examiner's gurney," said Felos at the press conference. "The Hospice chaplain said prayers. It was a very . . . emotional moment for many of us there." In responding to reporters' questions, Felos said that Terri had the stuffed tabby kitty under one arm and other stuffed animals were around her, just as the CBS News obituary had prophesied.

"It was absolutely disgraceful for us not to be allowed in there, and it was all staged so Michael could tell the media that he was there cradling his wife when she expired," said Bobby Schindler.[19]

"It's not that Mike didn't want them in there," Scott Schiavo defended his brother. "They've been throwing all these stones and saying all these bad things that aren't true. And you know, they've turned Mike into this monster, and now they want the media and the public to think Mike is, and he's not."

Many Schindler supporters believe that Terri passed away before Michael Schiavo arrived at her bedside. "We are convinced that she died while that dispute was going on out in the hallway. And the last thing she heard was that chant," said Anderson.

"That's what I'm going to believe just for my own peace of mind," agreed Bobby Schindler. "But, of course, the script had to be played out."

Many see "the script" as part of divine purpose. "We were all very hopeful until the end. But just as you watch what happened over the past couple of months, you realize that there's some other plan that God has because she was denied at every turn," said Nancy McGowan.

Attorney David Gibbs believes Terri Schiavo sent a clarion call. "As a nation, we once again need to adopt the heart of God toward the 'least of these,'" he said in a statement posted on his law firm's Web site, in a reference to the biblical passage in the gospel of Matthew. "We need to pray for America like never before. America is at a point of decision. Will Terri be the first of millions who are legally killed in our nation? Or will the heart of our nation be changed so that American law once again protects all life until the moment God decides to call us home? Terri's legacy has the potential to be millions more gruesome deaths by dehydration and starvation. Or it could be millions of lives spared because of her supreme sacrifice in raising this issue to the consciousness of the nation."

In the wake of Terri's death, the enmity between her family members remains. Michael Schiavo's cremation of his wife over the objections of her parents, his keeping them in the dark for months over the whereabouts of her remains, and the Schindlers' continued suspicions about his behavior the fateful night Terri collapsed fueled the raging rift beyond the autopsy and memorial services. After having had the upper hand in the court dispute, the guardian had the last word. Michael Schiavo arranged for Terri's cremated remains to be interred in a burial plot at a Clearwater, Florida, cemetery in June 2005. The bronze marker he purchased for the grave site lists the date "beloved wife" Theresa Marie Schiavo died, March 31, 2005, as the day she became "at peace." It lists the date of her brain injury as the day she "departed this Earth." The message engraved on the bottom reads, "I kept my promise."

NOTES

INDEX

NOTES

PREFACE

1. Ira R. Byock, “Patient Refusal of Nutrition and Hydration: Walking the Ever-Finer Line,” *American Journal Hospice & Palliative Care* (March–April 1995): 8–13.
2. George J. Felos, *Litigation as Spiritual Practice* (Nevada City, CA: Blue Dolphin, 2002), book jacket, inside back flap.
3. Ibid., 61.
4. Sophia A. Niarchos, “George Felos: Defending One's Right to Die,” *Greek-News,* April 25, 2003.
5. Bryan Jennett, *The Vegetative State: Medical Facts, Ethical and Legal Dilemmas* (New York: Cambridge University Press, 2002), 67.
6. *hOUR Tampa Bay,* Infinity/CBS Radio, April 20, 2004.

CHAPTER 1: TERRI SCHINDLER BECOMES TERRI SCHIAVO

1. Kelley Benham, “Terri's Two Lives: Elevated Life from Humble Beginning,” *St. Petersburg Times,* April 1, 2005.
2. Breed, “Inside Right-to-Die Case, A Woman's Real Life.”
3. *Paula Zahn Now,* CNN, March 28, 2005.
4. Benham, “Terri's Two Lives.”
5. *On the Record with Greta Van Susteren,* Fox News Network, March 21, 2005.
6. Terri Schindler-Schiavo Foundation Web site, http://terrisfight.org.
7. *Dateline NBC,* NBC News, April 25, 2000.
8. *Paula Zahn Now,* CNN, March 28, 2005.

CHAPTER 2: MYSTERIOUS COLLAPSE

1. *Dateline NBC,* NBC News, April 25, 2000.
2. Jackie Hallifax, “Bush Asks Prosecutor to Investigate Alleged Schiavo Discrepancies,” Associated Press, June 17, 2005.
3. *On the Record with Greta Van Susteren,* Fox News Network, June 17, 2005.

CHAPTER 3: BULMIA, BRUISES, AND BONE SCAN

1. WebMD.com, "Health Guide A–Z: Hypokalemia," February 2, 2003.
2. Ibid.
3. Breed, "Inside Right-to-Die Case, A Woman's Real Life."
4. Ibid.
5. Ibid.
6. *On the Record with Greta Van Susteren,* Fox News Channel, March 28, 2005.
7. Terri Schindler-Schiavo Foundation Web site, http://terrisfight.org.
8. Anita Kumar and William R. Levesque, "Subpoenas Miss Schiavo Witness," *St. Petersburg Times,* April 28, 2001.
9. Terri Schindler-Schiavo Foundation Web site, http://terrisfight.org.
10. Gael B. Strack and Dr. George McClane, "How to Improve Investigation and Prosecution of Strangulation Cases."
11. Daniel S. Moore, M.D., et al, "Heterotopic Ossification," eMedicine.com, May 7, 2002.
12. Thomas Boyle, M.D., "Terri Schiavo R.I.P. Part II: The Story in the Bones," CodeBlueBlog.com, April 7, 2005.
13. George J. Felos, *Litigation as Spiritual Practice,* 79–80.
14. Boyle, "Terri Schiavo R.I.P. Part II: The Story in the Bones."
15. Gael J. Lonergan et al., "Child Abuse: Radiologic-Pathologic Correlation," *Armed Forces Institute of Pathology,* April 4, 2003.
16. *Hannity & Colmes,* Fox News Channel, April 7, 2005.

CHAPTER 4: "I BELIEVE IN MY WEDDING VOWS"

1. Anita Kumar and J. Nealy-Brown, "Funds Meant for Schiavo's Care Dwindle," *St. Petersburg Times,* June 3, 2001.
2. *Larry King Live,* CNN, October 27, 2003.
3. Wendy Griffith, "Fighting the Culture of Death," CBN News, October 31, 2003.
4. Terri Schindler-Schiavo Foundation Web site, http://terrisfight.org.

CHAPTER 5: "GULAG OF GUARDIANSHIP"

1. Beth M. Gilbert, "The Gulag of Guardianship," *Money,* March 1, 1989.
2. Chris Tisch, "Ex-Lawyer Gets Six Months in Jail," *St. Petersburg Times,* May 18, 2005.
3. Jeffrey Good, "A Sorry Chapter in Local Legal History," *St. Petersburg Times,* December 19, 1993.
4. Op-Ed, "Guarding Assets," *St. Petersburg Times,* September 24, 2003.

5. U.S. Census Bureau, State and County QuickFacts, data derived from population estimates, 2000 Census.
6. Justice for Florida Seniors, "Sunny St. Petersburg Has a Dark Side," http://www.justiceforfloridaseniors.org.
7. Robert W. Melton, "Dirty Tricks of Guardianships: The Need for Change," http://www.justiceforfloridaseniors.org.
8. Justice for Florida Seniors, "Sunny St. Petersburg Has a Dark Side."
9. Candace Rondeau, "Authorities to Examine Guardian Agency," *St. Petersburg Times*, July 31, 2003.
10. Francis X. Gilpin, "Guarding the Guardians," *Gulf Coast Business Review*, April 30, 2004.
11. Barry Yeoman, "Stolen Lives: Thousands of Older Americans Are Being Robbed of Their Freedom, Dignity and Lives," *AARP: The Magazine*, January–February 2004.
12. Diana Lynne, "Court to Hear Petition to Remove Husband as Guardian," WorldNetDaily.com, November 5, 2003.
13. Diana Lynne, "Life, Death Tug of War in Florida Courtroom," WorldNetDaily.com, November 13, 2002.
14. Sarah Foster, "Terri's Money Used to Pay for Starvation Death," WorldNetDaily, March 26, 2005.
15. Mitch Stacy, "Money Evaporating in Terri Schiavo Right-to-Die Battle," Associated Press, March 16, 2005.
16. "Attorney: Michael Schiavo Vows to Carry Out Wife's Wishes," WFTS.com, October 23, 2003.
17. Press conference from the office of attorney George Felos in Dunedin, Florida, CNN, March 31, 2005.
18. "Ethics Laws May Stop Greer from Profiting from Schiavo Case," *Empire Journal*, August 2, 2005.
19. Sarah Foster, "Schindler Family Reunited with Terri," WorldNetDaily.com, June 4, 2004.
20. January 11, 2005, press release, Terri Schindler-Schiavo Foundation.
21. Diana Lynne, "Life, Death Tug-of-War in Florida Courtroom."
22. Maya Bell, "Guardians Laud Michael Schiavo for Fulfilling Wife's Wishes," *Orlando Sentinel*, August 5, 2005.

CHAPTER 6: TERRI'S WISHES

1. *Hannity & Colmes*, Fox News Network, March 31, 2005.
2. Art Moore, "Judge Greer Orders Terri's Starvation," WorldNetDaily.com, February 25, 2005.
3. Diana Lynne, "Michael Schiavo Pleads Case on CNN, WorldNetDaily.com, October 28, 2003.

4. *hOUR Tampa Bay,* interview, Infinity/CBS Radio, April 20, 2004.
5. Allen G. Breed, "Inside Right-to-Die Case, A Woman's Real Life," Associated Press, October 25, 2003.
6. "Judge's Error to Save Terri Schiavo?" WorldNetDaily.com, March 4, 2005.
7. Sarah Foster, "Terri's Money Used to Pay for Starvation Death," WorldNetDaily, March 26, 2005.
8. Wendy Griffith, "Fighting the Culture of Death," CBN News, October 31, 2003.
9. *Scarborough Country,* MSNBC, March 28, 2005.
10. George Felos, press conference, Dunedin, Florida, CNN, March 31, 2005.
11. "Terri's Death Wish or Michael's?" WorldNetDaily.com, March 20, 2005; *Larry King Live,* CNN, March 20, 2005.
12. *The Early Show,* CBS, March 21, 2005.

CHAPTER 7: "PLANT" OR DISABLED PERSON

1. Bryan Jennett, *The Vegetative State: Medical Facts, Ethical and Legal Dilemmas* (New York: Cambridge University Press, 2002), vii, 10.
2. Keith Andrews et al., "Misdiagnosis of the Vegetative State: Retrospective Study in a Rehabilitation Unit," *BMJ,* July 6, 1996, 13–16.
3. Multi-Society Task Force on the Persistent Vegetative State, "Medical Aspects of the Persistent Vegetative State," *New England Journal of Medicine,* May 26, 1994, 1499–1508.
4. James L. Bernat, "The Boundaries of the Persistent Vegetative State," *Journal of Clinical Ethics* 3 (1992): 176–80.
5. Jennett, *The Vegetative State,* 19.
6. *Truths That Transform,* Coral Ridge Ministries, http://www.coralridge.org, May 17, 2005.
7. Barbara J. Stock, "Terri Schiavo: The Fifteen Year Murder," RenewAmerica.us, posted on rense.com, March 26, 2005.
8. Jennett, *The Vegetative State,* 26.
9. Thomas Boyle, "CodeBlueBlog Issues $100,000 Challenge to Terri Schiavo Neurologist Experts," CodeBlueBlog.com, March 29, 2005.
10. Thomas Boyle, "CSI Medblogs: CodeBlueBlog Analyzes Terri Schiavo's CT of the Brain," CodeBlueBlog.com, March 21, 2005.

CHAPTER 8: DUELING DOCTORS

1. J. T. Giacino et al. "The Minimally Conscious State: Definition and Diagnostic Criteria," *Neurology* 58 (February 2002): 349–53.
2. Bryan Jennett, *The Vegetative State: Medical Facts, Ethical and Legal Dilemmas* (New York: Cambridge University Press, 2002), 20.

3. Jeff Johnson, "Schiavo's 'Dr. Humane Death' Got 1980 Diagnosis Wrong," CNSNews.com, April 13, 2005.
4. *CNN NewsNight with Aaron Brown,* CNN, March 30, 2005.
5. Terri Schindler-Schiavo Foundation, press release, September 16, 2003.
6. Amy Walsh, "Accident Victim Was 'A Very Gentle Person,'" *St. Petersburg Times,* August 8, 1995.
7. Sarah Treffinger, "Schiavo Autopsy Will Not Certify Vegetative State, Some Experts Say," *Cleveland Plain Dealer,* April 1, 2005.
8. Jeff Johnson, "Schindler Family Releases Video of Daughter," CNSNews.com, October 14, 2003.
9. Abby Goodnough, "Death Nears, Battle Persists; Family Feud Began over Money," *New York Times,* March 29, 2005.
10. Robert Johansen, "Starving for a Fair Diagnosis," *National Review Online,* March 16, 2005.
11. Sherry Eros and Steven Eros, "Terri Schiavo's Autopsy: The Blind Spot," Eros Colored Glasses weblog, http://eroscoloredglasses.blogspot.com, June 21, 2005.
12. Paula Story, "The Other Side of the Human Brain Is Understudy Waiting in the Wings," Associated Press, April 22, 1999 as cited by columnist Lionel Waxman in "Reconciling Terri's Autopsy," WaxmanMedia.com, June 16, 2005.
13. Cleveland Clinic, "Hemispherectomy for Pediatric Catastrophic Epilepsy," at http://www.clevelandclinic.org, June 16, 2005.
14. T. Duning et al. "Dehydration Confounds the Assessment of Brain Atrophy," *Neurology* 64 (2005): 548–50.
15. WorldNetDaily.com, "Autopsy Suggests Schiavo Cognizant," June 17, 2005.

CHAPTER 9: AT DEATH'S DOOR FOR 1,815 DAYS

1. "Medicaid, Medicare Fraud Evident in Schiavo Hospice Certification," *Empire Journal,* http://www.theempirejournal.com, March 8, 2005.
2. "Schiavo Hospice CEO Has Personal, Business Financial Woes," *Empire Journal,* http://www.theempirejournal.com, April 18, 2005.
3. Mitch Stacy, "Money Evaporating in Terri Schiavo Right-to-Die Battle," Associated Press, March 16, 2005.
4. George Anders, "U.S. Cracks Down on Hospices Treating Patients Who Aren't on Brink of Death," *Wall Street Journal,* January 8, 1997.
5. "Schiavo Hospice CEO Has Personal, Business Financial Woes," *Empire Journal,* http://theempirejournal.com, April 18, 2005.
6. William Levesque, "Hospice Let Home Sell Below Appraisal," *St. Petersburg Times,* March 8, 2003.
7. Charles R. Babcock, "Hospices Big Business, Thanks to Medicare; Exploitation of Some Patients Alleged," *Washington Post,* June 14, 1998.

8. Jeff Johnson, "Fired Nurse Claims Terri Feels Pain," CNSNews.com, March 23, 2005.
9. Courtney S. Campbell, Jan Hare, and Pam Matthews, "Conflicts of Conscience: Hospice and Assisted Suicide," *The Hastings Center Report,* May 1995.
10. "Wife Accidentally Backs Over Man," *St. Petersburg Times,* August 7, 1995.
11. Felos, *Litigation as Spiritual Practice,* 181–82.
12. Tubbs, "The Spirit and the Law."
13. Felos, *Litigation as a Spiritual Practice,* 60.
14. Ibid., 62–75.

CHAPTER 10: RIGHT TO DIE VS. NOT DEAD YET

1. "The Death of Nancy Cruzan," *Frontline,* PBS, March 24, 1992.
2. Ronald Kotulak, "Court Faces First 'Right to Die' Decision," *Chicago Tribune,* June 25, 1990.
3. "The Death of Nancy Cruzan," *Frontline,* PBS, March 24, 1992.
4. *The O'Reilly Factor,* Fox News Network, March 31, 2005.
5. Ian Dowbiggin, *A Merciful End: The Euthanasia Movement in Modern America* (New York: Oxford University Press, 2003), 1–2.
6. Alex Schadenberg, "Scholar Outlines Euthanasia Movement's Sordid History," review of *A Merciful End,* TheInterim.com, April 2003.
7. Ibid.
8. Norman L. Cantor, "Twenty-five Years After Quinlan: A Review of the Jurisprudence of Death and Dying," *American Society of Law and Medicine, Inc.,* June 22, 2001, 182.
9. Rita Marker, "Dying for the Cause: Foundation Funding for the 'Right-to-Die' Movement," *Philanthropy Magazine,* January 2001.
10. Alex Schadenberg, "Scholar Outlines Euthanasia Movement's Sordid History," review of *A Merciful End,* TheInterim.com, April 2003.
11. Ibid.
12. Letter to the editor from Charles E. Nixdorff, "Explaining Euthanasia: Proponent of Bill to Permit It Refers to Such Actions as 'Merciful Release,'" *New York Times,* January 30, 1939.
13. Rita L. Marker and Wesley J. Smith, "Words, Words, Words," International Task Force on Euthanasia and Assisted Suicide, http://www.internationaltaskforce.org.
14. Derek Humphry, "Why I Believe in Voluntary Euthanasia and Assisted Suicide," ERGO, http://www.finalexit.org.
15. Ibid.
16. Leslie Bond, "Hemlock Society Forms New Organization to Push Assisted Suicide Initiative," *National Right to Life News,* December 18, 1986, 1, 10.

17. Walter Owens, 1986 U.S. Civil Rights Commission Report, cited by Thomas Nerney in an unpublished essay, "Challenging Incompetence: The Meaning of Self-Determination."
18. Richard John Neuhaus, "The Return of Eugenics," *Commentary* 85 (April 1988): 15–26.
19. Beverly Beyette, "The Reluctant Survivor," *Los Angeles Times,* September 13, 1992.
20. Ibid.
21. Daniel Callahan, "On Feeding the Dying," *Hastings Center Report,* October 1983.
22. Diane Coleman, "Withdrawing Life-Sustaining Treatment from People with Severe Disabilities," *National Legal Center for the Medically Dependent and Disabled,* June 22, 1992, 55.
23. Joni Eareckson Tada, interview on *Truths That Transform,* Coral Ridge Ministries, http://www.coralridge.org, May 18, 2005.
24. Ceci Connolly, "Schiavo Raised Profile of Disabled," *Washington Post,* April 2, 2005.
25. Marker and Smith, "Words, Words, Words."
26. David Zeman, "Verdict Won't Stop Right-to-Die Efforts," *Detroit Free Press,* March 27, 1999.
27. Ibid.
28. Tim O'Brien, "Court Hears Physician-Assisted Suicide Case," ABC News, January 8, 1997.
29. Thomas Maier, "The Doctor Weighs In: A Prestigious Journal Becomes a Forum for Its Editor as She Shapes Public Debate over Controversial Issues," *NewsDay,* March 18, 1997.
30. Ira R. Byock, "Patient Refusal of Nutrition and Hydration: Walking the Ever-Finer Line," *American Journal Hospice & Palliative Care* (March–April 1994): 8–13.
31. Norman L. Cantor, "Twenty-five Years After Quinlan: A Review of the Jurisprudence of Death and Dying," *American Society of Law & Medicine,* June 22, 2001.
32. "Excerpts from the Supreme Court Oral Argument on Physician-Assisted Suicide," WashingtonPost.com, January 9, 1997.
33. Russell Hittinger, "Assisted Suicide: No and Yes, but Mainly Yes," *First Things* 71 (March 1997): 8–10.
34. Sharon Tubbs, "The Spirit and the Law," *St. Petersburg Times,* May 25, 2001.
35. Terri Schindler-Schiavo Foundation, press release, August 30, 2004.
36. "Attorney George Felos Carves Out Niche in Right-to-Die Law," Associated Press, March 31, 2005, posted on WHDH-TV Web site, http:www.whdh.com.
37. Tony Kennedy, "The Doctor's Message: Die with Dignity," Associated Press, February 11, 1991.

38. Marker, "Dying for the Cause: Foundation Funding for the 'Right-to-Die' Movement."
39. Theresa Tighe, "Doctors Conflict in 'Right-to-Die' Case, *St. Louis Post-Dispatch,* January 13, 1991.
40. Judy Mann, "When the Hospital Sues to Pull the Plug," *Washington Post,* May 31, 1991.
41. Tony Kennedy, "Judge Rules Against Doctors Who Sought to Unplug Patient's Respirator," Associated Press, July 2, 1991.
42. Barbara Dewey, "Brain-Damaged Patient in Right-to-Live Controversy Dies," Associated Press, July 5, 1991.
43. Op. Ed., "Oliver Wanglie Wins His Case," *Washington Times,* July 3, 1991.
44. "Schiavo Doctor a Right-to-Die Activist," *WorldNetDaily.com,* March 23, 2005.
45. Felos, *Litigation as Spiritual Practice,* 10.
46. Ibid.

CHAPTER 11: "TRANSFORMING THE CULTURE OF DYING"

1. Rita Marker, "Dying for the Cause: Foundation Funding for the 'Right-to-Die' Movement."
2. Carey Goldberg, "After 10 Years, $200M Effort on Dying Reaches Its Own End," *Boston Globe,* November 9, 2003.
3. Jeff Johnson, "Soros Foundation Given $30 Million by U.S. Government," CNSNews.com, April 25, 2005.
4. *Morning Edition,* NPR, May 9, 2005.
5. Jane Mayer, "The Money Man," *The New Yorker,* October 18, 2004.
6. George Soros, "Reflections on Death in America," PDIA, http://www2.soros.org, November 30, 1994.
7. "Two Decades to an American Culture of Death," http://www.lifetree.org.
8. David Stevens, *Truths That Transform,* Coral Ridge Ministries, http://www.coralridge.org, May 17, 2005.
9. *Scarborough Country,* MSNBC, March 29, 2005.
10. Wesley J. Smith, "Human Non-Person," *National Review Online,* March 29, 2005.
11. Lisa Belkin, "Doctors Debate Helping the Terminally Ill Die," *New York Times,* May 24, 1989.
12. Mary Loftus, "A Final Choice: Assisted Suicide Stirs Passionate Debates from Both Sides, *Lakeland Ledger,* February 14, 1998.
13. Liz Freeman, "Florida's Challenge: State on Front Lines of Battle to Improve the Final Months of Life," *Stuart News,* September 20, 1998.
14. National Conference of State Legislatures and the Center to Improve Care of Dying, "End-of-Life Commissions and Education."

15. Larry Keough, "Towey Applies Missionary's Zeal to Problems of Aging," *Florida State Times,* October 31, 1996.
16. Fran Hathaway, "Warning of the Coming Age Storm," *Palm Beach Post,* June 9, 1996.
17. Jury Gross, "Ambitious PBS Series Looks at Improving the Way We Die," *National Catholic Reporter,* August 25, 2000.

CHAPTER 12: STATUTORY SERENDIPITY OR SET-UP?

1. "Hemlock of Florida Legal Plans Update," *Hemlock Beacon Newsletter* (Florida Hemlock Society), Summer 1994.
2. Diane Lade, "Group Carefully Orchestrated Doctor-Patient Right-to-Die Test," *Fort Lauderdale Sun-Sentinel,* January 12, 1997.
3. John D. McKinnon, "Assisted Suicide Ruling Gives New Legal Life to a National Movement," *Miami Herald,* February 2, 1997.
4. Lade, "A Right to Die: Doctor Can Aid Patient with Aids."
5. McKinnon, "Assisted-Suicide Ruling Gives New Legal Life to a National Movement."
6. Gady A. Epstein, "Lawmakers Not Eager to Deal with Assisted Suicide," *Tampa Tribune,* February 4, 1997.
7. Sarah Foster, "Terri's Money Used to Pay for Starvation Death."
8. Ibid.
9. *Bryer v. Bryer,* No. 02-707-IN-04 (Fla. Pinellas Cir. Ct. March 21, 2002).
10. Felos, *Litigation as Spiritual Practice,* 249.
11. Tim Nickens, "Bill on Terminally Ill Vetoed," *St. Petersburg Times,* July 4, 1989.
12. Felos, *Litigation as Spiritual Practice,* 213.
13. Lindsay Peterson, "Comfort of Dying Patients Sought," *Tampa Tribune,* September 23, 1997.
14. Ibid.
15. Willamette College of Law, "Recent Developments in Physician-Assisted Suicide: October 1997," posted at http://www.willamette.edu, October 1997.
16. "Taking a Clear-Eyed Look at Death," *Tampa Tribune,* September 28, 1997.
17. Maya Bell, "Guardians Laud Michael Schiavo for Fulfilling Wife's Wishes," *Orlando Sentinel,* August 5, 2005.
18. L. L. Basta and H. D. McIntosh, "Project Grace: Guidelines for Resuscitation and Care at End-of-Life," *Clinical Cardiology* 23 (February 2000): supplement 2.
19. Bob Brooks et al., "Advancing End-of-Life Care: Lessons Learned from a Statewide Panel," *Journal of Palliative Medicine* 6 (October 2003): 821–29.
20. Bob Brooks, "Heart-Rending Decisions About End-of-Life Care," *Orlando Sentinel,* September 14, 1998.

21. Bebe Bahnsen, "The Quality of Life and Death; Panel Hears Views on Life's End," *Sarasota Herald-Tribune,* November 10, 1998.
22. Diane Lade, "Panel Discusses Giving Patients More Control over Life's End," *Fort Lauderdale Sun-Sentinel,* February 8, 1999.
23. "Overcoming the Reluctance to Face Mortality," *Palm Beach Daily Business Review,* March 26, 1999.
24. Susan R. Miller, "Living Wills Aren't Last Words," *Broward Daily Business Review,*" March 26, 1999.
25. Susan R. Miller, "Church Lobbying, Bush's Opposition Mean Compromise in Death Bill," *Broward Daily Business Review,* April 22, 1999.
26. Rachel La Corte, "Kin Fight over Fate of Woman," *Salt Lake City Deseret News,* December 26, 2002.

CHAPTER 13: "JUDICIAL HOMICIDE" OR RULE OF LAW?

1. Carolyn DuPree Hill, "Honorable George W. Greer" *Clearwater Bar Association Newsletter,* March 1998.
2. Joe Newman, "Victim's Co-Workers March Against Judge," *St. Petersburg Times,* March 17, 1998.
3. Jane Meinhardt, "Law No Shield for Slain Woman," *St. Petersburg Times,* March 13, 1998.
4. William R. Levesque, "Quiet Judge Persists in Schiavo Maelstrom," *St. Petersburg Times,* March 6, 2005.
5. WorldNetDaily, "Death Threats on Judge Lead to Federal Charges," April 6, 2005.
6. *hOUR Tampa Bay,* Infinity/CBS Radio, April 20, 2004.
7. Carol Marbin, "Pinellas Billed $4,130 for Cayman Trip," *St. Petersburg Times,* July 13, 1991.
8. Curtis Krueger, "City Okays Fine in Ethics Breach," *St. Petersburg Times,* December 5, 1989.
9. "Parks for Pinellas," *St. Petersburg Times,* October 7, 1987.
10. William R. Levesque, "Quiet Judge Persists in Schiavo Maelstrom."
11. Joseph Farah, "Meet Judge Greer's Pastor," WorldNetDaily, March 29, 2005.
12. Art Toalston, "Judge in Schiavo Case Withdraws Membership from Church," Baptist Press, March 18, 2005.
13. William R. Levesque, "Quiet Judge Persists in Schiavo Maelstrom."
14. Michael Sandler, "Local Republicans Back Greer," *St. Petersburg Times,* March 22, 2005.
15. Carol Marbin Miller, "Judge in Schiavo Drama Never Sought Political Spotlight," *Miami Herald,* March 18, 2005.
16. "Ending Life Support: Who Decides?" *TalkBack Live,* CNN, May 30, 2001.
17. "Judge's Error to Save Terri Schiavo?" WorldNetDaily.com, March 4, 2005.

18. *hOUR Tampa Bay,* Infinity/CBS Radio, April 20, 2004.
19. John Paul II, "Life-Sustaining Treatments and Vegetative State: Scientific Advances and Ethical Dilemmas," http://www.vatican.va, March 20, 2004.
20. Felos, *Litigation as Spiritual Practice,* 216.
21. *Truths That Transform,* Coral Ridge Ministries, May 17, 2005.
22. "Florida House Mum About Greer Impeachment Demands," *Empire Journal,* http://www.theempirejournal.com, May 11, 2005.
23. Jennifer Farrell, "Eyes on Judge in Schiavo Petition," *St. Petersburg Times,* November 3, 2003.
24. *The Abrams Report,* MSNBC, March 22, 2005.
25. *Hannity & Colmes,* Fox News Network, March 30, 2005.
26. *Scarborough Country,* MSNBC, March 30, 2005.

CHAPTER 14: TERRI'S LAW

1. Sarah Foster, "Petition Drive Launched for Terri Schiavo," WorldNetDaily .com, August 2, 2003.
2. David Kirkpatrick and John Schwartz, "List of Schiavo Donors Will Be Sold by Direct-Marketing Firm," *New York Times,* March 29, 2005.
3. *hOUR Tampa Bay,* interview with talk journalist John Sipos.
4. "Terri Lives!" WorldNetDaily.com, October 21, 2003.
5. Ibid.
6. Adam C. Smith, "Regret Plagues King After Schiavo Vote," *St. Petersburg Times,* February 10, 2004.
7. Allison North Jones and Elaine Silvestini, "Legislature Acts to Save Schiavo," *Tampa Tribune,* October 21, 2003.
8. Gary Fineout, "Governor Steps In," *Sarasota Herald-Tribune,* October 22, 2003.
9. *Buchanan & Press,* CNN, October 21, 2003.
10. *Good Morning America,* ABC, October 22, 2003.
11. *hOUR Tampa Bay,* interview with talk journalist John Sipos.
12. Anita Kumar, Alisa Ulferts, and Steve Bousquet, "Terri Schiavo: Decision Day," *St. Petersburg Times,* March 18, 2005.
13. "Lawmakers Intrude into Family Privacy," *Lakeland Ledger,* February 6, 2004.
14. Carol Marbin Miller, "Police 'Showdown' Averted," *Miami Herald,* March 26, 2005.
15. Dara Kam, "Governor, Lawmakers in Daily Contact on Schiavo, E-mails Show," *Palm Beach Post,* May 24, 2005.
16. *For the Relief of the Parents of Theresa Marie Schiavo,* S 686, 109th Cong., 1st sess., *Congressional Record* 151 (March 20, 2005): H 1706.
17. Sarah Foster, "Michael Schiavo to Bush: Come Down to Visit Terri," WorldNetDaily.com, March 21, 2005.

18. Michael Finnegan, "Dean Says Democrats Will Cite Schiavo Against GOP," *Los Angeles Times,* April 16, 2005.
19. Daniel Eisenberg, "Lessons of the Schiavo Battle," *Time,* April 4, 2005.

CHAPTER 15: CONSPIRACY THEORIES

1. Diana Lynne, "Political Corruption Alleged in Schiavo Case," WorldNetDaily.com, March 26, 2005.
2. Sarah Foster, "Schindler Family Reunited with Terri," WorldNetDaily.com, June 4, 2004.
3. The Terri Schindler-Schiavo Foundation, http://www.terrisfight.org.
4. Steven Ertelt, "Judge Strikes Down Law That Saved Terri Schiavo's Life," LifeNews.com, May 6, 2004.
5. *The O'Reilly Factor,* Fox News Network, March 28, 2005.
6. Levesque, "Quiet Judge Persists in Schiavo Maelstrom."
7. Robert Farley, "Scientology's Town," *St. Petersburg Times,* July 18, 2004.
8. Charles Stafford, "Church Entered Clearwater on Path of Deceit," *St. Petersburg Times,* 1980.
9. Thomas C. Tobin, "The Man Behind Scientology," *St. Petersburg Times,* October 25, 1998.
10. Felos, *Litigation as Spiritual Practice,* 20–21.
11. Robert Farley, "Church Requests That Trial Be Moved," *St. Petersburg Times,* May 23, 2003.
12. David Sommer, "State Drops Scientology Charges," *Tampa Tribune,* June 13, 2000.
13. Thomas Tobin, "The Man Behind Scientology."

CHAPTER 16: MEDIA MISINFORMATION

1. "Terri's Death Reported Too Early by CBS News," WorldNetDaily.com, March 30, 2005.
2. Felos, *Litigation as Spiritual Practice,* 238.
3. Diana Lynne, "Media Getting It Wrong on Terri Schiavo Story," WorldNetDaily.com, October 25, 2003.
4. Nat Hentoff, "A Woman's Life Versus an Inept Press," *Village Voice,* November 6, 2003.
5. Wesley J. Smith, "Life, Death, and Silence," *Weekly Standard,* October 31, 2003.
6. "Autopsy on the Schiavo Tragedy," *New York Times,* June 16, 2005.
7. "Jeb Bush Battles 'The NY Times' Over Schiavo Case," *Editor & Publisher,* June 18, 2005, http://www.editorandpublisher.com/eandp/news/article_display.jsp?vnu_content_id=1000964305.

8. Sherry Eros and Steven Eros, "Terri Schiavo's Autopsy: The Blind Spot," ErosColoredGlasses.blogspot.com, June 21, 2005.
9. *Truths That Transform,* Coral Ridge Ministries, May 18, 2005.
10. *Nightline,* ABC News, March 31, 2005.

CHAPTER 17: "I KEPT MY PROMISE"

1. Mitch Stacy, "Schiavo Spending First Full Day Off Tube," Associated Press, March 19, 2005.
2. *Larry King Live,* CNN, October 27, 2003.
3. *Scarborough Country,* MSNBC, March 28, 2005.
4. *Hannity & Colmes,* Fox News Network, March 30, 2005.
5. *Nancy Grace,* CNN, March 31, 2005.
6. *On the Record with Greta Van Susteren,* Fox News Network, March 28, 2005.
7. David Brown, "Little Known About Starvation Death," *Washington Post,* March 23, 2005.
8. *Truths That Transform,* Coral Ridge Ministries, May 17, 2005.
9. Anne Lindberg, "Hospice Pays Majority of Schiavo Police Bill," *St. Petersburg Times,* April 20, 2005.
10. *Weekend Edition Sunday,* National Public Radio, April 3, 2005.
11. Jill Smolowe, Steve Helling, and Jeff Truesdell, "Waiting for the End," *People,* April 11, 2005.
12. *Truths That Transform,* Coral Ridge Ministries, April 17, 2005.
13. Diane Lade, "Retirement Mecca Will Experience Extra Strain," *Fort Lauderdale Sun-Sentinel,* April 11, 1999.
14. *hOUR Tampa Bay,* Infinity/CBS Radio, April 20, 2004.
15. *Hannity & Colmes,* Fox News Network, April 7, 2005.
16. William Levesque, "Schiavo's Husband Says He'll Fight Back," *St. Petersburg Times,* October 24, 2003.
17. *Hannity & Colmes,* Fox News Network, May 6, 2005.
18. *Hannity & Colmes,* Fox News Network, March 31, 2005.
19. *Hannity & Colmes,* Fox News Network, April 7, 2005.

INDEX

www.ingramcontent.com/pod-product-compliance
Lightning Source LLC
Jackson TN
JSHW020014141224
75386JS00025B/519

* 9 7 8 1 6 8 4 4 2 1 8 3 1 *